Tourism and Memories of Home

TOURISM AND CULTURAL CHANGE

Series Editors: Professor Mike Robinson, *Ironbridge International Institute for Cultural Heritage, University of Birmingham, UK* and Dr Alison Phipps, *University of Glasgow, Scotland, UK*

Understanding tourism's relationships with culture(s) and vice versa, is of ever-increasing significance in a globalising world. TCC is a series of books that critically examine the complex and ever-changing relationship between tourism and culture(s). The series focuses on the ways that places, peoples, pasts, and ways of life are increasingly shaped/transformed/created/packaged for touristic purposes. The series examines the ways tourism utilises/makes and re-makes cultural capital in its various guises (visual and performing arts, crafts, festivals, built heritage, cuisine etc.) and the multifarious political, economic, social and ethical issues that are raised as a consequence. Theoretical explorations, research-informed analyses, and detailed historical reviews from a variety of disciplinary perspectives are invited to consider such relationships.

Full details of all the books in this series and of all our other publications can be found on http://www.channelviewpublications.com, or by writing to Channel View Publications, St Nicholas House, 31–34 High Street, Bristol BS1 2AW, UK.

TOURISM AND CULTURAL CHANGE: 50

Tourism and Memories of Home

Migrants, Displaced People, Exiles and Diasporic Communities

Edited by
Sabine Marschall

CHANNEL VIEW PUBLICATIONS
Bristol • Blue Ridge Summit

Library of Congress Cataloging in Publication Data
A catalog record for this book is available from the Library of Congress.
Names: Marschall, Sabine, editor.
Title: Tourism and Memories of Home: Migrants, Displaced People, Exiles and
    Diasporic Communities/Edited by Sabine Marschall.
Description: Bristol, UK: Channel View Publications, [2017] |
Series: Tourism and Cultural Change: 50 |
Includes bibliographical references and index.
Identifiers: LCCN 2016043701 | ISBN 9781845416034 (hbk : alk. paper) |
    ISBN 9781845416027 (pbk : alk. paper) | ISBN 9781845416065 (kindle) |
    ISBN 9781845416041 (Pdf) | ISBN 9781845416058 (Epub)
Subjects: LCSH: Heritage tourism—Social aspects.
Classification: LCC G156.5.H47 T685 2017 | DDC 338.4/791—dc23 LC record available
    at https://lccn.loc.gov/2016043701

British Library Cataloguing in Publication Data
A catalogue entry for this book is available from the British Library.

ISBN-13: 978-1-84541-603-4 (hbk)
ISBN-13: 978-1-84541-602-7 (pbk)

Channel View Publications
UK: St Nicholas House, 31–34 High Street, Bristol BS1 2AW, UK.
USA: NBN, Blue Ridge Summit, PA, USA.

Website: www.channelviewpublications.com
Twitter: Channel_View
Facebook: https://www.facebook.com/channelviewpublications
Blog: www.channelviewpublications.wordpress.com

The policy of Multilingual Matters/Channel View Publications is to use papers that are
natural, renewable and recyclable products, made from wood grown in sustainable forests. In the manufacturing process of our books, and to further support our policy, prefer-
ence is given to printers that have FSC and PEFC Chain of Custody certification. The FSC
and/or PEFC logos will appear on those books where full certification has been granted
to the printer concerned.

Typeset by Nova Techset Private Limited, Bengaluru & Chennai, India.
Printed and bound in the UK by Short Run Press Ltd.
Printed and bound in the US by Edwards Brothers Malloy, Inc.

In memory of my father, Hans-Jürgen Marschall,
whose family history inspired this book and who sadly passed away
shortly before it was published

Contents

Acknowledgements

This book would not have been possible without the intellectual contribution, proficiency, cooperation and patience of all individual authors, to whom I express my warmest gratitude. Special thanks to Nelson Graburn, whose kind offer to write the epilogue for this collection is most appreciated. I also thank all colleagues, near and far, who contributed their time and expertise to the double blind peer review of all individual chapters in this volume. Their thoughts, critiques and suggestions have been appreciated by the authors and shaped their revisions. Particular gratitude must be extended to Channel View's experts for their in-depth scrutiny of the Introduction chapter and the volume as a whole. Their constructive feedback is highly valued. I am moreover indebted to the production team at Channel View and most notably, Sarah Williams, who has lent her support and encouragement throughout the process.

Sabine Marschall

Contributors

Anna Arnone is a Research Associate at SOAS, University of London, working on the Italian island of Lampedusa as a space where different mobilities meet and show the contradictions of the regimes of movement. Her DPhil research at Sussex University (2010) was about Eritreans in Milan and the multitudes of agents constituting identities in a transnational context of sharp political tensions. Tourism and journeys among migrants and diasporas are an ongoing topic of interest. Her publications include 'Tourism and the Eritrean Diaspora' in *Journal of Contemporary African Studies*, 2011, 29 (4) and 'Talking about identity: Milanese-Eritreans describe themselves' in *Journal of Modern Italian Studies*, 2011, 16 (4).

Kalyan Bhandari, PhD, is a Lecturer in Events, Hospitality and Tourism in the School of Business and Enterprise, University of the West of Scotland, UK. He began his career in the tourism industry of Nepal before moving to the UK to pursue his PhD studies at the University of Glasgow, where he researched the aspects of 'nation' and 'nationhood' represented in Scottish tourism. His latest book is *Tourism and National Identity: Heritage and Nationhood in Scotland* (Channel View Publications, 2014). He maintains an equal interest in all aspects of tourism in Scotland and his native Nepal.

John Bieter, PhD, graduated with an undergraduate degree in Social Science and a concentration in Economics. His Masters thesis was published as An Enduring Legacy: A History of the Basques in Idaho. His book, *Showdown in the Big Quiet: Land, Myth and Government in the American West*, came out in April of 2015. John earned his doctoral degree from Boston College where he focused his research and teaching interests on Immigration and Ethnicity, the American West and American Catholicism. Currently, John serves as Professor in the College of Arts and Sciences and as Co-Director of the Basque Studies Center at Boise State University, Boise Idaho, USA.

Andrea Corsale is Assistant Professor of Geography at the Department of History, Cultural Heritage and Territory, University of Cagliari, Italy. He has a PhD in African and Asian Studies. His research interests include international migrations, ethnic minorities, rural and cultural tourism, participation and local development, particularly in Eastern Europe and the Mediterranean Region. His most recent publications include 'Jewish Heritage Tourism between Memories and Strategies. Different Approaches from Lviv, Ukraine', with O. Vuytsyk (*Current Issues in Tourism*, 2016) and 'Geografia delle minoranze fra Baltico e Mar Nero' (Franco Angeli Publisher, Milan, 2016).

Nelson Graburn earned his BA at Cambridge (1958), MA at McGill (1960) and PhD at Chicago (1963). He has taught at UC Berkeley since 1964 and held visiting positions in Canada, France, UK, Japan, Brazil and China. He has researched kinship, art and identity in 22 Canadian Inuit communities (1959–2010) and domestic tourism, multiculturalism and heritage in Japan (since 1974) and China (since 1991). His books include *Ethnic and Tourist Arts* (1976); *Japanese Domestic Tourism* (1983); *The Anthropology of Tourism* (1983); *Tourism Social Sciences* (1991); *Multiculturalism in the New Japan* (2008); 旅游人类学论文集 [Anthropology in the Age of Tourism], (2009); *Tourism and Glocalization: Perspectives in East Asian Studies* (2010); *Tourism Imaginaries: Anthropological Approaches* (2014).

Kevin Hannam is Professor of Tourism at Edinburgh Napier University, UK and a research affiliate at the University of Johannesburg, South Africa. Previously he was at Leeds Beckett University and the University of Sunderland, UK. He is founding co-editor of the journals *Mobilities* and *Applied Mobilities* (Routledge), co-author of the books *Understanding Tourism* (Sage) and *Tourism and India* (Routledge) and co-editor of the *Routledge Handbook of Mobilities Research* and *Moral Encounters in Tourism* (Ashgate). He has a PhD in geography from the University of Portsmouth, UK and is a Fellow of the Royal Geographical Society (FRGS).

Marjory Harper, MA, PhD, is Professor of History at the University of Aberdeen. Her most recent book, *Scotland No More? The Scots who left Scotland in the twentieth century* (Edinburgh, 2012) was awarded the Frank Watson Prize by the University of Guelph, and her previous monograph, *Adventurers and Exiles: The Great Scottish Exodus* (London, 2003), won the Saltire History Prize. She co-authored *Migration and Empire* (Oxford, 2010), and has recently published a multidisciplinary edited collection, *Migration and Mental Health: Past and Present* (Basingstoke, 2016). She is preparing two monographs: on Scottish emigrant testimony, and Scotland's heritage in the Antipodes.

Monica Iorio is Professor of Geography at the Department of Social Studies and Institutions, University of Cagliari, Italy. Her main research interests include rural and cultural tourism as a source of development for host communities, especially in marginalized areas. Her work has been based on extensive field work conducted in Romania, Morocco and Sardinia. Her publications include a number of peer-reviewed journal articles and book chapters. Heritage tourism and identity, tourism rejuvenation in Mediterranean mature destinations and international migrations are also ongoing topics within her areas of interest.

Patrick R. Ireland, PhD in political science (Harvard) and MPH (Texas), is a professor of political science at the Illinois Institute of Technology in Chicago. He has written extensively on cultural policy relating to the Scots-Irish; urban- and neighbourhood-level migrant integration in Europe, North America and Africa; female migrant domestic workers; and migrant health. His publications include several single-authored books and a number of peer-reviewed journal articles and book chapters. His work has been based on extensive field work conducted in Australia, Benelux, Canada, France, Germany, Ireland, the Philippines, Spain, Sri Lanka, Switzerland and North and sub-Saharan Africa.

Mustafa Kabha is a Professor at the Department of History, Philosophy and Judaic Studies, as well as Head of the JCM (Center of Relations between Jews, Christians and Muslims) at the Open University of Israel. As a researcher and lecturer in History and Communications, his main fields of research are the modern history of the Palestinian people, the history of the Arab press, oral history and Arabs in Israel. Recent publications include: *Towards a Historical Narrative of the Nakba: Complexities and Challenges*, Mada – Arab Center for Applied Social Research, Haifa, 2006 (Arabic); *Writing up The Storm – The Palestinian Press Shaping Public Opinion*. Vallentine Mitchell, 2007 (English); Kabha, M. and Caspi, D., *The Palestinian Arab In/Outsiders – Media and Conflict in Israel*. Vallentine Mitchell, 2011 (English); *The Palestinian People Seeking Sovereignty and State*. New York, 2014.

Noga Kadman, MA in Peace and Development Studies, is an Israeli researcher in the field of human rights and the Israeli-Palestinian conflict, whose main interest is to explore the encounter between Israelis and the Palestinian presence in the landscape and history of the country. She is also a licensed tour guide who deals mostly with the hidden Palestinian layers of the landscape in Israel. She is the author of *Erased from Space and Consciousness: Israel and the Depopulated Palestinian Village of 1948* (2015), and co-editor of *Once Upon a Land: A Tour Guide to Depopulated Palestinian Villages and Towns* (2012, in Hebrew and Arabic).

Carol A. Kidron is Associate Professor in the Department of Anthropology at the University of Haifa, Israel. Kidron has undertaken comparative ethnographic work with Holocaust descendants in Israel and children of Cambodian genocide survivors in Cambodia and in Canada. Her interests include personal, communal and collective Holocaust and Genocide commemoration. Kidron has also examined the glocalization of discourses on justice and reconciliation, victimhood and memory. Kidron's publications include: 'Toward an ethnography of silence: The lived presence of the past in the everyday life of holocaust trauma survivors and their descendants in Israel' (*Current Anthropology*, 2009) and 'Alterity and the particular limits of universalism: comparing Jewish-Israeli holocaust and Canadian-Cambodian genocide legacies' (*Current Anthropology*, 2012).

Sabine Marschall is Associate Professor in Cultural and Heritage Tourism (School of Social Sciences) at the University of KwaZulu-Natal, Durban (South Africa). She holds a PhD from the Eberhardt-Karls-University in Tübingen (Germany) and has published widely in the fields of South African art, architecture, cultural heritage (tangible and intangible), heritage tourism, monuments and memorialization. Major publications include *Landscape of Memory: Commemorative Monuments, Memorials and Public Statuary in Post-Apartheid South Africa* (Brill, 2010). Her current research interests revolve around the intersection of Memory Studies and Tourism Studies.

Jillian L. Powers, PhD, is a consultant at ReD associates and previously was a lecturer a lecturer in American Studies and Sociology at Brandeis University, Massachusetts. She is also the 2015–2016 Berman Early Career Fellow awarded by the Association of Jewish Studies. Working at the intersection of cultural sociology and racial and ethnic studies, Powers' current research focuses on how racial and ethnic identities are constructed and negotiated at the intersection of diasporic heritage and international travel. Selected publications include: 'Transnational encounters: Constructing diasporic bonds on homeland tours to China and Ghana' in *The Poetics of Travel*, edited by Garth Lean, Russell Staiff and Emma Waterton (Berghahn Books), and 'Chasing China: adoption tourism, Images of China and the negotiation of Asian American identity' in Chinese America: History and Perspectives – the *Journal of the Chinese Historical Society.*

Nina M. Ray, PhD, is Emeritus Professor of Marketing and International Business in the College of Business and Economics at Boise State University, Boise Idaho USA. Her undergraduate and Masters degrees are from Purdue University and her PhD in Marketing is from Texas Tech University. She has published in several journals in the field of ancestral, or 'roots'/'legacy' tourism and also battlefield tourism. One of her most recent publications on the latter topic appears in the *Oxford Journal: An International Journal of Business & Economics*. John Bieter and Nina have co-authored many publications about Basque identity, including one in the *International Journal of Cultural Policy* and a chapter in *Travel, Tourism and Identity.*

Julia Wagner studied History, Sociology and French at Humboldt University Berlin and at the Université Libre de Bruxelles. Her PhD thesis looked at post-war Nazi trials and the involvement of so-called 'Nazi hunters'. Between 2010 and 2014 she was part of the collaborative research project 'Reverberations of War in Germany and Europe since 1945', which was funded by the Arts and Humanities Research Council. Dr Wagner currently works for UCL's Centre of Multidisciplinary and Intercultural Inquiry (CMII). She is also completing a monograph about travel narratives by German post-war tourism and the reverberations of war entitled 'Invisible Luggage: Narratives of Germans Travelling in Post-war Europe – Perceptions, Experiences, Interpretations'.

Aaron Yankholmes, PhD, is a Visiting Assistant Professor at the Institute for Tourism Studies, Macau. His main research revolves around cultural heritage tourism and its management and marketing. Recent co-authored publications include 'Understanding slavery heritage tourism', *Tourism Management* 51, 22–32; and 'Rethinking slavery heritage tourism', *Journal of Heritage Tourism*. He currently leads two research projects focused on the representations and inter-relationships between people, places and spaces in tourism.

Ganna Yankovska holds a Master's degree in Tourism from the University of Sunderland, UK. She has guest lectured at tourism events and conferences and actively takes part in political debates about the tourism industry in Ukraine.

1   Tourism and Memories of Home: Introduction

Sabine Marschall

So identity, it seems, is also a question of memory, and memories of 'home'
in particular.
(Morley & Robins, 1993: 10)

Tourism was once defined as the journey away from home, the ritualized departure from the 'profane' realm of work and ordinary, everyday routine, to the extraordinary, 'sacred' realm of the touristic experience (Graburn, 1977; MacCannell, 1976). Tourists were believed to travel in search of novelty and authenticity, their 'tourist gaze' characterized by difference (Urry, 1990). Many of these conceptions have shifted in recent years, and the simple 'home and away' dichotomy is no longer seen as a defining marker of tourism. Today, different forms of travel and mobility intersect with touristic journeys (Cohen & Cohen, 2012; Urry, 2007) and the notion of 'home' itself has been problematized in the context of globalization, high mobility, displacement, migration and transnationalism as, increasingly, people have multiple homes, holiday homes, symbolic homes or no fixed abode at all.

The current collection inverts the 'home and away' conceptualization by exploring home as a destination; the longing for home and the desire to return as markers of identity; the sense of belonging – based on personal or collective memories – to a real, symbolic or imagined home(land) as travel motivation; the experience of the return visit and the encounter with the memory-laden home environment as stimulant of a unique form of touristic performativity. The types of mobility considered in this book include journeys to former homes and places associated with home by those who have moved away, voluntarily or involuntarily, within their home country or abroad; the return trips of migrants and their immediate descendants to their place of origin; the journeys of refugees and displaced people to the sites of their lost or destroyed homes; the travel to ancestral homelands of diasporic communities and ethnic minorities; the real travel to symbolic homes or symbolic forms of mobility towards the real home.

1

What characterizes many of these travellers is that they do not regard themselves tourists. Of course, tourists of all kinds and the world over commonly reject being labelled a tourist, preferring instead to see themselves in the 'more superior' category of 'traveller', as the terms tourism and tourists carry culturally derogative and negative connotations (McCabe, 2005). Most visitors discussed in this volume see themselves as crusaders, as pilgrims on an emotional 'sacred journey' to the place of their primordial belonging; as victims on a quest to see their lost home; or simply as individuals on a family visit. Many are even offended by being associated with tourists and consciously distance themselves – physically and ontologically – from touristic spaces and modes of behaviour (see especially Powers in Chapter 7). For those who have forcibly lost their homes and who can now only revisit as tourists, the journey also means psychologically coming to terms with being a tourist (see Wagner in Chapter 4). Migrants on return journeys to their homeland – what Oxfeld and Long (2004) call 'provisional return' – tend to distinguish their home visit from touristic visits of attractions undertaken during the same trip, as Bhandari illustrates with reference to Nepali migrants (Chapter 6).

Yet, in the eyes of the host community, most homeward-bound visitors are clearly evident as outsiders or 'foreigners', many even indistinguishable from the 'typical tourist', on account of their behaviour, dress code, possessions, mode of travel, activities, consumption patterns and perhaps use of hospitality and other touristic services. Oxfeld's (2004) observation that Chinese overseas migrants on home visits are seen as 'guests' as well as family by their relatives probably applies in many other contexts. The tourism industry and international tourism authorities typically capture these travellers as heritage tourists, Visiting Friends and Relatives (VFR) tourists and other niche market travellers. The ready presence of guides and interpreters, the entrepreneurial spirit of souvenir vendors and the overt or disguised commercial nature of other transactions with local people, expose the homecoming pilgrims as outsiders and tourists. This is well illustrated in Powers' chapter (Chapter 7). Extending Cave et al.'s (2013) exploration of souvenirs as expressions of culture and triggers of cultural change, Powers discusses souvenirs as complex, paradoxical artefacts that may rupture the experience of home and render the sense of belonging ambiguous for tourists in search of their roots.

This book argues that the trip 'home', be it a genuine return to an actual former home or a first time visit to an ancestral or imagined home(land), is instrumental in negotiating one's sense of belonging, identity and self-construal as it entails an exploration of the self, the personal past and one's relationship to home – both the remembered old home and one's current place of residence. Journeys inspired by memories and longing for home, journeys to real, ancestral and symbolic homes, associated with personal or collective memories, motivated by longing, homesickness, search for family roots, identification with collective memories and allied group identities, or by curiosity, social commitments, mundane and pragmatic reasons, constitute a considerable international travel phenomenon that deserves more systematic investigation and attention by tourism scholars, policy makers and the industry.

Home and homeland play a central role in diaspora consciousness, even if it exists only in memory, and the notion of return – permanent or temporary, desirable, feasible, or imaginary – is an integral aspect of transnationalism and the migration experience (Knott & McLoughlin, 2010; Long & Oxfeld, 2004). For the sake of convenience, the term 'migrant' is often used as an umbrella term, but strictly speaking the travellers referred to in this volume may be refugees; exiles; transnationals; immigrants; guest workers; expatriates; émigrés; members of diasporas; foreign residential tourists or members of expatriate retirement communities; sojourners; long-term travellers; expellees; second-generation migrants; members of ethnic, racial and religious minorities; internal migrants and internally displaced people; or simply those who have chosen to move within their home country. The systematic exploration of the entire range is salient in defining the analytical focus on home as a destination and longing for home as travel motivation. It contributes to and expands the tourism mobility spectrum explored by the emergent literature around the tourism-migration nexus, which has attracted increasing attention following the pioneering collection of Coles and Timothy (2004).

In addition, this book contributes to the tourism-memory nexus as it conceptualizes memory as underpinning touristic mobility, experience and performativity. The relationship between tourism and memory has been neglected both within Tourism Studies and the emergent field of Memory Studies, apart from investigations in the field of Heritage Tourism, where the focus is largely on collective or cultural memory embodied in sites and attractions. Personal or individual forms of memory may be mentioned, implied or tangentially touched upon in tourism research, but are rarely subject of more systematic investigation (among the exceptions are, e.g. Braasch, 2008; Braun-LaTour et al., 2006; Shaw et al., 2008). Memory is the basis of nostalgia and longing; emotion and affect; attachment and revulsion. Autobiographical and episodic memories, shared social memory and identification with collective memories are significant determinants in touristic motivation and experience, as well as in individuals' relationship to home and homeland.

Home

'Home', 'feeling at home' and the meaning of home have become important themes, dominating public discourse in the wider political and societal arena internationally and spawning a proliferating body of literature from multiple disciplinary perspectives (e.g. Blunt & Varley, 2004; Mallett, 2004; Sarup, 1994). Many societies in the Western World, having experienced cultural shifts on account of globalization, transnationalism and an influx of migrants and refugees, are increasingly obsessed with nostalgia, national identity, cultural belonging and notions of 'home' (Duyvendak, 2011; Morley & Robins, 1993). For the immigrants themselves, home is both here and there or neither here nor there, as they negotiate their emotional attachment to places, social relations and multifarious other spaces of belonging. As the identity of diasporic migrants, always simultaneously local and global (Brah 1996: 196), becomes reconfigured over time and increasingly defined by heterogeneity, hybridity, 'in-betweeness' or a 'third space' (Bhabha, 1994), they re-evaluate their relationship with the homeland and its significance for their identity, some of them by travelling there (Tie *et al.*, 2015). The role of tourism in hybridity and identity formation among diasporic communities has been identified as a neglected area of research (Coles & Timothy, 2004).

For any individual, traditional understandings of home, connection to places and even nations, are challenged by the present era's high mobility in search of employment and opportunities for life-style improvements (Coles & Timothy, 2004; Ralph & Staeheli, 2011). Home can mean the place that is so familiar (i.e. deeply rooted in memory) that it feels 'natural'. Home can also refer to a private place associated with safety, security, shelter and comfort ('home as Haven'), or a public, material or symbolic place where one can feel independent and freely express oneself ('home as Heaven') (Duyvendak, 2011: 4/5). The notion of home entails a sense of possibility or hope, 'an existential launching pad for the self' (Hage, 2010: 419). Home is widely understood as a multidimensional concept that can comprise a place, space, feelings, activities, a state of mind or a state of being (Mallett, 2004).

In the current collection, home as a destination for travel inevitably entails a geographical location, a spatial realm or a 'localizable idea' (Douglas, 1991), be it a person's place of birth, upbringing and kinship ties (the dwelling, the town, the region or country); a site associated with emotionally intense, formative events and periods of life; or an imagined terrain, a distant, experientially unknown place infused with deep feelings of cultural belonging. Memories, nostalgia and identification with shared histories are central themes in return journeys home. In the extensive literature on heritage tourism, nostalgia is commonly understood as longing to return to the past, envisaged as a better place (Boym, 2001), but in this book nostalgia refers to the literal meaning of the term, 'longing for home'. For some, the yearning for the old home is simultaneously an expression of the desire to return to one's own past (see Wagner, Chapter 4). However, home is not always where one longs to be. Home is invested with meanings and emotions, but not necessarily remembered fondly; it can be an ambiguous place, 'a space of belonging and alienation, intimacy and violence, desire and fear' (Blunt & Varley, 2004: 3).

Home is, in many ways, about family or kinship, universal human experiences of mating, birth and nurturing. The desire to foster social relations, to be with loved ones and members of the family is the driving force behind VFR tourism, whereas the need to find home by reconnecting with deceased relations and even distant ancestors engenders legacy, genealogical and various forms of roots tourism. The search for archival records, sites and material traces is often less about objective family history research than about subjective emotional identification with kin, whose life one imagines through the encountered traces and spaces, whose presence one feels in one's own identity and whose memory one appropriates for one's own sense of belonging and search for home. Moreover, as Powers shows in Chapter 7, kinship metaphors make homeland encounters meaningful in Chinese adoption tours to mainland China, both for American parents and their adoptive children who have no personal memories of home and biological kin. African American homecoming and roots tourists, whose kinship ties rely on genetic heritage, creatively modify kinship, turning strangers into distant relatives. Locals all too readily present themselves as 'instant kin' to these homecoming tourists, conveying a sense of home and welcoming, but also responsibility and obligation (Ebron, 1999).

Many scholars emphasize the social relationship aspect of home (Mallett, 2004) and indeed the notion of 'home is where the family is' motivates many of the journeys discussed in this volume. But the old saying 'home is where the heart is' posits home as the place one loves most and where one longs to be, which may not necessarily be the place where one's loved-ones are. For others, 'home is where I culturally belong', pointing to people's sense of identity and conception of self and their identification with cultural roots and spaces of belonging. Just as identity is today widely understood as fluid, dynamic, situational and socially constructed, home is a fluid, unstable concept, culturally constructed and always in a state of becoming, as individuals move through different life stages and invest places of belonging with meanings and emotions. Home may be located in space, but not necessarily fixed there (Douglas, 1991: 289).

Home may refer not only to one's actual or a remembered old home, but also to an imaginary terrain or one's ideas of the ideal home. Some people spend their lives searching for home; in fact, home can be more about where we are going than where we are from (Mallett, 2004: 77). The search for roots and ancestral home(land)s, the 'mother country' or 'fatherland', is always about the quest for identity and belonging, indicative of a sense of societal alienation and disaffection. Through identification with collective memories and chosen narratives, the identity and meaning of homeland and its significant places is constructed and imagined – 'home as a mythic place of desire' (Brah, 1996). The touristic experience of the longed-for place can reinforce and affirm one's relationship to the primordial home, but it can also shatter the myth.

Memory

The notion of home is intricately connected with and contingent upon memory. Home can be conceived of as a repository of autobiographical and episodic memories; as a place of remembered material objects, spaces, landscapes, social relations and sensory experiences. Migrants and diasporic groups without personal memories of the home(land) can be defined by the retention of a collective historical and cultural memory of the dispersion and a collective identity formed by memories and myths of the homeland (Shuval, 2000: 43; Stock, 2010). Members of ethnic groups may not even consider themselves as belonging to a diaspora, until they begin to identify with such collective memories, from which the desire to travel may arise.

In the context of tourism's association with concepts of personhood, such as identity, subjectivity and the self, Desforges (2000) shows how tourism consumption is mobilized for self-identity. Touristic practices, long associated with individualism and the pursuit of self-actualization, can contribute to shaping consciousness, affirming, contesting or forging new identities. Embarking on a return journey into one's own past and confronting the remembered old home, potentially inflects one's sense of self-identity, as one (re)negotiates the relationship with the remembered home, but also one's current place of residence.

For anyone who has relocated – voluntarily or by force – the desire to return to a former home/homeland, permanently or for a temporary visit, depends not least on the ways in which the home and the circumstances of its loss are remembered, because memories of home are 'fluid reconstructions set against the backdrop of the remembering subject's current positionings ...' (Stock, 2010: 24). The revisit can be a vehicle for the systematic pursuit of memories; an extension of the process of remembering itself; an opportunity for reconstructing one's own past and affirming or reshaping one's identity. As the traveller encounters the old home, memories are recaptured, refreshed and verified; distorted memories are exposed and adjusted; embodied memories are relived through bodily experiences; long-forgotten memories can suddenly resurface and cause deeply emotional reactions; memories may spontaneously be shared with companions. After the journey, memories are re-evaluated, consolidated, synthesized and narrated; in the process, they may be compared and partly merged with other people's memories and perhaps one's own memories from previous journeys.

An important motivation to remember is the desire to consolidate one's own sense of self. Memory is always mediated and actively reconstructed from a range of sources and shaped to be consistent with particular 'self-identity goals' our 'current working self' (Freeman, 2010; Rose, 2010; Schacter, 1996; Sutton et al., 2010). As this process of reconstruction is influenced by factors such as situational demands, personal and social motivations, a return journey to a former home, especially when undertaken with significant others, children, family members and selected friends, sets the stage for remembering and narrating memories 'in certain ways', subconsciously adjusting them to the context and the audience. The experience of the journey; the engagement in specific actions and behaviour; the encounter of familiar, remembered sites; and the narration of memories during and after the journey facilitate an exploration of the self and the reconstruction and representation of one's life history and identity in relation to others. This largely correlates with social-constructionist views of identity (Cerulo, 1997) and with the 'performativity' perspective in tourism studies, which analyses touristic behaviour as strategically deployed means of self-representation (Cohen & Cohen, 2012: 2183).

Immediate descendants lack personal experience and autobiographical memories of their parents' home, yet sometimes carry vivid, detailed images or 'memories' in their mind of a place they have never seen. Their journeys to the old home are motivated by the quest to authenticate these internal images. Tolia-Kelley (2004) refers to such 'second-hand memories' as 're-memory', recall that is not based on actual experience, but on the memories of others, notably parents and grandparents. Memories are absorbed by children through stories and day-to-day living, whereby photographs and material objects in the home play a catalytic role. Aron Mazel's (2014) account of his 'homecoming' trip to Lithuania is an excellent example of this. Born in South Africa, the author had never set foot in the country of his parents' birth, yet was surprised and almost confused about his experience of feeling a strong sense of 'return'.

Where parents take their children along on return trips, the memories of the home merge with the memories of childhood travel and possibly contact with grandparents and other social relations. As childhood experiences of family holiday travel tend to be happily remembered (Shaw *et al.*, 2008), such joint return visits assist in passing the parents' nostalgia and longing for return onto the descendants.

In cases where the loss of the home was associated with violence, trauma and victimization, the children, later generations of descendants and even some outsiders can develop 'prosthetic memory' (Landsberg, 2004), deeply felt memories of traumatic pasts that the individual has not personally lived through, but so strongly identifies with that they become part of his/her own memory, shaping that person's subjectivity.

Alterity and the relationship between the Self and the Other is probably the most researched aspect in the earlier mentioned nexus between tourism, identity and self (trans)formation. Picard and Di Giovine's (2014) recent collection explores the power, paradoxes and the many different forms of Otherness in the tourism context, drawing attention to the 'Other in Us'. For the most part, Self–Other relations in tourism refer to the encounter of 'other' people and 'different' times and places and their capacity to lead to introspection and the discovery of a renewed or transformed Other within our own self, implicitly conceptualized as a stable entity. For the returning home tourists, on the contrary, the interaction with familiar people and places, underpinned by autobiographical and episodic memories, as well as comparisons with their current 'home', reveals changes in their own life history and sense of self. The confrontation of their own remembered former self as Other and the resultant recognition of the instability and fluidity of the self, may be a deeply unsettling experience.

Jillian Powers, in Chapter 7, argues that the 'diasporic tourist gaze' of the homeland relies not on quintessential differences, but intrinsic similarities; the homeland tourist looks at 'an other that is also a representation of the self'. This adds an interesting dimension to Macleod's (2004) work, by raising the question how the presence of the diasporic tourist as Other affects the host community, not only socio-economically, but in terms of their own culture and sense of identity. Memory and the relationship to the home affect the 'tourist gaze' (Urry, 1990) and the unique characteristics of return journeys home warrant nuancing and redefining the concept. For 'homesick tourists' with personal memories of the old home, the gaze is defined by similarity and memory. Tourists who walk in the footsteps of their own remembered past, gaze systematically in search of the most ordinary familiar traces of their former everyday life-world. They 'see' what is no longer there, as internal images deeply imprinted in their brain superimpose themselves onto the external topography. The 'memory gaze' is not a detached, voyeuristic gaze, but deeply engaged and perhaps intensely emotional, as it is also a gaze into one's own past (Marschall, 2015a). The sense of authenticity caused by this unique experience is worth investigating more closely, as it potentially adds new perspectives to our understanding of this fundamental concept in tourism (Knudsen & Waade, 2010).

For some, home looks both familiar and surprisingly unfamiliar, as the encountered reality differs from the remembered and imagined images, causing confusion, alienation and even perhaps an affirmation of host-land belonging. This is especially true for members of diasporic communities removed by several generations, who realize their 'otherness' from homeland 'natives'. But in the tourism context alterity can also affirm belonging; Jackie Feldman (2016), himself a Jewish American immigrant to Israel, demonstrates how working as a Jewish guide for Christian pilgrims in the Holy Land 'made me Israeli'.

This brief introduction is meant to show that a systematic exploration of the triangular relationship between tourism, memory and home can result in new insights about touristic endeavours, open up novel avenues of enquiry and contribute to the development of new conceptual and theoretical perspectives. The following section will provide a contextual framework for this analytical lens, embedded in a comprehensive, but by no means exhaustive review of the literature.

Memory, Tourism and Home: Limitations

Tourism and Memories of Home does not include virtual forms of travel to an ancestral home; travelling in the mind and in one's dreams; or symbolic journeys home that do not engender real-life forms of travel. This book is also not about tourists returning to their place of residence after a holiday. The exception are long-term travellers, individuals who have spent a significant period of time abroad, and who – upon their return home – experience substantial shifts of consciousness. Their perception of home has changed and needs to be re-negotiated; some even feel a sense of alienation and struggle to re-integrate (Pocock & McIntosh, 2013).

Second home tourism, a field expertly explored in Hall and Müller's (2004) edited volume, constitutes another grey area in terms of the conceptualization of this book (see also Rogerson & Hoogendoorn, 2014). Most of these second homes, including holiday apartments and weekend cottages are located within a radius of less than 100km from the primary residence and are used for short-term recreation. However, some people own second homes much further away, even in other countries and genuinely divide their lives between two homes, possibly re-creating elements of their primary home in the second home and vice versa. Travelling to such homes, especially when they have been inherited within the family are important for reconnecting with memories of childhood and loved-ones. Second home tourism raises interesting questions about identity, sense of place and the meaning of home, especially as individual sentiments may clash with administrative practices for the purpose of taxation and citizenship rights that force households to state their primary residence.

Conceptually, *Tourism and Memories of Home* involves, in the first instance, the return journeys of people who have moved away from a former home, be it voluntarily in search of new opportunities or in accordance with new life stages, or involuntarily on account of political or socio-economic forces beyond their control. Not everyone wishes to see their old home again and not everyone who does, actually embarks on a journey to travel there. Understanding avoidance behaviour is as important for scholars of tourism studies as researching travel motivation. Some people prefer not to be reminded of past suffering and revile the thought of confronting the sites of their earlier trauma. Others avoid the return to their childhood home for fear of spoiling their happy memories. Yet others are simply indifferent about their former homes. They might miss specific aspects of their place of origin (e.g. the food, the weather), but have no further social or emotional ties to the place and do not care to revisit. Some people relocate precisely to burn all bridges and start out afresh somewhere else; they do not want to be reminded of where they came from and will not revisit, especially not with a significant other.

People may return to former homes or hometowns for entirely pragmatic, mundane reasons, perhaps to attend to a legal or financial matter or for a specific purpose connected to their livelihood (e.g. academics conducting fieldwork research in the place with which they are intimately familiar). The return 'home' may be completely coincidental – a person on a business trip or conference that happens to occur in one's former home town. Some of these tourists may use the opportunity to check up on familiar places and even delve into memories of their past life here, but others may attach no special significance to being in the location of their former home.

Likewise, not all descendants of migrants or refugees and members of diasporas are nostalgic about their family's place of origin; some neither wish to return there, nor visit. Their relationship with their family's former home or country of origin may be compromised, elusive or detached, depending not least on their level of attachment, integration and personal identification with their current place of residence or host country. The relationship of diasporic communities towards their ancestral homes is contingent on many factors, including the history and circumstances of the erstwhile migration; the level of (real or perceived) acceptance or alienation in the host country; the attitude of residents and the government in the homeland towards the diaspora and returnees; the migrants' sense of identity, ongoing support for and relationship with the homeland; their myths and memories of the homeland; and their desire to return permanently (Coles & Timothy, 2004: 6; Shuval, 2000).

Memories of the homeland refers not only to the personal and family memories held by individuals, but also prevailing 'societal frameworks of memory' (Halbwachs, 1992), i.e. larger discourses circulating in nations, societies or communities around how the past should be remembered. This is well illustrated by the case of German expellees (*Aussiedler, Vertriebene*), who lost their homes in the eastern parts of the German Empire at the end of World War II. By and large, the survivor generation's nostalgia for the homeland (and in many cases the longing to revisit) has not been passed on to their descendants. In the post-Nazi era, the younger generation has grown up distancing themselves from their parents' and grandparents' experiences of war and flight and identification with the lost homeland became sociopolitically undesirable in both East and West Germany. In other words, prevailing societal frameworks of memory and grand narratives of history communicated through the school curriculum and mainstream media may dominate over competing micro-narratives and personal memories encountered within the family (Marschall, 2015a; Wagner in Chapter 4).

Personal Memory Tourism

This book is about people who experience a curiosity or longing for home and who embark on journeys of various types to experience their own notions of home. Harper's historical research (Chapter 2) shows that the desire for the temporary return journey home is not a new phenomenon, but has accompanied the project of migration for a long time and given rise to organized commercial exploitation by the tourism industry since the early 20th century. This under-researched type of touristic mobility is also allied with and constitutes an aspect of 'personal heritage tourism' (Timothy, 1997), travel in search of sites related to one's own heritage and life history, including the old family home, but also significant places linked to one's professional development, religious conviction or hobbies. A similar range of potential travel destinations is covered by Pearce's (2012) concept of 'Visiting Home and Familiar Places (VHFP) Tourism', but with a stronger focus on previous experience and personal memories of the place. Based on a theoretical framework drawn from neuroscience, psychology and integrating insights from the study of human memory, cognition and emotions, Pearce argues that the exploration of this under-researched tourism phenomenon may offer new insights into existing tourism research on issues of identity and self-perception, as well as offering myriad opportunities for tourism marketers and the industry.

The experience of travelling in search of a former home is also part of what I have called 'Personal Memory Tourism' (Marschall, 2012, 2014, 2015b). A small-scale empirical study showed that many participants had indeed revisited former homes, especially in the company of their children or a new spouse, who they wanted to show 'where I come from'. In most cases, such trips were extensions of travel undertaken for other reasons, motivated by curiosity and underpinned perhaps by an attempt to recapture happy childhood memories. Where former homes are associated with experiences of fear, isolation or violence, the literal return to the site of suffering can be an attempt at coming to terms with disturbing episodic memories of trauma and potentially lead to catharsis and personal healing, mimicking psychoanalysis.

Tamara West's (2014) study of Germans returning to Displaced Persons' Camps illustrates the complexity of the notion of 'home'. These camps were set up at the end of World War II, but sometimes remained in operation well into the 1950s or even 60s, especially in West Germany. The camp was meant as a temporary shelter for those who had lost their homes, but for many it effectively became a new home, associated with shelter, security, family and community – complex sites of identity, belonging and difference. Today, the camps no longer exist or only in truncated form, yet people travel to see the remnants of these 'homes', deeply engrained in memory. Highlighting the enacted and embodied nature of memory, West draws attention to the role of photographs – cherished old photographs as *aide mémoires* and carefully framed new photographs taken during the revisit – in the process of remembering and narrating the past.

Internal Displacement

Throughout the 20th century, countless people lost their homes due to political violence and warfare, most especially in the wake of World War II and subsequent wars. Cohen's (1997) understanding of the 'victim diaspora' can be extended to all those people who were displaced and lost their homes due to political violence; warfare; genocide; ethnic, religious or other forms of persecution; natural or human-made disaster. In this context, Hannam and Yankovska (Chapter 3) engage with victims of the 1986 Chernobyl nuclear disaster, their memories, their relationship towards the lost home and their attitudes towards the emergent tourism around the 'ghost town' that was once their home. While recent literature covers the return journeys of some of these groups, much neglected from this discourse are the real or desired return trips by the internally displaced, including those evicted from their homes through economic pressures and imposed development measures. Large populations around the world, often indigenous communities, are resettled for the building of dams; the establishment of large-scale agricultural and industrial developments; the creation of nature conservation areas and game reserves; or other types of alternative land-use that erode their source of livelihood.

Even where people are compensated and persuaded to move voluntarily, the loss of their land may still be experienced as traumatic and a strong emotional attachment to the old home can linger and be transferred to the next generation. Indigenous communities are often tied to the land through spiritual beliefs, traditional cultural practices or the presence of ancestral graves. Many of these people may hold a deep yearning to revisit, not necessarily to see their old homestead again and dwell on memories, but perhaps to perform a ritual or pay respect at a burial site. Most will not have the means to travel there or are prevented from doing so, as the site is now destroyed or inaccessible. Others may pose as leisure tourists to a nature reserve or heritage site, but are in reality disguised return visitors, who clandestinely look for the plot that was once their home or secretly engage in a sacred rite at an unmarked grave. Researching this completely unchartered terrain, understanding these communities' unfulfilled longing to travel and perhaps facilitating such journeys 'home' could make a valuable contribution to fostering reconciliation and social cohesion, apart from benefiting the domestic travel sector.

The Return of the Victim Diaspora

Among all the population groups displaced through the impacts of World War II, the above mentioned German expellees have attracted the most scholarly attention. The phenomenon of *Heimattourismus*, 'homeland tourism' or *Heimwehtourismus*, literally 'homesick tourism' or 'travel prompted by longing for the homeland' refers to the return journeys of survivors and to a small extent their immediate descendants to their former homes in what is now Poland, Ukraine, western Russia and other Eastern European countries. This type of tourism became a trend in the 1970s and flourished in the 1990s, after the collapse of the Soviet Union, generating a considerable niche market tourism industry, which in turn spawned research interest (e.g. Peleikis, 2009). Two essential characteristics distinguish these expellees. First is their resettlement within their home country, theoretically facilitating fairly seamless blending in with their host communities in terms of nationality, language, culture and mutually shared history. Secondly, their former homes are now part of another country, inhabited by different people who have in many cases eliminated or modified the cultural traces of the German past. Most homesick tourists have no more family and friends in their old home town and reconnection with a familiar cultural environment is difficult. As they attempt to walk in the footsteps of their remembered past, traces of the old home and accustomed places may have to be researched and re-discovered.

Focusing on travel narratives of German expellees during the time of the Cold War, Wagner (in Chapter 4) compares the experiences of homesick tourists from East and West Germany, and how prevailing socio-political discourses, ideological forces and local cultures of remembrance relating to the lost homeland impact on the description of the return journey. The travel narratives from West German homesick tourists, for instance, tend to read like 'inventories' of the lost homeland, with their tendency to extreme detail in the descriptions of the remaining material traces of the past. For both groups, the return journey was experienced as an emotional and highly significant event. For some it confirmed that the lost home will forever remain their true home, a 'home of the soul', while others felt an acute sense of unbelonging, painfully acknowledging that this place is no longer home or 'home, but not home'.

Homesick tourism, currently mostly associated with the German context, is in reality a much wider phenomenon, as people in many parts of the world have similarly been displaced. For instance, thousands of Chinese men belonging to the Kuomintang forces, who fled to Taiwan in 1950 and were subsequently cut off from their homes, embarked on return visits after mainland China's political opening. As opposed to the German homesick tourists, the Chinese would predominantly focus on the reunification with members of their long-lost family. This alerts us to the fact that, despite similarities in the historical circumstances of the dislodgment, the return mobilities of survivors and their descendants are always contextually specific, dependent on larger socio-political and economic factors, societal relationships towards the past (or social frameworks of memory) and on the individuals' relationship with their old home and their current home.

Homesick tourism also takes place among Palestinians in exile, discussed in this volume by Noga Kadman and Mustafa Kabha (Chapter 5), who long to revisit their former homes, now inhabited by Jews, or the depopulated or erased traces of their former villages destroyed by Zionist forces during the *Nakba* in 1948. There is a growing trend of such visits by internally displaced Palestinians who became citizens of Israel, by West Bank Palestinians who manage to cross the Green Line, and by Palestinian who live abroad, mostly in western countries, and come to Israel as tourists. Unlike the descendants of German expellees, many young Palestinians have absorbed their parents' and grandparents' nostalgia for the lost home and their outrage at the injustice and victimization they suffered. The continuous demand for the return of the land renders the visit of the destroyed village a political statement, discouraged and inhibited by Israeli authorities. As the destroyed villages were often covered with a forest, some of which are now recreational tourist attractions, these visitors are not necessarily visible as homesick tourists (Kadman, 2010; Kaplan & Grunebaum, 2013).

The return of the victim diaspora is epitomized by Jewish survivors of the Holocaust in Israel and elsewhere in the diaspora who travel to Europe, often with their children. Some of these trips are even initiated by younger members of the family in an attempt to preserve the memory and bridge trans-generational gaps of communication and understanding. When these travellers visit synagogues, cemeteries, concentration camps and museums, they blend in with mainstream heritage tourists or 'dark tourists'. Although 'Holocaust tourism' is an established niche segment and a phenomenon well covered in the literature from multifarious disciplinary angles (e.g. Buntman, 2008; Kugelmass, 1994), the survivors' return to their lost homes in Western, Middle and Eastern Europe is rarely explored.

In addition to investigating the experiences of East and West German expellee homesick tourists, Wagner (Chapter 4) compares the return trips of German Jewish émigrés to their respective former homes in Poland. Members of each group may have virtually been neighbours in the past, yet for the Jewish return visitors, the Holocaust stands between the memory of the old home and the present. Although they engage in very similar behaviour – systematically searching for the remembered traces of their former homes – their attitudes towards the current inhabitants is very different. Some Jewish travellers even express a sense of satisfaction over their former homeland now being in Polish, rather than German hands and the visit instils in them a new appreciation of their current home, understood as a second chance in life. Linking with Wagner, Kidron's chapter (10), which focuses on Israeli descendants of Holocaust survivors who travel alone or accompanied by their survivor parents, will be discussed further below.

In many places, the wish by survivors and their immediate descendants to travel in search of memories and revisit their old home has spawned the emergence of specialized tour operators, social justice organizations and special interest groups, who facilitate such return travel (e.g. Zochrot in Israel). With the passing of the survivor generation, some increasingly cater for the descendant generation and reach out towards empathetic outsiders, i.e. heritage tourists with a special interest, conscience and perhaps 'prosthetic memory', who seek an emotionally touching educational experience or who visit in the name of reconciliation and cross-cultural understanding.

Perhaps more than any other type of diasporic return visit, the home journeys of victim diasporas take on the character of pilgrimage, a 'voyage of self-discovery and nurturance' (Ebron, 1999). Although many travellers actually say a prayer or engage in practices of religious worship when re-encountering the old home, especially on their very first journey back, pilgrimage here refers to secular, not religious forms of tourism. For many, the experience is a 'sacred journey' nonetheless. The tour with all its physical strains and sacrifices represents the culmination of a long-cherished desire; touching base with home is a historical moment, for some a life-changing experience, full of emotion, memories and symbolism. The performance of small private rituals or group rites of passage that affirm identity and belonging, acknowledge pain and suffering, perhaps foster forgiveness and reconciliation; the collecting of mementos such as stones or soil from the ground; their display and veneration as relics upon return; the perceived significance of the journey in attaining closure, a sense of salvation, symbolic regeneration and hope all echo core tenets of religious pilgrimage (Di Giovine, 2012; Picard & Di Giovine, 2014).

For refugees who return to their homes for the very first time, sometimes clandestinely and illegally due to their ongoing refugee status, the journey is a particularly memorable one, associated with anxieties, deeply emotional experiences and discoveries about their identity and the meaning of home (Muggeridge & Doná, 2006). On the other end of the scale are highly organized group tours, facilitating the return visits and homecomings especially of African American roots tourists. The more commercialized the tour, the more fervently is the notion of pilgrimage stressed by the guides and operators, hence allowing participants with all relevant trappings to distance themselves from their status as tourists (Ebron, 1999).

Migrant Return Travel

As opposed to refugees, émigrés, expellees and diasporic groups who were forced to resettle or violently lost their home, transnationals who migrate voluntarily in search of employment, better economic conditions or personal opportunities, as well as the proliferating number of foreign residential tourists or retirement expatriates (Levitt, 2010; McWatters, 2009) experience a comparatively less intense sense of loss. Most are theoretically able to return and may retain strong bonds with their former home, notably in the form of social relations and property, but also through the fostering and sharing of memories. Some feel a strong sense of nostalgia and long for a permanent return, which in reality remains largely illusory. Return trips home serve to maintain existing ties, introduce children to the homeland and theoretically prepare for the descendant generation's permanent return. Where descendants of migrants decide to move to the 'old country' ('return migration', 'counter-diasporic migration'), this usually occurs after one or several temporary return visits induced by the (grand)parents' nostalgia (King & Christou, 2010; Long & Oxfeld, 2004; Potter, 2005; Wessendorf, 2007). Yankholmes' chapter (Chapter 11) makes an important contribution to the literature on African American roots tourism in Ghana by focusing on those who have permanently 'returned'.

Modern information and communication technology greatly assists migrants to maintain transnational social networks and stay in touch with 'home', but for some, the actual visit remains important and prompts them to make financial and other sacrifices. For others, return visits home are low on the agenda, as they recreate their external homeland at their current place of residence through cultural practices, food preparation and eating rituals, images and artefacts in the home and various types of memory-based routines (Bhandari, Chapter 6; Hung et al., 2013; Tolia-Kelly, 2004). But this can suddenly change in response to dramatic events and external stimuli, as Bhandari discusses in Chapter 6, triggering patriotism and a new sense of pride, belonging and self-identity.

The touristic mobility patterns of migrants and especially their return visits home have attracted some scholarly attention in recent years (e.g. Dwyer et al., 2014; Rogerson, 2004; Scheyvens, 2007), but are still under-researched and especially neglected by policy makers, tourism authorities and the tourism industry. Some countries do not statistically capture or legally define visiting members of its diaspora as tourists (as Bhandari mentions with respect to Nepal). Many scholarly studies do not specifically distinguish transnationals or first-generation migrants and expatriates from diasporic communities more generally, which include successive generations of descendants without personal memories of the former home(land) and the migration experience. The home visits of transnationals are usually considered under the label VFR tourism and the motivations for such trips may be compared to family reunion travel (Kluin & Lehto, 2012), because the primary purpose of the journey is the fostering of social ties and the fulfilment of family commitments, such as attending weddings, funerals and traditional holidays.

VFR tourism itself has long been underestimated by tourism authorities and deserves more attention by researchers, especially from a social and cultural perspective (Backer, 2012; Hung et al., 2013; Shani, 2013; Uriely, 2010). Duval (2003) argues that the migrant 'return visit' is a rather special category of VFR tourism, distinguished by the need to maintain cultural ties with the external homeland and 'contextualise social and cultural backgrounds after migration' (Duval, 2003: 267; Baldassar, 2001). With reference to the Commonwealth East Caribbean community in Toronto, he illustrates how the relationship between the visiting migrant and the host community becomes a stage for the negotiation of identities. The return travel of migrants is about memory, nostalgia and longing for home as a specific localized place of belonging, but also more generally as an environment of cultural familiarity and significant social relations. In other words, there are different and additional dimensions to the visiting of family and friends when transnational migrants return home.

Many migrants travel specifically to introduce their children to their cultural home and provide them with an opportunity to meet relatives and reinforce relationships. Some send their teenage children to temporarily live with grandparents in the home country and children of marriageable age may be sent back home in the hope of finding a suitable spouse (King & Christou, 2010). Vietnamese families in Australia travel back home to enhance their children's familiarity with cultural values, religious norms and moral orders that the parents deem important (Nguyen & King, 2004). Traditional cultural principles (*guanxi*) impose relationship duties on Chinese people and compel them to perform ritual practices to foster familial ties as a contribution to the maintenance of social harmony. The need to observe filial piety, to attend to grave sites, pay respect to deceased family and ancestors and actively engage in remembrance, may instil a sense of obligation to visit home (Huang *et al.*, 2016; Lew & Wong, 2004; Oxfeld, 2004; Tie *et al.*, 2015). Hung *et al.* (2013) examined the return trips of Chinese migrants in Hong Kong as a way of maintaining social capital; for their participants, the trip was not about visiting friends, but rather a family-oriented journey for fostering kinship ties (i.e. VR, rather than VFR tourism). Powers' investigation of Chinese adoption homeland tours (Chapter 7) adds a unique dimension to these journeys, as the adoptive parents themselves have no connection with their child's homeland.

When spending time with friends and family, the exchanging of memories about the mutually spent past becomes a way of solidifying ties and re-establishing bonds, especially where a sense of alienation is noticeable due to the separation and resulting divergence of life worlds. Such social exchanges and observations about what is familiar and what has changed, induce reflection about one's former life here and comparisons with one's life at the current place of residence. Many return visitors, especially those returning for the first time, will experience a slight shift in their sense of identity at the end of the journey.

Return visits are socio-economically important for the country of origin, because migrants bring gifts for family and friends and are encouraged to sustain the practice of sending remittances (Asiedu, 2005; Duval, 2003; Hall & Duval, 2004), but the existing literature has not paid sufficient attention to the underlying cultural and social dimensions of such material exchanges (see Bhandari in Chapter 6; but see Baldassar, 2001). In subtle ways, such transactions redefine identities and nuance relationships between friends or parents and children. Similarly, diasporic return visits may be important in terms of political identity (Baldassar, 2001; 2011). Croatian migrants' return home can often be understood as an act of patriotism and affirmation of political, cultural and national identity in response to the country's attempts at establishing the nation as an extended 'imagined community' that includes the diaspora (Carter, 2004). In the case of Eritrean migrants discussed by Arnone (Chapter 8), the return trip is part of the remembering of their participation in and personal experiences of the Eritrean liberation struggle. The visit of museums and memorials commemorating the Eritrean liberation struggle, paying respect to the dead, are important components of the trip home for many travellers of the survivor generation and sites where their Eritrean identity can be asserted.

One of the important contributions of this book is to illustrate the diversity and uniqueness of the return visit home for individuals and groups. While many of the chapters arrive at similar and overlapping findings, each case of diasporic homecoming and migrant return is also different and associated with unique characteristics, based on the specific historical circumstances of the migration, the diasporic group's identity, as well as socio-political, economic and cultural factors in the host coutnry and the country of origin. An excellent example is Corsale and Iorio's chapter (9) with its focus on Transylvanian Saxons, an ethnic German population who, over a long period of time, experienced a double diaspora, first away from Germany and later away from Transylvania, Romania. The authors investigate the way Saxons perceived their homeland over the two diasporas and analyse the visits to the homeland made by the first generation of Saxons resettled in Germany and the influence of the rediscovered landscape on their sense of belonging to home(land).

The regular return home can be a coping strategy for migration related stress that migrants experience through cultural alienation in the host country (Iarmolenko, 2014). Stephenson (2004) found that members of the Afro-Caribbean diaspora in the UK experienced racist encounters and socially alienating situations during their domestic tourism journeys and indeed at destinations elsewhere in Europe. For these immigrant groups, a trip 'back home' to the Caribbean is partly motivated by the need for a sense of belonging, a desire to feel culturally at home and become (re)acquainted with their ethnic roots. The total immersion in a culturally familiar place includes the experience of cultural elements such as language, customary practices, food, religion and social behaviour; the multisensory encounter of remembered sounds, smells and familiar sights – mental images and cultural knowledge retained and transmitted within the diasporic community.

As much as the return visit can induce a feeling of 'home is where my culture is', it may equally reinforce a sense of belonging to the host country and result in further estrangement from one's roots, as tourists discover how much life in their old country has changed, or how much they themselves have changed (Tie *et al.*, 2015). Not all migrants return home to indulge in nostalgia, solidify their ethnic identities and affirm their sense of belonging to the country of origin. Eritrean migrants in Italy revisit their homeland specifically to perform touristic identities, visiting heritage sites and tourist attractions, to emphasize the contrast with their former lives and identities, still embodied by their friends and relatives who have remained behind (Arnone, 2011). Nepali migrants in Bhandari's study (Chapter 6) similarly combine family visits with the exploration of tourist attractions in their home country, but for his participants, comparisons with British friends and colleagues in the host country are more salient. Research on the touristic mobilities of immigrants in the UK adds nuance to Andrews' (2011) *The British on Holiday* and its insights into constructions of the self in relation to national, regional, class and gender identities.

Second Generation

Within the bourgeoning literature on migrant transnationalism, research on the second generation or the immediate descendants of migrants has been identified as particularly sparse (Huang *et al.*, 2016; King & Christou, 2010). It is important to understand why the younger generation decides to visit the old country, especially where this occurs independently of travel within the family context. First-generation migrants are always characterized by personal experience and memories of the homeland; they usually maintain social relations and a strong sense of nostalgia. For their immediate descendants, the connection with the parental homeland is believed to be based less on emotional and personal than on cultural and historical links (Tie *et al.*, 2015). Motivations include fostering remaining social relations, maintaining property, or conducting family history research driven by curiosity, without much sentimentality. Many of these descendants travel with their own children, spouse, friends or an organized group and combine their visit of the old family home with a larger exploration of the region and varied touristic activities. Focusing on Eritrean migrants in Italy, Arnone (Chapter 8) shows how the two generations revive the home country as an ideal identifier across borders in different ways, with each generation seeking spaces where to place nostalgic and idealized notions of the self.

Some members of the second generation opt to travel with members of the older generation, reversing the parent–child travel pattern discussed earlier. As Kidron shows in her case study of Israeli tourists travelling with their Holocaust survivor parents or older members of the family to visit childhood homes, hiding places and related family and community sites in Europe (Chapter 10 and Kidron, 2013), the initial aim of their journey is exploring family roots and gaining a historical understanding of the familial past.

However, the presence of the survivors and the joint witnessing of deeply personal authentic sites, the unlocking of suppressed memories *in situ*, induces profoundly emotional experiences, with the result that the quest for historical knowledge recedes behind the search for emotions that facilitate bonding, thick familial sociality and the intensification of psychological bonds with kin.

Apart from nostalgia and memories passed on by parents and grandparents, for second- and third-generation migrants the relationship toward the old homeland and the wish to travel there depend on various external factors. Education, language and religious affiliation have also been highlighted as critical in the context of Chinese migrants in Malaysia, as they impact on values and identity formation (Tie *et al.*, 2015: 207). Iarmolenko's (2014) study of the Ukranian diaspora in the US established that their exposure to media reports about Ukraine strongly influenced their imaginary of the old home. These images and ideas embedded in consciousness correlated with their desire to travel there. The Indian diaspora's imagination of India, their identity constructions, notions of home and 'return' travel to India has been shown to be influenced by Bollywood movies. For first-generation migrants, watching these movies creates nostalgia for the old homeland and a yearning to travel there, whereas the second generation seems to focus on the portrayal of modernity and affluence in Bollywood movies; they want to experience India as a new 'modern' country (Bandyopadhyay, 2008).

Travel to the Ancestral Home

The influence of movies, fiction writing and popular entertainment products on inducing touristic mobility is well known and the entire phenomenon of African American 'Roots tourism' is said to have originated with Alex Haley's 1976 novel *Roots* and the international success of the subsequent TV series. The 'ethnic homecoming' of the African-American diaspora now constitutes a major segment of the tourism industry in Ghana, Senegal, Benin and other West African destinations associated with the slave trade (e.g. Bruner, 1996; Schramm, 2010; Timothy & Teye, 2004). It is underpinned by a strong identification with collective memories and an emotional or spiritual connection with 'Mother Africa', a symbolic homeland, rather than specific, historically traceable places of origins. The slave castles and other 'attractions' of this type of tourism also draw more general heritage tourists from outside the African community.

Various scholars have cautioned against an over-emphasis on the ancestral homeland as reference point for diasporic groups (Tie *et al.*, 2015). Indeed, it will only ever be a minority that long to travel there and even fewer actually embark on a journey. Yet, the popularity of roots tourism and related niche area types of return travel to primordial homelands is indisputable; it has generated considerable tourism flows in various parts of the world and spawned thriving tourism industries. Tourism authorities in destinations with significant emigration histories have recognized the strategic importance of diasporas in targeting new markets (see e.g. *Die Welt,* 2009 for Germany).

Inspired by the growth of such trends and patterns in the tourism industry, roots tourism has engendered considerable scholarly attention and a host of typologies and sub-categories have been developed. A major geographical focal point of this research, apart from West Africa, is Scotland and Ireland with tourists coming mostly from the US, Canada, Australia, New Zealand and other parts of the world where these ethnic groups are prevalent. Those intending to engage in family history research in archives and libraries; gather oral testimony from kin; visit graveyards and retrace specific sites associated with their ancestors are referred to as genealogy tourists (Meethan, 2004), legacy tourists (McCain & Ray, 2003), or personal heritage tourists (Timothy, 1997). Others are more socially orientated with an interest in attending historical events; participate in family reunions and homecomings; and establish contacts with previously unknown members of the extended family (Basu, 2004). Yet others travel more casually in the footsteps of their ancestor. They do not conduct serious historical research, but rather desire an immersive experience in the country of their ancestors, attempting to experience the past and seek to re-discover the signs of their forebears in the landscape. They are fascinated with Ireland or Scotland and blend in with other heritage tourists, as they absorb the cultural icons, images, events and narratives that have been crafted to define identity and express a meaning of the nation (Bhandari, 2014; Cronin & O'Connor, 2003).

Harper (in Chapter 2) places the current scholarly interest in Scottish roots tourism, homecomings and genealogy tourism in historical perspective by investigating the return journeys of the Scottish diaspora since the 19th century. Although the general purpose of these tours has always been connection with roots and ancestry, the specific motivations and organizations of these returns home have changed over the years, giving rise to new tourism typologies and the increasing commercialization of 'homecomings'. Bieter *et al.* (Chapter 12) also focus on homecomings, which now constitute a significant niche industry in itself. They illustrate how the diasporic longing for an ancestral home is rendered more complex, where it cannot be matched with a specific destination, as in the case of the Scots-Irish diaspora or where the ancestral homeland is part of another country, as in the case of the Basques.

Israel is the destination of another major strand of diasporic roots tourism. Jewish-Americans and other members of the international Jewish diaspora undertake 'pilgrimages' to Israel, which may be combined with Holocaust tourism experiences in Eastern Europe (Ioannides & Ioannides, 2004). Israeli Birthright tourism (Kelner, 2010), Exodus tours (Cohen, 2004) and Youth

Tourism to Israel (Cohen, 2008) specifically attract a younger generation of Jews. Israel is not the home of their parents/grandparents, but the God-given ancestral homeland, the diasporic place of origin. These tours could be classified as study tours or heritage tourism products, except for the special relationship and emotional bonds of the target group. The purpose of these trips is just as much about heritage and roots, history and culture, as it is about religious, political and ideological consciousness shaping, i.e. identification with Israel, fortifying diasporic ties and political support in the diaspora.

Many roots tourists emanate from multicultural, melting pot or 'placeless' societies in the 'New World', where members of ethnic minorities face real or perceived discrimination and disempowerment that compromises their sense of belonging, or where members of mainstream populations and assimilated citizens begin to re-discover their ethnic roots, identify with collective memories and assert a group identity rooted in a distant homeland. The erosion of traditional values; depersonalizing effects of modernity; and 'atomized' existence in modern consumer society are said to cause disorientation, alienation and a problematized sense of belonging, a 'post-colonial unsettling of settler society' (Basu, 2005: 134), which prompt this search for identity and belonging. For some, the search culminates in the simulated 'return home', a roots journey to the ancestral homeland.

Motivations for visiting the old homeland are variously described in the literature as the quest for identity and belonging; to 'find oneself', to find out 'who am I' and 'where I come from'; the search for cultural roots and affirmation of ethnic origin; the desire to explore the past and gain a deeper understanding of the migration and diasporic existence; the yearning to experience and authenticate a place of internalized cultural narratives, memories and myths; the longing for 'primal' connections' or a spiritual link with ancestors; the yearning for an emotional, visceral, deeply meaningful and authentic experience through multisensory immersion in the place of ancestral origin (Basu, 2004, 2005; Bruner, 1996; Tie *et al.*, 2015).

Some of these homes are complete constructs of the imagination, based on romanticized notions and infused with myths. They are not founded in family memories passed on through the generations, but on stories constructed around the family's past and identification with wider cultural narratives acquired through books, popular media products, the internet or heritage centres (Basu, 2005). 'It seems to me that one has a more precise idea of *Heimat* [homeland] the further one is away from it', observed the German film director Edgar Reitz (cited in Morley & Robins, 1993: 7). Where people have mixed ancestry, they selectively embrace one strand of their heritage, often the one associated with narratives of trauma and victimization. Fuelling the identification with the lost home, they take on prosthetic memories of oppression and loss that may be completely non-factual, ignoring the particularities of historical realities and the real reasons for their ancestors' emigration (Basu, 2005). This social phenomenon prompts Basu (2005: 145) to draw parallels with the 'psychological phenomenon of false memory syndrome, where an identifiable – even though imagined – traumatic episode is believed to account for the symptoms of trauma, the true causes of which remain obscure.'

How exactly do tourists attempt to achieve a sense of home when travelling to countries, with which they have no personal connection? With respect to three very different case studies, Powers (Chapter 7) shows how tourists use kin concepts to transform essentially foreign homelands into familiar and comfortable home-spaces. Kinship metaphors articulate a sense of belonging and envision connections with the homeland by blurring boundaries between literal and imagined family. As the ancestral homeland is experienced against the foil of memories, myths and imagination, tourists feel 'at home' when the encounter of the visited place meets their expectations and imaginings, potentially resulting in extremely powerful, moving and life-changing experience. For others, the multifarious encounters and observations provided by the trip result in ambivalent, contentious or outright disappointing experiences, which lead to a critical reassessment of diasporic identity and the relationship towards the old home.

Travelling to the Symbolic Home and Symbolic Ways of Travelling to the Real Home

Some people travel to places that evoke memories of home, yet are geographically and historically unconnected to any family origins. Entire destinations can become substitutes or 'replacement homelands' based on similarity of tangible and intangible environmental characteristics. Leite (2005) illustrates this with respect to several different diasporic populations, where the touristic encounter of local landscapes seems to trigger 'genetic memory', i.e. reactivate long dormant emotions and the perception of an 'echo' of the tourist's ancestral collective memory (Leite, 2005: 294). Similarly, diasporic groups and ethnic minorities in Britain, notably the Turkish minority and Asians from Pakistan, are drawn to places in the UK that remind them of their home (Stephenson, 2004: 67ff). Remembered landscape features, characteristic vegetation types, smells, sounds and atmospheric effects are 'found' or discovered in the rural countryside and urban spaces, conveying a sense of home and triggering memories.

One of the characteristics of transnationalism is the propensity of migrants to recreate aspects of home in the private sphere of their household and public community spaces. Chinese diasporic communities, faced with the impossibility of the actual journey home, for instance, create institutions that allow them to fulfill their filial duties in terms of *guanxi* in their host country, hence meeting their obligation to return home symbolically (Lew & Wong, 2004). Of interest to tourism studies are members of diasporic groups who temporarily recreate 'home' in a destination other than their current place of residence. They organize the assembly of family, friends or specific communities in a place that facilitates immersion in a culturally familiar environment or encourages acting out performativity characteristic of home. In some places specific tours are designed to create such substitute home environments, drawing tourists who long for home, yet lack the means and opportunities to travel there. Bieter *et al.* (Chapter 12) examine the homecomings of the American based Basque diaspora in the city of Boise, Idaho, where a sense of home and an indulgence in collective memories is created through the condensation of cultural and social elements.

Apart from real travel to a destination temporarily defined as symbolic home, there are also symbolic ways of travelling to the real home, where the latter is inaccessible. The Trail of the Displaced commemorates the Karelian evacuation in Finland and represents a symbolic journey home (Kuusisto-Arponen, 2009). Walking on the road towards the Russian border, survivors and their descendants literally retrace the steps taken by those forcibly displaced at the end of World War II. It is precisely the experience of mobility, the rhythmic motions and kinetic aspects of moving through the material landscape that bring back experiential or narrated cross-generational memories and prompt narration. Some reported that 'journeying' had brought back long forgotten memories (Kuusisto-Arponen, 2009: 558). Obviously, from a tourism perspective this case is relevant only insofar as people actually travelled to take part in the commemorative trail.

Conclusion

Much of the literature covered in this survey is based on qualitative research, often involving interpretivist approaches and ethnographic methodologies, some featuring extensive verbatim accounts of participants' experiences. These quotations in themselves represent a valuable source, which can be mined for references to the role of memory in defining spaces of belonging when travelling home. Echoing Kuusisto-Arponen's (2009) findings, some interview testimony and travel narratives make explicit mention of memories being triggered through the kinaesthesia of walking around the hometown, travelling through remembered landscapes by train. This occurs because embodied memory is spontaneously recalled when specific bodily movements and mobility patterns are inadvertently re-enacted (e.g. travelling by train, or treading on familiar surfaces; see Marschall, 2015a). A sense of home, identity and belonging is attained through the physical re-encounter of sites and stimuli associated with episodic memories of momentous events, which one may have recalled and narrated many times before, and – perhaps more importantly – through the sudden, vivid recollection of long-forgotten mundane, trivial details of quotidian life back then, at home. The return visit is a journey back into one's own past to the roots of the self. As Wagner observed, some homesick tourists explicitly express this longing for a return to the past, a past that is always more positively remembered than it really was.

The process of reminiscing about home shifts into another gear, when the tourist begins to translate the desire to travel home into concrete action – planning and preparing the trip, reflecting on where to go and what to do. The dynamics of the journey and the concrete movements through familiar home territory by car, bus or train induce memories through the appearance of countless potential stimuli in rapid succession, as accustomed sounds and the sight of familiar landmarks and personal memory sites are flashing by the window. For diasporic return travellers and roots tourists who only have 're-memory' or collective memories of the old home, the journey facilitates the recognition of internal images and imagined multisensory characteristics of the homeland. As Basu (2004: 38) observes, '... the physical journey ... narrates and enables a corresponding inward journey, a cognitive homecoming, a recognition of identity, made possible through the material reality of the landscape.'

However, we must acknowledge that human beings are complex individuals with varied psychologies and diverse identities, cultures and histories, which preclude the development of any universally applicable theory of motivation, or generalizable conclusions about touristic behaviour, experience and the meanings attached to such journeys. We must be mindful to distinguish between different migrant communities in diverse contexts, different generations of the same diasporic group in the same host country, and even different waves of immigrants of the same generation in the same location, who may have had very dissimilar reasons for emigrating (Iarmolenko, 2014). More attention should also be paid to the ways in which individuals define and classify themselves. Whether someone considers him/herself an expatriate, a refugee or an immigrant says much about their sense of identity in relation to their place of origin, their current home and their potential desire to embark on a return journey.

The return into one's own past, the retracing of one's earlier footsteps and confronting of autobiographical memories looms large in the western popular imagination, featuring regularly in movies, novels, travel writings and other products of the media and entertainment sector. An appreciation for history and heritage conservation and the pursuit of heritage tourism, including multiple facets of roots tourism appear to be most prevalent among western societies. This is most obviously linked to socio-economic factors – heritage and tourism are essentially pursuits for the educated middle-classes – but the exploration of the personal and collective past and an interest in travelling in search of identity and self-actualization are also culturally learnt responses – heritage and tourism as habitus. However, as some of the secondary literature and the contributors to this volume illustrate, the longing for the old home and the practice of embarking on return journeys can be found among individuals and societies around the globe. The extent to which this occurs is still largely unknown.

The literature mentioned in this introduction cannot possibly cover the entire spectrum of diasporic identities, the diverse notions of 'home' people relate to, and the multifarious types of homeward bound journeys they long for and engage in. Rather it is meant to pull together some of the thematically related scholarly research and define an analytical focus on the return journey home underpinned by memories. From a tourism industry and policy perspective, this is warranted by the assumption that such return journeys are a significant, yet little recognized form of domestic and international touristic practice worldwide. Investigating this phenomenon more systematically and better comprehending its trends, dynamics and constraints may yield valuable insights that can lead to useful interventions. For instance, tourism marketers could promote the concept of return travel home and develop customized tours and services, which may be linked to educational outcomes, or reconciliation, psychological healing and cross-generational understanding. Such tourism can add to sustainability as it relieves pressure on key attractions and makes only minor demands on local cultures and infrastructure (Hall & Duval, 2004: 91).

From an academic perspective, this book contributes to Tourism Studies by providing an innovative analytical lens which helps us re-assess and nuance established concepts in the field and open up new perspectives on touristic mobility, motivation and experience. It establishes a frame of reference for the broader contextualization of many existing scholarly studies, which simultaneously allows us to identify gaps of research. The book complements the emergent body of literature on the tourism-migration link and in itself makes a contribution to the fields of Diaspora and Migration Studies, as well as the study of Transnationalism, Globalization and Identity by examining the role of memory and return travel in the negotiation of diasporic identity and relationship to home. Many chapters in this book moreover contribute to the emergent field of Memory Studies, which has thus far paid little attention to tourism, especially from the perspective of individual subjectivity and how different types of memory and practices of remembering are activated through touristic journeys home and patterns of mobility in familiar spaces.

This book represents only a first humble attempt at pulling together the strings around tourism, memory and home. Although the contributors have researched an impressive diversity of societal and geographic contexts, major lacunae remain to be explored, for instance the journeys of Africans on the African continent. All studies in this volume moreover employ qualitative methodologies, often relying on small sample sizes and foregrounding the experience of individuals; findings could be tested through triangulation with more rigorously conceptualized research approaches and much larger samples that may yield insights at the societal level and add new perspectives to the recurrent themes of this volume. Ultimately, we need more evidence, supplied by the tourism industry and government authorities, on the extent to which people desire to travel home and most especially actually engage in such forms of touristic mobility.

References

Andrews, H. (2011) *The British on Holiday: Charter Tourism, Identity and Consumption* (Vol. 28). Bristol: Channel View Publications.

Arnone, A. (2011) Tourism and the Eritrean diaspora. *Journal of Contemporary African Studies* 29 (4), 441–454.

Asiedu, A. (2005) Some benefits of migrants' return visits to Ghana. *Population, Space and Place* 11 (1), 1–11.

Backer, E. (2012) VFR travel: It is underestimated. *Tourism Management* 33 (1), 74–79.

Baldassar, L. (2001) *Visits Home: Migration Experiences between Italy and Australia*. Melbourne: Melbourne University Press.

Baldassar, L. (2011) Obligation to people and place: The national in cultures of caregiving. In L. Baldassar and D.R. Gabaccia (eds) *Intimacy and Italian Migration: Gender and Domestic Lives in a Mobile World* (pp. 171–187). New York: Fordham University Press.

Bandyopadhyay, R. (2008) Nostalgia, identity and tourism: Bollywood in the Indian diaspora. *Journal of Tourism and Cultural Change* 6 (2), 79–100.

Basu, P. (2004). My own island home: The Orkney homecoming. *Journal of Material Culture* 9 (1), 27–42.

Basu, P. (2005) Roots-tourism as return movement: Semantics and the Scottish diaspora. In M. Harper (ed.) *Emigrant Homecomings: The Return Movement of Emigrants, 1600–2000* (pp. 131–150). Manchester: Manchester University Press.

Bhabha, H.K. (1994) *The Location of Culture*. Routledge: London and New York.

Bhandari, K. (2014) *Tourism and National Identity: Heritage and Nationhood in Scotland* (Vol. 39). Bristol: Channel View Publications.

Blunt, A. and Varley, A. (2004) Geographies of home. *Cultural Geographies*, 11 (1), 3–6.

Boym, S. (2001) *The Future of Nostalgia*. New York: Basic Books.

Brah, A. (1996) *Cartographies of Diaspora: Contesting Identities*. London and New York: Routledge.

Braasch, B. (ed.) (2008) *Major Concepts in Tourism Research – Memory*. Centre for Tourism and Cultural Change (CTCC): Leeds Metropolitan University.

Braun-LaTour, K.A., Grinley, M.J and Loftus, E.F. (2006) Tourist memory distortion. *Journal of Travel Research* 44 (May), 360–367.

Bruner, E.M. (1996) Tourism in Ghana: The representation of the slave trade and the return of the black diaspora. *American Anthropologist* 98 (2), 290–304.

Buntman, B. (2008) Tourism and tragedy: The memorial at Belzec, Poland. *International Journal of Heritage Studies* 14 (5), 422–448.

Carter, S. (2004) Tourism and politics in the Croatian diaspora. In T. Coles and D.J. Timothy (eds) *Tourism, Diasporas and Space* (pp. 188–201). London & New York: Routledge.

Cave, J., Jolliffe, L. and Baum, T. (eds) (2013) *Tourism and Souvenirs: Glocal Perspectives from the Margins* (Vol. 33). Bristol: Channel View Publications.

Cerulo, K.A. (1997) Identity construction: New issues, new directions. *Annual Review of Sociology* 23, 385–409.

Cohen, R. (1997) *Global Diasporas: An Introduction*. London: UCL Press.

Cohen, E. (2004) Exodus and the case of diaspora education tourism. In T. Coles and D.J. Timothy (eds) *Tourism, Diasporas and Space* (pp. 124–138). London & New York: Routledge.

Cohen, E. (2008) *Youth Tourism to Israel: Educational Experiences of the Diaspora* (Vol. 15). Clevedon: Channel View Publications.

Cohen, E. and Cohen, S.A. (2012) Current sociological theories and issues in tourism. *Annals of Tourism Research* 39 (4), 2177–2202.

Coles, T. and Timothy, D.J. (eds) (2004) *Tourism, Diasporas and Space.* London & New York: Routledge.

Cronin, M. and O'Connor, B. (eds) (2003) *Irish Tourism: Image, Culture and Identity* (Vol. 1). Clevedon: Channel View Publications.

Desforges, L. (2000) Traveling the world: Identity and travel biography. *Annals of Tourism Research* 27 (4), 926–945.

Di Giovine, M. (2012) Padre Pio for sale: Souvenirs, relics, or identity markers? *International Journal of Tourism Anthropology* 2 (2), 108–127.

Die Welt. (2009) Kenne Deine Wurzeln. Das Geschäft mit dem Auswanderertourismus. 25 June. Retrieved from http://www.welt.de/3994514

Douglas, M. (1991) The idea of a home: A kind of space. *Social Research* 58 (1), 287–307.

Duval, D.T. (2003) When hosts become guests: Return visits and diasporic identities in a Commonwealth Eastern Caribbean community. *Current Issues in Tourism* 6 (4), 267–308.

Duyvendak, J. (2011) *The Politics of Home.* New York: Palgrave MacMillan.

Dwyer, L., Seetaram, N., Forsyth, P. and King, B. (2014) Is the migration-tourism relationship only about VFR? *Annals of Tourism Research* 46, 130–143.

Ebron, P.A. (1999) Tourists as pilgrims: Commercial fashioning of transatlantic politics. *American Ethnologist* 26 (4), 910–932.

Feldman, J. (2016) *A Jewish Guide in the Holy Land: How Christian Pilgrims Made Me Israeli.* Bloomington and Indianapolis: Indiana University Press.

Freeman, M. (2010) Telling stories: Memory and narrative. In S. Radstone and B. Schwarz (eds) *Memory. Histories, Theories, Debates* (pp. 263–277). New York: Fordham University Press.

Graburn, N.H.H. (1977) Tourism: The sacred journey. In V.L. Smith (ed.) *Hosts and Guests. The Anthropology of Tourism* (pp. 17–31). Philadelphia: University of Pennsylvania Press.

Hage, G. (2010) Migration, food, memory, and home-building. In S. Radstone and B. Schwartz (eds) *Memory, Histories, Theories, Debates* (pp. 416–427). New York: Fordham University Press.

Halbwachs, M. (1992) *On Collective Memory.* University of Chicago Press: Chicago.

Hall, C.M. and Duval, D.T. (2004) Linking diasporas and tourism: Transnational mobilities of Pacific Islanders resident in New Zealand. In T. Coles and D.J. Timothy (eds) *Tourism, Diasporas and Space* (pp. 78–94). London & New York: Routledge.

Hall, C.M. and Müller, D.K. (2004) Introduction: Second homes, curse or blessing? Revisited. In C.M. Hall and D.K. Müller (eds) *Tourism, Mobility, and Second Homes: Between Elite Landscape and Common Ground* (Vol. 15, pp. 3–14). Clevedon: Channel View Publications.

Huang, W.-J., Ramshaw, G. and Norman, W.C. (2016) Homecoming or tourism? Diaspora tourism experience of second-generation immigrants. *Tourism Geographies* 18 (1), 59–79.

Hung, K., Xiao, H. and Yang, X. (2013) Why immigrants travel to their home places: Social capital and acculturation perspective. *Tourism Management* 36, 304–313.

Iarmolenko, S. (2014) Bridging Tourism and Migration Mobilities: Diaspora Tourism as a Coping Strategy. PhD Dissertation. Pennsylvania State University.

Ioannides, D. and Ioannides, M.C. (2004) Jewish past as a 'foreign country': The travel experiences of American Jews. In T. Coles and D.J. Timothy (eds) *Tourism, Diasporas and Space* (pp. 95–110). London & New York: Routledge.

Kadman, N. (2010) Roots tourism – whose roots? The marginalization of Palestinian Heritage Sites in Israeli Tourism Sites. *TÉOROS* 29 (1), 55–66.

Kaplan, M.J. and Grunebaum, H. (2013) *Village under the Forest*. Documentary film production, 67 minutes. Directed by Kaplan, written and narrated by Grunebaum. South Africa.

Kelner, S. (2010) *Tours that Bind: Diaspora, Pilgrimage, and Israeli Birthright Tourism*. New York: New York University Press.

Kidron, C.A. (2013) Being there together: Dark family tourism and the emotive experience of co-presence in the holocaust past. *Annals of Tourism Research* 41, 175–194.

King, R. and Christou, A. (2010) Cultural geographies of counter-diasporic migration: perspectives from the study of second-generation 'returnees' to Greece. *Population, Space and Place* 16 (2), 103–119.

Kluin, J.Y. and Lehto, X.Y. (2012) Measuring family reunion travel motivations. *Annals of Tourism Research* 39 (2), 820–841.

Knott, K. and McLoughlin, S. (2010) *Diasporas: Concepts, Intersections, Identities*. New York: Zed Books.

Knudsen, B.T. and Waade, A.M. (eds) (2010) *Re-investing Authenticity: Tourism, Place and Emotions*. Bristol: Channel View Publications.

Kugelmass, J. (1994) Why we go to Poland. Holocaust tourism as secular tourism. In J.E. Young (ed.) *The Art of Memory: Holocaust Memorials in History* (pp. 175–183). New York: Prestel.

Kuusisto-Arponen, A.-K. (2009) The mobilities of forced displacement: Commemorating Karelian evacuation in Finland. *Social & Cultural Geography* 10 (5), 545–563.

Landsberg, A. (2004) *Prosthetic Memory: The Transformation of American Remembrance in the Age of Mass Culture*. New York: Columbia University Press.

Leite, N. (2005) Travels to an ancestral past: On diasporic tourism, embodied memory, and identity. *Anthropologicas* 9, 273–302.

Levitt, P. (2010) Transnationalism. In K. Knott and S. McLoughlin (eds) *Diasporas: Concepts, Intersections, Identities* (pp. 39–44). New York: Zed Books.

Lew, A.A. and Wong, A. (2004) Social capital and overseas Chinese tourism to China. In T. Coles and D.J. Timothy (eds) *Tourism, Diasporas and Space* (pp. 202–214). London/New York: Routledge.

Long, L.D. and Oxfeld, E. (eds) (2004) *Coming Home? Refugees, Migrants, and Those who Stayed Behind*. Philadelphia: University of Pennsylvania Press.

MacCannell, D. (1976) *The Tourist*. Macmillan: London and New York.

Macleod, D.V. (2004) *Tourism, Globalisation, and Cultural Change: An Island Community Perspective* (Vol. 2). Clevedon: Channel View Publications.

Mallet, S. (2004) Understanding home: A critical review of the literature. *The Sociological Review* 52 (1), 62–89.

Marschall, S. (2012) 'Personal memory tourism' and a wider exploration of the tourism–memory nexus. *Journal of Tourism and Cultural Change* 10 (4), 321–335.

Marschall, S. (2014) Tourism and remembrance: The journey into the self and its past. *Journal of Tourism and Cultural Change* 12 (4), 335–348.

Marschall, S. (2015a) 'Homesick tourism': Memory, identity and (be)longing. *Current Issues in Tourism* 18 (9), 876–892.

Marschall, S. (2015b) 'Travelling down memory lane': Personal memory as a generator of tourism. *Tourism Geographies* 17 (1), 36–53.

Mazel, A. (2014) Troubled 'Homecoming': Journey to a foreign yet familiar land. In I. Convery, G. Corsane and P. Davis (eds) *Displaced Heritage: Responses to Disaster, Trauma, and Loss* (pp. 151–161). Woodbridge: Boydell.

McCain, G. and Ray, N.M. (2003) Legacy tourism: The search for personal meaning in heritage travel. *Tourism Management* 24 (6), 713–717.

McCabe, S. (2005) 'Who is a tourist?' A critical review. *Tourist Studies* 5 (1), 85–106.

McWatters, M.R. (2009) *Residential Tourism: (De)constructing Paradise* (Vol. 16). Bristol: Channel View Publications.

Meethan, K. (2004) 'To stand in the shoes of my ancestors': Tourism and genealogy. In T. Coles and D.J. Timothy (eds) *Tourism, Diasporas and Space* (pp. 139–150). London/New York: Routledge.

Morley, D. and Robins, K. (1993) No place like Heimat: Images of home(land) in European culture. In E. Carter, J. Donald and S. Judith (eds) *Space & Place. Theories of Identity and Location* (pp. 3–31). Lawrence & Wishart: London.

Muggeridge, H and Doná, G. (2006) Back home? Refugees' experiences of their first visit back to their country of origin. *Journal of Refugee Studies* 19 (4), 415–432.

Nguyen, T.-H. and King, B. (2004) The culture of tourism in the diaspora: The case of the Vietnamese community in Australia. In T. Coles and D.J. Timothy (eds) *Tourism, Diasporas and Space* (pp. 172–187). London & New York: Routledge.

Oxfeld, E. (2004) Chinese villagers and the moral dilemma of return visits. In L.D. Long and E. Oxfeld (eds) *Coming Home? Refugees, Migrants, and Those Who Stayed Behind* (pp. 90–103). Philadelphia: University of Pennsylvania Press.

Oxfeld, E. and Long, L.D. (2004) Introduction: An ethnography of return. In L.D. Long and E. Oxfeld (eds) *Coming Home? Refugees, Migrants, and those who Stayed Behind* (pp. 1–15). Philadelphia: University of Pennsylvania Press.

Pearce, P.L. (2012) The experience of visiting home and familiar places. *Annals of Tourism Research* 39 (2), 1024–1047.

Peleikis, A. (2009) Reisen in die Vergangenheit: Deutsche Heimattouristen auf der Kurischen Nehrung. In W. Kolbe, C. Noack and H. Spode (eds) *Tourismus-geschichte(n): Voyage, Jahrbuch für Reise & Tourismusforschung* (Vol. 8, pp. 115–129). München: Profil Verlag.

Picard, D. and Di Giovine, M.A. (2014) Introduction: Through other worlds. In D. Picard and M.A. Di Giovine (eds) *Tourism and the Power of Otherness: Seductions of Difference* (Vol. 34, pp. 2–28). Bristol: Channel View Publications.

Pocock, N. and McIntosh, A. (2013) Long-term travellers return 'Home'? *Annals of Tourism Research* 42, 402–424.

Potter, R.B. (2005) 'Young, gifted and back': Second-generation transnational return migrants to the Caribbean. *Progress in Development Studies* 5 (3), 213–236.

Ralph, D. and Staeheli, L.A. (2011) Home and migration: mobilities, belongings and identities. *Geography Compass* 5 (7), 517–530.

Rogerson, C.M. (2004) Regional tourism in South Africa: A case of 'mass tourism of the South'. *GeoJournal* 60 (3), 229–237.

Rogerson, C.M. and Hoogendoorn, G. (2014) VFR travel and second home tourism: The missing link? The case of South Africa. *Tourism Review International* 18 (3), 167–178.

Rose, S. (2010) Memories are made of this. In S. Radstone and B. Schwarz (eds) *Memory, Histories, Theories, Debates* (eds) (pp. 198–208). New York: Fordham University Press.

Sarup, M. (1994) Home and identity. In G. Robertson *et al.* (eds) *Travellers' Tales. Narratives of Home and Displacement* (pp. 93–104). London/New York: Routledge.

Schacter, D.L. (1996) *Searching for Memory. The Brain, the Mind and the Past.* New York: Basic Books.

Scheyvens, R. (2007) Poor cousins no more valuing the development potential of domestic and diaspora tourism. *Progress in Development Studies* 7 (4), 307–325.

Schramm, K. (2010) *African Homecoming: Pan-African Ideology and Contested Heritage.* Walnut Creek, CA: Left Coast Press.

Shani, A. (2013) The VFR experience: 'home' away from home? *Current Issues in Tourism* 16 (1), 1–5.

Shaw, S.M., Havitz, M.E. and Delemere, F.M. (2008) I decided to invest in my kids' memories: Family vacations, memories, and the social construction of the family. *Tourism Culture & Communication* 8 (1), 13–26.

Shuval, J.T. (2000) Diaspora migration: Definitional ambiguities and a theoretical paradigm. *International Migration* 38 (5), 41–56.

Stephenson, M.L. (2004) Tourism, racism and the UK Afro-Carribbean diaspora. In T. Coles and D.J. Timothy (eds) *Tourism, Diasporas and Space* (pp. 62–77). London/New York: Routledge.

Stock, F. (2010) Home and memory. In K. Knott and S. McLoughlin (eds) *Diasporas: Concepts, Intersections, Identities* (pp. 24–28). New York: Zed Books.

Sutton, J., Harris, C.B. and Barnier, A.J. (2010) Memory and cognition. In S. Radstone and B. Schwarz (eds) *Memory. Histories, Theories, Debates* (pp. 209–226). New York: Fordham University Press.

Tie, C., Holden, A. and yu Park, H. (2015) A 'reality of return': The case of the Sarawakian-Chinese visiting China. *Tourism Management* 47, 206–212.

Timothy, D.J. (1997) Tourism and the personal heritage experience. *Annals of Tourism Research* 24 (3), 751–754.

Timothy, D.J. and Teye, V.B. (2004) American children of the African diaspora: Journeys to the motherland. In T. Coles and D.J. Timothy (eds) *Tourism, Diasporas and Space* (pp. 111–123). London/New York: Routledge.

Tolia-Kelly, D.P. (2004) Locating processes of identification: Studying the precipitates of re-memory through artefacts in the British Asian home. *Transactions of the Institute of British Geographers* 29 (3), 314–329.

Uriely, N. (2010) 'Home' and 'away' in VFR tourism. *Annals of Tourism Research* 37, 854–857.

Urry, J. (1990) *The Tourist Gaze: Leisure and Travel in Contemporary Societies*. London. Thousand Oaks. New Delhi: Sage.

Urry, J. (2007) *Mobilities*. Cambridge & Maiden, MA: Polity.

Wessendorf, S. (2007) 'Roots migrants': Transnationalism and 'Return' among second-generation Italians in Switzerland. *Journal of Ethnic and Migration Studies* 33 (7), 1083–1102.

West, T. (2014) Remembering displacement: Photography and the interactive spaces of memory. *Memory Studies* 7 (2), 176–190.

2 Homecoming Emigrants as Tourists: Reconnecting the Scottish Diaspora

Marjory Harper

Introduction

The return of emigrants to their homeland has been described as 'the great unwritten chapter in the history of migration' (King, 2000). Although recent scholarship has begun to rectify that Cinderella status, little attention has been paid to the historical context for temporary homecoming as tourism, let alone the relationship of such short-term travel to personal or collective memory or to identity formation in diasporic communities (Coles & Timothy, 2004; Dwyer et al., 2014; Scheyvens, 2007). Studies of diaspora tourism tend to address current issues, often related to policymaking and economic development, rather than the phenomenon's roots (Agunias & Newland, 2012).

This chapter is an empirically based historical analysis of the motives and experiences of Scottish emigrants who returned as tourists to the land of their birth or ancestry. The Scots are by no means unique in their conception and implementation of homecoming tourism (Iorio & Corsale, 2013; Leite, 2005; Lew & Wong, 2002), but a rich corpus of primary sources allows us to chart how a particular diaspora has reconnected with 'home' for more than two centuries (Harper, 2005; Varricchio, 2012). The study offers a typology of reasons for return, demonstrating – particularly through travel narratives – how different categories of visitors have chosen to remember Scotland since the mid-19th century. It also shows how those real or invented memories helped to shape their interpretation of the travel experience as well as their actual itineraries and encounters. Motives for return included visiting family, transacting business, recruiting other emigrants, enjoying recreation and seeking an alternative identity. Each of these themes is examined in a chronologically structured analysis which also considers the impact of improved communications and commercialisation on patterns and mechanisms of return, as well as the memorialisation of home.

Invented traditions lie at the heart of the homecoming experiences of Scottish emigrant tourists. At an individual level, their memories of Scotland were often fossilised in a time warp on the day of their departure, and became increasingly distorted with the passage of time. A return visit could therefore be an unsettling experience, particularly after a long absence with little communication. Collectively, emigrant tourists (and other visitors) were from the late 18th century bombarded with images of an ancestral homeland that owed much to the Romantic movement but had little in common with reality. The trend intensified in the Victorian era and persisted for much of the 20th century, as the tourist industry, in both Scotland and the diaspora, increasingly exploited the commercial potential of homecoming. Scotland, particularly the Highlands, had become Walter Scott-land, where tourists went 'to commune with the spirit of Scott communing with nature and with romantic history' (Smout, 1982–3: 117). Sightseeing embraced the quasi-religious 'ritual respect' identified by Dean MacCannell (1973), but, as he also points out, tourists were inevitably disappointed in their quest for authenticity in an invented landscape. In some cases, disappointment could turn into hostility, particularly among genealogical 'pilgrims', when invented memories were not borne out in their experiences of Scotland, or their encounters with its residents, who disparaged their fantasies and naive acceptance of a superficial 'staged authenticity' (MacCannell, 1973: 582, 595). Roots tourism, as we shall see, was not a neutral phenomenon.

Who were the visitors? Although England has always been Scotland's main tourist market, this study is concerned exclusively with the overseas diaspora. About a third of the 4 million Scots who emigrated in the 19th and 20th centuries returned permanently to their homeland (Devine, 2011: 93), while many other emigrants and their descendants reconnected with their roots through temporary – and sometimes multiple – visits. Initially most of these visitors came from North America, but colonists in the more recently settled and more distant Antipodes began to trickle back in the mid-19th century. Advances in transport generated an increased volume of movement, not least from Australia and New Zealand, but while technologies changed, practices and attitudes altered more slowly. Until recently the initiative was taken in the diaspora rather than in Scotland. For reasons of both confidence and cost, it was much more common for emigrants to visit people and locations in Scotland than for non-emigrants to travel in the opposite direction to reconnect with family or friends. Individuals who had already navigated the challenges of intercontinental travel were more comfortable with undertaking subsequent journeys, and some had greater means to do so.

Informal Reconnections: The Objectives and Impact of Private Tourism

Prospective visits to the homeland were commonly articulated and planned in personal correspondence, which was the most obvious conduit of information between emigrants and their families. One example will suffice. In 1842 William Fletcher left the Aberdeenshire parish of Logie Coldstone for Upper Canada, where, in the township of Tilbury East, he joined his brother John, who had emigrated in 1836. Both maintained a regular correspondence with their family back home, impressing on them the advantages of emigration. In 1860 William promised that if they decided to take the plunge, he would return to help with the removal. 'I have always liked Canada', he wrote to his brother-in-law, Charles Farquharson,

> and have never wished to be back in Scotland to live, but would enjoy a short visit very much; and although I am much pleased to hear of you all doing well in Scotland, I would welcome you all to Canada; and if you resolve to come, send me word and I will go home to help you pack your baggage, tell you what to bring and accompany you across the ocean, and introduce you to many kind friends here. (NRAS, 1860)

William Fletcher's return trip to Aberdeenshire, which had a practical as well as a recreational purpose, was subsequently described in a published family memoir which reported that 26 individuals from Logie Coldstone accompanied him back to Canada in 1866 (Farquharson, (undated [1930s]). Emigrant homecomings were also commonly reported in newspapers across the diaspora, and often marked by parting gifts. In 1892 the Reverend James Chisholm, who had emigrated from Kinross to Otago with his parents in 1858, was presented by his congregation at Milton with 'a purse of 125 sovereigns' on the eve of his second return trip to Scotland, and entrusted with the delivery of a number of letters (*Clutha Leader*, 20/5/1892). He used his parting sermon to assure his listeners that he was mindful of the emotional ties and memories that bound them to Scotland.

> I am going to the Home Country as you know, [and] I am taking with me many messages to your friends and relations. It has surprised me to find how many and close the ties are that bind so many of you to the old land. I have noticed with sympathy the light that has come into the eyes of many of you as you told me of father or mother, or other relations, and I have got a glimpse into many hearts during the last week or two. I have seen how much more of good news there is than I supposed, and wherever I go I shall be able to speak well of you. (*Bruce Herald*, 13/5/1892)

Chisholm had been granted a year's leave of absence for health reasons. His travels in Scotland, including encounters with the relatives of colonists, were regularly documented in the New Zealand press, and he was welcomed back publicly on his return in January 1893 (*Otago Witness*, 12/1/1893). The Australian, Canadian and American press was equally assiduous in reporting the travels of private individuals, some of whom were given a public send off by the Scottish associations to which they belonged.

Homing instincts were also evident in the early stages of World War I, when service personnel who had been sent back from the far corners of empire took the opportunity of embarkation leave to reconnect briefly with their roots. Indeed, some 'colonials' combined patriotism with pragmatism, one Aberdeenshire observer commenting that those 'with a roving inclination' welcomed the war 'as an opportunity of getting home to see the Old Country, and at the same time do their bit.' (*Aberdeen Journal*, 12/5/1915) Evidence that Scottish hospitality to servicemen on furlough was appreciated back in the Dominions is found in a letter to the press from representatives of five Scottish societies in New Zealand, offering 'their sincere and heartfelt thanks for the hospitality and kindness' of so many, and their gratitude 'for making dear "Auld Scotland" a second home to so many of our men while absent from their native land' (*The Scotsman*, 22/7/1919, quoted in Bueltmann, 2012: 153).

Public Celebrations of Return: Local Heroes and their Followers

Apart from reconnecting with family, and rekindling personal memories, how do we explain the Scottish diaspora's interest in the land of nativity or ancestry? In general terms it reflected a fascination with Scotland that had its origins in the late 18th century, when continental conflicts put an end to the European Grand Tour. The spotlight shifted to the aesthetic attributes of 'North Britain', which were being publicised by travellers such as Thomas Pennant, Samuel Johnson and James Boswell. Romanticism took root through the legends of Ossian, the poetry of Robert Burns, the novels of Walter Scott, and – after 1848 – the cult of Balmorality. Just as potential emigrants were lured overseas by literature, lectures and lantern slides, so the same devices wooed emigrants who could afford a trip home. Some of those who returned to Scotland from the Antipodes remodelled the Grand Tour – shorn of its original educational function – to travel across the Pacific and through North America. The romantic rhetoric was fuelled by the Scottish associations and clubs that often organised public farewells and returns, but which, more practically, provided a mechanism for homesick colonists who could not go back to Scotland to pass on greetings to family and friends and to connect vicariously with their native land. The pattern of public interest and gift-giving was echoed when the travellers reached Scotland, not least because most such tourism was one-directional, and those who had stayed behind were eager to hear verbal reports of their relatives' experiences.

Most public celebrations of emigrant tourism were modest affairs, but if they involved individuals who had made a name for themselves overseas, the civic bunting was brought out. In November 1882 the leading citizens of Adelaide treated Hugh Fraser MP to a public banquet and the valedictory gift of a 'handsome ring' on the eve of his departure for Europe. Twenty years earlier he had left Inverness for South Australia, and his homecoming itinerary included a visit to his native town, 'impelled partly by patriotic feelings and partly by the filial desire to see his parents' (*South Australian Weekly Chronicle*, 25/11/1882). Having assured his audience that 'he would tell his fellow-countrymen what a field there was for honest, enterprising, and intelligent Scotchmen in a new country like South Australia', Fraser was as good as his word. When we pick up the story from the other end in May 1883 Fraser was actively marketing Australia as a destination for emigrants, prompting the *Inverness Courier* to declare that he had 'awakened among the working classes an intense interest in emigration', so that there was 'hardly a workshop in town in which the prospects of tradesmen in the Colonies is not daily discussed with interest and intelligence.' (*Inverness Courier*, 19/5/1883). Interest was rapidly translated into action, for Fraser enticed around 150 emigrants to Adelaide, the departure of the first party of 50 being marked by a civic reception (*Inverness Courier*, 19/5/1883).

Meanwhile, across the Tasman Sea, John McKenzie, who had emigrated from Ardross in Easter Ross as a boy, had become Minister of Lands and Agriculture in New Zealand, where he implemented land reform policies that were based on his early experiences of Highland evictions (Brooking, 1996). His trip to Scotland in 1899, after an absence of 39 years, was similarly commemorated on both sides of the world. At a public meeting in Wellington in April, he was presented with a cheque 'for over a thousand pounds, subscribed by colonists throughout New Zealand', along with an illuminated address signed by 8000 individuals from Wellington and its hinterland (*Feilding Star*, 11/4/1899). A week earlier, in thanking a gathering of the Gaelic Society in his residential district of Palmerston for the gift of an album and a walking stick, he predicted that, back in his homeland, he would 'meet with Highlanders even as warm in blood towards us as we feel amongst ourselves here towards them', and assured them that, as the Society's chief, 'my never forgotten theme will be the Highlanders I have left behind me' (*Otago Witness*, 6/4/1899).

McKenzie's visit to Scotland was therefore infused with issues of memory and identity, some of which he may have cultivated for the benefit of his Scottish audience in New Zealand. But he was also a medical tourist, for his trip was triggered primarily by the need to undergo major surgery in London. Eight months later, after he had returned to New Zealand, the *Otago Witness* carried a 14-column interview, in which he recalled the highlights of his visit. He travelled with his family via the US, crossing from New York to Liverpool, from where he immediately took the train north to Glasgow. 'I asked my daughter how she liked the Home country', he recalled. 'She said it was lovely, but on pressing her to say it was lovelier than New Zealand she said it was pretty, but not equal to New Zealand' (*Otago Witness*, 7/12/1899). He spent a week in Glasgow, glad-handing civic dignitaries, and commented that 'The number of councillors for the City of Glasgow is about equal to the number of members of the New Zealand Parliament' (*Otago Witness*, 7/12/1899). McKenzie then made a brief visit to Dingwall, before heading to hospital in London. When he had recovered sufficiently to return to Easter Ross, his visit was publicly celebrated and widely reported in the local press, which described him as a man who had 'by his indomitable pluck and perseverance' worked his way up to high office in the New Zealand government. At his father's old home at Ardross, 80 people gathered for a celebratory dinner, chaired by the new owner of the local estate, Charles Perrins, a man who met with McKenzie's approval because of the benevolent way he treated his tenants. 'I only wish', McKenzie told his New Zealand interviewer later, 'the same good feeling existed between the landlords and tenants of other properties I visited' (*Otago Witness*, 7/12/1899). The publicity that surrounded McKenzie's visit was due partly, of course, to his reputation as a land reformer, at a time when the Highlands and Islands were convulsed by land agitation. When he was asked by a deputation from the Ross and Cromarty Ploughmen's and Labourers' Union to address a meeting on the conditions of land tenure and labour in New Zealand, he had to decline on health grounds, but added, 'if he were to express what he thought, perhaps some people in the county would not like it very much' (*Inverness Courier*, 15/9/1899; *Ross-shire Journal*, 25/9/1899).

Andrew Carnegie was another celebrity tourist – and self-styled 'exiled son' of Scotland – who made frequent return visits, and in 1898 purchased Skibo Castle in Sutherland as a Highland retreat. His travelogue was published five years later, but describes a stagecoach journey made in 1881, when he conducted a party of family and friends from Brighton to Inverness (Carnegie, 1903). By the 1880s Scottish itineraries were still dictated by the predilections of the Romantics who had begun to put the country on the tourist map almost a century earlier, and Carnegie's somewhat whimsical narrative documents a trip that incorporated some (but not all) the locations, identities and invented memories popularised in literature (Smout, 1982–3).[1] At Dunkeld, he wrote, they found themselves 'among the real hills at last … the very air breathes of Macbeth, and the murdered Banquo still haunts the glen' (Carnegie, 1903: 296). Two days later, in Badenoch, he heard 'the lament of Ossian in the sough of the passing wind', while also commenting appreciatively on the quality of catering and service in inns where the American flag was hung in honour of their visit (Carnegie, 1903: 307, 311, 327). Favourable comparisons were made with England, as at Drumlanrig, where 'we have a real castle at last; none of your imported English affairs, as tame as caged tigers', and he declared of his companions that 'they had admired England, but Scotland they loved' (Carnegie, 1903: 253, 273).

At the same time, Carnegie did not neglect the opportunity either to praise the educational attainments of the Scots, or to deplore the hierarchical class system which he believed still held them back. The sporting fraternity which was making its annual pilgrimage to the Highlands at the same time as the Carnegie party travelled north through a 'land of gamekeepers and dogs', came in for stinging criticism, and he bewailed the excessive deference that characterised Scottish society. 'Thank God! we have nothing like this in America' (Carnegie, 1903: 300, 322). The egalitarian parish school system, however, was the foundation 'upon which to predict the continued intellectual ascendancy of Scotland and an uninterrupted growth of its people in every department of human achievement' (Carnegie, 1903: 321). It was in Dunfermline that the world's first Carnegie library was established, the foundation stone being laid by the benefactor's mother during their 1881 visit (Carnegie, 1903: 283).

There was no more obvious way to commemorate return publicly than by setting it – literally – in stone. The Carnegie libraries were functional examples of that phenomenon. In other cases of returning emigrants, their descendants, or their communities of origin created symbolic shrines to which future generations of ancestral or ethnic tourists could make 'sacred journeys' or secular pilgrimages (Graburn, 1977: 17–31; Grimshaw, 2008). In 1911, for instance, 10 years after he had visited his father's birthplace of Badbea in Caithness, David Sutherland commissioned a memorial to family members who had emigrated from that barren, cliff-top location to New Zealand in the mid-19th century. Constructed from the stones of the community's abandoned houses, it speaks implicitly of the legacy of earlier land clearance, the settlement at Badbea having been formed in the late 18th century, largely by families who had been displaced by sheep from the nearby townships of Langwell, Ousdale and Berriedale (Harper & Constantine, 2010: 334).

A few miles to the south-west, a plaque in the wall of the old church at Kildonan commemorates the infamous clearance of that strath in 1813. Those forced into an arduous journey to Canada included the Bannermans, great-grandparents of Canada's 13th Prime Minister, John Diefenbaker (Hunter, 2015). During a personal visit to Sutherland in 1968, Diefenbaker unveiled both the Kildonan plaque and, 30 miles to the south, a cairn to commemorate Canada's first Prime Minister, John A. Macdonald, constructed from the stone of Macdonald's grandparents' family home at Rogart. That commemorative pilgrimage in July 1968 was Diefenbaker's second trip to the county. Ten years earlier, after attending a meeting of Commonwealth Prime Ministers in London, he had come north with his wife and brother to see the ruins of his ancestors' home and attend a ceremony at Kildonan church. He was, according to the *Northern Times*, 'especially proud of his connection with this crofting country' and described his visit as 'a wonderful experience' (*Northern Times*, 31/10/1958, 7/11/1958). It was hardly surprising that Canada's recently-elected premier was feted by a collection of local dignitaries and multiple Bannermans, or that his visit attracted huge public attention. 'Sutherland has seldom seen such a galaxy of reporters and cameramen', observed the local paper (*Northern Times*, 7/11/1958). When Diefenbaker's motorcade travelled up the strath from Helmsdale the official convoy of eight cars grew to 23 as local people joined the procession, but – perhaps symbolically – the 'sentimental journey' was impeded by a flock of sheep (*Northern Times*, 7/11/1958, 19/7/1968; Timespan, 2015).

Homecoming Recruitment Agents

High-profile return visitors could act as informal recruitment agents. But the advent of colonial self-government meant that from the mid-19th century settler colonies gained control of immigration, and it became common practice to send paid recruitment agents to locations with which they had a personal or family connection (Harper & Constantine, 2010: 277–305). In 1872 the New Zealand government despatched Thomas Birch to Lerwick. As a former mayor of Dunedin, MP, President of the Otago Caledonian Society, and a native of Fortrose in Easter Ross, Birch's visit attracted considerable press comment on both side of the world, and on 16 June he lectured at Lerwick to an appreciative audience, which 'completely filled' the hall (*Evening Star*, 27/9/1872). But the controversy that dogged his visit was evident in exchanges in the New Zealand newspapers, and in Birch's premature resignation in July 1873. Shortly after his appointment, a letter published in the *Bruce Herald* savaged the government policy of 'giving its favorites and supporters a trip home to the "old countrie" at the public expense'. Thomas Birch was allegedly just one such 'Government pet' who had been sent back to enjoy a 'little spree in the capacity of immigration agent' (*Bruce Herald*, 10/4/1872). In June 1873 he and a former agent, Peter Barclay, were described as simply 'tourists in Shetland' when they took up lodging at the Queen's Hotel in Lerwick (*Shetland Times*, 16/6/1873). In December, in response to continuing criticism of Birch's suitability, a letter to the *Otago Daily Times* defended the agent's record. Having accompanied Birch on some of his 'mission work' in Banffshire and Easter Ross, James McKay believed that an insight into his experiences would counter criticism that 'an emigration agency at home means a pleasure trip to the old country at Government expense'. On the contrary, 'he has to travel on a stormy coast, and from one island to another in a small steamer, with dirty passengers, pigs, and other livestock, live in hovels and pay double fare for everything, away from home and friends.' McKay's conclusion that 'Mr Birch works hard, is but poorly paid, and gets more abuse than praise for the valuable work he is doing'

(*Otago Daily Times*, 25/12/1872) was echoed seven months later, when Birch confirmed that his premature return to New Zealand was due to limited success and insufficient remuneration (*Wellington Independent*, 8/10/1873).

Similar controversy surrounded the year's leave of absence given to Colin Allan, Immigration Officer at Dunedin, to visit his native Isle of Skye in 1886. His objective was to capitalise on the land wars that were then raging in the Hebrides to encourage his fellow islanders to emigrate to Otago, although he tried to reassure the Agent-General in London that the crofters were suitable colonists by claiming they were now ashamed of the rent strikes and land seizures they had initiated, having been 'led astray by blatant agitators and unscrupulous journalists' (*Appendices to the Journals of the House of Representatives*, 1886). The New Zealand press was heavily sceptical about Allan's motives and the political agenda that allegedly underlay his trip, and scathing about the full salary of £325 and generous travelling expenses of £100 that were allocated to him as he pursued 'the absurd scheme' to recruit crofters (*Timaru Herald*, 13/7/1886; *Tuapeka Times*, 22/9/1886). Described as a parasite who was 'disporting himself … as a sort of volunteer emigration agent', he was criticised for enjoying a free holiday at government expense 'without doing anything in the shape of work for that liberal pay' (*Evening Star*, 9/9/1886; *Wairarapa Standard*, 12/7/1886). Allan's colonisation scheme did indeed fall by the wayside, owing to the Crofters' Holdings Act, as well as the high cost of settlement in New Zealand compared with the crofter colonies that were created on the Canadian prairies in the late 1880s (Norton, 1994).

Tourist Recollections

The itineraries of visiting recruitment agents were dictated by the need to drum up business, and they deployed memories of their homeland only as aids in their canvassing campaigns. While their reports reflect their perceptions of conditions and prospects in Scotland, it is primarily to a sample of the surviving diaries and letters of travellers and tourists that we turn for insights into the land of birth or ancestry to which they were returning with the central objectives of recreation and reconnection. It was not only high profile visitors such as John McKenzie and Andrew Carnegie who invoked memories or voiced opinions about Scottish political, social and economic issues.

Angus Mackenzie was 49 years old when in 1904 he made the first of several return visits to Scotland from Idaho. He had probably emigrated as a child, since his journal indicates that he had little memory of his native Highlands. 'It is', he wrote, 'the roughest and most picturesque place I ever saw.' The combination of beauty and utility, and the incongruity of some of the buildings, offered an implicit commentary on the economic and social context: 'You come around a high mountain and there below lies a beautiful lake and steamboats going right into the center of the country where least expected. Many fine mansions are to be found along these lochs where there is hardly room enough to build' (Mackenzie, 1904).

Mackenzie spent a month in his native parish of Applecross, visiting or identifying numerous relations, but his heart was not in the Highlands, for it was only as he approached the 'green meadows and suburbun (sic) homes' around Glasgow that he wrote 'I should like to change my home in Idaho for one in this place.' Lodging in the Waverley Temperance Hotel in Sauchiehall Street, for one shilling per night, he also ventured to Paisley, where he had 'the pleasure of inspecting' the cotton mills of Coats and Clark. In Glasgow he commended the impressive buildings ('witness to the skill and enterprise of its citizens'); glass-roofed 'railroad' stations ('large and commodious'); well-endowed university; numerous public parks; and streets that were 'mostly well laid out and spacious'. The double-decker tram cars were different from any he had seen in the US, and the police – perhaps also in contrast to the US – were 'very fine looking men & very polite and accomodating (sic) to strangers. Dignified in appearence (sic) and not officious.' The final part of the diary consisted of a review of Scottish agriculture – land tenure, crop rotations, soil, livestock, architecture, and implements ('much the same as with us except that the thrashing machines are altogether different'). His overall impressions were that 'People live comfortable, and I think are doing very well. They never seem to be in a hurry and take life easy. But depend, I think, too much on the baker ... in fact there are no stoves fit for baking of bread here.' (Mackenzie, 1904)[2]

Angus Mackenzie's comment about the general prosperity of the Scottish farming constituency was echoed 10 years later by James Innes, when, on the eve of the war, he and his wife came back from New Zealand on a three-week visit to Lossiemouth on the Moray coast. His memories were also of a practical nature. He itemised the changes that had taken place since his previous visit about six years earlier, including better accommodation for agricultural labourers and 'many new and good houses' in the suburbs of small towns. Even bigger changes had taken place in farm workers' wages since Innes had been in that position himself, with a 50% increase for men and a 100% increase for women. But while farmers 'appear to have a fairly comfortable life', their increased labour costs cancelled out any profit from higher prices. Turning to the herring fishing industry – a mainstay of Morayshire's coastal economy – Innes mused on the significant capital investment that was required to implement the switch from sailing boats to steam drifters that had taken place within the last two years, but added that – to his surprise – the role of the fisherwomen was 'unchanged'. They still carried heavy creels of fish on their backs, and 'their working dress is much the same as it was thirty years ago.' Recent developments in tourism and travel also caught his attention, notably the new 'health resort' of Stotfield, whose beach, golf course and two large hotels were 'largely frequented by more or less wealthy people'. At the same time, cheap fares offered by the railway companies meant that ordinary people 'travel about both in England and Scotland much more than they used to do' (*Poverty Bay Herald*, 29/8/1914).

Commercialising Routes to the Roots: Tartan Tourism in Inter-war Scotland

The examples of emigrant travel examined so far have been mainly private or family enterprises, or celebrity visits. Although they were an important ingredient in forging multiple reconnections with Scotland, they do not constitute the explicitly focused, commercialised ancestral tourism that became increasingly popular in the 20th century, and which relied more explicitly on invented traditions and memories.

'Tartan tourism', as it was dubbed by *The Scotsman* newspaper, was an enterprise made primarily in America. Almost biennially, between 1924 and 1938, the Order of Scottish Clans in the United States chartered Anchor line vessels to ship Scottish tradesmen back to their homeland for a holiday. Founded on St Andrew's Day 1878, one of the Order's objectives was 'to cultivate fond recollections of Scotland' among its membership, which by the mid-1920s numbered 24,000. The first transatlantic trip, in August 1924, saw 1000 visitors disembark at Glasgow, where they were formally welcomed by the presidents of *An Comunn Gaidhealach* and the Lewis and Harris Society, the minister of St Columba's Gaelic Church in Glasgow, the city's provost, magistrates and town council, and Sir Harry Lauder, who had been a schoolmate of Duncan MacInnes, Chief of the Order of Scottish Clans. In acknowledging the lavish and unexpected civic welcome, MacInnes – a Berwickshire man whose high-profile day job was chief accountant for New York City – said that the tourists 'were looking forward to making their trip not an exception but a habit' (*The Scotsman*, 5/8/1924).

That wish was fulfilled, as over the next 14 years, MacInnes arranged six further trips, most of which brought parties of between 1000 and 2400 emigrants or second-generation Scots on tours which extended from a fortnight to several weeks. There was usually a set itinerary that included Burns Country, Edinburgh and the Trossachs, but tourists could also make their own arrangements, which for many meant fanning out across Scotland to visit relatives. Perhaps it was the popularity of these trips that led the St Andrew's Society of Edinburgh to observe that the visit home was the 'great event of his lifetime to every Scot permanently settled overseas' and to pledge itself to 'extend a cordial welcome to brither [brother] Scots on their visit to the old country' (Otago Caledonian Society Scrapbook, quoted in Bueltmann, 2012: 156). In 1924 it agreed to improve the facilities at its Edinburgh headquarters so that visitors could be more appropriately welcomed and even billeted (*The Scotsman*, 29/11/1924).

By the early 1930s the depression had made its mark, not only by curtailing numbers but by reshaping the industrial landscape of Clydeside. These homecomings were very much public events, which attracted newsreel coverage and many column inches in the Scottish press. *The Scotsman's* description of the scene in July 1932 conveys the sentiments of both hosts and visitors, although the one passenger singled out seems to have pursued a rather unorthodox career in America.

From time to time as the liner steamed up river pleasure steamers went by, packed full, going down. The home-coming people cheered wildly and the passengers in the pleasure steamers cheered back. Elsewhere, at street ends and along the river banks, onlookers stood singly or in groups or crowds, and looked on, with handkerchiefs fluttering ... There was, I fancy, one passenger who must have felt thankful, as he looked at the empty shipyards and mouldy slipways, that he gave up working in a shipyard in Scotland some years ago, and went to America, where he now found life rather more prosperous, I gathered, as a bar tender in a club, dispensing alcoholic drinks with an entirely open mind on the question, if not always in an entirely open manner. (*The Scotsman*, 19/7/1932)

The Australians and Canadians too got in on the act. In 1932 a large party of Canadians attending the 'Great Natives of Glasgow Reunion' was entertained by the City Fathers, all dressed in full regalia. The Scottish Australian delegation four years earlier is better known. In April 1928 a crowd of 8000 in Melbourne waved off the vessel *Hobson's Bay*, with musical accompaniment from the Melbourne Highland Pipe Band and the Royal Caledonian Pipe Band. The ship's captain was described in the Australian press as a 'braw Hielan' man from up beyond Inverness', while 'practically every officer hails from the Land o' Cakes and Cookies' (*Northern Times*, WA, 26/11/1927).[3] The vessel was carrying, among others, over 600 Scots: 352 women and 251 men from every Australian State, and representing a range of trades, professions and industries: farming, teaching, retail, banking, hospitality and nursing. They were taking part in a delegation which was multi-tasked with promoting emigration and developing trade and commerce, as well as visiting family and having a holiday in the homeland (Wilkie, 2014). Delegates applied to take part, and places were allocated on the basis of state quotas, the biggest share being given to New South Wales (*Brisbane Courier*, 23/6/1927). The trip was organised by Archibald Gilchrist, general secretary of the Victorian section of the New Settlers' League, and the fare – subsidised by Scottish associations across Australia – was £200 for a berth on the ship, plus expenses in Scotland, but excluding the (compulsory) return voyage (*Brisbane Courier*, 28/6/1927; *Singleton Argus*, 24/3/1928).

The delegates were generally higher up the economic ladder than many transatlantic tourists, and the venture was soaked in imperial rhetoric and middle-class popular imperialism. In both Scotland and England, the party was subjected to a round of official receptions, at which politicians and civic dignitaries waxed lyrical on the virtues of the imperial relationship. But it was not only about men, money and markets. It was also an exercise in roots tourism and memory, the narrative of which demonstrates the importance of identity, even invented identity, to emigrants who were homesick or wanted to escape the arid heat of Australia. The trip therefore exemplifies Dean MacCannell's (1973) concept of 'staged authenticity', as the delegates sought out the 'back regions' of their own or their ancestors' homeland, and tried to share in the 'real life' of the places and people they visited.

After five days in London, the Australian tourists came north, where they spent a week in Edinburgh and Glasgow, respectively, before visiting Perth, Dundee, Aberdeen and Inverness, where the tour ended on 15 June. Part of the delegation's remit was to organise special 'Australia campaigns' in the main Scottish cities, where they circulated information about Australian industries. Modest exhibitions of products were laid on in smaller towns, and it was intended that each delegate would sponsor an emigrant. There were various perquisites along the way. In Perth, for instance, the General Accident Company offered free accident insurance to all delegates for the rest of their tour, and White Horse Distillers in Glasgow lubricated the wheels of commerce in the obvious way.

Writing from Aberdeen, the Reverend John Armour summed up the party's experiences half-way through the tour.

> It is amazing how much of Scotland we have seen in so short a time. On every side we have been met with the most elaborate hospitality, and the Scots have spared no pains to make our visit not only enjoyable, but also memorable. Rich and poor have greeted us ... Every day has been well arranged for, and points of historic interest and beauty have been visited in rapid succession. (*West Gippsland Gazette*, 27/11/1928)

He went on to describe how the Scottish hosts had joined enthusiastically in the publicity and marketing campaign.

> [In Glasgow] as in Edinburgh, were great calico posters, stretched across the streets, bearing the words, 'Welcome Australia, buy Australian Goods.' Balloons were also in the sky, bearing such statements as 'Buy Australian sultanas, the best in the world.' In many of the shop windows, there were special displays of Australian goods, and our delegation members were distributing great quantities of samples to their friends. Booksellers made special displays of Australian books and magazines, and altogether Australia has had a very good advertisement in Scotland's commercial city. (*West Gippsland Gazette*, 27/11/1928)

But not all the delegates had a business agenda. The passenger list included many family units, and a number of Australian newspapers claimed that the trip was 'primarily intended as a Back to Scotland picnic.' (*Canberra Times*, 1/11/1927). When the tour broke up in Inverness, and they were freed from their official duties, many of the party stayed on to visit relatives, or to make trips to tourist sites that had not featured in the official programme. The 1928 delegates subsequently recalled their trip through annual reunions in their various branches (*Sunday Mail*, Brisbane, 16/8/1931), but the only evidence of a further organised Australian visit to Scotland before the war was in 1936, when a party of 82 Scottish Australians who landed in London came north for a month's tour of their homeland, during which they enjoyed 'the height of Highland hospitality' (*Border Watch*, 1/8/1936; *The Scotsman*, 25/5/1936).

Promoting Genealogical Tourism in Post-war Scotland

The popularity of ancestral tourism increased markedly in the second half of the 20th century, when a growing constituency of well paid, mobile expatriates and their families energised the Scottish tourist industry. While straightforward family reunions were still the bedrock of such comings and goings, the tourist industry also addressed the fascination of the multi-generational Scottish diaspora with the land of its ancestors, and selected parts of Scotland began to be marketed as a mecca for genealogical pilgrims. Building on the foundations of 'tartan tourism', heritage holidays were promoted in the clearance hotspots of the Highlands, and week-long 'hamefarin' (homecoming) celebrations took place in Shetland in 1960, 1985 and 2010 (Shetland Hamefarin, 1960).

The inaugural Shetland event was the brainchild of John Arcus, an islander who had emigrated to Wellington, New Zealand. On a visit home in 1958 he suggested to the civic authorities that 'a grand return of Shetlanders from all parts of the world' should be organised for 1960 (Shetland Hamefarin, 1960). Despite – or perhaps because of – the uncertain economic climate and ongoing depopulation, his idea was adopted with enthusiasm, as a means of showcasing Shetland's products to the wider world, and fulfilling the remit of the recently-formed Shetland Development Council to promote tourism. A contingent of Shetlanders travelled to Southampton to welcome and accompany the 55-strong overseas party. The islanders would not have gone unnoticed, since they were dressed as Vikings in recognition of the enduring legacy of seven centuries of Norse culture in the Northern Isles (Fenton & Palsson, 1984).[4] Most of the tourists were New Zealanders, but others from Canada, America and Australia swelled the total to almost 90 (*Shetland Times*, 6/8/2010). Their debarkation at Lerwick on 20 May was greeted by the local Pipe and Brass bands, they were serenaded ashore with a specially composed anthem, and accorded an official address from the town's Provost. In the week that followed 'Lerwick's streets and public buildings became a temporary museum' within the framework of a Viking heritage (Church, 1990: 33). A plethora of exhibitions and entertainment culminated in a pageant, when 'hundreds of cars converged on the car park to the north of the arena, and by the time the programme started ... something like 3,000 people had paid ... hundreds more watched from a distance and paid nothing' (*Shetland Times*, 3/5/1985).

A similar pattern of activities was followed when the event was reprised in 1985, the main difference being that the transformation of Shetland's economy allowed for much more substantial investment by the oil-enriched local authority. Whereas in 1960 resident Shetlanders had travelled to the Lerwick pageant 'to witness the Hamefarers watch the representations of themselves', a quarter of a century later it was the 500 visitors who travelled throughout the islands. They attended a huge number of events planned and subsidised by civic authorities which injected the impact of oil into the rhetoric of a public welcome that emphasised the islands' prosperity (Church, 1990: 33–34). In urging the visitors to take time to reflect on their heritage, the convener of the Islands' Council highlighted his belief that memory was crucial to emigrant tourism.

> I do hope those of you who were born in Shetland have time to stand and stare and remember the Shetland you left when you look at the Shetland today. I hope that those whose parents or grandparents were born in Shetland that you will have time to stand and stare at the little crofts and tiny roofless croft houses where large families toiled, a hard life but in a happy family and community ... I hope you have time to stare and wonder what is in Shetland that causes this intense love for Shetland by Shetlanders. As Shetland, that could not provide a livelihood for its population, and one-third of the people born here had to leave Shetland to find a livelihood elsewhere, carried with them only memories of their homeland. But life really is not composed of years. Life is composed of memories, and I hope you'll carry away with you very happy memories of Shetland, memories that will walk beside you all the rest of your lives. (Church, 1990: 35)

Whereas Hamefarin had its roots in New Zealand, most ancestral tourism developments were steered from across the Atlantic. In the US the 1970s saw the beginning of a revival in celebrating Scottish ethnicity, at least among older immigrants and (especially) those of Scottish ancestry. The erosion of Scottish associational activity since the 1920s had begun to move into reverse as early as 1956 with the inauguration of Grandfather Mountain Highland Games in North Carolina, the formation of the Clan Donald Society USA and the establishment of the American-Scottish Foundation. Two decades later it accelerated dramatically as part of the wider American love-affair with genealogies, which was itself partly attributable to the success of Alex Haley's novel, *Roots*, and its television adaptation (Haley, 1976).

Part of that process, however, involved the escalation of a phenomenon that Hugh Trevor-Roper (1983) called a 'retrospective invention', the peddling of a spurious Scotland that existed only in the imaginations of pilgrims and promoters. His chapter is one of seven essays in an edited collection which analyses the pervasive power of invented traditions, particularly those which bolster nationalism or patriotism. According to Trevor-Roper (1983: 15–41; Trevor-Roper, 2008), the kilts and tartans that began to characterise Highland culture in the 18th century were a consequence of – and protest against – union with England. The invention of Scotland was demonstrated most memorably by Arthur Freed, the Hollywood film producer, when he was seeking a location for the first *Brigadoon* film in 1953. 'I went to Scotland but I could find nothing that looked like Scotland', he complained as he returned, disappointed, to Hollywood (Hardy, 1990: 1). In similar vein, some 'homecoming' tourists anticipated re-engaging with a country that only existed in their imaginations: either a completely fictional land, or (for first-generation emigrants) a land that remained frozen in the image they had created at the time of their departure, and which became increasingly divorced from reality the longer they were away. Descendants of the emigrant generation were more likely to be genealogical tourists searching for an invented identity, often in the ruins of cleared Highland townships.

The anthropologist, Paul Basu, has made innovative use of cyberspace to explore modern constructions of diasporic identity in a 'virtual' world (Basu, 2007: 94–121). In particular, he has scrutinised attitudes to sites of memory through the lens of internet chat rooms, where contributors discuss their Highland heritage, their desire to visit Scotland, and their subsequent impressions (Basu, 2007: 153). These early 21st-century 'returners' sometimes manipulate ancestral lines in order to highlight the most distinctive associations, particularly those which speak of victimhood, thereby giving the descendants' visits the extra dimension of pilgrimage. But that attitude can also cause disillusionment or a sense of displacement when Scotland has been unrecognisable, and its people cynical about the returners' quest to nurture an imagined identity. Some visitors complain that the dignity of their venture is diluted by inappropriate terminology. 'I am not, and never will be, a tourist in Scotland', declared one of Basu's Canadian correspondents. 'I felt Scotland many years before I was there.' (Basu, 2005, in Harper, 2005: 133). The passion of another correspondent sprang not from her own family history, but from the 'genocidal rhetoric' of a Highland Holocaust that had been fuelled by poetry, popular narratives and heritage sites. Referring to herself as 'a child of the outcasts', she was aghast at the Scots' indifference to – or even endorsement of – an alleged 'ethnic cleansing' of the Highlands that she likened to treatment of Canada's First Nations people.

When I first went to Scotland I was ready to enjoy the country, and to have some fun looking up all the places that I had heard about. When I got there and as I travelled north my thoughts began to change. *The place was empty, everyone was gone.* There were no places to see that I had heard so much about. No one even knew where they might be. *We weren't missed!* (Basu, 2007: 189; emphases added by Basu)

Conclusion: Legacies and Lessons

It is now widely recognised that ancestral and emigrant tourism is a money-spinner, with diaspora tourists being more likely than other travellers to engage with the host country's economy (International Diaspora Engagement Alliance, 2012). According to Scotland's national tourism organisation, 50 million people in the world have Scottish ancestry, with the biggest concentrations in North America, Australasia and other parts of the UK. An estimated 213,000 trips per annum, worth $101 million, are currently made by visitors who engage in ancestral research, and Visit-Scotland (2012) claims that, of the ten million people with Scottish ancestry who are interested in exploring their heritage, a remarkable 43% intend to spend time in Scotland within the next two years. Such visitors, they optimistically predict, could be worth around £2.4 billion by 2018.

The business of ancestral tourism has been actively promoted in Scotland since at least the 1920s, when transportation and travel companies began to entice emigrants and their descendants back from near and far. It has been demonstrated in a specific context in the 'hamefarin' excursions that took official root in Shetland in 1960, and most recently in the two nationwide 'Years of Homecoming' spearheaded by the Scottish government in 2009 and 2014. But, as we have seen, it has a much longer pedigree. It grew out of the cultural roots of Romanticism, coupled with advances in transport that embraced first the steamship and the train, and then the jet engine. Although the practical mechanisms and infrastructure of emigrant tourism have been transformed by technological developments, the impact of commercialisation, and most recently by a 'virtual' world of travel blogs and Facebook groups, the tourists themselves – from wherever they came – have continued to prioritise the quest to reconnect with real or invented roots. The legacy of the Romantic movement cast a long shadow, inspiring successive generations of visitors to construct similar memories, follow similar itineraries, and remark on similar phenomena. Other recurring themes included the contrast between architectural solidity and flimsiness, the warmth of the welcome, and the importance of making nostalgic reconnections, but the confident imperial rhetoric that characterised Victorian and Edwardian travelogues – and triggered the sometimes contentious visits of recruitment agents – faded markedly after World War I.

Emigrants revisited Scotland for many other reasons than holidaymaking, but recreation and the rekindling of memories were often key elements in a wider, multi-dimensional itinerary. By weaving the leisure experience into that bigger tapestry, we have been able to evaluate changes and continuities in its practice over several generations, assess the cumulative impact of the Scottish diaspora on the construction of the modern ancestral tourism industry and debate the significance of homecoming travel, particularly in terms of public perception and memory. This approach has also opened up a historiographical dialogue between tourism, memory and diaspora studies, since these scholarly disciplines – each vibrant in its own right – have never really explored their complementarity.

Finally, ancestral and emigrant tourism is also controversial, for the diasporic community is neither monolithic nor passive. Even among visitors whose specific objective is to investigate their ancestral heritage, knowledge, expectations and experiences vary considerably, not least because of the multiple and contested perceptions of home and identity that they construct, sometimes under the influence of overseas ethnic associations or family traditions. Consequently, as we have just seen, roots tourism can divide as well as unite, when cherished preconceptions – perhaps of eviction and exile, perhaps of the cosy kailyard – are not confirmed in the visitors' experiences of Scotland and their encounters with its residents. The ethical and practical challenge for the heritage tourist industry is to attract homecoming emigrants with a vibrant, authentic narrative that cultivates meaningful memories but avoids turning Scottish history into a Disneyfied theme park populated by ghostly caricatures.

Notes

(1) Edinburgh and Killiecrankie featured, but Burns' Country and the Trossachs did not.
(2) Mackenzie's unpublished journal was transcribed in 1983 by his great-nephew Wayne Oliver Mackenzie, and donated to the Applecross Heritage Society in 2009. The inadequate stoves were presumably in private households.
(3) Scotland was commonly described as a 'Land o' Cakes' (meaning oatcakes). The phrase appears in Robert Burns' poem, *On The Late Captain Grose's Peregrinations Thro' Scotland*.
(4) The King of Norway relinquished control of the Northern Isles to Scotland in 1468.

References

Aberdeen Journal (12 May 1915) Need for more recruits.

Agunias, D. and Newland, K. (2012) *Developing a Route Map for Engaging Diasporas in Development: A Handbook for Policymakers and Practitioners in Home and Host Countries.* Geneva: International Organization for Migration; Washington DC: Migration Policy Institute. See http://www.osce.org/secretariat/196621?download=true (accessed 12 December 2015).

Appendices to the Journals of the House of Representatives (1886) D4a. Agent-General to Minister for Immigration, 3 June 1886, enclosing letter from Colin Allan to Agent-General, 24 May 1886. See http://atojs.natlib.govt.nz/cgi-bin/atojs

Basu, P. (2005) Roots-tourism as return movement: semantics and the Scottish diaspora. In M. Harper (ed.) *Emigrant Homecomings: The Return Movement of Emigrants, 1600–2000* (pp. 131–150). Manchester: Manchester University Press.

Basu, P. (2007) *Highland Homecomings: Genealogy and Heritage Tourism in the Scottish Diaspora*. Abingdon: Routledge.

Border Watch (1 August 1936, p. 4) (Mount Gambier, South Australia). Australian Scots in Scotland. Trove. See https://trove.nla.gov.au/newspaper

Brisbane Courier (23 June 1927) Trove. See https://trove.nla.gov.au/newspaper

Brisbane Courier (28 June 1927) Trove. See https://trove.nla.gov.au/newspaper

Brooking, T. (1996) *Lands for the People? The Highland Clearances and Colonization of NZ: A Biography of John McKenzie*. Dunedin: University of Otago Press.

Bruce Herald (10 April 1872, p. 6) Fair Play: letter from 'Settler'. Papers Past. See http://paperspast.natlib.govt.nz/cgi-bin/paperspast

Bruce Herald (13 May 1892, p. 2) The Rev. James Chisholm's Farewell. Papers Past, http://paperspast.natlib.govt.nz/cgi-bin/paperspast

Bueltmann, T. (2012) 'Gentlemen, I am going to the Old Country': Scottish roots-tourists in the late nineteenth and early twentieth centuries'. In M. Varricchio (ed.) *Back to Caledonia. Scottish Homecomings from the Seventeenth Century to the Present* (pp. 150–167). Edinburgh: John Donald.

Canberra Times (1 November 1927, p. 4) Scottish Delegation. Trove. See https://trove.nla.gov.au/newspaper

Carnegie, A. (1903) *An American Four-in-Hand in Britain*. New York: Charles Scribner's Sons.

Church, J. (1990) Confabulations of community: The hamefarings and political discourse on Shetland. *Anthropological Quarterly* 63 (1), 31–42.

Clutha Leader (20 May 1892, p. 4) Untitled. Papers Past. See http://paperspast.natlib.govt.nz/cgi-bin/paperspast

Coles. T. and Timothy, D.J. (eds) (2004) *Tourism, Diasporas and Space*. London/New York: Routledge.

Devine, T.M. (2011) *To The Ends of the Earth. Scotland's Global Diaspora 1750–2010*. London: Allen Lane.

Dwyer. L., Seetaram, N., Forsyth. P. and King, B. (2014) Is the migration–tourism relationship only about VFR? *Annals of Tourism Research* 46, 130–143.

Farquharson, D. (undated [1930s]) *Tales and Memories of Cromar and Canada*. Chatham, Ontario, n.p.

Evening Star (27 September 1872, p. 2) An Old Colonial at Home. Papers Past. See http://paperspast.natlib.govt.nz/cgi-bin/paperspast

Evening Star (9 September 1886, p. 2) Untitled. Papers Past, http://paperspast.natlib.govt.nz/cgi-bin/paperspast

Feilding Star (11 April 1899, p. 2) The Minister of Lands. Papers Past. See http://paperspast.natlib.govt.nz/cgi-bin/paperspast

Fenton, A. and Palsson, H. (eds) (1984) *The Northern and Western Isles in the Viking World: Survival, Continuity, and Change*. Edinburgh: John Donald.

Graburn, N.H.H. (1977) Tourism: The sacred journey. In V. Smith (ed.) *Hosts and Guests: the Anthropology of Tourism* (pp. 17–31). Philadelphia: University of Pennsylvania Press.

Grimshaw, M. (2008) *Bibles and Baedeckers: Tourism, Travel, Exile and God*. Abingdon: Routledge.

Haley, A. (1976) *Roots: The Saga of An American Family*. Garden City, NY: Doubleday.

Hardy, F. (1990) *Scotland in Film*. Edinburgh: Edinburgh University Press.

Harper, M. (ed.) (2005) *Emigrant Homecomings. The Return Movement of Emigrants, 1600–2000*. Manchester: Manchester University Press.

Harper, M. and Constantine, S. (2010) *Migration and Empire*. Oxford: Oxford University Press.

Hunter, J. (2015) *Set Adrift Upon The World: The Sutherland Clearances*. Edinburgh: Birlinn.

International Diaspora Engagement Alliance (2012) *Diaspora Tourism: Building Economies through Cultural Connections*. See http://www.diasporaalliance.org/diaspora-tourism-building-economies-through-cultural-connections/ (accessed 11 December 2015).

Iorio, M. and Corsale, A. (2013) Diaspora and tourism: Transylvanian Saxons visiting the homeland. *Tourism Geographies: An International Journal of Tourism Space, Place and Environment* 15 (2), 198–232.

Inverness Courier (19 May 1883).

Inverness Courier (15 September 1899) The Hon. John Mackenzie (sic) in Ross-shire.

Leite, N. (2005) Travels to an ancestral past: On diasporic tourism, embodied memory, and identity. *Antropologicas* 9, 273–302.

Lew, A.A. and Wong, A. (2002) Tourism and the Chinese diaspora. In C.M. Hall and A.M. Williams (eds) *Tourism and Migration: New Relationships Between Production and Consumption* (pp. 205–209). Dordrecht: Kluwer Academic.

King, R. (2000) Generalisations from the history of return migration. In B. Ghosh (ed.) *Return Migration: Journey of Hope or Despair.* Geneva: International Organization for Migration, 7.

MacCannell, D. (1973) Staged authenticity: Arrangements of social space in tourist settings. *The American Journal of Sociology* 79 (3), 589–603.

Mackenzie, A. (1904, transcribed 1983) Unpublished journal of Angus Mackenzie of Moscow, Idaho.

National Register of Archives Scotland (NRAS) (1860) survey no. 1345, letter of William Fletcher to Charles Farquharson.

Northern Times (31 October 1958) (Golspie, Sutherland).

Northern Times (7 November 1958, p. 2) (Golspie, Sutherland). No direct success in tracing forebears, but it was 'wonderful experience'.

Northern Times (19 July 1968, p. 2) (Golspie, Sutherland). Tributes to Canada's First Prime Minister.

Northern Times (26 November 1927) Carnarvon, WA. Trove, https://trove.nla.gov.au/newspaper

Norton, W. (1994) *Help Us to a Better Land: Crofter Colonies in the Prairie West.* Regina: Canadian Plains Research Centre.

Otago Caledonian Society Scrapbook II. (Hocken Library, Dunedin, MS-1045/031).

Otago Daily Times (25 December 1872, p. 3) Mr Birch in Scotland. Papers Past. See http://paperspast.natlib.govt.nz/cgi-bin/paperspast

Otago Witness (12 January 1893, p. 21) Milton. Papers Past. See http://paperspast.natlib.govt.nz/cgi-bin/paperspast

Otago Witness (6 April 1899, p. 22) Presentation to the Hon. J. McKenzie. Papers Past. See http://paperspast.natlib.govt.nz/cgi-bin/paperspast

Otago Witness (7 December 1899, p. 22) The Home Trip of the Minister for Lands. Papers Past. See http://paperspast.natlib.govt.nz/cgi-bin/paperspast

Poverty Bay Herald (29 August 1914, p. 7) Impressions on revisiting Scotland. Papers Past. See http://paperspast.natlib.govt.nz/cgi-bin/paperspast

Ross-shire Journal (25 September 1899) Hon. John Mackenzie (sic), Minister of Land, New Zealand.

The Scotsman (22 July 1919).

The Scotsman (5 August 1924).

The Scotsman (29 November 1924).

The Scotsman (19 July 1932).

The Scotsman (25 May 1936).

Scheyvens, R. (2007) Poor cousins no more valuing the development potential of domestic and diaspora tourism. *Progress in Development Studies* 7 (4), 307–325.

Shetland Hamefarin *(20–27* May 1960) Official Programme, foreword by G.W. Blance, Chairman, Hamefarin Committee. See http://copac.jisc.ac.uk/search?title=shetland%20hamefarin%201960&rn=1

Shetland Hamefarin (2010) See http://www.shetlandhamefarin.com/2000–shetland-hamefarin (accessed 16 October 2015).

Shetland Times (16 June 1873).

Shetland Times (3 May 1985) supplement, p. 7.

Shetland Times (6 August 2010) History: the first Hamefarin.

Singleton Argus (24 March 1928) See https://trove.nla.gov.au/newspaper

Smout, T.C. (1982–3) Tours in the Scottish Highlands from the eighteenth to the twentieth centuries. *Northern Scotland* 5, 99–121.

South Australian Weekly Chronicle (25 November 1882).

Sunday Mail (16 August 1931) (Brisbane). Trove. Seehttps://trove.nla.gov.au/newspaper

Timaru Herald (13 July 1886, p. 3) Disinterested Service. Papers Past. See http://paperspast.natlib.govt.nz/cgi-bin/paperspast

Timespan Museum (2015) Diefenbaker's North. See http://www.heraldscotland.com/news/13146491.Museum_project_s_tribute_to_former_Canadian_PM/ (accessed 15 November 2015).

Trevor-Roper, H. (1983) The invention of tradition: The Highland tradition of Scotland. In E.J. Hobsbawm and T.O. Ranger (eds) *The Invention of Tradition* (pp. 15–41). Cambridge: Cambridge University Press.

Trevor-Roper, H. (2008) *The Invention of Scotland: Myth and History.* New Haven and London: Yale University Press.

Tuapeka Times (22 September 1886, p. 2) Untitled. Papers Past. See http://paperspast.natlib.govt.nz/cgi-bin/paperspast

Varricchio, M. (ed.) (2012) *Back to Caledonia. Scottish Homecomings from the Seventeenth Century to the Present.* Edinburgh: John Donald.

VisitScotland (2012) *Summary of Ancestral Research* (TNS, 2013). See http://www.visitscotland.org/pdf/Ancestral%20Research%2016%20Jan%20vs.org_pptx.pdf (accessed 21 October 2015).

Wairarapa Standard (12 July 1886, p. 2) Some Waiters Upon Providence. Papers Past. See http://paperspast.natlib.govt.nz/cgi-bin/paperspast

Wellington Independent (8 October 1873, p. 2) Untitled. Papers Past. See http://paperspast.natlib.govt.nz/cgi-bin/paperspast

West Gippsland Gazette (27 November 1928) Trove. See https://trove.nla.gov.au/newspaper

Wilkie, B. (2014) The tie that binds: Commerce, migration, and the Australian Scottish delegation of 1928. *International Review of Scottish Studies.* Guelph: University of Guelph.

3 You Can't Go Home Again – Only Visit: Memory, Trauma and Tourism at Chernobyl

Kevin Hannam and Ganna Yankovska

> *All of us had the same fear 'what if we can't come back' the authorities were trying to convince us that it was a short term evacuation but we could all feel that things will never be the same.... I felt that we will never return home. This was our destiny.*
>
> (Respondent B)

> *It's the world's weirdest day trip; one for extreme tourists and a once-in-a-lifetime experience you probably won't want to repeat. A package tour to the Chernobyl exclusion zone will take you to the heart of an apocalypse and sear itself into your memory.*
>
> (Di Duca & Ragozin, 2011: 68)

Introduction

The quotations above sum up what this chapter is about, namely the tensions inherent in memories of trauma. The first quotation is from a former resident of Chernobyl and clearly reflects a memory about the past, *what happened* and the fear of loss of home. The second quotation, from the *Lonely Planet Guidebook* to Ukraine emphasises memory in terms of the future; touring Chernobyl *will be* seared into your memory. It is the tensions between different types of memory that we aim to explore in the context of Chernobyl through the memories of former residents – who were told that they could not go home again, only visit. Chernobyl has become something of a sought-after tourism destination in recent years for those pursuing aspects of what has become known more widely as 'dark tourism' or 'toxic tourism' (Pezzullo, 2007; Yankovska & Hannam, 2014). Hence, it is against the wider commercialised backdrop of tourism to Chernobyl that residents voice their memories.

The name 'Chernobyl' has become a synonym for one of the worst nuclear accidents and technological disasters of all times. The nuclear accident at the Chernobyl power station occurred on 26 April 1986 as an accident during an experiment, allegedly due to inexperienced staff and a weak security backup system (for a detailed review see Petryna, 2003; Perez, 2009). The roof of the reactor came off due to an explosion, emitting radioactive material which soon turned into a radioactive cloud spreading over Ukraine, Russia, Belarus and most of Europe. The immediate result was significant ecological harm due to the spread of radioactive ions in the environment, four hundred times more than the Hiroshima and Nagasaki nuclear bombs. Within a few days, hundreds of thousands of people were evacuated from the most contaminated areas around the Chernobyl site (UNDP, 2002). Most of the evacuees were residents from Pripyat, the nearest town to Chernobyl and a model Soviet settlement with many leisure facilities. Pripyat is now known as a 'ghost town' (see Figure 3.1). The residents were misinformed by the Soviet Government about the accident and promised to be allowed to return within a few days; they hence left all their personal belongings in their homes. However, once the scale of the disaster was recognised, it became clear that they would never be able to return. The negative health impacts (cancer, leukaemia, circulatory diseases and other chronic diseases) have so far claimed an estimated 600,000 people's lives in the contaminated zones (International Atomic Energy Agency, 2006).

Figure 3.1 Leisure facilities in Chernobyl
Source: Kevin Hannam

The most radioactively contaminated area around the Chernobyl power plant was officially designated as The Chernobyl Nuclear Power Plant Zone of Alienation, known as the 'Chernobyl Exclusion Zone' or the 'Zone', located in the northern territory of Ukraine (see Figure 3.2). The exclusion zone extends approximately 30 km in radius from the Chernobyl nuclear

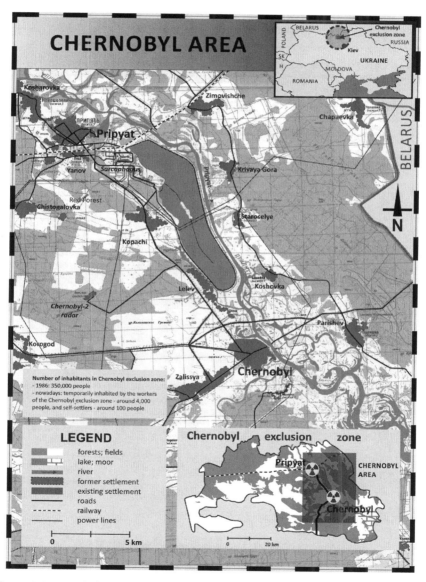

Figure 3.2 Map of Chernobyl. Reproduced with permission from Chernobylwel.com

reactor and covers around 2600 square kilometres of the Ukrainian mainland. It includes Chernobyl city, the town of Pripyat and roughly 180 villages that were evacuated and placed under the military control due to the disaster. Mycio (2005: 2) in her book *Wormwood Forest*, describes the exclusion zone as 'Europe's largest wildlife sanctuary' and explains that 'radiation is no longer "on" the zone, but "of" the zone. It is part of the food chain.' Twenty-seven years on, Ukrainian scientists are still evaluating Chernobyl-related problems as environmental and health issues in the contaminated areas continue to pose a real challenge (Liashenko, 2013).

The first tourists in Chernobyl appeared in the mid-1990s, after the level of radiation had significantly fallen (Steshyn & Cots, 2006). At this time, 'Chernobylinterinform' was the only legal tourism organisation allowed to arrange excursions to the zone. Initially, the 'radioactive' tourist destination was especially popular among foreign tourists from the US and Western Europe. According to the head of the administration of the exclusion zone (officially called the zone of absolute resettlement), visitors of the zone can be classified into three categories: foreign scientists, Ukrainian and foreign journalists and former residents of the territory visiting the remains of their homes and graves of relatives and friends (Golovata, 2010). In this chapter we focus on the latter visitors. However, as Phillips and Ostaszewski (2012: 127) note: '[l]ax surveillance and a lack of security, along with shoddy and broken-down fencing in places around the zone's perimeter, mean that the zone of alienation has very porous borders. Wildlife and people roam in and out. In short, the area has never truly been an "exclusion zone".' Some areas in and around Chernobyl still have high radiation levels and all tourists must follow an official tourist guide and adhere to strict health and safety requirements. A small number (around 100) former residents have now returned to live in the exclusion zone.

In recent years, Chernobyl has seen an increase in the number of visitors, consisting mainly of (dark) tourists, but also former residents returning to visit their former homes. Recent academic work has analysed photographic representations of Chernobyl and the anxieties that these may suggest in terms of their symbolism for industrial decline (Dobraszczyk, 2010), the postmodern sublime (Goatcher & Brunsden, 2011) or as a heterotopian space (Stone, 2013). Indeed, Stone (2013: 91) asserts that, 'Chernobyl is a heterotopia that allows us to gaze upon a post-apocalyptic world, in which the familiar and uncanny collide.' Nevertheless, many of these studies lack an engagement with the actual experiences of Chernobyl, which this study seeks to understand from the perspective of former residents making what Marschall (2015) has called 'memory-trips'.

Conceptualising Traumatic Memories

The literature on dark tourism has sought to understand tourist's engagement with a range of sites that are associated with various traumatic events.

Indeed, in an earlier paper we interpreted the Chernobyl site from the perspective of dark and toxic tourism (Pezzullo, 2007; Yankovska & Hannam, 2014). A key problem with much of the literature on this form of tourism is that it has a tendency to conceptualise such sites as being fixed or static when, in fact, they are open to multiple interpretations – moreover often highly fluid and mobile. The fluidity of memory itself becomes evident when we consider people's personal memories of such sites.

The dynamic role of memory can be traced back to the earlier work of Bartlett (1932: 213) who argued that memories are influenced by the presence of others and by the social and cultural worlds we inhabit: '[r]emembering is not the re-excitation of innumerable fixed, lifeless and fragmentary traces. It is an imaginative reconstruction, or construction, built out of the relation of our attitude towards a whole active mass of organized past reactions or experience.' The term 'collective memory' was introduced by Halbwachs (1992) who argued that individual memories are conceived and mediated by some form of collectivity such as families or communities: 'individual memory cannot be seen as detached from social factors and social influences' (Ferron & Massa, 2014: 23). Although an individual may recollect an event, such remembering is influenced by the wider social environment to which the individual belongs. Halbwachs (1992) emphasised how social institutions and contexts made possible certain memories while discouraging others (see Legg, 2005). Thus 'sites of memory' may hold communal identities together or divide them (Crang & Travlou, 2001).

Heritage tourism research has focused on the active contestation of performances of collective memory (Browman & Pezzullo, 2010; Crang, 1996; Hannam, 2013). This has led to further research on the material mobilities of photographs, postcards, letters, images, guides, souvenirs and all sorts of gifts in terms of the memories that they create for visitors or consumers (see for example Lury, 1997; Selwyn, 1996). More recent work has also examined the kinds of pictures and objects that people carry with them and use to reassemble memories, practices and even landscapes, thus remaking the materiality of places of heritage tourism and migration (see Staiff & Bushell, 2013; Tolia-Kelly, 2006). In this context, Basu and Coleman (2008: 313) note that:

> We are not only concerned with … the material effects of having moved, perhaps many years earlier, to a new place, and with the inter-relatedness of the movements of people and things. In addition, we want to convey the sense that a 'world' – an often fragmented and fragile set of material and non-material assumptions and resources – can itself be made mobile, seemingly translated from one geographical location to another, even as it is transformed in the process.

Here, Basu and Coleman (2008) are emphasising the notion that heritage moves people emotionally and imaginatively to think about their own pasts through different material sensations which themselves can be both tangible and intangible – something we can see in the re-enactment of the past through living history projects (Hannam, 2013) and in residents' travelling memories of sites that have become tourist sites (see Erll, 2011). Reflecting on heritage, as the migrants that Basu and Coleman (2008) refer to, can also be related to contested traumatic events such as leaving one's home behind in search of a better life.

Trauma as a cultural process is also closely connected with the formation of collective memories. Cultural trauma may affect a whole social group and does not need to be experienced by every group member. Events may not be traumatic by themselves but they are attributed a traumatic meaning collectively (Alexander, 2004; Ashworth, 2008; Eyerman, 2004). Ferron and Massa (2014: 23) have argued that 'studying how collective memories are formed, particularly in the case of trauma, is important because they persist for entire generations and they play a crucial social role, in that the interaction of the cultural elements involved can influence attitudes not only toward the past but also toward the present of current societies.' Traumatic events, nevertheless, can be conceptualised as a fundamental 'disruption' of social life in some form (Birtchnell & Buscher, 2011). Philosophically, traumatic events can also be considered as the 'intrusion of something new which remains unacceptable for the predominant view' (Zizek, 2014: 77).

In terms of understanding the collective memories of traumatic events, empirical research has focused on how such events can produce widespread collective mourning, commemorative ceremonies as well as the construction of physical monuments as sites of remembrance (Johnson, 1995; Knox, 2006). While monuments are usually symbols of only one person or one ideal, war memorials and 'memory landscapes' such as cemeteries, commemorate many people or whole communities (Heffernan, 1995). War memorials can be seen as ways in which to commemorate those men and women who gave their lives for others as well as for specific ideals, such as democracy, freedom and justice that attach to particular military campaigns (Hannam & Knox, 2010). Memorials and the events associated with them may serve the needs of a community in the present, connected to its collective identity in order to overcome a past trauma (Johnson, 1995).

More critically, Legg (2005) has drawn attention to the ways in which such traumatic remembering is socially contested and further suggests that trauma should be understood as a collective social, political, and aesthetic condition. Legg (2005) also emphasises the embodied power relations in any form of remembering: that we remember through our bodily actions which combine moments of stillness and movement. As Hebbert (2005: 581) asserts, 'memory and identity are rooted in bodily experiences of being and moving in material space.'

Methodology

Data collection in the form of in depth semi-structured interviews with former residents was conducted in the Ukrainian capital Kiev located around 100 km from the Chernobyl exclusion zone in July 2012, November 2014 and August 2015. In addition, one of the authors (Hannam) took part in a guided tour of the Chernobyl exclusion zone in December 2013. In total, 12 former residents agreed to be interviewed. It should be noted that these former residents had revisited Chernobyl not as members of the commercial tours but either on their own or as part of smaller tours organised by former residents. The interviews were conducted in Russian or Ukrainian (depending on the interviewee), later translated into English for coding purposes. Each interview lasted between 45 minutes and one and a half hours. All interviewees were assured of the confidentiality of their responses to protect their identities. The participants were interviewed regarding their memories of Chernobyl as former residents, their interpretations of the Chernobyl site, and their views on tourism. The former residents that were interviewed had all worked and lived at Chernobyl, had been present during the disaster and had subsequently been evacuated and relocated.

Although, the interview sample was relatively small, the qualitative depth of the responses was significant. Further, we do not seek to make grand generalisations regarding the data gathered but instead illustrate theoretical points regarding respondents' emotional responses to memories of home in the context of tourism developments in Chernobyl. Indeed, the quotations from the interviews have been left intentionally lengthy, in order to convey the full response to the reader. Given the focus of this book, we do not include interview data from tourists themselves.

The interview transcripts were coded using principles of open coding and axial coding to reveal particular themes. Open coding refers to analysis in terms of labelling and categorising data by asking questions and making comparisons; similar incidents are grouped together and given the same conceptual label. Axial coding, meanwhile, puts the data back together by making connections between a category and its sub-categories (Strauss & Corbin, 1990). Using these data analysis procedures two key themes emerged from the data which we discuss below, namely the trauma of the event itself and the ways in which it is remembered collectively and individually, and the ways in which tourism has been developed both by former residents and by other tour companies.

It should be noted at the outset that all of our respondents had positive memories of their former lives in Chernobyl. They variously commented about the beauty and attractiveness of the place before the catastrophic event. In terms of our analysis we consider memories which are concerned with looking back, i.e. the reflections and remembering of the traumatic event itself which have been termed 'spectro-geographies' (Maddern & Adey, 2008). We then relate these to memories concerned with the present; how is Chernobyl remembered collectively today; how is it memorialised; in what ways is it forgotten? Finally, we reflect on how memories are connected with processes of looking forward, in terms of former residents' reflections on tourism at Chernobyl.

Memories Looking Back: Trauma and Hauntings

Consider Figure 3.3. Chernobyl consists of a largely abandoned landscape of houses, apartments, offices, a school and various leisure facilities. It is a haunted space where the material remnants of the past lives of former residents are to be found. Figure 3.3 shows the material remains of the gas masks of the 'liquidators' who were there to contain and clean up the initial effects of the explosion. As such the landscape of Chernobyl can be considered as 'beyond the real' where 'events continue to reverberate ... long after they have occurred so that

Figure 3.3. Gas masks at Chernobyl
Source: Kevin Hannam

time is rendered "out of joint"' (Maddern & Adey, 2008: 291). But the landscape also conjures various materialities in terms of the memories of the trauma of being at Chernobyl for the former residents. Respondent A reflected that:

> I remember the blanket of sand covering all that we could see, people running in all directions, it was a terrifying experience. At that time I was 27 years old and I remember people walking like zombies (dazed and confused). At the time when we started working as a liquidator, all the livestock was culled, all wells were closed with a special material, everything was closed and we were not allowed any movement in certain areas where we had a permission to enter with special passes provided by the government. I could never forget the scenes of the whole town covered in a layer of sand in scorching heat. ... the streets were barren; it seemed like everything had died and vanished. I was young and couldn't understand anything at that time, it was all new to me. The radiation is a totally different thing no one knew about. I remember going out camping with my friends and I felt sick whilst lighting the fire in the forest. I felt tightness in my head and my nose started bleeding. There were no beetles on the trees which was very unusual at that time of the year.

The above quotation raises a number of points. Firstly, there is reflection on mortality which develops the felt 'hauntedness' and confusion of the memory in the landscape (Pinder, 2001). Secondly, the memory conveyed is fundamentally an embodied one: the effects of the radiation on the human body as well as the local environment are noted. Thirdly, the participant reflects upon the effects of stillness and how mobility was curtailed during the event (Hebbert, 2005; Legg, 2005). More broadly, this talks to the materialities of the event itself: the blanket of sand and the livestock being culled evoke memories that describe a different 'world' (Basu & Coleman, 2008).

Respondent C further commented that:
I remember that day very well [he laughed], because I was working that day. We treated it as any emergency situation, we were used to it as part of our usual health and safety drills. When I was at my shift, they told us that an experiment was going on. We didn't know the reasons behind the accident; we couldn't understand what had happened. There were no windows and we were surrounded by thick walls on all sides. ... During the same night, we saw some new starters working and most of them lost their lives there in the first night. Two of them died straight away, and the remaining absorbed a very high level of radiation and they were taken straight to Moscow where they passed away ... Although we received lesser amounts of radiation, most of us were sick for a very long time and even now I have major radiation related health issues. I don't want to talk about this anymore ... don't want to remember any of that.

In this quotation we can see the individual memory of the trauma of the accident being conveyed, as well as the notion of mortality and the embodied sense of memory through reference to the sickness caused by the radiation. At the end, the participant emphasises the individual need to forget these memories, of himself not wanting to remember. Petryna's (2003: 3) respondents from Chernobyl similarly described themselves as the 'living dead' who wanted to forget everything. Traumatic memories then are not always about remembering; they are also there to be forgotten. The Proustian distinction between voluntary and involuntary memories (Crang & Travlou, 2001) becomes important in this context where the act of forgetting is used to curb the involuntary memories of the trauma.

Just like remembering, collective, rather than individual forgetting, however, is more politically charged and can be contested. Nuala Johnson (1995) has called attention to the ways in which memorials may help constitute 'circuits of memory' through which the collective remembering can take place as individual memories become part of a collective consciousness. Figure 3.4

Figure 3.4. Monument to the Liquidators of Chernobyl
Source: Kevin Hannam

shows the monument to the liquidators of Chernobyl. Such monuments argu-
ably function more as 'circuits for tourism' than as 'circuits of memory', as in
the context of Chernobyl they are only rarely visited by former residents.
Respondents argued that such monuments are representative of and reflect
the power of the State rather than their own collective memories.

Many of the respondents were, however, concerned with the collective
process of remembering Chernobyl in the present. There was a strong sense
that the State had largely forgotten them and there had been a lack of commemoration despite the building of State monuments. Respondent G argued
that rather than build monuments, he had expected the State to clean up
Chernobyl and re-build the infrastructure: 'A lot of years have gone by and
no one has built anything here. At the start we had some kind of hope and
we were waiting for this to happen and expected that people come back to
live their normal life but not anymore.' Furthermore, respondent B (who had
recently returned to live within the exclusion zone) commented that:

> It is sad that no one wants to do anything about this place ... I don't
> think many people thought we would be able to live here for long but
> against all odds we have defied the science and managed to survive hap-
> pily in this radiation filled land. I would be very happy if some people
> decided to invest in this place and redevelop it. Having said that, we
> started here with a small temple and hopefully one day a new town will
> be redeveloped just like this spiritual rebirth.

Most former residents, though, had not returned to live in Chernobyl and
reflected on the impossibility of return and of not wanting to return:

> No, I didn't want to return. The work completely changed after the
> explosion and the people in our team were also different. We were treated
> like a bunch of nobodies. It became much harder to work, so I didn't
> want to stay there anymore. The town Chernobyl was still very beauti-
> ful though, but I didn't feel like I wanted to return. (Respondent C)

These statements can be related to wider conceptualisations of the loss of
home through migration and the so-called 'myth of return' (Ali & Holden,
2006; Basu & Coleman, 2008). Other respondents also noted their social and
emotional dislocation within Ukraine: 'A lot of the people didn't feel welcomed in their new roles or places where they moved; there was a lack of
acceptance in other parts of the country for the sufferers of this catastrophe'
(former resident D). Two former residents developed a nostalgic perspective
on those that had returned, for example: 'The people who have settled back
in Chernobyl grow their own food and live happier. I think they are happy
because they are home, at their own home and at peace more importantly'
(Respondent B).

In terms of these memories of Chernobyl as home, we can note how in the present 'the past is resurrected by less-than-dead presences that narrate and also disrupt the telling of history at odds with the commemorative practices of the state' (Maddern & Adey, 2008: 293). Official commemorations are less concerned with the former residents and more with the construction of monuments and collective political events in order to gather international support for ameliorating the continued after effects of the event – what Zizek (2014) has termed an event transition where the event itself becomes transformed into a process. This transition and transformation opens up the space of Chernobyl for tourism in terms of various types of tours. Hence we now focus on the return tours organised by former residents as well as their reflections on contemporary tourism to Chernobyl as a visitor attraction.

Memories Looking Forward: Reflections on Tourism

Former residents reflected on their return visits to Chernobyl as a form of collective rather than individual pilgrimage, in which the local church, rather than to the monuments were most significant:

> After we enter the Zone, we go straight to the church in Chernobyl. We always buy gifts, candles and icons to bring there. The Holy Father and his wife usually meet us there. In the beginning, they were cold to us and unwelcoming. This church is from Moscow Patriarchate, but we (people in the group) were from different churches like Catholic, Greek and Ukrainian orthodox. Once when we entered the church, the Holy Father fell on his knees and we all fell after him. Since then we are all good friends, as we understand that our misfortune has united us. (Respondent A)

Although ostensibly organised as a tour, they also commented on their visits being distinct from tourism in terms of the way they remember and the significance of it being a pilgrimage to their place of home:

> Sometimes I don't even tell my wife and kids, I just pack and go to visit the Zone. ... What is really amazing is how people who live there (in the Chernobyl zone) treat us. They are always happy to meet us. They know we come to 'free our souls' and calm down here. We are not like those tourists who travel there to play; we go there to remember. ... When I organise a tour for the former residents and the others that are interested, I usually warn them that we are not going there for an excursion or walking around but for pilgrimage only. (Respondent H)

Such pilgrimages may have a religious element but are hyper-meaningful, ostensibly secular and intimately bound up with remembering the past in terms of the future (Di Giovine, 2011; Knox & Hannam, 2014). Indeed, Crang and Travlou (2001: 168) have argued that '[m]emories are organised and called up by attention to the present and the future [rather than the past]; what Bergson calls "attention to life", or we might say being-towards.' Indeed, practices of tourism have been conceptualised as learned experiences of becoming in the world (Herbert, 2001; Hannam & Knox, 2010). The former residents' tours at Chernobyl disrupt conventional notions of linear temporality; as former residents, their understandings of time attempt to make sense of the past in terms of the future. Respondent B, for example, noted that:

> I am very glad tourists are coming here a lot. I am always happy to meet them. A lot of people who come here for fun and adrenaline don't know about this place much and about its history and culture. I always try to speak to them and educate them about the catastrophe because I feel they know nothing about what happened to the ordinary people and the liquidators. They just think this place is a dump where strange mutant animals can be found.

He reflects on the ways in which his memories can be used to educate tourists and to challenge their interpretations in the future, but he remains negative about their motivations to visit. Another former resident also felt that tourists could never comprehend the former residents' experiences:

> Tourists are coming just because of their curiosity, they didn't lose anything, and they didn't go through the same pain in their life, like we did. When I go to my native city, my heart aches and I feel so hurt about what happened with my city. The tourists will never be able to understand the pain and the heartache of residents of the Zone; they can never comprehend our experience. (Respondent G)

These respondents' statements are an attempt to connect their past memories with the future, 'allowing distant presences, events, people and things to become rather more intimate' (Maddern & Adey, 2008: 292).

Conclusions

This chapter has specifically examined former residents' memories of Chernobyl based upon qualitative in depth interviews. Former residents return to visit their previous homes in the Chernobyl exclusion zone primarily as a form of pilgrimage but retain positive memories of their lives in what was a model Soviet urban industrial development. Moreover, they see their memories as having educational value for tourists despite their ambivalence about the motivations of these visiting outsiders. Their memories are shaped by the trauma of the past, re-written through attempts at pilgrimage and return in the present, and contested through tourism practices which look towards the future through complex temporal interpretations of the ruins of the Chernobyl landscape. Further, their memories disrupt linear understandings of time and space such that, as Edensor (2005: 829) has suggested, their memories 'act as an antidote to the fixed, classified, and commodified memories purveyed in heritage and commemorative spaces.' Former residents grapple with their nostalgic desires for a lost community/home/time through memorialising visits, while simultaneously harbouring mixed feelings about visitors who engage in 'dark tourism' for pleasure as well as those outsiders who lack respect for what the former residents have lost.

The analysis of specific places such as Chernobyl is important for understanding the relations between different forms of tourism and different conceptualisations of home (Blunt & Dowling, 2006). In the case of Chernobyl, the forced evacuation dislocated many residents from being able return home but as discussed above, those that have returned echo many of the ambivalences of contemporary migration and the 'myth of return'. Williams and McIntyre (2001, cited in White & White, 2007: 90) have argued that, 'the question of where one lives or dwells ... is not a simple matter of residential geography. It is also a matter of emotional geography. Where does one's heart, one's identity, reside? Where is one's emotional home?' Memories of home convey both individual and collective emotional connections and may be developed through further research in terms of the past, present and future imaginings of tourism.

References

Alexander, J.C. (2004) Toward a theory of cultural trauma. In J.C. Alexander, R. Eyerman and B. Giesen (eds) *Cultural Trauma and Collective Identity* (pp. 1–29). Berkeley: University of California Press.

Ali, N. and Holden, A. (2006) Post-colonial Pakistani mobilities: The embodiment of the 'Myth of Return' in tourism. *Mobilities* 1 (2), 217–242.

Ashworth, G.J. (2008) The memorialization of violence and tragedy: Human trauma as heritage. In B. Graham and P. Howard (eds) *The Ashgate Research Companion to Heritage and Identity* (pp. 231–244). Aldershot: Ashgate.

Bartlett, F.C. (1932) *Remembering: A Study in Experimental and Social Psychology*. Cambridge: Cambridge University Press.

Basu, P. and Coleman S. (2008) Introduction: Migrant worlds, material cultures. *Mobilities* 3 (3), 313–330.

Birtchnell, T. and Büscher, M. (2011) Stranded: An eruption of disruption. *Mobilities* 6 (1), 1–9.

Blunt, A. and Dowling, R. (2006) *Home*. London: Routledge.

Browman, M. and Pezzullo P.C. (2010) What's so 'Dark' about 'Dark Tourism'? Death, tours, and performance. *Tourist Studies* 9 (3), 187–202.

Crang, M. (1996) Magic kingdom or a quixotic quest for authenticity. *Annals of Tourism Research* 23 (2), 415–431.

Crang, M. and Travlou, P.S. (2001) The city and topologies of memory. *Environment and Planning D: Society and Space* 19, 161–177.

Di Duca, M. and Ragozin, L. (2011) *Ukraine*. London: Lonely Planet.

Di Giovine, M. (2011) Pilgrimage, communitas, contestation, unity and difference – an introduction. *Tourism* 59 (3), 247–270.

Dobraszczyk, P. (2010) Petrified ruin: Chernobyl, Pripyat and the death of the city. *City: Analysis of Urban Trends, Culture, Theory, Policy, Action* 14 (4), 370–389.

Edensor, T. (2005) The ghosts of industrial ruins: Ordering and disordering memory in excessive space. *Environment and Planning D: Society and Space* 23, 829–849.

Erll, A. (2011) Travelling memory. *Parallax* 17 (4), 4–18.

Eyerman, R. (2004) Cultural trauma: Slavery and the formation of African American identity. In J.C. Alexander, R. Eyerman and B. Giesen (eds) *Cultural Trauma and Collective Identity* (pp. 61–111). Berkeley: University of California Press.

Ferron, M. and Massa, P. (2014) Beyond the encyclopedia: Collective memories in Wikipedia. *Memory Studies* 7 (1), 22–45.

Goatcher, J. and Brunsden, V. (2011) Chernobyl and the sublime tourist. *Tourist Studies* 11 (2), 115–137.

Golovata, L. (2010) Chornobyl Stalkers (in Ukrainian; «Чернобильські Сталкери») Zaxid News. See http://zaxid.net/home/showSingleNews.do?chornobilski_stalkeri &objectId=1101343 (accessed 24 April 2013).

Handbook of International Economic Statistics (1996) *Radiation Hotspots Resulting from the Chernobyl' Nuclear Power Plant Accident.* See http://www.lib.utexas.edu/maps/common wealth/chornobyl_radiation96.jpg (accessed 25 May 2012).

Halbwachs, M. (1992) *On Collective Memory*. Chicago: University of Chicago Press.

Hannam, K. (2013) The mobilities of living history: A case study of Viking heritage. In B. Garrod and A. Fyall (eds) *Contemporary Cases in Heritage*. Oxford: Goodfellow.

Hannam, K. and Knox, D. (2010) *Understanding Tourism*. London: Sage.

Hannam, K., Rickly-Boyd, J. and Mostafanezhad, M. (eds) (2016) *Event Mobilities*. London: Routledge.

Hebbert, M. (2005) The street as locus of collective memory. *Environment and Planning D: Society and Space* 23, 581–596.

Heffernan, M. (1995) For ever England: The western front and the politics of remembrance in Britain, *Ecumene* 2, 293–323.

Herbert, D. (2001) Literary places, tourism and the heritage experience. *Annals of Tourism Research* 28 (2), 312–333.

International Atomic Energy Agency (2006) *Chernobyl's Legacy: Health, Environmental and Socio-Economic Impacts and Recommendation to the Governments of Belarus, the Russian Federation and Ukraine.* The Chernobyl Forum 2003–2005. Vienna: International Atomic Energy Agency. See http://www.iaea.org/Publications/Booklets/Chernobyl/ chernobyl.pdf (accessed 10 May 2012).

Johnson, N. (1995) Cast in stone: monuments, geography, and nationalism'. *Environment and Planning D: Society and Space* 13, 51–65.

Knox, D. (2006) The sacralised landscapes of Glencoe: From massacre to mass tourism, and back again. *International Journal of Tourism Research* 8 (3), 185–197.

Knox, D. and Hannam, K. (2014) Is a tourist a secular pilgrim or a hedonist in search of pleasure? *Tourism Recreation Research* 39 (2), 235–267.

Legg, S. (2005) Contesting and surviving memory: Space, nation, and nostalgia in Les Lieux de Memoire. *Environment and Planning D: Society and Space* 23, 481–504.

Liashenko, A. (2013) *News Analysis: Chernobyl disaster poses long-term environmental challenges.* See http://news.xinhuanet.com/english/indepth/2013–04/26/c_132342756. htm (accessed 26 April 2013).

Lury, C. (1997) The objects of travel. In C. Rojek and J. Urry (eds) *Touring Cultures: Transformations of Travel and Theory* (pp. 75–95). London: Routledge.

Maddern, J. and Adey, P. (2008) Editorial: Spectro-geographies. *Cultural Geographies* 15, 291–295.

Marschall, S. (2015) Touring memories of the erased city: Memory, tourism and notions of 'home'. *Tourism Geographies* 17 (3), 332–349.

Ministry of Emergencies (2011) Procedure of Visiting of the Exclusion Zone. State Agency of Ukraine. See http://dazv.gov.ua/en/index.php?option=com_content&view=article&id=184:order-moe-of-ukraine-on-november-2-2011-1157-approving-the-visiting-of-the-exclusion-zone-and-zone-of-unconditional-mandatory-resettlement&catid=80:norma tivno-pravov-akti-z-pitan-scho-nalejat-do-kompetenc-dazv&Itemid=156 (accessed 12 June 2012).

Mycio, M. (2005) *Wormwood Forest: A Natural History of Chernobyl*. Washington DC: Joseph Henry Press.

Park, C. (1989) *Chernobyl: The Long Shadow*. London: Routledge.

Perez, J.R. (2009) Uncomfortable heritage & dark tourism at Chernobyl. In S. Merill and L. Schmidt (eds) *A Reader in Uncomfortable Heritage and Dark Tourism* (pp. 31–47). Cottbus: Brandenburg University of Technology.

Petryna, A. (2003) *Life Exposed: Biological Citizens after Chernobyl*. Princeton: Princeton University Press.

Pezzullo, P.C. (2007) *Toxic Tourism: Rhetorics of Pollution, Travel, and Environment Justice*. Alabama: The University of Alabama Press.

Phillips, S. and Ostaszewski, S. (2012) An Illustrated Guide to the Post-Catastrophe Future. *The Anthropology of East Europe Review* 30 (1), 127–140.

Pinder, D. (2001) Ghostly footsteps: Voices, memories and walks in the city. *Ecumene* 8, 1–19.

Schindlauer, S. (2008) *Chernobyl, Nuclear Energy and Risk Perception: Can Risk Management Be Prosperous?* Norderstedt: GRIN Verlag oHG.

Selwyn T. (ed.) (1996) *The Tourist Image: Myths and Myth Making in Tourism*. Chichester: Wiley.

Staiff, R. and Bushell, R. (2012) Mobility and modernity in Luang Prabang, Laos: Re-thinking heritage and tourism. *International Journal of Heritage Studies* 19 (1), 98–113.

Steshyn, D. and Cots, E. (2006) The 'Komsomolska Pravda'. See http://www.kp.ru/daily/23696/52367/ (accessed 20 May 2012).

Stone, P. (2013) Dark tourism, heterotopias and post-apocalyptic places: The case of Chernobyl. In L. White and E. Frew (eds) *Dark Tourism and Place Identity: Managing and Interpreting Dark Places* (pp. 79–93). Abingdon: Routledge.

Strauss, A. and Corbin, J. (1990) *Basics of Qualitative Research: Grounded Theory Procedures and Techniques*. London: Sage.

Tolia-Kelly, D. (2006) Mobility/stability: British Asian cultures of 'landscape and Englishness'. *Environment and Planning A* 38 (2), 341–358.

UNDP, United Nations Development Program (2002) 'The Human Consequences of the Chernobyl Nuclear Accident: A Strategy for Recovery' Chernobyl Report-Final. Commissioned by UNDP and UNICEF. See http://www.unicef.org/newsline/chernob ylreport.pdf (accessed 15 June 2012).

White, N. and White, P. (2007) Home and away: Tourists in a connected world. *Annals of Tourism Research* 34 (1), 88–104.

Yankovska, G. and Hannam, K. (2014) Dark and toxic tourism in the Chernobyl exclusion zone. *Current Issues in Tourism* 17 (10), 929–939.

Zizek, S. (2014) *Event: Philosophy in Transit*. Harmondsworth: Penguin.

4 Emotional Inventories: Accounts of Post-war Journeys 'Home' by Ethnic German Expellees

Julia Wagner

Introduction

In Ilse Tielsch's novel *Heimatsuchen* (1995: 172) ['Searching for the Homeland'] the protagonist describes how, with her mother, she journeyed back to the Central European town where she had been born and where her family had lived before they were expelled in 1945. She explains the yearning that lay behind this trip: 'We ... wanted to encounter the past and ourselves in the past. We wanted to turn back time and recover what happened back then.' Their motivation, therefore, was more than simply a wish to revisit a place: they wanted to go back to a vanished period of time in an emotional journey that would take them to the roots of the self.

This desire to 'go back in time' was shared by thousands of real-life Germans who spent their holidays visiting their old homelands. Using first-hand accounts, this chapter examines how those who went back reacted during such visits. First, it draws on travel narratives describing journeys 'home' undertaken in the 1950s, 1960s and 1970s by ethnic Germans expelled from the eastern parts of the disintegrating German Reich and now living in the Federal Republic of Germany (West Germany). The experiences recounted by these West Germans are contrasted with those revealed in a smaller sample of accounts by tourists from the German Democratic Republic (East Germany) and, in the final section, by German Jewish émigrés, who had left those same areas several years earlier in order to escape Nazi persecution, returning to visit their former homes in Central and Eastern Europe.

The ways these groups framed their travel stories were influenced both by the circumstances in which they had had to leave their original homes and by the later contexts of their lives. However, despite these significant differences, a large number of the travel narratives have a common theme: the visitors were taking stock. Many of the accounts contain passages that read like inventories. There are detailed descriptions of all the things the travellers paid attention to while touring their old homelands – the current condition of the streets, the buildings, the public places and the memorials. The visitors generally sought out places that held special meaning for them or were connected with special times in their lives. They looked for remnants of the past they could recognise, traces of the former communities and their cultures. They also noted aspects that now seemed 'different' or 'foreign', but their engagement with contemporary life was usually very limited. Their focus lay on their own changing emotional relationship to these places. By reviewing their memories of how things used to be, their expectations for their visit and the experiences and impressions they gained while actually there, the visitors took stock of the differences and considered what these might mean for their own evolving sense of identity and belonging.

The Aftermath of War

Between 1944 and 1950 some 12–14 million ethnic Germans were uprooted from their homes in Central and Eastern Europe. Either they fled west from the approaching Red Army or they were forcibly expelled. The expulsions affected three groups: The first group were Germans from territories that had belonged to the German Reich until 1945; the second group were ethnic German from other territories in Central and Eastern Europe, including Poland, Czechoslovakia, Hungary, Yugoslavia, Romania and the Soviet Union; the last group were Germans who had migrated to occupied territories during the war. The decision to realise forced migrations of Germans from the Soviet zone of influence had been made by Soviet, British and American leaders during the Yalta conference in February 1945. The bulk of the refugees and expellees came from the territories east of the Rivers Oder (Odra) and Neiße (Nysa) that had been part of the German Reich since 1871, but which were now absorbed into Poland or the Soviet Union by the terms of the Potsdam Agreement of 2 August 1945.[1] These territories included East Prussia, Pomerania, Upper Silesia, parts of Brandenburg, Königsberg and the free city of Danzig. Another large group came from the Sudetenland region of Czechoslovakia, which had been annexed by Germany in 1938 but which was restored to the Czechs after 1945. Smaller groups of ethnic Germans came from other areas of Poland and Czechoslovakia as well as Hungary, Romania and Yugoslavia (Röger, 2011: 32). The refugees and expellees[2] were resettled within the new national borders of post-war Germany. By 1950, approximately 8.1 million – two-thirds of them – were registered in the Federal Republic (FRG) and 4.1 million – the remaining third – in the

German Democratic Republic (GDR) (Schwartz, 2006: 92–106). At this time, many of the new settlers regarded their situation as temporary: they hoped they would return home in due course. Gradually it became clear that their resettlement was permanent (Engelhardt, 2006: 17). There was only one way they could ever see their old homes again – as tourists.

Because of the divisions imposed on Europe by the Cold War, many had to wait for years before they could make a trip back to their birthplaces (Schlögel, 1986: 24–25). During the first decade after 1945, travel opportunities were highly restricted and it was almost impossible to visit Central and Eastern Europe. For West Germans this situation was alleviated in the later 1950s due to a *détente* in diplomatic relations. Poland became the most visited destination for expellees. In 1956 the Leo Linzer travel company started organising bus tours to areas of that country that had previously been German. In that same year, over 9000 visa requests from citizens of the FRG were made to the consular division of the Polish military mission in West Berlin alone – an indicator of the growing desire the exiles had to see their homelands again. By 1966 the number of West Geman tourists going back to Poland exceeded 31,000 (Demshuk, 2012: 186). They went largely in organised group tours which were closely monitored by the Polish secret services. Those who wanted to explore areas of Poland on their own, by car, were still often refused a visa. The real shift in the tourist pattern took place after the ratification of treaties with several Eastern Bloc states made by Willy Brandt's government in the 1970s. This set in motion a new wave of West German tourists going back to the places where they had spent the years of their childhood and youth (Knütel, 2002: 149–150).

GDR citizens had to wait until 1954 before they could apply for a tourist visa to travel abroad during their holidays. Official figures show only a few hundred people actually making it to other Eastern European countries as holiday-makers in the mid-1950s (Bundesarchiv Berlin DM 102 342), although some managed detours to their old homes while travelling on business in Poland and Czechoslovakia or while attending trade congresses and conferences in these countries. Only 430 GDR tourists visited other socialist countries in 1954 on trips arranged by the official GDR travel agency. However, the numbers rose steadily and conditions were alleviated in 1961 after the Wall had been erected. Otherwise, the easiest way to travel abroad was to book an organised group tour via the *Reisebüro der DDR* – the East German state travel agency – but this gave the tourists little opportunity for excursions to their own towns and villages. If they wanted to travel abroad independently, East Germans had to show the authorities an invitation from a host in the country they sought to visit and get official permission to travel (Irmscher, 1996: 55). These restrictions eased dramatically in the second half of the 1960s, when the GDR signed bilateral treaties with Czechoslovakia (1967) and Poland (1972) allowing visa-free cross-border tourism (Politisches Archiv des Auswaertigen Amtes, B 57 498).

Post-war Travel Narratives

The data collection and analysis in this chapter are based on a sample of 62 first-hand accounts describing visits back to the expellees' homelands that took place between the early 1950s and the mid-1970s. With one exception, all the accounts were written in German. The vast majority were published in West German newspapers or magazines, but the sample also includes descriptions in travel books and from published and unpublished memoirs, some of them written much later. These accounts vary considerably in length and style. They are supplemented by three oral history interviews conducted by this author. In addition, several transcripts or verbatim quotations made accessible by earlier scholars in archives or books and archives, notably the *Archiv Deutsches Gedächtnis* were consulted (see also van Hoorn, 2004). The inclusion of unpublished texts and interviews is of particular importance because it ensures greater diversity than would otherwise be possible – especially with respect to accounts from people who lived in the GDR, where open public discourse on the experience of expulsion was not permitted. All quotes in this chapter were translated by the author.

Although there are differences in the specific contexts, reach and ambition of the accounts in the sample, they also share many commonalities, both in content and in structure. With one exception all are related in the first person and all describe real-life journeys to places where the expelled narrators had lived as Germans or German Jews before the end of World War II. Most of the texts and interviews describe journeys to areas that, before 1945, were part of the German Reich but had since then been ceded to Poland, the Soviet Union or Czechoslovakia. However, accounts of trips to Hungary and Romania have also been included.

Travel accounts of journeys 'home' have to be considered against the backdrop of contemporary discourses, in this case the historical contexts of East and West Germany during the Cold War. In the FRG, descriptions of journeys to the 'old East' formed a niche genre that was popular with certain readers. They were not only regularly published in the various outlets and newsletters of expellee organisations and clubs, but appeared in mainstream newspapers. In addition, there were books and articles by well-known publicists and prominent creative writers chronicling journeys and experiences in Central and Eastern Europe (Dornemann, 2005: xxiii). Expellees formed more than 15% of the population of the FRG and were distributed across the country. According to Karoline von Oppen and Stefan Wolff (2006: 194–196), the expellees' sense of victimhood 'provided an additional impetus for a collective identity to be formed among refugees and expellees … and it remained a potent source of mobilisation through the decades'. However, as time passed the subject of expulsion – and especially the demand for a redrawing of the border with Poland and restoration of the former German lands – moved from a subject enjoying wide societal consensus to one that was regarded as dangerously right-wing, as Maren Röger (2011: 42) outlines. This change in perception took place in the late 1950s and early 1960s. Röger suggests four main reasons. There had been substantive progress in the socio-economic integration of the refugees and there was a growing realisation that demands for a return were unrealistic. There was also a decrease in international support for the German demands. By the early 1960s the history of National Socialist persecution and violence had come more strongly into focus, and this put the argument that the expulsions had been 'unjust' into a different perspective – expellees were no longer considered 'victims' in the same way (also Schlanstein, 2005: 17–18). Finally, insistence on a right of return to former homelands, on a redrawing of the de facto border and on compensation for lost possessions appeared increasingly to put obstacles in the path of the reconciliation and rapprochement process that culminated in the new *Ostpolitik* [new eastern policy]. Such demands rapidly became 'marginal to public debate' (von Oppen & Wolf, 2006: 195).

In general, West German travel accounts of journeys 'home' do not reflect this shift in public perception. The desire for a return home, and the emotional attachments to 'home' apparently stood outside the dominant public narrative of the changing social conditions of West Germany at the time. Many of the narrators continued to use the old politically coloured language, referring to their former homelands as parts of Germany that had been 'occupied' or put 'under the administration' of other states, and voicing hopes – even convictions – that the lands would 'rightfully' (Blank, 1962: 10) be returned to Germany as many articles in the German press the late 1950s and early 1960s, many collected into a book edited by the Bonn-based political journalist Ulrich Blank. As Corinna Felsch (2015: 153) shows, basing her observation on a study of travel accounts written between 1970 and 1989, there is surprisingly little change in attitudes over the decades in this question.

Discourse in the GDR on expulsion and the 'lost East' was very different. It was unthinkable to have any open discussion on the experience of losing one's homeland or having nostalgia towards it. Nor could there be debate on the relationship with Poland and the placing of the border (Lotz, 2007: 110). The self-image of the GDR was based on being in the anti-fascist and anti-Nazi tradition of the Communist Bloc. Forced migration and the loss of territories east of the Oder and Neiße were regarded as corollaries of the victory against these forces. Besides, the 'lost East' was now under socialist control and a close friendship with the USSR and other socialist states central to the identity of the new East German state. Memories of their role in taking territories away from Germany and forcing German populations to leave – often with threats or overt violence – were held to be 'undesirable'. Instead of the terms 'expellees' and 'refugees', the GDR government used the euphemism 'resettlers'. Homeland organisations and clubs were banned; songs from the old German East were not played on the radio; street names were changed (Röger, 2011: 18). However, despite the 'socialist tabooization' (Wohlfahrt, 2006: 103) of the subject, many GDR citizens remained privately very interested in maintaining a link with the places of their past and dreamt of travelling there. About a quarter of the whole East German population had been born and brought up in the territories that were now outside German borders. They employed 'a multifaceted network of contacts' (Irmscher, 1996: 58) to organise trips abroad to see remaining relatives or revisit the places they remembered. However, they could not write openly about their travel experiences. Most published texts about journeys to Eastern Europe and areas where expellees had lived before 1945 are not personal accounts describing individual impressions, but embody the official viewpoint, with its propaganda – and this is especially so when the authors were commissioned to write about their travels by the state (e.g. Krzoska, 2006: 438–440). Even so, despite having to adhere to an official line and use the official vocabulary, some East German travel accounts manage to convey a more nuanced picture (e.g. Krzoska, 2006: 441). This chapter is furthermore able to draw on interviews with former East German citizens or texts which were published after the demise of the GDR when the issue of censorship was no longer relevant.

The Journey East

Displaced Germans had many reasons for wanting to revisit their old homelands. Nostalgia and a desire to reconnect with the past; a curiosity about what had become of the places they remembered; a wish to see living relatives and pay their respects to the dead – these were just some of the motives for going back. Some tourists wanted to mourn and come to terms with the loss of their one-time homes; others sustained a hope of eventual return (e.g. Demshuk, 2011: 62–63; Krzoska, 2006: 424). There were also many reasons for *not* wanting to undertake a journey back. Some would-be tourists felt mistrustful of the locals and were concerned for their own safety. Some did not want to expose themselves to the pain and grief of revisiting what was 'irretrievably lost': they preferred to keep memories alive without confronting the new reality (Engelhardt, 2006: 18).

Those Germans who did decide to make the trip back to their homelands often describe their journeys there as highly significant events in their lives, awakening strong emotions. Many had been thinking about returning for a long time, had made protracted plans, and had gone to considerable efforts to obtain the necessary paperwork, apply for visas and book tours or arrange alternative transport or accommodation. Often they had ambivalent feelings – on the one hand, positive anticipation and curiosity; on the other hand, apprehension (Knütel, 2002: 154). Some used the journey by train or bus to reflect on such thoughts, feelings and expectations. For example, the moment when they approached and then crossed the border often drew them into musings about the political status quo and expressions of dismay about borders which 'cut through' the land (Beute, 1956: 5). This sentiment comes out not only in accounts of crossing the still contested border between the GDR and Poland but also, among visitors to Kaliningrad, when crossing the Soviet one (Blank, 1962: 10–11).

By contrast, in published East German accounts, there could be no questioning of the legitimacy of borders. There is a clear sense that 'the East' was now 'a different country', no longer German. Crossing the border is celebrated as a joyful experience and an achievement. In one travel account describing a visit to Poland in the early 1950s, the author, the writer Armin Müller (1953: 5), fails even to mention that he was born in Silesia. His mission was not to revisit the past, but to admire the new Poland. But even accounts that were published after the GDR regime had come to an end by those who travelled to see their old homelands again describe positive excitement rather than ambivalence (e.g. Deutsches Tagebuch Archiv, 822; von Haupt, 2007: 11).

Aside from thoughts about the political situation, the tourists were occupied by more personal reflections. One West German tourist, setting off for Poland in 1961 to visit the estate his parents had once owned, describes his thoughts in this way:

> Pent-up in the train all night, I have time to realise that I am not 'coming home'; that this is maybe the last time in my life that I will see the place where I was born and lived my first happy years; that my home is now somewhere in the West; and that, as an engineer, I am not suited to running an agricultural business. (Blank, 1962: 84–85)

He tried to readjust his expectations by reminding himself that he no longer really belonged in Silesia, and attempted to resign himself to being just a visitor.

The question of belonging also occupied another visitor who took a train through Poland in 1954 – the ophthalmologist Georg Günther (1989: 221), who came from Greifswald in the GDR. He was attending a medical congress in Warsaw, and the train journey there was the closest he could get to his former home town. When the train neared the region where he had grown up, he stood by the window hoping to catch a glimpse of it:

> Emotion overcame me and I stood by the window for a long time, gazing at the familiar streets until we reached open fields again. I knew that I would feel like a stranger but at the same time it felt as though I still belonged [in this place]. (Günther, 1989: 221)

When their journeys drew to an end, several tourists describe how moved they were simply to be standing in the place they had known many years before. One writes that it was a 'strange feeling to enter the familiar building of the railway station in Hirschberg [Jelenia Góra, J.W.] again after so many years' (Blank, 1962: 30). Another admits to being left speechless: 'My heart was in my mouth. I was standing in my home railway station. Are there words to describe this experience?' (Blank, 1962: 26).

A Devastating Sight

A characteristic feature of many accounts of journeys 'home' is the extraordinarily detailed description of how places now appeared, in the visitors' eyes. This is a particularly pronounced feature in West German narratives written for a readership of fellow expellees who had perhaps not themselves made the same journey. (Sometimes advice is offered, should they decide to travel after all.) Willi Michael Beute was among the first journalists from the FRG to visit Poland after the thaw in political relations in the mid-1950s. His account of the visit, published in 1956 in *East Prussia Today*, is a good example of the tendency to provide comprehensive descriptions of everything found even remotely striking. Beute (1956: 5,12) describes his trip as 'a sad reunion with a home that has almost become an alien place [*Fremde*]'. His long article gives a blow-by-blow account of his tour around various small towns and villages in one of the Polish regions. At times it resembles an inventory. He details with precision what has been damaged in the war, what has been rebuilt and what still lies in ruins, meticulously recording the state of cemeteries, bridges, monuments and special landmarks, often with 'sad surprise'. Besides recording how things look in the present, Beute is interested in the former German occupancy of the region, and visits several German memorials, which he finds changed or dilapidated (Beute, 1965: 7–10).

A similar tendency to extreme detail is visible in many of the articles published in the West German press. On arrival at their destinations, the first reflex of the authors is to compare what they see with what they remember from before the war and before their departure from these places. They tend to provide very thorough assessments of the condition of specific streets, squares, buildings and monuments. The tone often conveys shock and disappointment at how desolate many of the towns and cities have become. Numerous accounts mention deserted, empty factories, decaying houses with their paint peeling, and neglected public buildings. Although they comment positively on reconstruction efforts in old city centres, like those of Danzig [Gdansk] and Breslau [Wrocław], the authors notice how, only a few streets away from the centres, they find uncleared rubble, and buildings in near-ruin. Words used over and over in a great many of the accounts are: 'neglected', 'dirty', 'uncared for', 'derelict' 'desolate', 'decline', 'heaps of rubble', 'disrepair' and 'deserted'. Another recurrent word is one attesting to the authors' emotional reactions on seeing certain sights: they describe themselves as 'devastated' (e.g. Blank, 1962: 12, 18, 20, 25, 56, 61, 68, 71, 72, 101).

Positive comments in the reports of these trips are rare and, when they do occur, they are frequently framed by negative judgements (e.g. Blank, 1962: 14, 15, 61, 45). There is general agreement in the accounts collected in Blank's volume and elsewhere in the West German sources that these former German areas had lapsed into decline since the pre-war years. Interpretations differ only in their nuances. Either explicitly or implicitly, several authors blame the foreign authorities. In their opinion, war damage should by now have vanished and the cities and towns should have been restored to their former dignity (Blank, 1962: 14, 26). They compare what they see in the former Eastern territories not only with the images they remember from the past, but also with the situation in the FRG, where there had been huge investment in rebuilding the cities and where, due to the economic boom, there was a much higher standard of living. Only a small minority of accounts point out that such comparisons are unfair and misleading (Blank, 1962: 101).

By choosing to focus on the insufficiency of efforts to clear and repair war damage and the failure to rebuild and restore towns and cities to look just as they once did, the authors communicate several messages. They express a desire to see the scars of war eradicated, but assign blame to the locals, avoiding any discussion of the actual reason why these places were reduced to such a state – a disastrous global war started by Nazi Germany that killed more than 60 million people, obliterated entire villages and led to bombing campaigns that devastated cities across much of Europe, especially in Central and Eastern Europe. This stands in stark contrast to the travel accounts published in the GDR, which acknowledge this fact frankly and which praise reconstruction efforts. Some of this East German positive attitude may be explained by the authors having to bow to the work of socialist regimes, to please the censors and meet official expectations. The unpublished accounts, although still positive in tone, do betray some disgruntlement at the sight of neglected buildings and of once-flourishing farms with hardly any livestock (e.g. interview with Irene B. 21.3.2013 and 26.3.2013, interview Günter R., 23.4.2013; Haupt 2007: 30).

As we have seen, the West German visitors to the old homelands were not just curious; a great many of their narratives display an almost obsessive need to record the exact state of the towns, villages, houses, churches and farms that once meant 'home' to them. Indeed, some contain little but 'descriptions of condition' and have nothing to say about the authors' experiences, reflections, political views or thoughts about recent history. This has led Corinna Felsch to exclude them from her *Reisen in die Vergangenheit* [Journeys into the Past] (2015: 148). However, the sheer frequency of these descriptions is remarkable, and they are worth studying, if only to gain a better understanding of the expectations and perceptions of these tourists. There are several possible explanations that could account for their desire to record the state of their surroundings so minutely. One of these may have been a need to hold on to the concrete, visible and tangible in order to counterbalance inner turmoil, sadness and upset feelings when they saw their former homes again. By focusing on what could be precisely described, the authors could avoid discussing more difficult matters – to engage in a process of mourning, confronting their sense of loss, the reasons that had led to it, the impact on themselves and others. However, another possible explanation, proposed by Andrew Demshuk, is that an assessment of 'before' and 'after' differences may have actually helped them come to terms with their losses (Demshuk, 2012: 186). Yet another explanation is that some of the authors may have been looking at the state of their former properties with an eye on reclaiming them at a future point in time.[3]

The tourists' tendency to inspect everything they saw in their old homelands so closely did not go unnoticed and was not always welcome. Some tourists report run-ins with the police. Klaus Granzow and his family had left their former home in a small Pomeranian village in 1947. In the mid-1970s he signed up for a tour organised by an agency specialising in trips for expellees wishing to see their former homes again. The party he went with consisted of 50 people, almost all of whom had been born in the town of Stolpe [Słupsk]. Once they had arrived in Stolpe, Granzow took a taxi to his old home village. His first stop was the farm which had once belonged to an uncle now living in Bremen. When he attempted to take photographs of the house, he was arrested on the spot. The police searched him, confiscated his camera and put him in a prison cell (Granzow, 1976: 158–159). He was subsequently interviewed by the local police and also by members of the secret police, who were not satisfied with his explanations. However, when Granzow recounted this experience to the Polish tour guide leading his party, the guide was very apologetic and insisted that they would, together, go back to the farm the next day, so that he could have a good look around and take as many pictures as he liked. The guide wanted to be sure that his guest went back to the GDR with 'friendly memories'. Back in the village, the Polish farmer who now lived in the farmhouse welcomed Granzow cordially, gave him a tour of the place and even invited him for lunch (Granzow, 1976: 160–161).

Since this type of experience was relatively common (Knütel, 2002: 155), other tourists were more savvy. Johann R. visited the Hultschiner Ländchen [Hlučínsko] in Czechoslovakia in 1964. While on this visit he stayed at the home of his former servant, who was a member of the ethnic German minority. During his ten-day trip, R. and his friend made an excursion to a small town where an acquaintance had once lived. The acquaintance herself did not want to travel to Czechoslovakia because her father had been mayor of the town and she feared resentment from the locals. Aware that their arrival might raise suspicions, R. and his friend took some precautions. 'So as not to attract any attention', R. used his friend's car, which had a Czech number-plate; he parked at some distance, and was very discreet. He was therefore able to take pictures of the former mayor's house, the cemetery and a few other places, unchallenged (Interview with Johann R., 22.4.2013). In both cases described above the local authorities were perceived as hostile while civilian locals and a tourism agent cooperated and helped the travellers in their quest to revisit places of the past and provide them to experience exactly what they had come for.

Home, but not Home

Two themes that come up repeatedly in the travel accounts might appear entirely contradictory at first glance but, on closer inspection, we can see that they are both, one way or the other, explorations of the boundary between the familiar and the foreign. One is the conviction that almost everything had changed; and the other, the conviction that nothing much had changed. Many visitors, particularly those going to the bigger cities, found their surroundings very much altered and sometimes barely recognisable. This was not only because of the new structures that now replaced those destroyed in the war, but also because of a street life that seemed strange and unfamiliar (e.g. Blank, 1962: 61, 62, 64). However, even those authors who focus most on apparent differences and aspects that look foreign to them may, on occasion, find themselves unexpectedly moved by encounters with places or situations that seem utterly familiar. Turning a corner in a city, they may be struck by a view that seems just as they remembered it. 'Many things have changed,' writes one visitor, describing the square in front of the railway station in Hirschberg [Jelenia Góra], 'but you can still take a tram to Warmbrunn and Hermsdorf like you used to' (Blank, 1962: 26). A visitor to Katowice [previously Kattowitz] reports that, when he stopped for a coffee in a café that he remembered from the past, it suddenly felt 'as though time had been turned back' (Blank, 1962: 31).

Those who visited villages and the smaller towns that had suffered less from wartime destruction often comment that the landscapes and settlements look exactly the same as they remember them. According to Verschaeve and Wadle (2014: 90), the imaginary of a place frozen in time became a topos in narrations of West European tourists about the European East that transcended Socialist times and is perpetuated in travel guides and descriptions until this day.

Under communism, the appearance of many places was preserved – in stark contrast to what many visitors had become accustomed to in the rebuilt urban areas of West Germany (Dornemann, 2005: xxiv). A lot of the accounts remark on the fact that things looked just 'like before the war' and that 'hardly anything has changed' (...). But the writers also noticed that certain other aspects – especially the people – were very different (Blank, 1962: 28–29, 65).

It is striking how little interest in people these accounts reveal, as which they focus almost exclusively on descriptions of farms, buildings and landmarks. The people inhabiting the territories often appear merely as an anonymous mass of faceless 'foreigners' without individual characteristics. However, there are some accounts that quote from conversations with locals, and these locals often seem to be intensely curious about living conditions in West Germany and are sometimes (reportedly) critical of the situations in their own countries (e.g. Blank, 1962: 53, 72, 106). When visitors from Germany wanted to see their old properties again, they had no choice but to contact the new owners and explain their intentions. In numerous cases, the new owners welcomed the Germans cordially, with no resentment (Knütel, 2002: 154–155). The following three examples give an idea of how tourists might describe the experience of revisiting their former homes, now in the hands of others.

We have already encountered Klaus Granzow, who was allowed to return to his uncle's farmhouse after being arrested for taking photographs. He describes the moment when he stepped inside this once-familiar building: 'Of course it wasn't like it used to be. Inside the house there was little that brought to mind our former life – only an old marriage certificate of my relatives still hanging in the front corridor.' The owners were happy to give this certificate to him, and they also served him an ample meal, inviting him to return the following year (Granzow, 1976: 160–161).

Family S. from East Germany had a similar experience. Gisela S. had left her home town, in Pomerania, in 1947 and returned for a visit in 1971. She went with her brother, father and husband, who recounted what happened in a memoir. In advance, the family had written to the people who now owned their former property and they had been invited to visit. When they arrived, they were greeted enthusiastically and plied with quantities of homemade schnapps. To their astonishment the S. family found that the house still contained its old furniture, unchanged except for being covered in a coat of green paint. Gisela's father was aghast at how laxly the farm was run and disapproved of the scarcity of livestock; but the overall experience was reported as being very cordial and cheerful, with no feelings of sadness or nostalgia (Deutsches Taebuch Archiv 822, 1).

By contrast, a West German visitor who returned to the estate his parents once owned reports how he struggled to keep his composure. When the new administrator picked him up in a horse cart and they drove along the country road which led to the estate, he felt his heart pounding:

[W]herever I look, I feel it's my home. The old water tower is not just any tower, it is *our* water tower. ... I would like to jump off the cart and hug the nearest tree and simply gaze across the vast fields. The land stretches out as though time has stood still – and it is only two hours' drive to Berlin. (Blank, 1962: 84–85)

When visiting the stables, this visitor felt transported back to the past. 'The door opens and everything is like it used to be' (Blank, 1962: 48); he even found a white horse behind the last partition, just like the one he was so fond of when he was a child. The emotion was so overwhelming that he had to leave immediately and concentrate on what has changed. To distract himself, he focused on the facts, noticing the dirt on the road and discussing with the administrator the estate's productivity and the numbers of livestock (Blank, 1962: 85–86).

The question of foreignness or familiarity seems to have become especially pressing when tourists visited places that once meant a great deal to them – churches, schools, special landmarks and, above all, homes. As in the three accounts cited above, descriptions of the moment when the authors re-encountered these special places form the emotional climax of many of these travel narratives. Despite the fact that many elements have changed, the authors focus on what has stayed the same. This can be seen in the three examples just given – in the first account, the certificate of marriage; in the second, the furniture; and in the third, so many aspects that the author had to make an effort to pull himself together. Axel Dornemann has emphasised the importance for travellers of 'real relics that memories could be hinged on' (Dornemann, 2005: xxiv). Certain objects or buildings acquire special meaning, becoming symbolic of the lost past.

Tourists who still had relatives or friends living in their former villages or houses narrate their travel experiences quite differently. Although they have heightened emotions and may express some degree of nostalgia, they appear to be less homesick and less focused on the past. Instead, they talk about current situations, especially about the hardships and challenges their relatives may be facing (van Hoorn, 2004: 272–279; Schlotis, 1962: 9, 29).

Journey to the Land of Death

Several years before ethnic Germans were expelled from areas of Central and Eastern Europe, Jews from an even wider area had had to leave their homes and emigrate abroad to escape the Nazi regime and its policy of persecution. Up to 1933 the city of Breslau [Wrocław] in Silesia had been the third largest (after Berlin and Frankfurt am Main) centre of Jewish life and culture in Germany. The Jewish community there, which counted 23,000 members, ran several synagogues and schools, a Jewish cemetery, a Jewish old people's home and a well-known hospital (United States Holocaust Memorial Holocaust Encylopedia). After the progrom of 1938, this vibrant community had to withdraw its religious, educational and other activities. As from other areas of Nazi Germany, there were several waves of Jewish emigration before even emigration was outlawed in October 1941. By 1939 two-thirds of the Jewish community had gone; most of those remaining were deported to concentration camps and ghettos and were murdered (Bräu, 2008: 100). Those who managed to get abroad settled in other European states or emigrated further afield, to Israel, North America and other places. A few of these Jewish émigrés returned to visit their old homes after 1945.

Andrew Demshuk has studied several accounts by Jews who travelled back to Wrocław after 1945. He observes that, like the ethnic German expellees, Jewish travellers also sought to find traces of their community and lamented the loss of their homes and the vanishing of the old culture of their homeland. But, in addition, they had often been victims of persecution by the Nazi regime and lost relatives and friends in the Holocaust. For this reason, Jews who returned to Wrocław were generally 'more ready to attribute its loss to German crimes' and were 'more acceptant of the city's new Polish life' (Demshuk, 2007: 311–335; 2011: 78).

Nevertheless, there are exceptions to this and some accounts are very critical of Polish rule and betray nostalgia for pre-war times. Markus Krzoska cites an account by Erwin Hirschberg, a Jewish entrepreneur from Breslau [Wrocław] who had emigrated to the Netherlands in 1935 and who came back to visit in 1954. According to Krzoska, Hirschberg paints 'a picture of a derelict country whose new inhabitants ... are primarily destroyers of the old, peaceful order' (Krzoska, 2006: 426). On the other end of the spectrum is an account by the Jewish philosopher and journalist Günther Anders, who published an article entitled 'Journey to Hades' in the West German magazine *Merkur* in 1967. Anders had been born in Breslau [Wrocław], where he had spent the first 13 years of his life before moving to Hamburg. In 1933 he had emigrated to Paris, later moving on to New York, but returning to Europe in 1950 to settle in Vienna. In contrast to the accounts by ethnic German expellees and by Hirschberger, which deal in loss, nostalgia and the desire to reconnect a happier past, Anders' account takes death as its key theme. To Anders:

> all of this area is a cemetery ... an enormous mass grave, an untended one of course, one that does not call itself so and which does not reveal the names of its dead – but does it make a difference? (Anders, 1967: 749–50)

Awareness of the Holocaust stands immovably between him and the past; it affects every aspect of his perception of the city. When visiting a park, he suddenly remembers a childhood friend called Robert Triest, who lived nearby and who used to play the violin very well. Immediately Anders adds detail which changes this happy childhood memory to a much darker story.

Robert Triest emigrated to Paris, where he had to sell his violin to buy food just to survive; and Anders recalls that, when he visited the museum at Auschwitz, he saw a suitcase with the name 'Triest' on it, and he wonders whether this could have been a relation (Anders, 1967: 750–751).

Like so many of the other visitors 'home,' Anders took himself to places he remembers from his childhood. In many ways, this is akin to revisiting his former self. When browsing in second-hand bookstores, for instance, he half expected to find his own name inscribed on the first page of some of the German-language volumes. But he is not idealising the past, nor looking to relive it; this is not a search for a lost paradise. At one point in Anders' journey, the past became uncomfortably alive and close. In a part of Breslau changed beyond recognition, he was seeking, with 'desperate determination,' to find the house his family used to live in, and he stopped to ask the way:

> The attendant, although an old Breslauer, [is] apparently not old enough to know Hollenzollernstraße under the name 'Hohenzollernstraße' [and] he asks – unblinkingly, as if implying Nazi solidarity as a matter of course – whether I mean 'SA Alley'. (You should bear in mind: that he is saying this to a Jew in Breslau, which has been Polish for twenty-one years.) It startles me to such an extent that I do not answer him. (Anders, 1967: 753)

Anders felt some satisfaction that Breslau is now a Polish city. Nevertheless, he was surprised that he is far less bothered than he had previously imagined at finding the city where he learned to speak German no longer German at all. He concludes:

> Can you expect patriotic feelings from someone who has only Chance to thank that his fate was not to join those on the [trains] rumbling over the Oppen Bridge to the ovens of Auschwitz and who did not, like them, become smoke rising into the Upper Silesian sky? (Anders, 1967: 765)

This sentiment is echoed in the memoirs of the historian Fritz Stern, who returned to this same native city in 1979 from the USA. Stern writes that he had 'suffered too much in Breslau to have regretted that the city had passed to new masters or to feel compassion for the Germans expelled from it' (Stern, 2007: 5). He admitted to finding it 'easier' to go back to a Polish city than to a German one: seeing Germans continue to live there 'as if nothing had happened, would have stirred resentment'. Returning to a place so utterly changed, he could recall the past, feel 'possessive of some corners', even regret how much has been lost, but be in no doubt, throughout his visit, that the city is no longer 'his' (Stern, 2007: 8–9). He wrote that his 'sense of loss [was] overlain by an all-pervasive gratitude for having found a second, better home' (Stern, 2007: 5).

Conclusion

To ethnic German expellees and German Jewish émigrés alike, 'home' signified more than a place. It was also an emotion, an experience. And it could be a destination. For many of the expellees, regardless of whether they had settled in East or West Germany, the places from which they had been evicted remained their 'true homes' – 'homes of the soul' – for the rest of their lives (Altmann cited in van Hoorn, 2004: 272–279). They may subsequently have put down roots elsewhere, but they remained deeply attached to their places of birth. This often went along with an idealisation of the past. The writer Gertrud Fussenegger, born in Pilsen, observes this tendency to portray the past in a golden light and to emphasise the positive aspects. 'The stony field behind the house remain[s] forgotten, and the creaky pump in the courtyard. They [do] not fit into the gilded image of memory' (Fussenegger, 1997: 26). For many expellees who made the journey east, the prime interest was not to visit Poland or Czechoslovakia or wherever their trip took them. They wanted to go back to the past, relive happy moments in their life before the great trauma of expulsion.

For Jewish émigrés such as Anders and Stern, idealisation of the past to this degree was not a possibility: they could not forget why they were forced to leave Germany and what had happened afterwards. Acute awareness and memories of the suffering the Germans had caused their families and of the many lives that had been lost in the Holocaust stood between them and the past and prevented excessive nostalgia or longing to relive it.

Journeys 'home' were important events for members of both groups. Many German visitors came to the realisation that the 'homes' they remembered had been irrevocably transformed and that they no longer belonged there (Demshuk, 2012: 186–187). Although some of the Jewish travellers also felt a deep attachment to their native cities, they found that their bond to them had already been severed beyond repair years before the Germans were expelled by earlier experiences of persecution and by the destruction of their communities. To at least one Jew revisiting Breslau, for example, the realisation that the city had morphed from a German metropolis to a bustling Polish city seemed a relief.

Both groups were mourning the loss of a place from which they were cut off through historic events, mass violence and suffering. Yet they were mourning almost largely in isolation, without taking into account the experiences of others which were also traumatic, but different to their own. Doris L. Bergen (2000: 173) asked whether a kind of mourning was possible that 'grieves for one's own losses but also acknowledges the suffering of others, suffering occasioned by crimes to which one was a witness and perhaps even a perpetrator?' The travellers studied in this chapter felt little desire to engage or even acknowledge with the loss and mourning of other communities. Their journeys were attempts to come to terms only with their own losses.

Dieter Arendt writes that, in literature, the return home is always also an opportunity to confront the self. The self is called to make an 'inventory and justification in front of the tribunal of consciousness' (Arendt, 2001: 29). 'Only if the retrospect allows insight into the hidden reasons for flight and homelessness, [is] the question of the meaning of the return home or the claim to home ... justified' (Arendt, 2001: 29). A true self-confrontation is absent in most accounts by ethnic German expellees visiting their homelands after the war. They show little awareness, or interest in, the reasons for their expulsion. By contrast, accounts by Jewish return visitors are often motivated by a desire to better understand the past. Nevertheless, travelling 'home' was not just an inspection of the physical world for any of them. The return forced them to examine their own identity and their own changing relationship to the place that had once been 'home'.

Acknowledgements

I would like to express my gratitude to the AHRC who generously funded this research. I would also like to thank Dr Gaelle Fisher, who brought several accounts of journeys to Romania and Hungary to my attention.

Notes

(1) Although the wording of the agreement left the possibility of further changes of the borderline open, the signatories 'expected the *de facto* border agreement to become permanent'(Ahonen, 2003: 15). In July 1950, shortly after the foundation of the German Democratic Republic (GDR), the East German government recognised the new eastern border with Poland. The Federal Republic of Germany (FRG) followed suit when, with reservations, it ratified the Warsaw Treaty of 1970. Following reunification in 1990, Germany signed a treaty recognising the Oder-Neiße line as the legitimate border between Germany and Poland and gave up all claims to areas beyond it (see for example Krozska, 2006: 423).

(2) In the following I will refer to them under the summary title of 'expellees', although it should be noted that not all of them were subjected to explusions. Some fled to safety when the war front moved closer or chose to migrate to other areas before 1944/45. However, despite their heterogeneous backgrounds and the diverse circumstances of their migration, they were cut off from their homelands after 1945 and tended to self-identify themselves as 'expellees'.

(3) A good example is an article by the Polish journalist Eugeniusz Guz which appeared in the Polish newspaper *Zycie Warszawy* in 1971. It implied that these tourists had revisionist intentions (Politisches Archiv des Auswaertigen Amtes B 57 873).

References

Ahonen, P. (2003) *After the Expulsion. West Germany and Eastern Europe 1945– 1990.* Oxford: Oxford University Press.
Anders, G. (1967) Fahrt in den Hades. *Merkur. Deutsche Zeitschrift für europaeisches Denken* 21, 748–765.

Arendt, D. (2001) Vom literarischen "Recht auf Heimat" oder: Das Motiv der Heimat in der Literatur. In S. Feuchert (ed.) *Flucht und Vertreibung in der deutschen Literatur.* Frankfurt am Main: Peter Lang.

Bergen, D.L. (2000) Mourning, mass death, and the gray zone: The ethnic Germans of Eastern Europe and the Second World War. In P. Homans (ed.) *Symbolic Loss. The Ambiguity of Mourning and Memory at Century's End* (pp. 171–193). Charlottesville, VA: University Press of Virginia.

Beute, W.B. (1956) 1.500 km durch das polnisch besetzte Ostpreußen. Eine Fahrt im Sommer 1956. In *Das heutige Ostpreußen. Ein Bild-und Reisebericht aus dem polnisch besetzten Teil Ostpreußens herausgegeben in Zusammenarbeit mit der Landsmannschaft Ostpreußen e.V.* München: Aufstieg.

Blank, U. (ed.) (1962) *Wo Heute Fremde Wegweiser Stehen. Die Deutschen Ostgebiete im Spiegel der Westdeutschen Presse (1959–1962).* Leer: Verlag Gerhard Rautenberg.

Bräu, R. (2008) *'Arisierung' in Breslau – Die 'Entjudung' einer deutschen Großstadt und deren Entdeckung im polnischen Erinnerungsdiskurs.* Saarbrücken: VDM Verlag Dr. Müller.

Demshuk, A. (2007) 'Wehmut und Trauer': Jewish travellers in Polish Silesia and the *foreignness* of Heimat'. In *Jahrbuch des Simon Dubnow Instituts* (pp. 311–335). Göttingen: Vandenhoeck & Ruprecht.

Demshuk, A. (2011) Heimweh in the Heimat: Homesick travelers in the lost German East, 1955–70. In J. Beinek and P.H. Kosicki (eds) *Re-mapping Polish-German Historical Memory. Physical, Political, and Literary Spaces Since World War II* (pp. 57–79). Bloomington: Slavica Publishers/Indiana University.

Demshuk, A. (2012) *The Lost German East. Forced Migration and the Politics of Memory, 1945–1970.* Cambridge: Cambridge University Press.

Dornemann, A. (2005) *Flucht und Vertreibung in Prosaliteratur und Erlebnisbericht seit 1945. Eine annotierte Bibliographie.* Stuttgart: Anton Hiersemann Verlag.

Engelhardt, M. (2006) Biographien deutscher Flüchtlinge und Vertriebener des Zweiten Weltkriegs. In Stiftung Haus der Geschichte der Bundesrepublik Deutschland (ed.) *Flucht, Vertreibung, Integration* (pp. 14–21). Bielefeld: Kerber Verlag.

Felsch, C. (2015) *Reisen in die Vergangenheit? Westdeutsche Fahrten nach Polen 1970–1990.* Unpublished manuscript.

Fussenegger, G. (1997) Verlust und Rückgewinn. Notizen zur Literatur der Vertriebenen. In Frank-Lotahr Kroll (ed.) *Flucht und Vertreibung in der Literatur nach 1955.* Berlin: Gebr. Mann Verlag.

Granzow, K. (1976) Wiederbegegnung mit einem Dorf in Pommern. In Hanns Gottschalk (ed.) *Autoren reisen. Prosa und Lyrik.* München: Delp, 158–161.

Günther, G. (1989) *Gewinne das Leben. Autobiographie.* Berlin: Verlag der Nationen.

Von Haupt, A. (2007) *Meine Reise in die alte Heimat. Erinnerungen.* Eichwalde: Raku Verlag.

van Hoorn, H. (2004) *Neue Heimat im Sozialismus: die Umsiedlung und Integration Sudetendeutscher Antifa-Umsiedler in die SBZ/DDR.* Essen: Klartext.

Irmscher, G. (1996) Alltägliche Fremde. Auslandsreisen in der DDR. In Hasso Spode (ed.) *Goldstrand und Teutonengrill. Kultur-und Solzialgeschichte des Tourismus in Deutschland 1945 bis 1989* (pp. 51–68). Berlin: Moser.

Knütel, W. (2002) *Verlorene Heimat als literarische Provinz. Stolp und seine Pommersche Umgebung in der Deutschen Literatur nach 1945* (pp. 149–150). Frankfurt am Main, Berlin, Bern, Bruxelles, New York, Oxford, Wien: Peter Lang.

Krzoska, M. (2006) Das deutsche Bild von den ehemaligen Ostegbieten und von Polen in Reiseberichten der fünfziger und sechziger Jahre des 20. Jahrhunderts. In *Die Quarantäne. Deutsche und österreichische Literatur der fünfziger Jahre zwischen Kontinuität und Neubeginn* (pp. 423–441). Wroclaw/ Dresden: Neisse Verlag.

Lotz, C. (2007) *Die Deutung des Verlusts. Erinnerungspolitische Kontroversen im geteilten Deutschland um Flucht, Vertreibung und die Ostgebiete (1948–1972).* Köln, Weimar, Wien: Böhlau.

Müller, A. (1953) *Sommerliche Reise ins Nachbarland. Ein junger Schriftsteller erlebt das neue Polen.* Weimar: Thüringer Volksverlag.
von Oppen, K. and Wolff, S. (2006) From the margins to the centre? The discourse on expellees and victimhood in Germany. In B. Niven (ed.) *Germans as Victims. Remembering the Past in Contemporary Germany* (pp. 194–195). Basingstoke: Palgrave Machmillan.
Röger, M. (2011) *Flucht, Vertreibung und Umsiedlung. Mediale Erinnerungen und Debatten in Deutschland und Polen seit 1989.* Marburg: Verlag Herder-Institut.
Schlanstein, B. (2005) Neue Wurzeln, alte Wunden. In *Als die Deutschen weg waren. Was nach der Vertreibung geschah: Ostpreußen, Schlesien, Sudetenland* (pp. 7– 21). Berlin: Rohwolt.
Schlotis A. (1962) *Reise nach Polen.* München: Biederstein.
Schlögel, S. (1986) *Die Mitte liegt ostwärts. Die Deutschen, der verlorene Osten und Mitteleuropa.* Berlin: Siedler.
Schwartz, M. (2006) 'Umsiedler' – Flüchtlinge und Vertriebene in der SBZ und DDR. In Stiftung Haus der Geschichte der Bundesrepublik Deutschland (ed.) (pp. 91–101). *Flucht, Vertreibung, Integration.* Bielefeld: Kerber Verlag.
Stern, F. (2007) *Five Germanys I have Known.* New York: Farrar, Straus and Giroux.
Tielsch, I. (1995) Heimatsuchen (extract). In L.F. Helbig, J. Hoffmann and D. Kraemer (eds) *Verlorene Heimaten – neue Fremden. Literarische Texte zu Krieg, Flucht, Vertreibung, Nachkriegszeit* (pp. 172–174). Dortmund: Veröffentlichungen der Forschungsstelle Ostmitteleuropa an der Universität Dortmund.
United States Holocaust Memorial Museum. Germany: Jewish Population in 1933, http://www.ushmm.org/wlc/en/article.php?ModuleId=10005276 (accessed 3 October 2015).
Verschaeve, M. and Wadle, H.C. (2014) Tourism and post-socialist Heterotopias: Eastern Europe as an imagined rural past. In D. Picard and M.A. Di Giovine (eds) *Tourism and the Power of Otherness: Seductions of Difference* (pp. 74–91). Bristol: Channel View Publications.
Wohlfahrt, P. (2006) Das Thema "Umsiedler" in der DDR-Literatur. In Stiftung Haus der Geschichte der Bundesrepublik Deutschland (ed.) *Flucht, Vertreibung, Integration* (pp. 103–107). Bielefeld: Kerber Verlag.

5 'Home Tourism' within a Conflict: Palestinian Visits to Houses and Villages Depopulated in 1948

Noga Kadman and Mustafa Kabha

Introduction

During the War of 1948 and its aftermath, which Palestinians refer to as the Nakba (catastrophe), most Palestinians became refugees. Israel demolished most of their houses and repopulated some of the remaining ones, mostly with Jews. Owing to Israeli border control and restrictions on movement, most Palestinian refugees have no access to their family house or village; however, different groups of refugees in different periods do manage to visit their former homes, the memory of which is very much alive and central in their lives and identity, as well as in their political consciousness.

Palestinian visits to depopulated villages and towns are well dealt with in academic writings, which analyse private memoires and interviews from different angles: for instance, Ben-Ze'ev (2004) focuses on the significance of taste and smell in refugee village visits; Ben Ze'ev and Aburaiya (2004) write on the transformation from individual or family memory visits into organized group visits of political commemoration among Palestinians in Israel; Piroyansky (2014) analyses the discourse of property and ownership in Palestinian autobiographical narratives of return visits to urban houses.

Following a short historical background, this chapter will map the phenomenon of Palestinian 'home tourism', documenting different groups of visitors and the places they can visit; this form of travel is presented as part of the Palestinian memory culture, as well as a form of protest. Using verbatim testimony, the second section will elaborate on several central themes that arise from accounts of Palestinian visits to depopulated places, related to the ways visitors cope with destruction, change and repopulation. Throughout the chapter we will point at the changes and developments Palestinian 'home tourism' has undergone over time, and place them in relevant political, social and demographic contexts. We will highlight what is unique about Palestinian 'home tourism' – that it occurs in the context of an ongoing, living conflict. We will conclude by locating aspects of memory and home of these Palestinian visits in the wider field of 'roots tourism,' which, as Handley wrote (2006: 28): 'consciously disturbs the polarities of "home" and "away" and "here" and "there".'

Methodologically, we used both original interviews and published testimony as source material. Fourteen semi-structured interviews were conducted, mostly in 2015, with nine internally displaced Palestinians who are Israeli citizens, among them activists in associations who organize such visits; two non-refugee Palestinians who are Israeli citizens; and three Palestinian refugees living in the West Bank. The published testimonies we reviewed were found in personal memoirs published in books, journals and websites, as well as in interviews quoted by researchers. Autobiographical books and articles include six testimonies written by first-generation refugees, living mostly in the US or in Europe and originating from Palestinian urban quarters (usually Jerusalem); two written by refugees living in the West Bank, who visited their urban house in Acre and Ramla; and one by a first-generation refugee living in the West Bank, about his visit to his demolished village. In two cases, second-generation refugees wrote about their visits to the family home in Jaffa: one lives in the US and one in the West Bank. Three other second-generation refugees, living in Europe and the US, wrote in online magazines about visiting their obliterated village. Several testimonies were found in articles or books of authors who interviewed first, second or third-generation refugees in Lebanon, Jordan, London, the West Bank and Israel. Almost all the published testimonies we used appeared in English, sometimes in Hebrew, and rarely in Arabic. This reflects both the wish of the refugees to be heard among wider audiences (see Piroyansky, 2014: 100), and their access to the financial, social or educational resources needed in order to get published. This bias is somewhat compensated for by the use of our interviews, which were conducted in Arabic; quotations below are our translations.

Historical Background

Following the 1947 United Nations (UN) decision to divide Palestine into a Jewish and an Arab state, hostilities began between Palestinian and Jews, which escalated to a full-scale war. Its gravest consequence was that most Palestinians within the territory that became the State of Israel in May 1948 – some 750,000 people – became refugees; they were forced to leave their homes mostly due to military and militia attacks, deportations or fear of being attacked. Most fled across the Israeli borders – to the West Bank, the Gaza Strip, Jordan, Syria and Lebanon; some spread later to other countries. Others remained within Israel after being internally displaced and became

Israeli citizens. All displaced persons were prohibited from returning to their homes, based on an official Israeli decision.

Everything the refugees had to leave behind – land, houses and belongings in over 500 villages, towns and urban quarters – was appropriated by Israel. Israel demolished most of the Palestinian structures in these places, among other to prevent the return of the refugees and to de-Arabize the landscape (Morris, 2004: 342–360; Shai, 2006). For similar motives, European-like forests were planted on vast areas, including the remains of some of the depopulated villages (Kadman, 2015: 112–113).

Several dozen depopulated Palestinian villages and quarters were settled by Jews, mostly refugees in their own right – either Holocaust survivors from Europe or Jews from Arab countries that had to leave without their property. Internally displaced Palestinians also settled in houses depopulated from other Palestinian refugees, in cities and villages that continued to exist after the war, while their population mostly changed.

Who Can Visit?

De Santana Pinho (2008: 70) observes that one type of inequality entailed by roots tourism – conducted by descendants in search of their ancestral origins – is 'the disparity between those who have access to travel and those who do not'. This observation is particularly true concerning Palestinian refugees and their descendants – numbered over 5 million people today – spread globally and differing widely in their ability to access their former homes. Over the years, changes in Israeli restrictions on entry and movement determined these different groups' capability of access and the following will provide a brief overview.

Israel

While remaining in their homeland and receiving Israeli citizenship, internally displaced Palestinians (IDPs) settled in Palestinian communities close to their village of origin. Subjected to the military rule imposed on Palestinian citizens of Israel between 1948 and 1966, for 18 years the IDPs could legally or easily visit their village only on Israeli Independence Day (Wakim, 2002). Since 1966, IDPs and their descendants – over 250,000 today – visit their home villages regularly (Ben-Ze'ev, 2004: 157, note 4). Other Palestinians who are citizens of Israel can also visit the depopulated places, which they see as central to their national identity.

West Bank and Gaza Strip

In the aftermath of the war and well into the 1950s, Palestinian refugees in Jordan-controlled West Bank and in the Egypt-controlled Gaza Strip managed to cross the poorly marked borders into Israel, attempting to take belongings from their houses and harvest their fields. This gradually became impossible, due to the strict Israeli policy to forcibly block 'infiltrators' (Morris, 1993). Following the Israeli occupation of the West Bank and Gaza in 1967, these refugees fell under Israeli military rule, which opened the borders between the newly Occupied Territories (OT) and Israel. Tens of thousands of Palestinians, both inhabitants of the OT and visitors from neighbouring countries, conducted visits to the sites of their former homes within Israel (Rubinstein, 1991: 62–63). As part of the Oslo agreement between Israel and the PLO, thousands of Palestinians exiled in Tunisia and Arab countries were allowed to return to Palestine in the mid-1990s – not to their places of origin but to the West Bank. Some of them managed to enter Israel and visit their family's home for the first time since 1948 (Hammer, 2003; Sa'di, 2002: 189–192; Tamari, 2003). Visits from the OT dwindled over time with the increasing restrictions on Palestinian entry to Israel, especially since the 1990s. Today, refugees in the OT number over 2 million, and most have no access to Israel. Visits can be carried out only by the few who get entry permits by the Israeli authorities, or by those initiating them clandestinely from the West Bank.

Jordan

After occupying the West Bank in 1967, Israel allowed entry there from Jordan. Palestinian refugees living in Jordan – most of which hold Jordanian citizenship – could cross to the West Bank and from there to Israel, to visit their homes. With the termination of this 'open bridges' policy in late 1987, and the increasing restrictions on movement from the West Bank to Israel, Palestinians in Jordan – over 2 million today – can no longer visit their former homes.

Lebanon and Syria

As their compatriots in the OT, some refugees who fled north, especially to Lebanon, managed, till the early 1950s, to cross the border and visit their former homes in Palestine (Khoury, 2007; Sayigh, 2005: 33). After its invasion of South Lebanon in 1982, Israel granted entry permits to some people from Lebanon, and let them into its territory. An unknown number of Palestinian refugees entered Israel that way until 1994, when the Lebanese government declared travel to Israel illegal (Allan, 2007: 267–268; Khalili, 2005: 33; Sayigh, 2005: 33). Following the Israeli withdrawal from South Lebanon in May 2000, Palestinian refugees began to travel to the border zone (inaccessible to most of them since 1982), so they can see their family villages in the Galilee across it. After a few months, Hizballah allowed only those it had granted permits access to the border, and itself bused refugees there for planned demonstrations (Khalili, 2004: 10). Currently, there are some 1 million Palestinian refugees in Lebanon and Syria, most have no citizenship there, all are incapable of entering Israel.

Western countries

Palestinians holding foreign passports, usually after moving to North America and Europe, can enter Israel with a tourist visa and visit their former homes. Permission is conditional to passing border control checks, which are usually very strict when pertaining to Arab visitors. (U.S. Department of State, Bureau of Public Affairs, 2015)

To conclude – even though at times home visits were possible for Palestinians from the OT, Jordan and even Lebanon, in more recent times, and definitely today, they are available almost exclusively to Palestinians holding Western passports or Israeli citizenship.

What Can They Visit?

According to Khalidi (1992: xviii–xix), nearly 300 depopulated Palestinian villages were already totally destroyed in the late 1980s, and over 100 more were mostly destroyed. Only in 15 villages did most of the structures survive, he notes, and some of the latter were populated by Jews. Falah (1996) concludes that two-thirds of the villages in the same period suffered high levels of destruction, and nearly a third were destroyed to a significant degree and were partly repopulated by Jews. Falah found that most of the villages do have some kind of reminder in the landscape – a cluster of ruins, remains of walls, or parts of structures. He found intact but unpopulated homes in 74 villages across the country. Although over 25 years have passed since Khalidi's and Falah's field surveys, their figures can still be seen as valid, since most village sites are neglected by Israeli authorities – for better or worse – since the last demolition project carried out in the 1960s (Shai, 2006). Though destruction did take place in depopulated urban areas as well (mostly in Lydda, Tiberias, Jaffa, Haifa and Acre), many houses there were left intact and repopulated.

Importantly, the previously built up area of almost half (182) of the depopulated Palestinian villages is today included within Israeli tourism and recreation sites (Kadman, 2015: 112) and in some cases, remains of the Palestinian village are being preserved by the tourism authorities as tourist attractions (i.e. agricultural terraces in Sataf, orchards in Dayr Ayyub, structures in al-Zeeb); in many others, they are being neglected.

Palestinians who manage to enter Israel, then, can either visit their original houses, now inhabited mostly by Jews (principally in cities and towns), or the site of the former home, which was completely destroyed, leaving rubble at best; those within contemporary tourist sites would be more accessible and identifiable. In the vicinity of the house, some other remains of the Palestinian past might be observed, such as orchard trees and prickly pear cacti (mostly in rural areas), or other depopulated houses and structures (mostly in urban areas). All are within the borders of a state that has caused the uprooting, and whose current residents, beneficiaries of the appropriated property, are generally labelled as 'the enemy' in the context of an ongoing conflict.

Palestinian Home Visits: Memory, Commemoration and Protest

Family memories, the remembrance culture of Palestinian refugees, and their political demand of return are among the driving forces behind Palestinian visits to their lost homes. A central component of the personal and collective memory of Palestinian refugees is naturally the Nakba – the sequence of events that caused their uprooting, dispossession and exile. For Palestinian refugees, the Nakba is centred mostly in their own lost village or town (Masalha, 2008: 142). They often tell their offspring every detail about their place of origin and recount glorifying stories of their lives there (Karmi, 2002: 199–200; Rubinstein, 1991: 25–26).

Different remembrance and commemorative practices have evolved throughout the years among Palestinians in exile, all emphasizing concrete places of origin. When asked where they are from, refugees, including those from the second and third generation, often present themselves as coming from the family's original village (Peteet, 2005: 190. But see Allan, 2014: 218); quarters, streets, schools and shops in refugee camps are named after the villages of origin of their residents (Bisharat, 1997: 214; Hamzeh, 2001: 111; Khalili, 2007: 80; Peteet, 2005: 95, 111, 190); village names are given to Palestinian daughters, adopted as surnames, as well as chosen as nicknames by youth on the internet (Khalili, 2005: 28; Masalha, 2012: 207); keys of the original homes are kept and displayed on walls, and sometimes worn as necklaces; deeds of the house are also retained (Bisharat, 1997: 214; Khalili, 2005: 28; Shakkour, 2015: 190–191). In the 1980s, refugee descendants began to publish self-written and -financed historical ethnographies of lost villages, following the example of such books published earlier by different institutions (Davis, 2011; Khalili, 2005: 29–30; Slyomovics, 1998: 1–14). The practice of visiting the depopulated home or village of origin became another practice of remembrance for individuals and families who had access.

In the 1990s, with negotiations between the Palestine Liberation Organization (PLO) and Israel focusing almost solely on the OT, commemorative practices among refugees have gained new momentum by the second and third generation, in order to advocate for inclusion of refugees' rights – above all the right of return – in the agreements (Khalili, 2004: 7–9; Sayigh, 2005: 32). The attachment to the village of origin was being cultivated by political factions, NGOs, and the media, and was sometimes used as a mobilizing political tool (Khalili, 2005: 26). This process reached its peak in 1998, around the 50th anniversary of the Nakba, with a proliferation of Nakba-related commemoration practices such as oral histories, plays, art exhibits, village history books, memoirs, archival websites and films (Allan, 2007: 254–255; Ben-Ze'ev & Aburaiya, 2004: 640; Masalha, 2008: 143; Tamari, 2003: 173).

The increased practice of visits to Palestinian depopulated villages is another aspect of the growing Palestinian commemoration activity since the 1990s, as well as the spreading of accounts of such visits (Sayigh, 2005: 37): photos from visits are shown in living rooms and are posted on Palestinian websites, as are descriptions of the visits; videos of visits are screened to family and friends in the diaspora. Ben-Ze'ev (2004: 155) sees it as 'a shift away from remembrance to commemoration'. This growing 'tourism' takes place among those who have access to the depopulated sites – mostly IDPs and other Palestinians in Israel – and is part of a general process of reclaiming the right of return of IDPs to their villages (Cohen, 2000: 11–15; Jamal, 2011: 100). Although this process was triggered by the Oslo accords, which have ignored the IDPs (Ben-Ze'ev & Aburaiya, 2004: 647), it was also boosted by a shortage of housing and land among IDPs, and by the growing political awareness among second-generation IDPs and Palestinians in Israel in general (Jamal, 2011: 122; Schechla, 2001: 27–28).

Since the 1990s, IDPs' associations, as well as other Palestinian organizations in Israel, have been organizing group visits and parades to depopulated Palestinian villages, particularly on specific dates of national importance, such as Nakba day (15 May), targeting IDPs and their descendants, as well as the general Palestinian public. Different motivations stand behind such mass visits: advocating the return of IDPs to their villages of origin, strengthening Palestinian national identity among Palestinians in Israel, increasing their familiarity with the Nakba history, and raising their political awareness regarding current Israeli abuses towards Palestinians in Israel (Ben-Ze'ev & Aburaiya, 2004; Gutman, 2011: 68; Jamal, 2011: 100). Other activities in the depopulated villages became prevalent, including youth 'roots and belonging summer camps', and prayers as well as cleaning and restoration projects in deserted mosques (Ben-Ze'ev & Aburaiya, 2004: 648–649; Magat, 2000).

The organized visits and activities, which sometimes include waving of the Palestinian flag and singing national Palestinian songs (Jamal, 2011: 100–101), are part of the development towards what Ben-Ze'ev and Aburaiya (2004) coined 'middle-ground politics': it links abstract national Palestinian notions with concrete daily concerns and localities of Palestinians. The commemoration of the depopulated sites has become a more collective act, public, organized and political, with the personal connection to the lost home or village serving as a symbol and a tool in an ongoing political struggle.

Coping with Destruction, Change and Repopulation

In the following sections we will examine some of the difficulties and challenges faced by refugees who consider visiting their former places, and their ways of coping. The generation difference, the current location of visitors and the current status of their former home are all reflected in the personal accounts of such visits.

Fears and reluctance to visit

For Palestinian refugees, thinking about the possibility of visiting their former house often involves anxiety and stress: how would they cope with the inevitable changes? Will they feel like strangers in their own home? Can it still be considered their home? (Lindholm Schulz & Hammer, 2003: 211). Some refugees choose not to visit at all: they don't want to arrive as visitors rather than repatriates, they want to retain the memory of their home – and of Palestine – intact, they prefer to avoid the painful experience of visiting the house that was forcibly taken from them, or they don't want to enter Israel. Some of those who did make the journey to their still standing houses prefer to see it only from the outside.

Shakkour interviewed Palestinian refugees exiled in London. Some of them, 'hoping to avoid the pain they saw their friends experiencing,' have never come to visit (Shakkour, 2015: 189). Hasan Karmi, exiled in London after being uprooted from his house in the Qatamon quarter in Jerusalem, refused to use his British passport and visit as a tourist. His daughter, Ghada, born in Jerusalem in 1939, wrote that her parents 'preferred to preserve the memory of their home as it had been before they left, intact. ... Seeing the place altered in alien custody would tarnish the image' (Karmi, 1994: 39). Even IDPs, who live only a short distance from their original village, sometimes refuse to go there: Wakim, head of the Association for the Defense of the Rights of the Internally Displaced in Israel, says that many first-generation IDPs refused to visit their villages for some time after hearing of the destruction of their houses (Wakim, 2002; see also Grossman, 1993: 73–74).

According to Karmi (2002: 214), for decades, scarcely any exiled Palestinian went to Israel, even when they were legally able to, because even contemplating this was conceived as 'the worst treachery any Palestinian could commit'. This was the case with Ibrahim Abu-Lughod, who fled to Jordan in 1948 and from there moved to the US. For years after obtaining his American passport, he refused to go and see his former home in Jaffa. In the words of his daughter, Lila – herself, an eminent anthropologist, studying the politics and culture of memory (Abu-Lughod, 1986, 2001): 'he could not imagine placing himself at the mercy of and under the authority of the state that had overrun his entire country; to come face to face with the people who contaminated and devastated the everyday lives of Palestinians' (Abu-Lughod, 2007: 78). Later on, in 1991, Ibrahim Abu-Lughod moved to the West Bank, and often visited Jaffa from there.

The encounter with the Israelis who came to occupy the family house was another deterrent factor. Karmi's brother and sister refused to visit because they 'feared their own reactions to seeing the new proprietors' (Karmi, 1994: 39). Overcoming all those fears and hesitations, and reaching a decision to visit after all, isn't easy, as Karmi (1994: 39) recalls:

> The prospect of going to Palestine filled me with dread, partly because I was infected with my parents' feelings, and partly because I too had my own little precious memory that I was reluctant to soil. ... But the day came when I decided to return. In August 1991, after 43 years, I took a journey to Jerusalem to face the monster I had been hiding from all my life.

Some refugees who did make the journey to their former house, preferred to see it only from outside and not to enter, avoiding the close encounter with the loss: Serene Husseini Shahid's family had left Jerusalem for Beirut in 1936. They came in 1972 to stay in Jericho, and from there went to visit their old home in the Musrara neighbourhood. Serene and her sisters refused to enter the house and stayed in the car, saying: 'we could not stand the sight of the house which was ours, and is no longer. ... Mom entered, but none of us had the courage to join her' (Husseini Shahid, 2006: 147–149).

Second- or third-generation refugees have no personal memories of their parent's home and sometimes don't feel related to it. Some are reluctant to visit – feeling alienated, apprehensive of getting attached, or wanting to avoid seeing their parents' distress. Tareq, born in 1967 in Jordan, travelled with his father to Palestine, but refused to come with him to the ruins of their village of origin, al-Tira:

> It's my dad's country. ... I didn't want to see my father in pain ... I thought that if I did [go the village], I would be too much related to it. ... I don't want to live in the past. ... I am looking ahead for the future. (in Ben-Ze'ev, 2005: 130–131)

Although refugees in general might be reluctant to visit their ruined or appropriated former home, for the Palestinian refugees there is another burden – and deterrent – associated with such visits: the visit has to be carried out within the boundaries of the 'enemy', who caused the destruction and shaken off responsibility for it.

From the Idealized Past to the Painful Present Reality

First-generation refugees were left with cherished memories, nostalgia and yearning, often describing their lost house, village or town to their off-spring in terms of a lost paradise (Hammer, 2003: 182–185; Lindholm Schulz & Hammer, 2003: 109). Visiting may hence create a painful clash between the sweet memories and the home's contemporary state (see Ali & Holden, 2011: 81). Indeed, Palestinian refugees from different generations recount big disappointment and shock at the sight of the gap between their parents' descriptions and the current reality. As Rema Hammami, born in Saudi Arabia to a family from Jaffa, says: 'Going to Jaffa for someone who grew up with it as an iconic myth, a place that no other place can ever measure up to is bound to bring disappointment' (Tamari & Hammami, 1998: 67).

Encountering the still standing home

Hala Sakakini visited her house in Qatamon in July 1967, 19 years after fleeing with her family in April 1948. She recalls that upon their departure the house was 'in perfect condition ... Bright and shiny ... The garden was well kept'. Describing her impressions during the visit, she mourns the pain-ful transformation her house had gone through: 'How different we found the house and the garden now ... the walls seemed so dusty, the paint on the shutters had worn off, the stairs were dirty ... The garden was dry and brown and covered with litter.' She compared the encounter to 'meeting a dear person whom you had last seen young, healthy and well-groomed and finding that he had become old, sick and shabby', or 'coming across a friend whose personality had undergone a drastic change and was no more the same person' (Sakakini, 1990: xi, xiv).

Sometimes the visiting refugees observe their house didn't change much, but its surroundings did completely, spoiling both the visit and the memo-ries. Mariam, a Palestinian refugee who lives in London, describes visiting her house for the first time since 1948:

> I burst out crying. ... It hadn't changed much, but it looked small among all the big buildings around it. Ours was the only house there when I was young... I regretted going there because I regretted losing my childhood memories of the beautiful place. (Interviewee quoted in Shakkour, 2015: 189)

Apart from the surroundings, the population had changed completely, fur-ther estranging the place for its visiting former residents. Sakakini (1990: xiv) recounts 'everything was so different. It was no more home. ... It is people that make up a neighbourhood and when they are gone it will never be the same again.'

Seeing the family place after living most of their lives elsewhere made visitors feel like strangers in what was supposed to be 'their' town: Turki, who exiled from Haifa to Lebanon as a child and later moved to Australia and the US, visited the city in 1991, concluding: 'I was a stranger in a strange city that under different circumstances I would find boring, tacky, and uptight' (Turki, 1994: 7); Ibrahim's daughter, Lila Abu Lughold, born in 1952 in the US, felt as a 'stranger' and even as a 'vulnerable intruder' while visiting Jaffa, her father's hometown (Abu-Lughod, 2007: 88, 91).

Perhaps even more difficult is coping with the fact that others are using your own home. Elias said: 'To see my house being lived in by others, it disturbed me ... to see the things that I have used as a child being used by another family, it was very painful' (interviewee quoted in Shakkour, 2015: 189). Visiting refugees are forced to communicate and negotiate with current residents in order to enter the house. This sometimes ends with quarrels, rejection, denial of entrance and even calls to the police, and in other cases with witnessing the house from the inside as the contemporary home of others, and sometimes conversing with those others, mostly Jewish, often refugees or displaced themselves (see Al-Khairi, 1997: 27–52; Kanafani, 1995: 40–42; Karmi, 2002: 448–450; Katz, 2000: 132; Khalili, 2005: 33; Peteet, 2005: 213–214; Piroyansky, 2014: 105–107, 110–114; Rubinstein, 1991: 63–64; Turki, 1994: 6).

In some cases, refugees found a Palestinian family in their former home, who had repopulated it after being displaced from its own house. For Nu'man Kanafani, visiting his family's house in Acre from Denmark and interacting with its current Palestinian residents, this was a sort of relief:

> There was a tacit consensus among us, a deep implicit feeling that we are all victims and that we should be somewhat satisfied that the house is occupied mainly by Palestinian rather than by Jewish families. (Kanafani, 1995)

Some refugees discovered that their re-used house no longer serves as a residence. Abu Firas was relieved to find out that his former house in Ramla served as a school at the time he visited in 1967, believing it will be easier to gain access to it (which he did) (Al-Khairi, 1997: 33); Hammami realized that her family's house in Jaffa was turned into a kindergarten for retarded children, and later into residence for incapacitated old people. She recounts: 'This made the visits even more painful ... Our house had become a dumping ground for unwanted people – God's waiting room' (Tamari & Hammami, 1998, 69). Raymonda Hawa Tawil, visiting her childhood house in Acre in 1967, found out to her dread that it had been turned into a museum. This fact enabled her to enter the place, but caused much frustration and grief, learning that 'new' memories are being transferred about it to tourists: 'As the guide led the visitors around, he explained blandly that this house, our home, used to belong to an eminent Jewish family. What a humiliation! I felt my blood rise' (Hawa Tawil, 1980: 113–114; see also Bisharat, 2003).

Facing destruction

Rural refugees who returned to their completely erased village were terrified and shocked; some regretted ever coming. Sirhan was born in 1937 in the village of al-Sindiyana, south of Haifa, from which he exiled in 1948 to Jordan. He visited his demolished village in 1998, and laments:

> Indeed this is al-Sindiyana. ... which I always imagined in its peak of beauty, but found a mound emptied of its inhabitants, quiet as graves ... I wish I wouldn't make this sad visit. What have I done to myself? I came to meet the bride, and met the mummy. (Kabha & Sirhan, 2004: 176–178; see also Slyomovics, 1998: 17; Rubinstein, 1991: 66)

In contrast, Safiyya Shbeitah, exiled in 1948 from the village of Miska to nearby a-Tira within Israel, says that the frequent visits she has been conducting to her demolished village throughout the years, gave her 'the strength to get rid of the shock which was the result of seeing the destruction' (S. Shbeitah, personal communication, 22 August 2010).

Refugees arriving at their demolished village are sometimes so disoriented, they refuse to believe this is indeed where they used to live. Tareq, who was displaced from Suhmata and lives in nearby Buquei'a inside Israel, visited with a fellow former-villager. He describes to Rania, a student from Buquei'a who interviewed him:

> We sat in a ruined house surrounded by trees. I asked him: where do you sit? He answered that he doesn't know, and I told him he sits in his own house. He said it's impossible, no way. He got alarmed and began looking around and checking the place, but couldn't remember. ... It happened to many people. (in Katz, 2000: 200)

For descendants of refugees, who didn't see the house or village with their own eyes prior to its destruction, the encounter with the site might be less devastating. Wafa, born in 1974 in the West bank, had continuously heard from his parents and grandparents about Bayt Shanna, the family village of origin. Assia Ladizhinskaya, an Israeli decade-old-friend of Wafa, accompanied him on his first visit to the village. She wrote: 'Wafa kept looking back into the past; his longing for the perfection of Bayt Shanna refused to dissipate'. Though he found Bayt Shanna completely destroyed and nothing like the description of his parents, the transgenerational memory was so power-ful that he exclaimed during the visit: 'This is the happiest day of my life. I am happier than I was at my wedding!' (Ladizhinskaya, 2014).

Struggling between past and present

Many visitors find it extremely difficult to accept the dramatic trans-formation of their former places. Some try to focus on the remains of the past, ignoring what was added or changed. Jamil Toubbeh, visiting his former home in Qatamon, recounts (1998: 149): 'The concrete presence of a multistoried structure did not obstruct the mental image of my home. It was there in time and space.' Sometimes, overlooking the new reality can only work for a short time. Nader recalls his first visit to the village of Zakariyya:

> I looked at the peak of a hill and imagined building a house for myself there. But, it was a very brief and momentary dream when I looked around and saw the Israeli houses built on Zakariyya's land, the roads and the schools. I said to myself: who are we fooling, this doesn't belong to us anymore. (Hamzeh, 2001: 112)

Hammami, in her repeated visits to Jaffa, aspires to experience the city dif-ferently, but is torn by an ideological dilemma:

> I would love to be able to walk through the city without being weighed down by its past and my duty to that past – just to be able to be fasci-nated by the architecture and the people who live there now, ... Alas, to do so would mean being burned at the stake for collaborating with a reality built on the demolition of dreams. (Tamari & Hammami, 1998: 67)

Accompanying Visitors

Visiting with family members

Many refugees visit their old homes accompanied by others, especially members of their family. IDPs, who visit their nearby former villages fre-quently, often bring their children or grandchildren along. At the site, they provide them with details about the village, its customs and its history; they visit the former home, cemetery, mosque or church together (Ben-Ze'ev & Aburaiya, 2004: 644; Magat, 2000: 29–30), thereby transferring their memo-ries to their descendants, enhancing the latter's identification with the place, and mobilizing them to continue the struggle to return.

Second-generation refugee travellers are aided by their parents, who once lived there, but these parents do not necessarily join them physically: they may have passed away, live in exile, or are unable or unwilling to make the journey. The visitors seek their company from afar during the trip, either in their mind (through active recollection of shared memories) and nowadays also through cellphones.

Kanafani, born in 1948, expresses vividly his lack of memories, yearning for the company of his father: 'I'm here ... to touch a country woven from memories, from songs, from stories of elders, ... oh, if my father was with me. I have no memoires to come back to, only his memories' (Kanafani, 1995. See also Turki, 1994). Husein Chawich, born in Syria to a Palestinian family from the Galilee village of Qabba'a and living in Berlin, visited the village site in 2010, with his father in his thoughts and his heart: 'I knew that the eyes crying were not mine. They belonged to my father, who saw his dead Qabba'a and mourned' (Chawich, 2011: 15).

While visiting the house or village, the visitors sometimes realize that the stories and details they have heard about it once and again from parents and grandparents helped them find their way around or identify objects they encounter. Wafa, visiting his family's village of Bayt Shanna, knew his way around there: 'Here was the mosque, here was the school, there was my parent's house', he mumbled. With unfathomable confidence, he was walking in a village in which he had never been before. (Ladizhinskaya, 2014). After finding two cisterns, Wafa insisted there ought to be a third one. 'Wafa made his way through the shrubs and thorns towards the missing cistern. His mother and grandfather were instructing him in his head, whispering to turn left and right. ... eventually, we stood over the opening of the third cistern. Wafa ... smiled victoriously' (Ladizhinskaya, 2014).

Rula 'Awwad-Rafferty came from Idaho, USA to participate in a Peace Education project in Israel/Palestine and while there, visited her mother's village of Qula. Her parents, living in Jordan, accompanied her from afar:

> I called my parents, announcing that I was walking on the earth of Qula. They asked what I could see, my mother's voice quivering. ... There would be numerous calls, some would have answers, laughs, and some would bring tears, memories, and hopes. ('Awwad-Rafferty, 2008)

In one of the conversations her father told her for the first time a painful story about old people who were left behind in the village in 1948 and were later found burnt. Rula writes:

> My father is a stoic man, but the emotions and tears in his voice were unmistakable. ... Someone [from those accompanied Rula in the visit] said that it was necessary for me to be there in Qula that day for my dad to share this painful memory, and it really was. ('Awwad-Rafferty, 2008)

Israelis as mediators

Many Palestinians visitors are not familiar with the location of the home or village, feel uncomfortable to move around alone in Israel or are reluctant and apprehensive communicating with Israelis who inhabit the house or the area. Some of them seek the company of Palestinian Israelis (i.e. Kabha & Sirhan, 2004: 176–178); others make the journey together with an Israeli Jew acquaintance or friend, who is familiar with the area and can serve as a mediator between fellow Israelis and the visitor. For instance, when Wafa, a West Bank resident, found himself in Israel for work, he suggested to his Israeli friend Assia to dedicate one Saturday for a visit in his family's village Bayt Shanna together. She happily agreed. That Saturday she struggled with him to find the obliterated place, accompanied him for hours touring the site, and shared with him her own home visit experience in Moscow, where she was born (Ladizhinskaya, 2014; see also Karmi, 2002: 444–448).

Hege Haeier from Norway contacted Eitan Bronstein from Zochrot, an Israeli non-profit organization which aims to 'promote acknowledgement and accountability for the ongoing injustices of the Nakba ... and the recon-ceptualization of the Return as the imperative redress of the Nakba' (Zochrot, n.d.; see also Gutman, 2011, 2016). She explained that the parents of her husband Josef – born in 1965 in a refugee camp in Lebanon – are from the Palestinian depopulated village of al-Qubab. She asked Eitan to help them locate the place and visit there. In July 2013 Eitan toured with them around the village and conducted all the communication with its current Jewish dwellers. Josef Haeier's (2013) written account expresses the family's feelings regarding Eitan's direction and mediation:

> We depend on Eitan to communicate with the residents because he speaks the language. ... Another house of the village was nearby ... Eitan went forward ... We waited by the gate, watching tensely, surprised at how smoothly and quickly the discussion went. They called to us. We came forward, greeted the man, he greeted us and offered us a drink. ... Eitan's presence during our first visit to al-Qubab village had a huge effect on us and made it much easier. ... Eitan made our dream a reality. We wouldn't have been able to visit the homes and take photographs without him. (Haeier, 2013; see also 'Awwad-Rafferty, 2008)

The idea of returning to one's obliterated family village accompanied by an Israeli is not always easy to digest. Chawich, who was invited to a conference in Ramallah, decided to visit his family village of Qabba'a in the Galilee for the first time. He contacted Tomer, an Israeli working in Zochrot. After their joint visit to the village site, Chawich wrote (2011): 'Was al-Qabba'a laughing or crying when it saw me coming from afar in a car driven by an Israeli?'

Visiting in an organized tour

As mentioned above, Palestinian associations in Israel have been organizing group tours to Palestinian depopulated villages in the last twenty years. Most of the guides of those tours have a university degree in history, geography or political studies, many regularly work as teachers, or were certified by the Israeli tourism authorities, according to the official Zionist narrative. In the tours, however, unlike most official Israeli tour guides, they consciously choose not to follow the national information policy, which tends to silent and ignore Palestinian sites and past in Israel (Gutman, 2016; Kadman, 2010).

The association Deiritna (Arabic: our homeland), for example, organized some 40 visits to demolished villages between 2008 and 2010. Around 60 people of different ages participated in each tour, led by Prof. Mustafa Kabha: they visited central locales of the obliterated village, learnt about its history, social composition, and depopulation, as well as heard testimonies from village refugees. The guide, therefore, serves as a cultural mediator for the visitors, as he interprets and enhances the otherwise ruined, silent site (see Katriel, 1997: 27–29).

Sleiman Buwayrat, among the organizers of such tours, notes that participants emphasized the new knowledge they gained through the visits on the Palestinian society before 1948 and on the refugee issue as a whole, stressing the visits' contribution to their enhanced connection to the land and strengthened national identity (S. Buwayrat, personal communication, 20 August 2015).

A 42-year old woman, whose parents were displaced from the village of Qumya, describes her experience of participating in the annual return march that took place on Nakba day, 2015 to the nearby ruined village of Hadatha:

> I felt deep identification. For the first time I could sing [the national song] 'my homeland' without hesitation and out loud. I know I have a flag, but never before have I raised it or even touched or drew it! (Anonymous, personal communication, 21 June, 2015)

While IDPs frequently visit their own village of origin independently, they go on organized tours to learn about other depopulated villages. Dawud Bader, for example, was displaced from al-Ghabsiyya when he was six, and settled with his family in nearby Sheikh Dannun. He used to visit his former village since childhood. As an adult, he became aware of the struggles of displaced Palestinians from other villages to return there, joined the Association for the Defence of the Rights of the Internally Displaced, and helped organizing tours to depopulated villages. He recalls:

> During the visits I loved to hear details about the villages and felt very emotional as a reaction to the stories of the displaced people. It was very

moving to see them entering their yards and eating fruits of orchards their forefathers had planted there. (D. Bader, personal communication, 3 August 2015)

Palestinians in Israel who are not part of the refugee population take part in such tours as well, seeing the depopulated village sites as important markers of their nation's history. A.I., born in 1975 in Kafr Qari' to a non-refugee Palestinian family, began joining village tours at the age of 38. She says:

> This tour, and the one that followed, caused me lots of grief. For the first time I felt that I deeply understand the Palestinian question. I felt growing identification with the refugee demand for return. I felt more Palestinian, developed strong sentiments of belonging to the Palestinian people. (Anonymous, personal communication, 20 August 2015)

The visits of refugees in the company of others can also be seen in the unique prism of the conflict: refugees bring their children and grandchildren so that they carry on the continuing struggle for return; during their visits, Palestinians connect to their parents, who were directly expelled and dispossessed in the heat of the conflict; being unwanted guests in Israel, visitors seek the aid of individual Israelis, who sometimes assist, perhaps in a potential gesture of remorse or reconciliation; others visit the depopulated sites in organized groups, as part of an attempt to enhance national identity and conduct a political struggle for return.

Discussion and Conclusion

In this chapter we mapped the phenomenon of Palestinian 'home tourism' – visits of Palestinian refugees and their descendants to their former home or village. We described the different groups of refugees who are able to visit, their motivations, experiences and the current state of their destinations. We portrayed several themes that run through the accounts of the emotionally loaded encounter between refugees and their obliterated or repopulated homes; memory and the meaning of home are central to most.

Memory

As Palestinian exile has persisted for almost 70 years, Palestinian visitors come from different generations; this significantly affects the nature of their visit. First-generation refugees carry first-hand memories of their home and its surrounding, based on actual experiences; their visit to their appropriated former home triggers and confronts concrete old memories. The next generations only have 'second-hand' memories, delivered to them mostly through idealized stories of parents and grandparents. When they visit the family's house, the place turns from abstract and imagined to real and concrete (Ben-Ze'ev, 2005; Marschall, 2015; Tamari, 2003: 176–179). IDPs, as well as non-refugee Palestinians inside Israel, visit homes appropriated from others, which they see as an important part of their national collective memory.

The depopulation as a result of the ongoing national conflict turns the memory of home to another arena in this conflict: Israel is trying to erase this memory by demolishing the depopulated places, neglecting their remains, repopulating them by Jews, Hebraizing their names and removing them from official maps (Kadman, 2015). At the same time, Palestinians try to keep the memory of their lost places alive by using their names, seeking and publishing information and testimonies about them, keeping and presenting keys and deeds, as well as visiting them in person or in groups. Writing about these visits and publishing these accounts to wider audiences – even if not intended by each specific author as such – can be viewed as part of a continuing struggle to keep the memory of the Nakba alive and to seek its redress.

Home

All visits are carried out in pursuit of 'home', but there are notable differences between urban refugees, who can often visit tangible remains, and rural ones, who can usually see only rubble. Rosemary Sayigh (2005) argues that this destruction, which doesn't allow rural visitors to dream of visiting their actual home, is one reason that the visitors she interviewed, as opposed to urban refugees, did not mention the individual home in their visit accounts. Another reason, she believes, is that for rural refugees, memories of 'home' are not limited to an individual structure, but to 'a cluster of houses and their inhabitants,' and their visits are '... a reconnecting with a territory, a landscape, and a social body that form the prescriptive context of the "beit" [home].' (Rosemary Sayigh, 2005: 36, 38). This is true also of the testimonies we reviewed, in which visitors to obliterated villages mostly emphasize the village as a whole as home, while often being unable to recognize the site of the specific family house.

The accepted notion is that the place of origin continues to be the primary form of identification among Palestinian refugees and their descendants, who don't feel at home in their host countries (Khalili, 2005: 26; Peteet, 2005: 195). For them, according to Lindholm Schulz and Hammer (2003: 94), 'Home is somewhere else, from where you once came or where you originated, but where it is impossible to reach.' Therefore, when they manage to visit, it is to their 'real' home. Yet, this real home was taken from them and was destroyed or repopulated; visitor accounts do not express relief and satisfaction about coming back home, but mostly sentiments of shock, anger, frustration and pain.

As opposed to generally accepted notions, Allan (2014: 198) believes that Palestinian refugees of the younger generation don't actually retain the connection to their family's place of origin, since their dynamic adaptation to current daily life and present reality 'has weakened mnemonic communities more than is generally recognized'. She expresses concern that the focus on 1948 and on the strife for return to Palestine actually comes from the elite of the Palestinian diaspora, who put the 'burden of remembrance' on the younger generations. They are expected to 'miss keenly something that they themselves have not experienced losing.' It makes it harder for them to forge a 'sense of identity and belonging' in their place of birth and residence (Allan, 2007: 256–257, 271). Writing about refugees in Lebanon, who cannot visit their former places nowadays, Allan's words can be true also regarding younger generation IDPs in Israel: the growing political awareness among IDPs in the last two decades, expressed also in frequent visits to former villages, enhances the pressure on younger generations to avoid assimilating into their host communities, and keep aspiring to return to their original village, of which they only ever saw ruins (see Magat, 2000).

The struggle for the right of return is a central basis of Palestinian nationalism; Israel's shaking off the responsibility for the refugee problem, the refusal of central host countries to grant citizenship and equal rights to their Palestinian refugee residents, and the Oslo accords which pushed the matter aside – all keep this struggle alive. Visits of refugees and their descendants to former homes in Palestine can be seen as part of this struggle, even if that was not each visitor's intention; more strategically, such visits are indeed used by various Palestinian groups as a political tool in the struggle for return. In the heat of this collective struggle, personal connections to contemporary homes – in refugee camps, host countries or host villages – might be perceived as illegitimate and going against the national interest, sometimes at the expense of individual young refugees, as Allan (2007, 2014) shows.

Tourism?

Can the phenomenon of Palestinian home visits be classified as 'tourism'? Palestinian refugees and their descendants, who visit their place of origin, don't see themselves as tourists, but as returning to or visiting their own place (see Piroyansky, 2014: 120), in a country they would not choose otherwise as a tourist destination (see also Marschall, 2015: 336). Ben-Ze'ev (2011: 104, 107) argues that the Palestinian return visit is not tourism, but 'pilgrimage to a site of family mourning', a journey which ought to be difficult. Visits also have a clear political aspect, as they take place in a non-resolved conflict; personal visits 'articulate persistent claims for restitution' (Piroyansky, 2014: 120), and organized ones are built around resisting Israeli policies and mobilizing political goals.

Israel, on its part, does not want this kind of 'tourism': it doesn't grant visit permits to most of these potential travellers, and hence there is hardly any international 'tourism' of this sort. Israel's destruction of the villages was, among other, carried out to prevent visits to such 'destinations'. The Israeli authorities fail to acknowledge the significance of most sites of the Palestinian past in terms of archaeology, architecture, heritage and commemoration; they ignore and neglect them, if not demolishing them altogether (Falah, 1996: 277; Fenster, 2004: 408–408; Kadman, 2015: 33–51; Kletter, 2006; Shai, 2006).

Moreover, popular tour guide books, such as Lonely Planet or Bradt, do not consider depopulated Palestinian villages and towns as tourist destinations; only alternative tour guides refer tourists to those sites: the Palestine guidebook of the Alternative Tourism Group (2005) is defined by its authors as describing 'places rooted in Palestinian memory', and sites of contemporary tragedies and importance of the Palestinian people, such as the destroyed villages of 1948. Another unique guidebook focuses solely on depopulated Palestinian villages and urban quarters (Gardi *et al.*, 2012). Written mainly by Israeli Jews and directed primary at an Israeli audience. Amal Eqeiq, in her epilogue of the guide, notes that in some of the tours 'the readers are literally asked to walk into the shoes of the Palestinians who lived in these villages until the Nakba' and to experience the refugees' 'loss, nostalgia and dream of return' (Gardi *et al.*, 2012: 504–505). Thus, the Israeli tourists are invited here to a special kind of roots tourism – tracing the roots of the 'other' in their homeland (Kadman, 2010).

While Palestinian visits to their former homes cannot be easily accommodated in traditional definitions of tourism, they can certainly fall under its extended categories presented in more recent literature: 'Homesick Tourists' are defined as survivors (and their descendants) who travel to places from which they were forcibly removed, that may be completely destroyed; the driving forces for their journey are memories of home, and emotions associated with identity and a sense of origin and belonging (Marschall, 2015: 333, 346–347). This description suits first, second and sometimes third-generation Palestinian refugees, but what is unique about them is that their visits take place in the context of a living conflict, a fact which makes their visits more difficult and grants them an aspect of a political declaration and demand.

For third-generation Palestinian refugees, visits to depopulated sites can also be characterized as 'roots tourism', conducted by descendants in search of their ancestral origins, family history and a sense of identity and belonging or 'home' (Marschall, 2015: 336). In the literature, 'roots tourism' often refers to visits of African Americans to Africa or of the Jewish diaspora to Israel, seeking the ancestors' presence of hundreds or thousands of years earlier. Palestinian depopulation, on the other hand, took place only few decades ago, and visitors who are third-generation refugees might still have directly heard personal memories of the real home from their family members. They do not just visit a place of collective memory and significance in their remote national history, but rather a site of central importance in their family memory and personal heritage. At the same time, the visit bears significance in their collective national memory and their nation's political struggle.

Second- and third-generation Palestinian refugees in exile who visit their family house can also be seen as taking part in 'Diaspora Tourism', some of which goals, as detailed by Coles and Timothy (2004), are relevant to Palestinian visits: retracing the lives of one's ancestor, understanding the circumstances surrounding one's ancestors' emigration, and reaffirming one's identity. Ali and Holden (2011: 80–81) suggest that Diaspora tourism is formulated to influence the construction of national identity and has a role in 'reforging links with the ancestral homeland to sustain "imagined communities" and to preserve the illusion of return.' The organized visits initiated by Palestinian associations to depopulated villages indeed serve as a tool for national mobilization and identity building (Ben-Ze'ev & Aburaiya, 2004: 639), but since most Palestinians in the 'real' Diaspora cannot make such visits due to lack of access, their participants are Palestinians who are citizens of Israel. Writing about Pakistanis living in the UK, Ali and Holden (2011: 80) argue that the 'myth of return' – common among many migrant communities arriving in host societies – drives Diaspora tourism. Such myth or desire to return is highly significant among Palestinians in exile, particularly since, unlike many other refugees or migrants, most Palestinians don't enjoy equal rights and civil status in their host countries, and lack implementation of their groups' right for self-determination. Their visits to their former houses, then, can be called 'Return Tourism', since, as Ben-Ze'ev and Aburaiya note (2004: 644), these visits serve as a 'kind of temporary return' for the Palestinian visitors: concrete return to the family's home, and politically symbolic national return to the homeland.

Within the ongoing Israeli-Palestinian conflict, the rights of return and compensation are issues that were left painfully open and unresolved, and are central in the Palestinian national discourse. Palestinian 'home tourism', therefore, touches an open national wound. Viewing it through the prism of a living conflict explains some of the main characteristics of this kind of tourism: the ability of only a fraction of the displaced to visit, the state of home appropriation and destruction encountered by the visitors, and the political context of the national struggle that surrounds the visits, implicitly or explicitly.

Being carried out in the context of the conflict, visits of refugees and their descendants to the appropriated family house or village – whether triggered by pure personal and family motives, or organized by a national association – can be seen as political actions (see Ben-Ze'ev & Aburaiya, 2004; Piroyansky, 2014). Writing and publicizing accounts of such visits is yet another political act, as these texts keep alive the memory of destruction and human pain it continues to cause, beyond the immediate environment of the visitors and their families. Palestinian 'home tourism' is thus distinguished from other kinds of homesick, Diaspora, or roots tourism, which take place after a conflict has been resolved or faded away, and can be labelled also as return tourism or political tourism. While often deeply personal, it is also a part, and sometimes a tool, in an ongoing, unresolved collective struggle for home.

References

Abu-Lughod, L. (1986) *Veiled Sentiments: Honor and Poetry in a Bedouin Society*. Berkely: University of California Press.

Abu-Lughod, L. (2001) *Dramas of Nationhood: The Politic of Television in Egypt*. Chicago: University of Chicago Press.

Abu-Lughod, L. (2007) Return to half-ruins. In A.H. Sa'di and L. Abu-Lughod (eds) *Nakba: Palestine, 1948, and the Claims of Memory* (pp. 76–104). New York: Columbia University Press.

Al-Khairi, B. (1997) Mikhtavim le'etz halimon [*Letters to the Lemon Tree*]. (D. Brafman, trans.). Jerusalem: The Alternative Information Center.

Ali, N. and Holden, A. (2011) Tourism's role in the national identity formulation of the United Kingdom's Pakistani diaspora. In E. Frew and L. White (eds) *Tourism and National Identity: An International Perspective* (pp. 79–93). New York: Routledge.

Allan, D.K. (2007) The politics of witness: Remembering and forgetting 1948 in Shatila camp. In A.H. Sa'di and L. Abu-Lughod (eds) *Nakba: Palestine, 1948, and the Claims of Memory* (pp. 253–282). New York: Columbia University Press.

Allan, D. (2014) *Refugees of the Revolution: Experiences of Palestinian Exile*. Stanford, CA: Stanford University Press.

Alternative Tourism Group (2005) *Palestine and Palestinians: Guidebook*. Beit Sahour, Palestine.

'Awwad-Rafferty, R. (2008, July) Being in place, of place, in Qula... [Web log post]. Retrieved from http://zochrot.org/en/article/52197

Ben-Ze'ev, E. (2004) The politics of taste and smell: Palestinian rites of return. In M.E. Lien and B. Nerlich (eds) *The Politics of Food* (pp. 141–160). New York: Berg.

Ben-Ze'ev, E. (2005) Transmission and transformation: The Palestinian second generation and the commemoration of the homeland. In A. Levy and A. Weingrod (eds) *Homelands and Diasporas: Holy Lands and other Places* (pp. 123–139). Stanford, CA: Stanford University Press.

Ben-Ze'ev, E. (2011) *Remembering Palestine in 1948: Beyond National Narratives*. New York: Cambridge University Press.

Ben-Ze'ev, E. and Aburaiya, I. (2004) 'Middle ground' politics and the re-Palestinization of places in Israel. *International Journal of Middle East Studies* 36 (4), 639–655.

Bisharat, G.E. (1997) Exile to compatriot: Transformations in the social identity of Palestinian refugees in the West Bank. In A. Gupta and J. Ferguson (eds) *Culture, Power, Place: Explorations in Critical Anthropology* (pp. 203–233). Durham, NC: Duke University Press.

Bisharat, G.E. (2003, May 18) Rite of return to a Palestinian home. *San Francisco Chronicle*, section D.

Chawich, H. (2011) Ten days of return: A segment of the diary of rebirth of a Palestinian diaspora. *Sedek: A Journal on the Ongoing Nakba* 6, 1–19.

Cohen, H. (2000) Hanukhahim nifkadim: Ha-plitim ha-falastinim me-1948 [*The present absentees: The Palestinian refugees in Israel since 1948*]. Jerusalem: Institute for Israeli Arab Studies.

Coles, T. and Timothy, D.J. (eds) (2004) *Tourism, Diasporas and Space.* New York: Routledge.

Davis, R. (2011) *Geographies of the Displaced: Palestinian Village Histories.* Stanford: Stanford University Press.

de Santana Pinho, P. (2008) African-American roots tourism in Brazil. *Latin American Perspectives* 35 (3), 70–86.

Falah, G. (1996) The 1948 Israeli-Palestinian war and its aftermath: The transformation and de-signification of Palestine's cultural landscape. *Annals of Association of American Geographers* 86 (2), 256–285.

Fenster, T. (2004) Belonging, memory and the politics of planning in Israel. *Social and Cultural Geography* 5 (3), 403–417.

Gardi, T., Kadman, N. and Al-Ghubari, U. (eds) (2012) Omrim yeshna eretz *[Once upon a land: A tour guide].* Tel Aviv: Zochrot-Pardes.

Grossman, D. (1993) *Sleeping on a Wire: Conversations with Palestinians in Israel* (H. Watzman, Trans.). New York: Picador.

Gutman, Y. (2011) Transcultural memory in conflict: Israeli-Palestinian truth and reconciliation. *Parallax* 17 (4), 61–74.

Gutman, Y. (2016) *Memory Activism: Reimagining the Past for the Future in Israel-Palestine.* Nashville, TN: Vanderbilt University Press.

Haeier, J. (2013, December) I come from there, from al-Qubab [Web log post]. See http://www.zochrot.org/en/article/55191

Hammer, J. (2003) A crisis of memory: Homeland and exile in contemporary Palestinian memoirs. In K. Seigneurie (ed.) *Crisis and Memory: Representation of Space in Modern Levantine Narrative* (pp. 177–198). Wiesbaden: Reichert Verlag.

Hamzeh, M. (2001) *Refugees in our Own Land: Chronicles from a Palestinian Refugee Camp in Bethlehem.* London: Pluto Press.

Handley, F.L. (2006) Back to Africa: Issues of hosting 'roots' tourism in West Africa. In J.B. Haviser and K.C. MacDonald (eds) *African Re-genesis: Confronting Social Issues in the Diaspora* (pp. 20–31). Walnut Creek, CA: Left Coast Press.

Hawa-Tawil, R. (1980) *My Home, My Prison.* New York: Holt, Rinehart & Winston.

Husseini Shahid, S. (2006) Yerushalmit *[Jerusalem Memories]* (M. Baruch, Trans.). Tel Aviv: Andalus.

Jamal, A. (2011) *Arab Minority Nationalism in Israel: The Politics of Indigeneity.* New York: Routledge.

Kabha, M. and Sirhan, M. (2004) Bilad al-Ruha fi fatrat al-intidab al-Britani: al-Sindiyana namuzajan *[Bilad al-Ruha during the British mandate, al-Sindiyana as a model].* Ramallah: Dar al-Shuruq lil-Nashr wa-al-Tawzi.

Kadman, N. (2010) 'Roots Tourism – Whose Roots?' The marginalization of Palestinian heritage sites in Israeli tourism sites. *Téoros* 29 (1), 55–66.

Kadman, N. (2015) *Erased from Space and Consciousness: Israel and the Depopulated Palestinian Village of 1948.* Bloomington: Indiana University Press.

Kanafani, N. (1995) Homecoming. *Middle East Report, 194/195*, 40–42.

Karmi, G. (1994) The 1948 exodus: A family story. *Journal of Palestine Studies* 23 (2), 31–40.

Karmi, G. (2002) *In Search of Fatima: A Palestinian Story.* New York: Verso.

Katriel, T. (1997) *Performing the Past: A Study of Israeli Settlement Museums.* Mahwah, N.J.: Lawrence Erlbaum Associates.

Katz, K. (2000) Mifgashim shel zikaron *[Memory encounters].* Jerusalem: The Alternative Information Center.

Khalidi, W. (ed.) (1992) *All that Remains: The Palestinian Villages Occupied and Depopulated by Israel in 1948.* Washington D.C: Institute of Palestine Studies.

Khalili, L. (2004) Grass-roots commemorations: Remembering the land in the camps of Lebanon. *Journal of Palestine Studies* 34 (1), 6–22.

Khalili, L. (2005) Commemorating contested lands. In A.M. Lesch and I.S. Lustick (eds) *Exile and Return: Predicaments of Palestinians and Jews* (pp. 19–40). Philadelphia: University of Pennsylvania Press.

Khalili, L. (2007) *Heroes and Martyrs of Palestine: The Politics of National Commemoration.* Cambridge: Cambridge University Press.

Khoury, E. (2007) *Gate of the Sun: Bab al-Shams* (H. Davies, Trans.). New York: Picador.

Kletter, R. (2006) *Just Past? The Making of Israeli Archeology.* London: Equinox.

Ladizhinskaya, A. (2014) Two journeys back in time to a place called home [Web log post]. See http://972mag.com/a-palestinian-journey-back-in-time-to-a-place-called-home/88378/ (accessed 15 March 2014).

Lindholm Schulz, H. and Hammer, J. (2003) *The Palestinian Diaspora: Formation of Identities and Politics of Homeland.* London: Routledge.

Magat, I. (2000) Bir'am: Kehilat zikaron meguyeset *[A Conscripted Community of Memory and the Maintenance of Voice].* Giv'at Haviva: Peace Research Institute.

Marschall, S. (2015) Touring memories of the erased city: Memory, tourism and notions of 'home'. *Tourism Geographies: An International Journal of Tourism Space, Place and Environment* 17 (3), 332–349.

Masalha, N. (2008) Remembering the Palestinian Nakba: Commemoration, oral history and narratives of memory. *Holy Land Studies: A Multidisciplinary Journal* 7 (2), 123–156.

Masalha, N. (2012) *The Palestine Nakba: Decolonising History, Narrating the Subaltern, Reclaiming Memory.* London: Zed Books.

Morris, B. (1993) *Israel's Border Wars 1949–1956: Arab Infiltration, Israeli Retaliation, and the Countdown to the Suez war.* Oxford: Clarendon Press.

Morris, B. (2004) *The Birth of the Palestinian Refugee Problem Revisited.* Cambridge: Cambridge University Press.

Peteet, J. (2005) *Landscape of Hope and Despair: Palestinian Refugee Camps.* Philadelphia, PA: University of Pennsylvania Press.

Piroyansky, D. (2014) Retrouver son foyer: Propriété et dépossession dans les récits de visite des exilés palestiniens à leur ancienne maison [Reclaiming home: Property and ownership in narratives of return visits to the Palestinian urban house]. *Revue d'Histoire Moderne et Contemporaine* 61 (1), 97–122.

Rubinstein, D. (1991) *The People of Nowhere: The Palestinian Vision of Home* (I. Friedman, Trans.). New York: Random House.

Sa'di, A.H. (2002) Catastrophe, memory and identity: Al-Nakbah as a component of Palestinian identity. *Israel Studies* 7 (2), 175–198.

Sakakini, H. (1990) *Jerusalem and I: A Personal Record.* Amman: Economic Press.

Sayigh, R. (2005) A house is not a home: Permanent impermanence of habitat for Palestinian expellees in Lebanon. *Holy Land Studies* 4 (1), 17–39.

Schechla, J. (2001) The invisible people come to light: Israel's 'internally displaced' and the 'unrecognized villages'. *Journal of Palestine Studies* 31 (1), 20–31.

Shai, A. (2006) The fate of abandoned Arab villages in Israel, 1965–1969. *History and Memory* 18 (2), 86–106.

Shakkour, S. (2015) Return to Palestine. In T. Gale, A. Maddrell and A. Terry (eds) *Sacred Mobilities: Journeys of Belief and Belonging* (pp. 181–197). Surrey: Ashgate.

Slyomovics, S. (1998) *The Object of Memory: Arab and Jew Narrate the Palestinian Village.* Philadelphia, PA: University of Pennsylvania Press.

Tamari, S. (2003) Bourgeois nostalgia and the abandoned city. *Comparative Studies of South Asia, Africa and the Middle East* 23 (1–2), 173–180.

Tamari, S. and Hammami, R. (1998) Virtual returns to Jaffa. *Journal of Palestine Studies* 27 (4), 65–79.

Toubbeh, J.I. (1998) *Day of the Long Night: A Palestinian Refugee Remembers the Nakba.* Jefferson NC: McFarland.

Turki, F. (1994) *Exile's Return: The Making of a Palestinian-American*. New York: The Free Press.

U.S. Department of State, Bureau of Public Affairs (2015) U.S. Citizens at Israeli ports of entry [press release]. See www.state.gov/r/pa/prs/ps/2015/08/246170.htm

Wakim, W. (2002) The exiled: Refugees in their homeland. *Palestine-Israel Journal of Politics, Economics & Culture* 9 (2), 52–57.

Zochrot. (n.d.) Who we are. See http://zochrot.org/en/content/17

6 Travelling at Special Times: The Nepali Diaspora's Yearning for Belongingness

Kalyan Bhandari

Introduction

Tourism, diaspora and mobility are inextricably linked. Whereas tourism is temporary mobility, diasporic feelings are the result of long-term or permanent dispersion from the place of original residence. Describing tourism as a form of mobility, Sheller and Urry (2004) argue that different mobilities inform, shape and drive tourism. This chapter looks into forms of mobility in the daily practices of the Nepali diasporic community in the UK and their association with 'home' and belongingness. The purpose of this is to examine how diasporic memories and performances act as a repository of diasporic consciousness. It will then examine how such consciousness produces 'memory' and belongingness during Nepalis' 'homeland' travel. This chapter argues that the realm of the diasporic 'everyday' consists of routine conditioning of 'home' atmosphere through the mobilisation of memory and belongingness and that such conditioning helps reaffirm Nepalis' root identity which finds its expressions in their homeland travel.

The study of memory has not received enough attention from tourism scholars (Marschall, 2012a), though memory is strongly connected to tourism in various ways: for example, tourism is often seen as something to be remembered (Braasch, 2008); memory can influence travel experience when tourists compare their present tour with the memories of earlier journeys, and memory can inspire individual destination choices, for instance, people travelling to sites connected with their own past (Marschall, 2012b). The latter is associated with diasporic travellers, whose desire for travel is the outcome of remembering their own past. The context in which such journeys take place can influence how a particular visit is remembered, how its details are recalled and how such memories are shared (Marschall, 2012b). In such scenarios, a calamity such as the April 2015 earthquake in Nepal is important because 'people vividly recall their own thoughts and actions at a moment of public crisis because they jump at the chance to connect themselves with a meaning' (Lowenthal, 1995: 197). Lowenthal (1995) further argues that people who are witness to important events many years later remember their own circumstances at that time: 'where they were, who told them, what they were doing, how they reacted, what they did next' (Lowenthal, 1995: 197). The April earthquake calamity is a landmark event in the history of the Nepali nation that every member of the diaspora, irrespective of whether or not they were in the home nation at the time, can presumably recollect, share and identify with.

Sharing of memory is important in the expression of group identity. Urry (1996) argues that memory is social in nature, that is, people remember together. Some scholars take the view that as a form of awareness, memory is wholly and intensely personal; it is always felt as 'some particular event (that) happened to me' (Lowenthal, 1995: 194). Nevertheless, every recollection, however personal it may be, even that of events of which we alone were the witnesses, even that of thoughts and sentiments that remain unexpressed, exists in relationship with a whole ensemble of notions which many others possess (Connerton, 1989: 36). Such sharing of recollections is important because through them we recover consciousness of former events. For the diasporic community this is even more important because the remembering of the past is crucial for their sense of identity; recalling past experiences links us with our earlier selves, however different they may since have become (Urry, 1996). Thus, the aim of this chapter is to look into the recollections of diasporic visits 'home' after Nepal's devastating earthquake and to see how they contribute to the traveller's homeland memory.

There has been increasing interest in the aspect of return visits by diasporic groups which is studied under the guise of different names, for example, personal heritage (Timothy, 1997), roots tourism (Basu, 2007; Wright, 2009), legacy tourism (McCain & Ray, 2003), genealogical tourism (Santos & Yan, 2010), diasporic tourism (Leite, 2005), ethnic tourism (King, 1994), ancestral tourism (Fowler, 2003) or homesick tourism (Marschall, 2015a). Though they may be termed differently, there is a common denomination in that they all entail a certain level of personal and emotive connection to places and artefacts (Stephenson, 2002; Timothy, 1997, 2008; Timothy & Boyd, 2003). Such experience of return travel is often perceived as personal enrichment and gives visitors a sense of being 'at home' (Stephenson, 2004: 62).

The concept of home and homeland can be varied in scope and meaning. One strand of research on home posits it as a fixed and bounded place that plays an important role in grounding people to a particular place (Ralph & Staeheli, 2011). Another approach treats home as a mobile concept where the idea extends and connects people and places across time and space (Brettell, 2006; Datta, 2010); this is very relevant for the present study on migrants. Speed, intensity, frequency and volume of human mobility and migration have so much changed the world that both place of origin and destination influence migrants' routine practices and everyday lives (Al-Ali & Khoser, 2002; Baldassar, 1997; Urry, 2000). According to this view, home is built through a dynamic process of localising particular sets of relationships that do not necessarily depend on the essential qualities of a particular geographical place (Nowicka, 2007). Thus, home is a process involving both the people we share home with and the material objects therein (Ralph & Staeheli, 2011: 519).

The above idea of home is inextricably linked with the notion of belongingness, because the same relationships and processes that construct 'home' are also involved in creating identities and feelings of belonging (Ralph & Staeheli, 2011). To belong means to find a place where an individual can feel 'at home', whereby home stands for a symbolic space of familiarity, comfort, security and emotional attachment (Antonsich, 2010). For diasporic communities, home is a way to express their belongingness which is articulated through their sense of self. Place-based attachments take a key part in this process, as belonging to a place becomes one and the same as belonging to a group of people; belonging becomes synonymous with identity, both social and individual (Brown, 2011; Christou, 2011). Thus, belongingness can be understood as a representational practice of the diasporic condition which provides a strong emotional sense of support and identity (Bess et al., 2002).

Such practices give rise to diasporic tourism: a sense of self-identity and the search for 'ancestry' are among the reasons for people to take return journeys (Wright, 2009). Such journeys can rouse diasporic consciousness, often associated with myths, nostalgia, imagined and actual histories of the group (Coles & Timothy, 2004: 13) and can function as a means to 'renew, reiterate and solidify familial and social networks' (Duval, 2004: 51). As there are many reasons for people to travel to their homeland, most studies on diasporic travel are concerned with motivations. Many conclude that diasporic consciousness and longing for root identity is the main reason for 'homeland' travel (Basu, 2007; Bhandari, 2013; Leite, 2005). If we consider that in many cases homeland travel could be triggered not by intrinsic desire or longing for home alone but by external factors, then the question arises whether such travel can still provide room for the articulation of identity and belongingness. Thus, I will look not only into the production of 'home' and 'memory' in the daily performances of the Nepali diasporic community, but also examine how the sense of home and belongingness is articulated during homeland travel imposed by a powerful external stimulant, in this case the above-mentioned devastating earthquake.

Research Context

Nepal was struck by a massive earthquake of 7.8 magnitudes on the 25 April 2015 that killed more than 8800 people and injured another 23,000.

Hundreds of thousands of people were made homeless, with many villages flattened in some parts of the country (National Planning Commission, 2015). Centuries-old buildings were destroyed, including some very important tourist attractions such as the UNESCO World Heritage sites in the Kathmandu Valley. The earthquake invited an unprecedented level of engagement of the Nepali diasporic community with their homeland throughout the world. The events provided a setting for the expression of feelings and show of patriotism and love for the home country; this resulted in a considerable number of Nepali diasporic community members visiting 'home' in the immediate aftermath. Those who could not return to visit their families sent back money; the Asia Foundation (2015) found a considerable increase in remittances in some places in the weeks following the earthquake. Many Nepali diasporic organisations helped raise money through charities and some of them sent contingents of volunteers to directly engage with rescue and relief operations in Nepal. Nepali medical practitioners in the UK sent nurses and doctors to Nepal with medical and other emergency supplies to help the rural poor. Similarly, the Non-Resident Nepalese Association mobilised its chapters across the world to raise money and sent their volunteers to help in the relief and rescue. Many other emigrant Nepalis acted in their individual capacity (personal communication with members of Glasgow Nepalese Association in July 2015).

There are several reasons for choosing the Nepali diasporic community for this chapter. Firstly, outward migration of Nepalis is relatively recent and diasporic consciousness is still evolving; as a result, very little is known of the Nepali diaspora's homeland travel tendencies. Secondly, most of the existing studies of diaspora have been conducted in the post-colonial context and very little is known of more recently migrated societies. This chapter is based on both primary and secondary sources. The primary data were collected in the UK from people who recently visited Nepal during the aftermath of the earthquake in April 2015. They were interviewed in order to ascertain their views about their sense of 'home', their feelings towards their homeland identity and their experience of their most recent home visit. A total of 11 individuals, identified through snowball sampling, were interviewed between June and October 2015 in their respective current homes in Glasgow and Reading; the interviews lasted from 15–45 minutes. All interviews were conducted in Nepali and were translated and transcribed by the author. They were supplemented with data collected from a study of media articles written by Nepali diasporic communities after their visit to Nepal. A total of 10 such articles were reviewed. The reason for interviewing was premised on the assertion that 'human experience has a crucial narrative dimension' (Kleres, 2010: 184), that is, people have knowledge of how things have come about which is best expressed in narrative form through their own stories. The narrative account also gives us access to the identity constructions of individuals and is relevant for studying minority groups like diasporas (Elliott, 2005; Halberstam, 2005; Riessman, 2003).

Additionally, visits to the residences of some of the respondents were carried out to see expressions of their sense of loss, memories and belongingness through encounter of objects and the general atmosphere of their home. This helped the author to note interesting signs or indicators to validate verbal expressions and relate them to actual manifestations in the participants' home. The study was largely carried out against the backdrop of the earthquake and as such the findings are influenced by it. As the purpose of this study is not to show absolute truth, but to see how there are sometimes contradictory truths and different versions of the truth (Rapley, 2007: 128), the findings presented here must be read in the same light.

Outmigration in the Nepali Context

Separation from home or homeland is relatively new to Nepalis. Though Nepalis have migrated from their ancestral villages to newer pastures, this has been mostly confined within their national border. Very limited outside migration that took place in the medieval period was largely to India for religious purposes and to Lhasa in Tibet for trading purposes. The modern form of migration only started in the last quarter of the 20th century and much of it for economic reasons. Traditional destinations were India, Hong Kong, Japan and other areas in the Asiatic mainland. This pattern of migration began to change from the 1990s, when Nepalis opted for Gulf countries such as Kuwait and Qatar. Later on this triggered a movement further west, since immigration laws in Hong Kong and Japan began to tighten (Gellner, 2013).

As such, migration to the US and Europe is fairly new. Earlier migrants to the US belonged to a group that dared to 'dream big' and those who succeeded had certain objectives, notably, to study in an advanced educational environment. People with this desire were and are still facilitated by agencies which provide guidance and counselling back home. Other migrants were attracted by the prospects of work and earning money (Gellner, 2013). Another important factor that has aided increased migration to the US is the Diversity Visa (DV) lottery system. The programme is congressionally mandated and allows up to 55,000 persons from nations that are historically under-represented in terms of migration to the US to qualify each year for immigrant visas. Since Nepal is on the eligibility list, a large number of Nepalis immigrate to the US through this system every year. These immigrants secure their Green Card, become permanent residents and join the ranks of the 'diaspora' (Gellner, 2013).

The situation differs to some extent in the UK. Migration to that country during the 1970s and 80s related to scholarships offered to Nepali medical doctors and civil servants. The number of Nepalis started to increase after 1997, when Gurkhas, Nepali men serving in the British Army, were allowed to settle in the UK upon retirement (see Gellner, 2013). The trend continued further since May 2009, when the government conceded the right for all ex-Gurkhas with four years of service to settle in the UK. Today, Nepalis are the fastest growing ethnic minority in the UK (Adhikary, 2012). According to the 2011 UK census the estimated number of Nepalis in the UK is 60,202 which is a significant rise from the 5938 recorded in the 2001 census. Even the 2011 census data are considered to be below the actual number, since a study in 2008 already estimated the Nepali population in the UK to be 72,173 (Adhikary, 2012). Though ex-servicemen form a large portion, the Nepali community in the UK is diverse, comprising of more than two dozen ethnic groups (see Gellner, 2015).

The presence of different ethnic groups has great implications for the study of the Nepali diaspora. An important aspect of diaspora is orientation to homeland; however, the presence of more than 100 ethnic groups in Nepal that have their own claim over separate territories as 'homeland' makes it problematic to study the Nepali diaspora. These groups have discrete ethnic homeland movements in Nepal and have undergone different migratory trajectories. Barth (1981) takes the view that ethnic groups are categories of ascription and identification by the actors themselves and the nature and continuity of their self-identity depends on the maintenance of a boundary with the 'Other' or the outsider. In such cases, 'homeland' is not always remembered in the same way and reference to 'home' or 'homeland' by members of different ethnic groups could significantly vary in meaning because of increased ethnic polarisation in Nepal. This has also been supported by Brusle (2012), who states that diasporas can never be homogenous; the author has shown that the structure of the Nepali diasporic community reflects the tensions of Nepali society. Thus, the various ethnic groups in the UK may be speaking in the name of their 'homeland', but this is understood as a place of their specific ethnic identity and origin, not as a place of Nepali national identity.

To overcome the above difficulty, I will investigate the 'diasporic stances, claims or practices' (Brubaker, 2005: 13) that for each of these constituencies represent 'home'. Brubaker (2005) states that the proliferation of 'diaspora' in the last two decades has expanded the meaning of the term so much that it is scattered in all directions. There is a tendency to conceptualise all emigrant groups as diasporas, including those from Nepal. However, Subba (2008) argues that Indian Nepalis are not diaspora as most of them were born in India, have no memories of Nepal and no wish to visit Nepal. This cautions us to avoid the fallacy of a blanket approach that treats all overseas Nepali communities as diaspora. Thus, drawing on Brubaker, I take diaspora to mean a category of practice, rather than a bounded group. A similar approach is suggested by Hausner and Gellner (2012); their study of 'Nepali religion' has shown that the religious practices of Nepalis in the UK involve a ritualised behaviour that may or may not fit into fixed religious categories as defined by the census.

Tourism and the Nepali Diasporic Communities

Contrary to many other diasporic communities, Nepalis immigrated to the UK voluntarily, i.e. without a direct act of coercion. They are free to go back to their home country and the sense of loss is presumably comparatively lower than for certain other groups, such as refugees. Schiller and Fouron (2002: 357) note that an 'increasing number of states are developing legal ways of reclaiming emigrants and their descendants', though this is not the case in Nepal. Since the migration itself has happened because of people's desire rather than compulsion, the question of return visits does not appear high on the diasporic agenda. Pariyar *et al.* (2014), however, report that among the ex-British Gurkha servicemen of the UK, there is some intention to return to Nepal after seeing their children settled here. Even if there is a fair number of people returning, this will hardly find any place in Nepal's tourism strategy because, according to existing definitions, Nepalis are not considered tourists. Nepal's Tourism Act of 1978 defines tourists as those non-Nepali citizens coming to Nepal for a visit from a foreign country, i.e. even Nepalis travelling in their own country are not recognised as domestic tourists. The association between tourism and diaspora has been geared more towards mobilising diaspora to promote Nepal as a destination for foreign tourists. For example, the Nepal Tourism Board appoints Nepali entrepreneurs based in the host country as its honorary PR representatives. For entrepreneurs this is a privilege, as reflected in a restaurant owner's statement (R1): 'this is the way I am fulfilling my duty towards my motherland'.

The mobilisation of diaspora was attempted in a 'Send Home a Friend' campaign in 2007. This was not intended for Nepalis as tourists, but they were asked to send their friends to visit Nepal. It was a well thought-out programme at the time when Nepal was battling with a poor image due to internal political instability. The use of the word 'home' was carefully chosen to appeal to the diasporic sentiment and was aimed at garnering support from the vast network of Nepalis scattered around the world. The programme provided free promotional collaterals to the diasporic Nepali community and friends of Nepal. However, the campaign was neither fully owned by the tourism board nor the diasporic communities and was not a success. For example, an influential Trekking Agents Association of Nepal claimed that less than 20 visitors came to the country through the campaign in the fiscal year 2007/08 (TAAN, 2009). The campaign was originally conceived by a top bureaucrat in the tourism ministry who later headed the Nepali bureaucracy; as a result, it was extended to 2009 and 2010 in the run-up to the 'Nepal Tourism Year' celebration in 2011. During the promotion of Nepal Tourism Year 2011, a television advertisement was prepared where some youths along with Miss Nepal 2010, were shown discussing their next plan to visit their ancestral home in rural Nepal. But this was intended for domestic consumption and targeted at the population displaced internally owing to various socio-economic factors (personal communication with a senior officer in Nepal Tourism Board).

Routine Conditioning of the 'Home' Environment

According to Urry (2002) there are countless mobilities: physical, imaginative and virtual; voluntary and coerced. There are increasing similarities between behaviours at home and away from home. In the case of Nepali diasporic communities, everyday practice is made close to 'home' through the conditioning of routine. Routines are part of the ongoing processes through which a home, its ambience and the living of everyday domestic life are constituted and experienced (Pink & Mackley, 2014: 7). The Nepali case shows that such practices are suspended in time: though they have travelled thousands of miles away from home, their routine practices are much closer to their roots. These routines are their inheritance: a strong part of their personal heritage and, according to them, 'home' is embodied in their everyday ritual. Thus, home in this case does not only take a physical form but rather resides in one's mind (Santos & Yan, 2010: 3). A respondent (R5) informed that her daily routine begins with waking up at 5 am in the morning and then tuning to old Nepali *bhajan* (Hindu devotional songs) on YouTube. To her the *Sankha dhun* (the conch tune) of Radio Nepal is very much part of her routine that makes her dwelling 'homely'. She states, 'You know every morning I turn this Radio Nepal morning *bhajans* on YouTube. The *sankha dhun* and all old Nepali *bhajans* make me feel 'home'. I never feel I am away [from Nepal].'

Another woman in her forties is very devoted to her daily *puja* (religious prayer). She left Nepal in the early 1990s and has maintained her morning ritual the way she would have done it in Nepal. She appreciates that her daily performance does not hold the same level of spiritual purity; however, it gives her an immense self-satisfaction and sense of fulfilment of her duty towards ancestors, their spirits, or her roots, hence reinforcing her cultural identity. She further adds,

> The main reason that I do this *puja* is a great sense of satisfaction and security. I feel this has kept my home away from evil spirits and protects my home and family. There is another reason; I really miss the *puja* atmosphere of home, humming of *mantras* and the smell of incense. This *puja* takes me back to my flashback memories of my childhood. (R8)

The above examples bring the importance of everyday practice as a means to 'travel' in their memory. Urry (1995) argues that in a post-modern society tourism becomes blurred with many forms of production, consumption and mobility and people are for the most part tourists, 'whether they are literally mobile or only experience simulated mobility' (Urry, 1995: 148 cited by

Gale, 2009: 122). The daily routine in the above examples show such simulated mobility to root identity, because, according to Ehn and Lofgren (2009: 100) the word 'routine' is actually the diminutive of route, the making of small paths in everyday lives.

The examples show that sitting at home they travel down memory lane through 'routine' that provides strong attachments to Nepal and a strong sense of identity and belonging. This coincides with Nash (2002) who argues that such practices are a form of imaginative self-making and guarantees of truth about individual identity. Tolia-Kelly (2004: 316) terms this concept 're-memory' where sensory stimuli such as scent, sound or sight play a role in reminding people of their 'root' identity and are critical in the formation of their cultural identification. The above case illustrates the role of memory in shaping cultural practices: for example, memories of how they did things in Nepal and how this informs current routines. Additionally, it exemplifies the engagement of less tangible and sensory elements such as smells or performances in bringing back the memory of home.

Boundary Erosion and Boundary Creation

Boundary maintenance is an indispensable criterion of diaspora (Cohen, 1997: 24). Scholars of diaspora maintain that the diasporic consciousness involves the preservation of a distinctive identity vis-à-vis the host society (Brubaker, 2005). Barth's (1981) theorisation of ethnicity views ethnic groups as socially constructed and a form of boundary which is framed through interaction with the 'Others'. Barth (1981) further argues that an ethnic group cannot exist in isolation: its formation and continuation is dependent upon interaction with 'Others', which plays an important role in creating the boundary. This can be witnessed in the case of the diasporic Nepali community, where there is a constant switching between boundary creation and boundary erosion. The various everyday routines discussed in the previous section are examples of the consciousness of this boundary. Another female respondent (R9) endorses the above point when she says 'you may not be able to keep the purity of the stuff; you do like the way you would do *puja* in Nepal, but it keeps the cultural part intact ... one should never forget one's root and identity.' She adds,

> I celebrate *Dashain* every year. Celebrating one's culture is the way to assert our distinctiveness. ... See this *Tika Jamara* has great cultural and emotional significance.

> Putting this with red *Tika* (vermilion spot on the forehead) reminds me where I come from ... Its smell brings back my memories of my parents and grandparents ... it reminds me of my school days ... my friends. It is a sort of time machine for me.

The above case highlights the importance of memory and its relation to cultural heritage and identity. It reasserts the point that memory can be encapsulated in non-material heritage and can circulate far outside the nation, in a way creating a boundary with the host society. In the case of the Nepali diasporic community, the idea of boundary or ethnicity has an important implication in their travel behaviour both vis-à-vis the host society and home society. The residential status in a foreign country can account for social mobility: those who live abroad feel raised in class status and are seen as such in their home country. This inspires the diasporic communities to make regular visits to Nepal, as doing so would reinforce their newly acquired social status. This is what Gale (2009: 122) refers to when he says, 'people construct their identities through consuming *and being seen to consume* a particular set of commodities whose sign-values correspond to a desired lifestyle, and not so much by means of what they do in work or at home...' (italics in original). Such practice has given rise to a new leisure travel culture in the Nepali diasporic community. Though travelling for religious purposes has long been part of cultural life in Nepal, leisure travel or trekking to Nepal's mountainous terrain has been mostly left to foreign tourists. According to Barth (1981), the cultural features that signal the boundary may change over time: with greater interaction and exposure, the cultural characteristics of the members may likewise be transformed. This has been seen in the case of the Nepali diaspora, who have acquired a new cultural trait of travelling for leisure. There are two notable trends: first, many Nepalis visiting their homeland now consider a short leisure break in the Himalayas, and, second, many members of the Nepali diaspora take a holiday abroad. One respondent (R6) gave the following reason for taking a trekking trip to upper Mustang:

> I never thought of going to [the] high Himalayas when I was in Nepal. After coming here I realised that most of my colleagues or friends in the department where I work have been to the Annapurna and the Everest region. It was then [that] I realised the importance of [the] great wealth of my nation. I would now go to at least one trek on my every visit; I have been doing this for [the] last five years.

Another respondent (R9) opined, 'See, I work in the NHS. All of my colleagues go on holiday each year. I felt why not use part of my time in Nepal as a tourist.'

Identifying oneself as a 'tourist' by the above respondent is important. In Nepali cultural life the notion of 'tourist' has wider significance. It does not signify simply a traveller, but it is often associated with a higher species or ethnic designation (Hepburn, 2002). It is also a means through which Nepalis differentiate people or visitors in their own terms. Thus, a short break to an established 'tourist' route as part of a 'home' visit can have a wider social meaning. It can bring with it a raised social profile and create a new ethnic boundary between the diasporic visitor and their local relatives. Scholars have noted for some time that tourism can create a special kind of ethnic relationship, because tourists generally come from affluent societies and are envied for their wealth (van den Berghe & Keyes, 1984).

Supporting the above idea, Barth reminds us that 'ethnic relations and boundary constructions in most plural societies are not about strangers, but about adjacent and familiar "others"' (Barth, 1994: 13 cited in Wood, 1998). There is another instance where this divide is created in Nepal. Many respondents in this study confirmed that they would normally take gifts to their friends and families back home when they visit. One respondent (R4) stated, 'you know it feels good to take them some gifts and see them happy ... I believe it is also a way to give them respect ...'. Smart (1993) suggests that gifts are associated with the imposition of imperial values, as the act of giving creates thankfulness on behalf of the receiving party. In contrast to the claim by the respondent above, gifts can be more than simply an issue of social embeddedness and social connections; they can be part of a system of favours in which obligation and indebtedness are created (Yang, 1994). Gifts in Nepali society are a form of social institution called *Chakari* (see Bista, 1996). Traditionally, the concept of *Chakari* meant to appease or seek favour, however, in the modern context, gifts can be a medium to display disparity of wealth and can act more to dominate the person to whom gifts are offered. It distinguishes between the giver and the receiver: creating a boundary between those who can and cannot afford gifts.

Diasporic Travel to the Homeland During the Earthquake

The above paragraphs show how mobility of culture and cultural objects can help create feelings of 'home' and belongingness and how some forms of travel, notably leisure trips to established tourist routes in the home country and gifts that travel from the host to the home destination can be associated with creating boundaries. How does such construction of boundaries impact on the immigrants' feelings and emotions when they travel to the homeland in the wake of the April earthquake? In the following section I will show in more detail how the idea of home or belongingness and cognition of boundary or self-identity inform, and are embedded in, Nepalis' homeland travel in the aftermath of the earthquake. The following quote from an emigrated Nepali who visited the country after the earthquake indicates that she is aware of the boundaries between herself and her home society, but this does not diminish her love for her country. She writes,

Though our countrymen may regard us as an emigrated bunch, we could not remain aloof to the decapitated grieving Nepali heart after the destruction caused by the April earthquake. There is no word to express love for one's motherland at this time of pain and suffering to my country. (Siwakoti, 2015)

Many respondents approached by the author took the view that they did not travel to Nepal for a normal visit or celebration but primarily for the purpose of being with fellow countrymen at a time of need. They emphasised that it creates a very different and special feeling, a great deal of self-fulfilment and sense of achievement when you go back to your home on such a mission. They thought that it was a different and difficult trip but they felt proud of having travelled to Nepal at this historical time. To many of them this visit has made them re-realise their self-identity and where they come from. There was a deep sense of pain and belongingness in the expressions of many people who travelled to Nepal. A former tourism entrepreneur, who now lives in the UK, said the following of her love for the country,

Not only Nepal is grieving at this time, Nepali hearts all over the world have been broken along with the historical and natural heritage that [was] lost in this tragedy (...) We are grieving because we have lost our heritage bequeathed to us by ancestors; we are also grieving because pride and dignity have been shattered. The whole nation has grieved from the plains of the south to the high Himalayas in the north. (R6)

Loss of some of Nepal's iconic monumental and sacred buildings is a huge set back to the nation's heritage that relies on the notion of memory being bound to a place and captured in an artefact or historic objects, as well as the heritage industry that is of crucial economic importance to Nepal. To the above respondent the demolition of such objects and heritage icons implied the destruction of the homeland's 'containers of memory' (Marschall, 2015b: 336).

Another respondent (R2), a nurse, who volunteered in the remote villages to work for the earthquake victims, had the following to say for her compulsion to live in a foreign country,

We settled in here because of desire at first, but soon it became a compulsion. Despite immense love for the country, there are many Nepalis who are living abroad because there is very little opportunities back home.

The above expression shows a great sense of loss, an inevitable condition of diaspora. Mensah (2015) has shown in the case of the African diaspora visiting Ghana that homeland travel can be an emotional journey where expressions of grief, sorrow and loss are extensive. In fact, emotional engagement is the reason for home travel, argues Leite (2005). A respondent (R6) described the beginning of her journey this way, 'with heart filled with love and eyes with tears, we embarked on our journey to Nepal'. She feels being there is different to hearing about it from others,

> There is a great difference between hearing from others and seeing it, probably facing it yourself would ... be different. Even now my imaginations are filled with flattened heritage sites and peoples' grieving pain. I keep [being] reminded of the injured people. The [uncertain] future seen in the eyes of innocent children keeps me waking up.

Returning to the homeland is a journey through memory, moments of cultural (re)discovery and experiences of longing and belonging (Vathi & King, 2011). According to Marschall (2012b) such journeys can involve revisiting one's lost family home, one's old school, the place one used to play as a child, and many other sites where key moments in one's life occurred. The following example testifies to the above view and shows the feelings of a US based Nepali politician upon seeing the extent of devastation in one of his childhood haunts,

> My heart was filled with tears after seeing the devastation in the Basantapur durbar square where I was brought up, where I played, did my school assignments and spent my childhood. It was lifeless like a war torn region. All its history was eclipsed by the devastation. (Rauniyar, 2015)

In a study of Irish immigrants to the UK, Hughes and Allen (2010) found that a desire to visit was expressed by some older informants as an opportunity to recapture childhood memories and in that sense Ireland was interpreted as 'home' – a place of origin. For the above individual the visit also offered a chance to restore his 'childhood through memories' (Vathi & King, 2011). On many occasions travel home arouses 'reflective nostalgia' (Boym, 2001) in which one cherishes fragments of memory which could be objects, stories or texts. The devastation created by the earthquake was one such stimulus for the above respondent.

While nostalgia is a yearning for the past, a different place and time, possibly our childhood when time appeared to move more slowly (Boym, 2001), visits home can sometimes foster a yearning for a better future as well. This is often seen in the form of nationalistic feelings. Rauniyar (2015) writes, '(t)his is the time to do something for the country, this is the time to wake up the country and take it to prosperity. It is the time to transform the country, time for a new leader to emerge'. It is well established that diaspora travel and other transnational activities can play a role in the development of nationalism (Mulligan, 2002). 'Homeland nationalism', according to Brubaker (1996: 111), is

> directed 'outward' across the boundaries of territory and citizenship, towards members of people's own ethnic nationality, that is, towards

persons who 'belong' (or can be claimed to belong) to the external national homeland by ethno-national affinity, although they reside in and are (ordinarily) citizens of other states.

Hutt (1998) argues that a diasporic consciousness is more conspicuously present in the literary productions of nationalist intellectuals than it is in the minds, hearts and actions of working class cosmopolitans. However, there were many instances where such expressions were equally common in the opinion of ordinary members of the Nepali diaspora. The following is an example,

> I felt [a] great sense of pride for having this opportunity to touch the hundreds-of-years-old bricks during the rescue in Tripureshwor. I was overwhelmed by my patriotic feelings. This is time to show love for your motherland – to express your patriotism. It is during the time of pain that you heal your country through your love and care. (R5)

In the case of diaspora there is always an element of 'travel down memory lane'. Sheller and Urry (2004) argue that tourism and other types of mobility are part of the same complex and interconnected system, each producing the other. According to them, there is a proliferation of countless discourses, forms, and embodiments of tourist places and tourist performance and as such tourism sometimes can be 'unreal'. This reinforces the idea that holidays do not have to involve physical travel, we can move between different modes of doing; being a tourist is not necessarily place or time specific (Gale, 2009; Larsen, 2008). Some expressions evoke this element of mobility where travel is still continuing in the mind even after the completion of the physical journey. A respondent expressed it this way,

> Though my body is in the US, my heart is always loitering in Nepal. Let alone the patriotic Nepalis, anyone would not be untouched by the suffering of the Nepali citizens at this time. (Siwakoti, 2015)

The above example illustrates well that a cultural sense of belonging is often maintained by bringing back visual reminders and memories, as argued by Vathi and King (2011). The case of the Nepali diaspora shows that it can also be brought back with the element of 'experience' retained in the form of memory. A similar example is seen in the following expression,

> The suffering the country is facing has put every Nepali living abroad in pain. It does not matter where one lives physically, but it is the heart which is greater than this. My body is in the UK but my soul is still wandering in Nepal all the time. (R11)

Discussion and Conclusions

In this chapter I have shown the interplay of memory, belongingness and travel within the context of mobility in the Nepali diasporic community. I have considered the role of routine in exemplifying the idea of 'home' and 'homeland' and discussed the articulation of memory, home and belongingness in the context of diasporic travel to homeland. It was found that notions of 'home' and personal memory play an important part in negotiating the bonding with and the sense of belonging to the Nepali nation; and return travel is an expression of this belongingness.

The Nepali diasporic community shows a strong sense of identity which is rooted in the idea of the 'routinising' Nepaliness in their everyday lives. This is maintained through the organisation of a 'homely' atmosphere in the host country, that is, the creation of a resemblance to home back in Nepal. The Nepali case supports Bohme (1993: 122) who argues that it is necessary to understand atmosphere not as separate from things and people. The UK dwelling of the diaspora is a recreated 'home'. For the Nepali diasporic communities, the 'routines' discussed in this chapter are rituals which are 'a crucial part of generating belonging' (Pariyar et al., 2014: 2) where 'home' is the 'locus' (Basu, 2004: 28). To the Nepali diasporic community home is where people, things and environments are tied together to articulate a sense of belongingness (Pink & Mackley, 2014: 8).

This study shows that the homely environment is a medium through which the Nepali diasporic community travels to Nepal every day, not physically but emotionally. In this, culture plays an important part. Pariyar et al. (2014) have argued that for a Nepali cultural life, a house is more than a physical space for dwelling. Their study of the Nepali diasporic community in Oxford reported that a family did not feel at home because they believed their deities and ancestral spirits were not living in their dwelling as it had not been consecrated through rituals. This is similar to one of the respondents of this study for whom cultural performance is a way to make their dwelling 'homely': this is why she feels her home is protected by gods and her family deities. This also affirms that cultural performance and rituals are an important way in which diaspora identities are formed (Levitt, 1998) and that elements of cultural practice or belief seem to travel when diasporas take them forward.

Through these cultural practices Nepalis engage with Nepal every day. These routines are the repositories of their cultural identity and sense of belongingness. At times of 'national crisis' these feelings are galvanised into the allegiance to home that stimulates and shapes their 'homeland' travel. The experiences of memory and belongingness produced during the national crisis strongly follow the path of nationalist discourse. Homeland visits in essence are the expression and mobilisation of memory and belongingness that help reaffirm their root identity and sense of diasporic consciousness.

An important aspect of this account is its contribution to the study of newer and less researched diasporic groups. The Nepali case represents a valuable addition to the body of scholarship on diasporic consciousness and its embeddedness in homeland travel narratives. It elucidates the important interaction of 'home', memory and belongingness in everyday diasporic practices and its articulation in homeland travel narratives. It also showed us how memory is transmitted through tangible objects and intangible practices. However, it must also be appreciated that the expressions in this chapter are influenced by the devastating April earthquake and it can be fairly assumed that the results could be different at ordinary times: future studies should focus on this in the normal 'home' context.

References

Adhikary, K. (2012) *Nepalis in the United Kingdom: An Overview.* Reading: Centre for Nepal Studies United Kingdom.

Al-Ali, N. and Khoser, K. (2002) *New Approaches to Migration? Transnational Communities and the Transformation of Home.* London: Routledge.

Antonsich, M. (2010) Searching for belonging – an analytical framework. *Geography Compass* 4 (6), 644–659.

Armstrong, J.A. (1976) Mobilised and proletarian diasporas. *American Political Science Review* 70 (2), 393–408.

Baldassar, L. (1997) Home and away: Migration, return and 'transnational' identity. *Communal/Plural* 5, 230–249.

Barth, F. (1981) Ethnic groups and boundaries. In *Process and Form in Social Life: Selected Essays of Fredrik Barth: Volume* (pp. 198–227). London: Routledge & Kegan Paul.

Barth, F. (1994) Enduring and emerging issues in the analysis of ethnicity. In H. Vermeulen and C. Govers (eds) *The Anthropology of Ethnicity: Beyond Ethnic Groups and Boundaries* (pp. 11–32). Amsterdam: Het Spinhuis.

Basu, P. (2004) My own Island home: The Orkney homecoming. *Journal of Material Culture* 9 (1), 27–42.

Bess, K., Fisher, A., Sonn, C. and Bishop, B. (2002) *Psychological Sense of Community: Theory, Research, and Application.* New York: Plenum Publishers.

Bhandari, K. (2013) Imagining the Scottish nation: Tourism and homeland nationalism in Scotland. *Current Issues in Tourism.* DOI:10.1080/13683500.2013.789005

Bista, D.B. (1996) *Fatalism and Development: Nepal's Struggle for Modernisation.* Patna: Orient Longman.

Bohme, H. (1993) Atmosphere as the fundamental concept of a new aesthetics. *Thesis Eleve* 36, 113–126.

Boym, S. (2001) *The Future of Nostalgia.* New York: Basic Books

Braasch, B. (2008) *Major Concepts in Tourism Research – Memory.* Leeds: Centre for Tourism and Cultural Change (CTCC), Leeds Metropolitan University.

Brettell, C. (2006) Introduction: Global spaces/local places: Transnationalism, diaspora, and the meaning of home. *Identities* 12 (3), 327–334.

Brown, J. (2011) Expressions of diasporic belonging: The divergent emotional geographies of Britain's Polish communities. *Emotion, Space and Society* 4, 229–237.

Brubaker, R. (1996) *Nationalism Reframed: Nationhood and the National Question in the New Europe.* Cambridge: Cambridge University Press.

Brubaker, R. (2005) The 'diaspora' diaspora. *Ethnic and Racial Studies* 28 (1), 1–19.

Brusle, T. (2012) Nepali diasporic websites: Signs and conditions of a diaspora in the making. *Social Science Information* 51 (4), 593–610.

Christou, A. (2011) Narrating lives in emotion: Embodiment, belonginess and displacement in diasporic spaces of home and return. *Emotion, Space and Society* 4, 249–257.

Cohen, R. (1997) *Global Diasporas: An Introduction.* Seattle: University of Washington Press.

Coles, T. and Timothy, D.J. (2004) 'My field is the world' conceptualising diasporas, travel and tourism. In T. Coles and D.J. Timothy (eds) *Tourism Diasporas and Space* (pp. 1–29). London: Routledge.

Connerton, P. (1989) *How Societies Remember.* Cambridge: Cambridge University Press.

Datta, A. (2010) The translocal city: Home and belonging among East-European migrants in London. In K. Brickell and A. Datta (eds) *Translocal Geographies: Spaces, Places, Connections* (pp. 10–27). London: Ashgate.

Duval, D.T. (2004) Conceptualising return visits: A transnational perspective. In T. Coles and D.J. Timothy (eds) *Tourism Diasporas and Space* (pp. 50–61). London: Routledge.

Ehn, B. and Lofgren, O. (2009) Routines made and unmade. In E. Shove, F. Trentmann and R. Wilk (eds) *Time, Consumption and Everyday Life: Practice, Materiality and Culture* (pp. 99–114). Oxford: Berg.

Elliott, J. (2005) *Using Narrative in Social Research.* London: Sage.

Fowler, S. (2003) Ancestral tourism. *Insights*, March, D31–D36.

Gale, T. (2009) *Urban Beaches, Virtual Worlds and 'the End of Tourism', Mobilities* 4 (1), 119–138.

Gellner, D. (2013) Warriors, workers, traders, and peasants: The Nepali/Gorkhali diaspora since the nineteenth century. In D. Washbrook and J. Chatterjee (eds) *Routledge Handbook of South Asian Diasporas* (pp. 136–150). Abingdon and New York: Routledge.

Gellner, D. (2015) Associational profusion and multiple belonging: Diaspora Nepali in the UK. In N. Sigona, A. Gamlen, G. Liberatore and H. Neveu Kringelbach (eds) *Diasporas Reimagined: Spaces, Practices and Belonging* (pp. 78–82). Oxford: Oxford Diasporas Programme.

Halberstam, J. (2005) *In a Queer Time and Space.* New York: New York University Press.

Hausner, S. and Gellner, D.N. (2012) Category of practice as two aspects of religion: The case of Nepalis in Britain. *Journal of American Academy of Religion* 80 (4), 971–997.

Hepburn, S.J. (2002) Touristic forms of life in Nepal. *Annals of Tourism Research* 29 (3), 611–630.

Hughes, H. and Allen D. (2010) Holidays of the Irish diaspora: The pull of the 'homeland'? *Current Issues in Tourism* 13 (1), 1–19.

Hutt, M. (1998) Going to Mughlan: Nepali literary representations of migration to India and Bhutan. *South Asia Research* 18, 195–214.

Jaworski, A. and Coupland, N. (1999) Introduction. In A. Jaworski and N. Coupland (eds) *The Discourse Reader* (pp. 1–44). London: Routledge.

King, B. (1994) What is ethnic tourism? An Australian perspective. *Tourism Management* 15 (3), 173–176.

Kleres, J. (2010) Emotions and narrative analysis: A methodological approach. *Journal for the Theory of Social Behaviour* 41 (2), 182–202.

Larsen, J. (2008) De-exoticing tourist travel: Everyday life and sociality on the move. *Leisure Studies* 27 (1), 21–34.

Leite, N. (2005) Travels to an ancestral past: On diasporic tourism, embodied memory, and identity. *Antropologicas* 9, 273–302.

Levitt, P. (1998) Local-level global religion: The case of U.S.-Dominican migration. *Journal for the Scientific Study of Religion* 37 (1), 74–89.

Lowenthal, D. (1995) *The Past is a Foreign Country.* Cambridge: Cambridge University Press.

Marschall, S. (2012a) Tourism and memory. *Annals of Tourism Research* 39 (4), 2216–2219.

Marschall, S. (2012b) Personal memory tourism and a wider exploration of the tourism-memory nexus. *Journal of Tourism and Cultural Change* 10 (4), 321–335.

Marschall, S. (2015a) 'Homesick tourism': Memory, identity and (be)longing. *Current Issues in Tourism* 18 (9), 876–892.

Marschall, S. (2015b) Touring memories of the erased city: Memory, tourism and notions of home. *Tourism Geographies* 17 (3), 332–349.

McCain, G. and Ray, N.M. (2003) Legacy tourism: The search for personal meaning in heritage travel. *Tourism Management* 24 (6), 713–717.

Mensah, I. (2015) The roots tourism experience of diaspora Africans: A focus on the Cape Coast and Elmina Castles. *Journal of Heritage Tourism*, DOI:10.1080/1743873X.2014.990974

Mulligan, A.N. (2002) A forgotten 'greater Ireland': The transatlantic development of Irish nationalism. *Scottish Geographical Journal* 118 (3), 219–234.

Nash, C. (2002) Genealogical identities. *Environment and Planning D: Society and Space* 20 (1), 27–52.

National Planning Commission (2015) *Post Disaster Needs Assessment Executive Summary.* Government of Nepal: Kathmandu.

Nowicka, M. (2007) Mobile locations: Construction of home in a group of mobile transnational professionals. *Global Networks* 7 (1), 69–86.

Pariyar, M., Shrestha, B.G. and Gellner, D. (2014) Rights and a sense of belonging: Two contrasting Nepali diaspora communities. In J. Pfaff-Czarnecka and G. Toffin (eds) *Facing Globalisation in the Himalayas: Belonging and the Politics of the Self* (pp. 134–158). New Delhi: Sage.

Pink, S. and Mackley, K.L. (2014) Moving, making and atmosphere: Routines of home as sites for mundane improvisation. *Mobilities* DOI: http://dx.doi.org/10.1080/17450101.2014.957066

Ralph, D. and Staeheli, L.A. (2011) Home and migration: Mobilities, belonging and identities. *Geography Compass* 5 (7), 517–530.

Rapley. T. (2007) *Doing Conversation and Document Analysis.* London: Sage.

Rauniyar, D. (2015) Samsmaran, Bhukanpapachi America dekhi Nepal samma. See http://www.onlinekhabar.com/2015/06/285942/ (accessed 20 July 2015).

Riessman, C.K. (2003) Performing identities in illness narrative: Masculinity and multiple sclerosis. *Qualitative Research* 3 (1), 5–33.

Santos, C.A. and Yan, G. (2010) Genealogical tourism a phenomenological examination. *Journal of Travel Research* 29 (1), 56–67.

Schiller, N.G. and Fouron, G. (2002) Long-distance nationalism defined. In J. Vincent (ed.) *The Anthropology of Politics* (pp. 356–365). Oxford: Blackwell Publishing.

Sheller, M. and Urry J. (2004) *Tourism Mobilities: Places to play, Places in Play.* London: Routledge.

Singh, R. (2015) Man mailo ra bicharma birko laagepachi. See http://global.setopati.com/america/710/ (accessed 22 July 2015).

Siwakoti, S.L. (2015) Tan Americama bhayepani man Nepalmai ghumirahancha. See http://global.setopati.com/america/713/ (accessed 14 August 2015).

Smart, A. (1993) Gifts, bribes, and guanxi: A reconsideration of Bourdieu's social capital. *Cultural Anthropology* 8 (3), 388–408.

Stephenson, M.L. (2002) Travelling to the ancestral homelands: The aspirations and experiences of a UK Caribbean Community. *Current Issues in Tourism* 5 (5), 378–425.

Stephenson, M.L. (2004) Tourism, racism and the UK Afro-Caribbean diaspora. In T. Coles and D.J. Timothy (eds) *Tourism Diasporas and Space* (pp. 62–77). London: Routledge.

Subba T.B. (2008) Living the Nepali diaspora in India: An autobiographical essay. *Zeitschrift fur Ethnologie* 13 (2), 213–232.

TAAN (2009) Send Home A Friend campaign to run till 2010. See http://www.taan.org.np/news/755-send-home-a-friend-campaign-to-run-till-2010 (accessed 20 June 2015).

The Asia Foundation (2015) *Aid Recovery in Post-Earthquake in Nepal: Independent impacts and recovery monitoring phase 1*. Kathmandu: The Asia Foundation.

Timothy, D.J. (1997) Tourism and the personal heritage experience. *Annals of Tourism Research* 24 (3), 751–754.

Timothy, D.J. and Boyd, S.W. (2003) *Heritage Tourism*. England: Prentice Hall.

Timothy, D.J. (2008) Genealogical mobility: Tourism and the search for a Personal Past. In D.J. Timothy and J.K. Guelke (eds) *Geography and Genealogy: Locating Personal Pasts* (pp. 115–136). Aldershot: Ashgate.

Tolia-Kelly, D. (2004) Locating processes of identification: Studying the precipitates of re-memory through artefacts in the British Asian home. *Transactions of the Institute of British Geographers* 29 (3), 314–329.

Urry, J. (1995) *Consuming Places*. London: Routledge.

Urry, J. (1996) How societies remember the past. In S. Macdonald and G. Fyfe (eds) *Theorizing Museums* (pp. 45–65). Oxford: Blackwell.

Urry, J. (2000) *Sociology Beyond Societies: Mobilities for the Twenty-first Century*. London: Routledge.

Urry, J. (2002) Mobility and proximity. *Sociology* 36 (2), 255–274.

Urry, J. (2007) *Mobilities*. Cambridge: Polity Press.

Van den Berghe, P. and Keyes, C. (1984) Introduction: tourism and re-created ethnicity. *Annals of Tourism Research* 11 (3), 343–352.

Vathi, Z. and King, R. (2011) Return visits to the young Albanian second generation in Europe: Contrasting themes and comparative host-country perspectives. *Mobilities* 6 (4), 503–S18.

Wood, R. (1998) Touristic ethnicity: A brief summary. *Ethnic and Racial Studies* 21 (2), 218–241.

Wright, A.S. (2009) Destination Ireland: An ancestral and emotional connection for the American tourist. *Journal of Tourism and Cultural Change* 7 (1), 22–33.

Yang, M.M.H. (1994) *Gifts, Favors, and Banquets: The Art of Social Relationships in China*. Ithaca: Cornell University Press.

7 Collecting Kinship and Crafting Home: The Souveniring of Self and Other in Diaspora Homeland Tourism

Jillian L. Powers

Introduction

Homeland tourism is a growing industry where organizations representing a variety of American diasporic communities now sponsor group tours in order to provide further context regarding unknown, lost or broken ancestral links (Newland & Taylor, 2010). These structured tours (facilitated by tour agencies and mediated by tour guides) combine leisure travel with pilgrimage, bringing groups of travellers both to standard landmarks commonly seen by all tourists (such as the Wailing Wall in Jerusalem and the Great Wall of China) and to places of particular interest to those looking for connections to their heritage (such as the slave castles in Ghana and particular orphanages in China). More than just a journey to witness sights and sites, the homeland tour invites tourists to discover commonality and articulate a natural and ineffable connectedness – a fundamental kinship with those they encounter. Working within the controlled and structured tourist landscape, homeland tourists are encouraged to develop understandings of place, self, society – and the relations of these three with each other – in an environment that is both foreign and familiar. Examining the categories they inhabit, and primed for transformative self-reflexive inquiries, homeland tourists negotiate and explore the boundaries of Self and Other.

Homeland tourism can be understood as a subset of personal heritage tourism (e.g. Timothy, 1997). These sorts of journeys include family reunions and travels to places associated with one's past or religious beginnings. Sabine Marschall has defined personal heritage tourism as journeys in search of roots where travellers visit 'sites associated with one's family or community heritage,' in order to 'delve into the past' and find 'new context for

132

understanding their own self in the present' (2012: 329). These memories of the past provide the raw material from which heritage travellers craft their identities. However, 'if the memories are of one individual's, their associations extend far beyond the personal' (Kuhn, 2002: 4). Memory is a social activity that binds individuals together into larger social groups (e.g. Dwyer, 2000; Edensor, 1997; Till, 2001). Thus, individuals use memory to find a sense of rootedness and imagine their communities into being.

There are homeland tours to many locales, including tours to Scotland (e.g. Birtwistle, 2005), Israel (e.g. Kelner, 2010; Powers, 2011), China (e.g. Louie, 2004), Armenia (Darieva, 2011), the Philippines (Garrido, 2010) and Ghana (e.g. Bruner, 1996; Holsey, 2008) among others, only beginning to pique the interest of researchers. To date, however, scholarship on the genre is limited and mainly evaluative and case-specific in nature. Research has found that homeland tourists from America work out their identity as Americans (Garrido, 2010; Louie, 2004), connect (or fail to connect) transnationally (Hartman, 2008), rewrite their pasts by shaping their ancestral biographies (Kelner, 2010), and position themselves in the future as environmental global custodians (Darieva, 2011). They also contribute to transnational political agendas (Carter, 2004) and are crucial for burgeoning homeland development projects like state-sponsored investments in infrastructure (Newland & Taylor, 2010). Yet, no study to date has yet to examine findings from across ethnic groups and homeland tours in an effort to reconcile, integrate and challenge these various claims. Regardless of the particularities of each place and tourist population, do tourists understand their experiences and journeys in similar frameworks? Can we work to understand homeland journeys outside of an ethnic lends in order to 'account for the ways in which – and conditions under which – this practice of reification, this powerful crystallization of group feeling, can work' (Brubaker, 2004: 10)?

Informed by recent constructivist scholarship, I treat ethnicity, nation and race as one integrated domain (e.g. Brubaker, 2009; Wimmer, 2013). In this framework, foundational categories do not reflect shared traits or commonalities, but rather larger processes of classification and categorization that accomplish specific aims. This allows me to expand the social field and go beyond case specificity.

I examine the homeland tour experiences of three groups of Americans[1] – Jewish American college-aged participants of Birthright-Israel, African-Americans travelling to Ghana, and adopted Chinese children and their American families travelling to China – in order to uncover any shared frameworks of interpretation (e.g. Strauss & Corbin, 1998: 80–81). As I show, homeland tourists from all three of these groups negotiate the substance of their ancestral and personal histories by strategically and creatively modifying kinship – an idiom of relatedness that draws, in varying degrees, from the universal human experiences associated with family. Family, as a social category resonates because it appears to represent and reflect the most fundamental form of belonging. 'Most of us imagine the family as a place of safety, closeness, intimacy; a place where we can comfortably belong and be accepted just as we are' (Kuhn, 2002: 1). By envisioning homeland natives as distant kin, tourists bridge the distance between Self and Other and create liminal communities of remembrance (Winter, 1999). This enables these tourists to access ancestry and thus root themselves to larger social groups that extend through time and space. By creating fictive kinship bonds and imagining family, homeland tourists transform homelands into home-spaces.

Familial stories, as Winter explains, are powerful because they are part of a wider code, 'perhaps even a "master code" of stories' that define who we are and how we got there (1999: 42). Yet, the creation of small-scale fictive kin-groups is a form of remembrance that is 'both powerful and brittle' (Winter, 1990: 60). As these imaginary kinsmen age – or in this case, as tourists return home – the 'substrate' that holds these 'cells of remembrance together' atrophy and lose their hold (1999: 60). However, the homeland tourist has a way to capture these moments. Like an insect preserved in amber, the traces of fictive kinship can live on in the souvenir.

Although souvenirs are 'often disregarded as impermanent in nature and lacking in value' (Collins-Kreiner & Zins, 2011: 19) to their possessor, they are imbued with hidden significance (Gordon, 1986; Hitchcock, 2000; Love & Kohn, 2001). They are intentionally purchased to commemorate the journey (Swanson & Timothy, 2012), and remind us of the people, places, experiences, and events that defined our time away (Cohen, 2000; Gordon, 1986; Love & Kohn, 2001; Stewart, 1993). By acquiring souvenirs, travellers 'freeze passing moments' (Collins-Kreiner & Zins, 2011: 18). Thus, souvenirs facilitate memory work; they serve as tangible reminders of our fleeting travel experiences (Smith & Reid, 1994). According to Love and Kohn (2011: 53) 'The souvenir tends to encourage and mediate the dialectic between Self and Other'. In the stories told around the souvenir, the boundaries between Self and Other blur. By collecting souvenirs, travellers capture traces of the Other that they can appropriate and incorporate into their own identity narratives upon return. Souvenirs therefore do more than just define the place visited; they characterize the tourist. By capturing or collecting traces of our journeys we reveal who we are, how we identify ourselves, and who we identify with (Anderson & Littrell, 1996; Fairhurst et al., 2007; Littrell, 1990; Littrell et al., 1994). The souvenir thus becomes a way to remind the traveller of a 'coherent identity ... a place in the world' (Said, 2000: 179). When we come across a souvenir resting upon a shelf, it can trigger a variety of sensorial memories (Haldrup & Larsen, 2006). In fact, in French, the word souvenir means 'to remember'. However, the word souvenir can also mean 'to get back to myself' (Collins-Kreiner & Zins, 2011: 18). For the homeland tourist, these two definitions rest comfortably together. In this chapter I show how homeland tourists travel to remember – they journey in hopes of accessing an ancestral, personal, or natal past and idealize the bonds of family in the process. Yet, in their travels, they add their traces to the initial story. The memories of both are held within the souvenir.

Methods and Cases

Ghanaian slavery/ancestry tours

Only 9.7% of captured and enslaved black bodies left for the Americas and the Caribbean from Ghanaian ports from 1700–1809 (Richardson, 1989: 17). Yet, Ghana has attracted the most diaspora repatriates (Dunbar, 1968; Jenkins, 1975: 152) and diasporic tourists owing to its economic stability and claim as the 'gateway to the Homeland' (Ghana Tourist Board). Inspired by Alex Haley's *Roots*, the aptly named Ghanaian Ministry of Tourism and Diasporan Relations began capitalizing on the increased interest and financial success of the diaspora and began organizing activities, events and constructing memorials designed to attract African-Americans and Afro-Caribbean tourists by focusing on Pan-African heritage and the trans-Atlantic slave trade (Ghana Ministry of Tourism). Forty castles and lodges (as described in official tourism material) used for the slave trade are located in Ghana with three sites designated by UNESCO as World Heritage sites. According to estimates, 10,000 African Americans visit Ghana each year (Zachary, 2001).

In 2007, I travelled with Sankofa Travel, a tour agency based in the capital city of Accra, and joined roughly 600 members of the African diaspora as they travelled for the Ministry of Tourism's diasporan events. These tours involved trips to landmarks, treks of natural wonders, visits to traditional native villages, and guided tours and ceremonies at slave castles and memorials. Consistent with recent literature, those travelling with Sankofa represented a well-educated middle class segment of the African American population (Bruner, 1996; Ebron, 1999; Holsey, 2008).

Sankofa relies on trip organizers to recruit participants. Barbara Jones, the coordinator of my Sankofa homeland tour, organizes tours to Africa every two years (interest permitting). The excursion I joined was around two weeks, and my tour group consisted of 21 African-Americans. While most of the tour was made up of retired women, there were two husbands and two single men. Sankofa tours had multiple groups travelling during our voyage, and we were frequently grouped together for meals, lodging and daily activities. Among these groups were alumni organizations from two universities, a loosely knit family reunion/church group, a group of retirees, and another group consisting of young professionals. Travellers on all of these tours ranged in age from 21 to 90.

At first, my fellow travellers had reservations about my involvement. Yet, by the end of our journey, my outsider status led to close bonds. Since my tour group consisted of mostly older women, I became a sort of adopted child. Gender worked to my advantage as well. The women on my tour made a concerted effort to watch over me in order to mitigate my obvious difference. For example, I was directed to keep close to the group when we stopped to shop at craft markets. If I showed interest in an item, someone would engage with the vendors on my behalf, acting as mediator and elder. Therefore, as an outsider both by age and race, I was allowed to ask the 'naïve' questions engaging with my fellow travellers as an inquisitive and respectful pupil.

Chinese adoption/heritage tours

Between 1971 and 2001, US citizens adopted 265,677 children from other countries, and more than one-quarter of those adopted came from China. Parents of adopted foreign-born children are generally white, in their late 30s to early 40s, college educated, and have high levels of income (e.g. Register, 1990). Transnational adoptive parents engage in what sociologist Heather Jacobson (2008) has called 'culture keeping' – the practice of incorporating aspects of the child's culture of origin in family rituals and activities. Exploring what it means to be Chinese primarily through the international adoption community, families attend heritage camps, participate in activities sponsored by groups such as Families with Children from China (FCC), eat at Chinese restaurants, watch films and television shows about China and celebrate holidays such as Chinese New Year. Although involvement in these communities and activities vary, the homeland tour is seen as a natural extension and the ultimate form of familial engagement with China.

Families embark on heritage tours lasting for 7 to 14 days, when their children are roughly between the ages of 6 and 14. Accompanied by English speaking guides, families visit tourist sites such as the Great Wall, the Summer Palace, the Terra Cotta Soldiers, adoption-specific sites such as the child's orphanage/welfare center, and iconic adoption cities such as Guangzhou. Homeland tours also schedule age-appropriate activities and performances. Although private tours do occur, as in other cases of homeland tourism, specialists encourage group tours since it is understood that excited travellers develop close bonds from the reflexive conversations around issues of significance and subjectivity (Turner, 1966).

I travelled to China with three families in 2008 with Panda Tours. In total, there were five Chinese daughters, two birth children and five parents. The children on this trip ranged in age from 8 to 12. Only one family visited the orphanage/welfare center where their daughter spent her first few months, and I was able to accompany the Elms family during their time in Farah's home city. Because I was younger than the parents, but older than the children, I existed as both an older kid and a younger adult.

As an adult, I was tasked with watching children and holding hands. However, since I was younger and unattached, I was also not quite seen as a full-fledged authority figure so I could joke, share in the private cultural worlds of children and play and tease with ease. I conducted in-depth and semi-structured interviews with seven of the participants travelling to China (both children and adults). To supplement such a small sample size, I also analysed news articles with user comments, adoption blogs and list-serves, homeland tour brochures and printed material provided by tour agencies.

Taglit-Birthright Israel

Now a half-billion-dollar joint initiative between the State of Israel, diaspora Jewish organizations and individual philanthropists, Taglit-Birthright Israel launched in 1999 to 'encourage Jewish continuity, foster engagement with Israel, and forge a new relationship among Jews around the world.'[2] Created by Michael Steinhardt and Charles Bronfman to 'plug the dam of assimilation' (Wohlgelernter, 2000) seen occurring in the United States, Birthright sponsors ten-day complimentary tours of Israel for Jewish young adults ages 15 to 26 throughout the diaspora. Although concern over Jewish-American identity is not new (Rawidowicz, 1987), directing resources towards the unaffiliated was seen as risky. Yet, by the end of the summer of 2007, more than 160,000 young Jews from North America went on Birthright.[3]

On tour, participants see old and new, the devout and the secular. They gaze upon Holocaust memorials and museums, contemporary Jewish life and Zionist and biblical Jewish history. Birthright works to present Israel as a diverse nation, an exemplar of the pluralism and possibilities of Judaism, while still presenting the Jewish people as possessing distinct values and rituals. This representation allows those who might not see themselves as traditional or exemplar models of Jewish living feel a connection to a foreign land and a similarity with those speaking a different language.

In 2005, I travelled to Israel with a campus-based Jewish organization. Joining the other Taglit-Birthright tour groups from around the globe, our bus consisted of Jewish undergraduates from two different American universities. While I travelled with college students, I interviewed a mix of college and graduate students, as well as young professionals between the ages of 19 and 24 from across the US travelling with Taglit between 2005 and 2011. Primarily recruited through snowball sampling and my own Birthright trip in 2005, these young adults travelled with independent tour companies with affiliations to campus-based Jewish organizations such Hillel or Chabad, or toured Israel in regional and age-specific groups.

Souveniring Lives and Identities

Traces of a 'tribe;' Jewish essentialism

Homeland tourists have many similarities with leisure tourists. They too travel away from home for short periods of time in order to experience something outside the confines of the everyday (Graburn, 2004). Interacting as excited observers, tourists gaze upon towns and cities for classic examples of their already preconceived notions of place (Urry, 1990). For example, the first contact Birthright tourists have with Israeli sights such as the Western Wall in Jerusalem is not necessarily the site itself, but some representation thereof. If there is one image burned into the psyche of every Hebrew school attendee, it is some variation of an image of the old city of Jerusalem. Tacked to classroom walls or bulletin boards, a frayed and possibly sun-damaged poster has become utterly ubiquitous. However, even when this image becomes banal and overly familiar, the golden Dome of the Rock demands one's attention.

'You can't ignore it,' Zach, one young professional stated. However, the attraction that Zach speaks of here exists below this shining edifice. Beneath that golden dome in the Old City of Jerusalem sits the most unassuming and most potent Jewish landmark. Built by Herod the Great in 19 BCE, the Western Wall or Kotel 'was once the retaining wall for the Temple's foundation,' one Hillel travel guide detailed. Yet, 'all that is left of the entire ancient Temple complex is this single simple structure.' For Jews, the Western Wall has been a site of prayer and pilgrimage for centuries. Owing to the gravitas of place and its significance in shared Jewish collective memory, travellers are prepared and anticipate moments of intensely felt spirituality. 'It's just such an important place to go see, everyone tells you,' Zach declared. 'I grew up hearing about the Wall in Hebrew school,' Ben shared. 'This is a place you've learned about and heard about,'[4] another confirmed. To Zach and these other American Birthright travellers, the Western Wall is Jewish canon, thus no trip to Israel is complete without a visit.

Tourists blend kin concepts (incorporating elders, extended family, ancestors, childhood routines and family rituals) with Jewish signifiers to articulate these affective and indescribable connections. For example, Gaby, a recent college graduate, explained the overwhelming emotions she felt at the Western Wall and the transformation that occurred when she came face to face with one of the most significant sites of Jewish history and Jewish symbolism. She begins with her Jewish American life. 'This was the Wall that I was facing from New Jersey for the last twenty-five years,' she shared. 'It's been in the Torah, and has been known by all of my ancestors, and here I am touching it.'

The worn stones feel durable under Gaby's palm as she traces her fingers around the crumbling mortar. For Gaby and others, this is a sacred space because it's a lasting space. The Wall's very materiality allows her to expand her consciousness and travel back through time. As she works to connect to a past, she claims these ancient homeland natives as kin. This is a place where ancestors, 'thousands of years ago,'[5] might have walked, stood, and prayed. As Gaby's fingers linger, centuries melt away as she envisions direct routes to the people of the past. 'I had a hard time believing that I had ancestors so long ago,' she shared. 'But I could just picture thousands of people, more than thousands, millions of people, from biblical times to modern times coming here and crying and asking questions.' With one hand upon the Wall, she discovers that Jewish roots have great depth – she finds ways to extend imagined schemas of relatedness. Gaby however, doesn't just travel back in time; she travels *through* time. 'From biblical times to modern times,' she envisions a fundamentally bound somewhat unchanging social collective that traverses temporal boundaries (Mead, 1929).

'When I touched the Wall, it was empowering,' Jacob, a young man from the Midwest explained. 'I felt myself grow strong and weak at the same time. Weak with how much history there was and how in the scope of everything, how insignificant I felt in the history of Judaism, and empowered at the same time because here was this holy symbol still standing, everyone was gathered around it. It was one of the most incredible things I've ever seen.' When Jacob recalls his experience he combines a variety of frameworks, all with ineffable undertones, to describe the Wall, and his relationship to it. First, Jacob, like many others, highlights the holiness of this space. While the divine appears beyond description, by touching the stone, the ineffable becomes clear and the symbolic becomes tangible. Through touch he can envision his place within a larger fundamentally connected group. However, like other homeland encounters with sacred spaces that facilitate movements through time and space, he speaks in contrasts. Jacob explains how he feels both strong and weak. He explodes the boundaries of Jewish identification and roots himself to a people with an unending presence.

Taglit travellers speak with confidence and reverence when they talk about their time at the Kotel. 'I remember when I first walked up to the Kotel, it was almost like the wind struck at just that moment,' Nicole stated as she worked to create a sense of fundamental significance by painting a multi-sensory memory. However, when we were in Israel, Nicole approached the Wall with hesitation. She's an easy going and kind young woman with a tall athletic build. She talks often about her basketball playing days in high school. At the Kotel, due to her height, she felt noticeable. She pushed the long bangs that she's trying to grow out of her forehead and kept her hands busy by restyling her messy ponytail. As she fidgeted, she watched, trying to absorb any necessary yet unspoken cues regarding codes of conduct. She shifted her weight awkwardly and stared openly at the women gathered around – they clutched their tattered prayer books then intimately placed their foreheads on the stone. Amidst all the solemnity, Nicole felt inept. 'I wanted to say a prayer,' she explained

> but I didn't know what to say. So I went up to a woman who was with her family and asked her if there was a prayer I could say. She grabbed for my hands and held them when she told me that anything I said, God would hear. She was holding my hand as she told me this. That made me tear up because I felt like I was her daughter and she was helping me.

At the Kotel, without much to go on, she felt unable to appropriately commemorate her experience because she is unfamiliar with Hebrew prayers. While Israel is a secular nation, Nicole envisions a fundamentally religious space; and as a secular and American Jew, she struggles to find a way to extend relatedness.

While Nicole identifies as Jewish, she's not very religious. Ever since she moved out of her parents' home to attend college, she's let her religious practice lapse. While her parents attend synagogue regularly, and have made the trip to Israel a few times, she never had an interest. 'That was their thing,' she explained. She's not involved in her campus Jewish organizations, and had to be 'strongly encouraged' to go on Birthright. With distance between herself and her actual family, Nicole turns towards a stranger and creates kin. The woman rewards Nicole's choice; this fictive mother reassures her – there is no right answer or right prayer. Nicole walks away from this encounter with confirmation that her Jewish self (and a Jewish imagined community) does not hinge on her knowledge of religious practice; it exists at a more fundamental level deep within the core of her being.

Paradoxically, to Nicole, the response of this imagined mother-figure contrasts the mundane ritualized participation demanded by family back home. 'All these years our parents taught us all these things,' Liz, one young woman similarly explained. In their everyday lives these personal heritage tourists passively accept their parents' approaches. 'I wasn't very religious, I never got the connection, but my family was. I was only Jewish because my parents were,' Nicole shared. Yet, like many Birthright participants, Nicole felt obligated to participate. 'I think everyone, a lot of people, feel pressure to be Jewish from their parents, grandparents, and great-grandparents,' stated tour facilitator Rachel. Back home, Jewish engagement feels like work. In her daily life, Nicole doesn't feel any control or individualized connection to formal ceremonial Jewish rituals. However, by travelling away to Israel, she can connect to something more fundamental – she reaffirms the primordial nature of a bond she has only ever experienced as something religious and formulaic.

'I feel more Jewish now, it's almost like you feel like yourself or you understand part of who you are more,' Nicole concluded. Separated in time and space from her every day, this brief encounter feels transcendent and contains elements of the sacred. 'I think that anytime somebody understands where you come from, it's just like if you are an orphan and you finally meet your grandparents after 18 years – you find a little bit of yourself inside that,' she concluded. By imagining this woman as kin, she bridges any sort of distance between Israelis (assumed to be religious) and travelling secular Jewish-American Birthright participants. 'Coming to Israel it doesn't matter what kind of Jew you are, religious or Reform. If you're a Jew, you're a Jew, and you're accepted,' another participant exclaimed. Kin concepts thus turn homelands into home-spaces, since 'everyone treats you as family.'

'I've been to youth groups, I've been to synagogue. I've experienced a sense of family, of course. Just not like that,' Jacob shared. Jacob is a thoughtful and sensitive young man. However, if you were to look at him, you'd probably dismiss him as an apathetic holdover from the day's metal and grunge ruled the airwaves. He's a musician with longish curly hair, a penchant for heavy metal and rock band t-shirts, and still sports a metal chain-link wallet chain. In our interview after his Hillel-organized tour, he spoke frequently about feeling like an outsider in multiple spaces. He talked at length about how isolated he felt as a Jew in his hometown. According to Jacob, as a member of a religious minority, he found it hard to make friends in a predominately Christian town. He hoped college would be different; he joined a Jewish fraternity and tried to get involved with Jewish campus-based organizations. Yet, Jacob still felt like he didn't belong. When others spoke about their lavish Bar or Bat mitzvahs or summers spent at camp or in Israel, Jacob kept silent. He couldn't relate since he did not have a similar privileged upbringing like many of his Jewish peers. Not only does Jacob feel marginalized as a Jew in America, he believes he exists on the margins of Jewish communal life as well. However, in Israel, Jacob finds something he's been searching for – a sense of belonging and a rightness to his Jewish self.

The moral remaking that Jacob refers to, as Durkheim explains, 'can be achieved only by means of meeting, assemblies, or congregations in which individuals, brought into close contact, reaffirm in common their common feelings.' ([1915] 2001: 322). Although Jacob is familiar with the religious foundations of Judaism and goes (albeit sometimes) to synagogue, in Israel he learned something 'they can't teach you in Hebrew School.' Instead of passively engaging in Jewish communities, here he participates. In contrast to Hebrew school or synagogue, these embodied practices are sensory and thus offer more insight regarding ways to be Jewish. To communicate the feelings of intensely felt solidarity, Jacob deploys kin concepts to link past experiences to his newfound present embodied self. When he needs to be reminded of this after his 10-day tour, Jacob turns to one particular souvenir.

'I find it to be a beautiful and exhilarating thought. I can make a home for myself there, it's given to me as my home. Sitting on my nightstand is the Birthright necklace they gave us shopping in one of those malls in Jerusalem. They gave it to everybody, but I still have mine,' Jacob exclaimed proudly.

This little trinket enables him to construct and reconstruct his sense of self on demand.

The necklace Jacob refers to is simple: dangling from a matte metal chain is a small charm with Birthright's logo. Yet, Jacob finds value in this mass-produced trinket because of how it was acquired (Gordon, 1986). It was given to him as a commemorative memento of his experience. Not everyone who travelled on our tour found this necklace to be meaningful. Many thought it was cheap, silly and a trite reminder of a heavy-handed journey. Yet, for Jacob, the necklace reminds him of a positive experience of being home-while-away. For Jacob, the souvenir is a way for him to collect traces of kinship and signal a shared identity. For Jacob, this necklace works as an 'intangible reminder' (McKercher & du Cros, 2002: 230) of a liminal experience where kin felt enduring and solid. Whenever he looks upon this necklace he can recall the memories of a brief time when the imagined community felt particularly tangible.

Tourists like those who participate in the Taglit program are driven to travel by the memory of iconic images (Urry, 1990). And, like all tourists, they collect souvenirs while away to not only remind themselves of the places they visited, but to prove that they were there (Gordon, 1986; Hitchcock, 2000; Love & Kohn, 2001). Yet, the souvenirs Nicole and Jacob collect do more than just remind them of the Kotel, or any other landmark, they serve as tangible relics of intangible experiences where they were able to feel the bonds of relatedness and thus actively create the substance of heritage. The souvenirs become ways to recall the feelings of home and connectedness they felt as they reshaped relational ties while away.

Collecting racial kinship

In Ghana there was always more time for shopping. We shopped covertly in hotel rooms, at open-air markets and while exiting and entering our bus. We had a running joke; counting down the days of our trip by how many shopping days remained. We showed off our wares to the other members, discussing where we would display it in our home, what we were going to use it for upon return and who would be receiving each piece. Like Christian pilgrims, we spent a significant proportion of our time shopping (Kaell, 2012). We tried on 'traditional' African clothes, commenting on which pattern looked better and where each dress could be worn. Experiences in the homeland become reportable through the narratives told around the souvenir (Stewart, 1993). The souvenirs we returned with reflected the connections we made and the identities we wanted to craft. In addition, whether it was a bracelet, a woodcarving, a replica of an Ashanti stool, or African clothing, shopping provided us with a sense of comfort and homelike stability. While Swanson and Timothy (2012) suggest that shopping helps tourists connect to their familiar routines, for us, shopping served as a way to connect two worlds. In Ghana, expressions of kinship both exposed the underlying tensions within our journey and opened up space for new frameworks of relatedness.

More than just an indicator of the culture in which it was created, the souvenir, as an object, 'transforms intangible experiences into tangible memories and enables us to freeze a passing moment' (Collins-Kreiner & Zins, 2011: 18). For many homeland tourists, these passing moments involve intensely felt feelings of collective solidarity. To put these affective experiences into words, like travellers to Israel, homeland tourists in Ghana idealized the bonds of kinship and family. For example, recent college graduate Anita encountered an older woman she called a 'grandmother.' Her reading of this moment demonstrates the power of extended and imagined racial kinship.

> During a festival in Ghana, thousands of miles away from my home ... I met my 'grandmother' ... [she] could hardly speak English and we could not make out [her] language either. But in that moment, I showed [her] a necklace I had recently purchased for my [real] grandmother ... At that moment, the tears fell. They fell not because I was sad or happy or angry but just because it was one of those moments where your spirit is full of joy because something so unexpected becomes expected. At that moment, my grandmother asked a question that rattled my soul. She asked where were my handkerchiefs to wipe my tears. In that moment, the tears flowed even more because in a country that holds my ancestry but is viewed by those in my own country as inferior, weak, and uncivilized – my grandmother taught me what it truly means to be a lady.

Back home, Anita cannot help but feel 'on the fringes' of society. She is unable to trace her ethnic origins in a country that reifies ethnic heritage and glorifies immigrant assimilationist success stories. In the US, racial classification has historically excluded African Americans from ethnic assimilation models (Alba & Nee, 2003; Glazer & Moynihan, 1970; San Juan, 1992). Excluding large segments of the population from celebrated discourses of multicultural diversity maintains the racist myth of black cultural inferiority (e.g. Pierre, 2004). Constantly aware that her historical traces are missing, devalued and dismissed, Anita is unable to access the value and import imbued within America's immigrant ethos.

Yet, at a festival in Ghana, surrounded by tourists and locals, Anita connects to one woman, and in the process, is able to heal some of the trauma she feels as a descendant of the trans-Atlantic slave trade. As Anita recalls, amidst the bustle that surrounded them, she showed this woman a necklace she has bought for her grandmother. For Anita, in that moment, time slowed as they created a 'family of remembrance.' While they could not communicate through words since they did not share a language, Anita envisions a connection based on a shared experience (Winter, 1999).

Anita reads kindness as kinship. Yet, this woman is not just kin; she's a *grandmother*, a sagacious elder capable of imparting wisdom. However, Anita's experience with this fictive grandmother differs from Nicole's experience with her fictive mother. While both appear wise, for Nicole, this encounter allows her to recast her own experience – she sees *herself* as deficiently Jewish and uses kin to craft new forms of Jewish relatedness that reaffirm the tribal or primordial character of the 'Jewish people.' Anita, on the other hand, rewrites racist ideologies depicting blacks as inferior, uncivilized, and a people without a significant history (Gordon & Anderson, 1999). To do this, Anita uses kinship to blur the borders between the representation of the Other and representations of the Self. This 'grandmother' stands as a symbol for Africa itself and embodies the inherent dignity and power stored within the black body (e.g. Harris, 1992). Unfortunately, their time together is brief. Nevertheless, Anita returns with a powerful totem. The necklace Anita carries back with her for her actual grandmother is now imbued with a 'golden memory' (McKercher & du Cros, 2002: 230).

By crafting kin, Anita discovers she can feel grounded 'thousands of miles away' from home. Unfortunately, the very medium used to encourage tourists such as Anita to feel attached and see Ghana, a foreign country, as home also contains within it forces that create distance and estrangement. Anita (like others travelling with Sankofa tours) sticks to well-worn paths and spends her time mainly in the touristic border zone – the pre-approved touristic settings meant to offer the traveller a comfortable introduction to place (Bruner, 2005). While Anita met a fictive grandmother at that itinerary-included festival, she also encountered many Ghanaians working within the tourist economy. For those working in the border zone, these are sites of work and opportunities for income; for tourists, they're places to discover and explore kinship and primordial belonging. These two contradictory intentions sometimes do not rest comfortably together.

In Ghana, tourists were not the only ones to creatively modify the relational web of kinship to suit their needs and desires. Craft retailers in touristic spaces use a variety of methods to attract interested buyers (Kean *et al.*, 1996; Popelka *et al.*, 1992). For example, children in Ghana swarmed our tour bus calling us Father, Mother, Auntie and Sister. They would approach as we exited the bus and ask for our name and where we were from, overwhelmed by the attention, we would dismissingly answer, trying to make polite conversations as we tried to hurry to the next attraction. Upon exiting, these child/vendors would then present us with personalized souvenirs adorned with our name, residence and kin-salutation and then give us the suggested price for this commemorative piece.

This overt use of the emotional and affective aspects of kinship was off putting to tourists. Souvenirs such as these were unwanted; they felt forced upon us since 'souvenirs are often attached to locations and experiences that are not for sale' (Stewart, 1993: 140). The commodification of kinship ties corrupted the moment and uncomfortably revealed how most of our encounters in the homeland existed within the 'calculative rationality of the market' (Shepherd, 2002: 192). By turning kinship into a commodity, these children transformed something sacred into the profane. Travelers dismissed the children because it made a spectacle of their desires. But, if a knick-knack is personalized, can you really say no to a disadvantaged child hailing you as a relative? Members of my tour group begrudgingly paid the children and thanked them.

The host/guest relationship is fraught with challenges because 'it is based upon obligatory reciprocity that moves hospitality and connection into the economic domain' (Cohen, 1984: 380). When I spoke to one young professional, Ryan, who travelled with a family reunion, about his time in Ghana, he struggled with the paradoxical pulls of banal returnee and celebrated tourist. 'I encountered individuals that reminded me of people that I knew or family members. It was like, wow, I'm in Ghana. I'm in West Africa but it felt like I was home to some degree.' He confirms roots by transforming Ghanaians into distant relatives. For Ryan, physical and behavioural parallels confirm shared sensibilities, yet it does more; it suggests a natural and effortless comfort when visiting a strange and new place. However, not all of Ryan's experiences in Ghana are pleasantly welcoming. 'I felt like a rock star and I didn't like that kind of greeting ... I didn't like the pseudo fame. I didn't like being approached [like] I was someone who was important or larger than life. Folks were always grabbing at you and reaching for you. I got really tired of it really quick,' Ryan exclaimed. Unlike a returning family member intimately welcomed into the fold, he cannot blend in because he's seen as someone important, someone 'larger than life.' In Ghana, Ryan feels exposed and uncomfortable. He wants to feel a sense of fundamental connectedness, but the reception he receives exposes him as an outsider. If kinship is associated with home, and home-spaces are routinely mundane, then Ryan is definitely not home. Tensions arise for Ryan because he cannot be both a celebrated tourist and a returning kinsman.

Other travellers in Ghana also had similar experiences. Jessica, a young woman travelling with Anita and her college alumni group, had a particularly revelatory experience with one local vendor in Ghana. Here, she was able to reconcile touristic distance with her desires for connection.

> I met one of the local artists who set up shop wherever he went ... He was trying to sell me his goods but by that time [I decided] I'm going to have to have a mean look on my face because ... I just [couldn't] handle it every time I got off the bus. He stopped me and I had my little face on. And he said, you know, you can still be nice. It hit hard. I pride myself on trying to be a good person to people. What ended up happening over the course of the trip was I would see him and I would tell people the story and point to his things so he actually sold a lot as a result.

Like Ryan, Jessica kept her guard up while walking through the border zone. The demands and assumptions of touristic economic power were laid bare during her repeated interactions with this aggressive vendor, and she doesn't like how it makes her feel. The persistence of vendors and their celebratory demeanour toward homeland tourists expose the tourist as outsiders, but most importantly, outsiders with money to burn. In these spaces of interactional intimacy, tourists worry that they are seen by homeland natives as inconsequential interlopers, superficially interested in the places they visit, comfortable consuming hyperreal simulacra, and easily separated from their disposable income. To prove that she is not someone who can be easily taken advantage of, Jessica changes her affect to one of haughty estrangement. As she explained, 'she put her little face on.' Jessica, thus, is now cast in the role of the tourist. She no longer feels like a welcomed relative and approaches all of her interactions with sceptical distance. He calls her out on her behaviour – 'you know you can still be nice,' he reminds her. In this moment, Jessica realizes that she has gone too far in her attempts to maintain and retain her sense of control while away.

As Dean MacCannell explains, when tourists commit gaffes, 'they are no longer innocent bystanders,' they are exposed as individuals requiring handling and thus learn 'how the tourist is seen by the other' (2011: 219). Feelings of disjuncture and disconnect, or 'unhomeliness,' are powerfully uncomfortable and not easily forgotten (Bhabha, 1994: 9). While Jessica feels uncomfortably vulnerable, she works to right her wrongs. Instead of focusing on her hurt feelings and further entrenching the distance between Self and Other, this encounter becomes a teachable moment. She 'tells people the story,' and as a result, he winds up selling a great deal of his art.

However, his art is not valued for its intrinsic aesthetic qualities (Brulotte, 2012; Graburn, 2004). The art from this particular vendor reminds buyers of a unique acquisition story (Littrell et al., 1993), and most importantly, a personal relationship. Fixed to his paintings is the memory of Jessica's uncomfortable encounter – and its ultimate resolution. Those travelling with Jessica purchase his work intentionally as a commemorative icon (Swanson & Timothy, 2012). Once they return to their everyday, whenever they look upon his art, homeland tourists can recall and share Jessica's revelatory experience. Thus, those who purchase from this particular vendor engage in a practice of collecting and souveniring an identity transformed.

Origin stories, adoptees, and others

'We'll never know anything about Farah's birth family,' Karen Elms, one adoptive mother explained to me, yet she ventured to China with her family to find context, connect to tender memories, and explore a country that gave her a daughter. Besides visiting standard 'touristy' sites, the Elms family also travelled back to Farah's Social Welfare Institute (SWI). At her orphanage, they hoped to find answers, and Karen saw them everywhere as she worked to construct and fill in a natal biography and chain of care. She scrutinized the environment 'in search of the smallest most elusive remnant of the past' (Marschall, 2012: 330). In China, Karen was on an exploratory journey to find evidence that, despite being abandoned, her child had never been truly discarded.

For example, at Farah's orphanage we were able to meet with the woman who had originally cared for her 12 years ago. Through our interpreter, Farah's *ayi* (caretaker) shared stories about her first year of life. The stories this woman shared were not extraordinary; there were no large revelations or sensational accounts, yet her fond recollections of the banality of family routine were familiar. Owing to idealized images of kinship, Karen found her meeting with this woman comforting.

> The best part for me was meeting Farah's nanny. I didn't expect her to remember Farah, yet it turned out that she remembered quite a bit about her and was able to answer some of the questions we've always had about those first several months of her life. It helped us make sense of her story. It was also wonderful to see that there is someone in China who really cares about her – someone who is emotionally attached to her.

Karen can't place her daughter in China until she can imagine Farah as part of her nanny's family. She can see Farah growing up in the nanny's apartment and interacting with her children. Karen thus expands the boundaries of kinship relationally and envisions an unbroken global chain of care (Hochschild, 2000; Parrenas, 2001). She comes to terms with Farah's abandonment by imagining a settled alternative that hinges on the genuine feelings of Farah's *ayi*. Nurturing becomes the most salient aspect of relatedness as Karen herself crafts kinship in China.

By finding and reconnecting to Farah's nanny, the Elms family was able to transform a foreign space into a home space. Molly Elms, Farah's older sister and Karen's biological daughter, also uses kinship to understand her relationship to Farah's caretaker. As Molly explains:

> I have never had a personal connection to someone in China before. It seemed like everyone there was like strangers to me, and that we didn't have very much in common. However, meeting the nanny and her family showed me that I did have a connection with China, that a family there actually shared a sister with me, at least for a short while.

As a white American teenager, most of China was foreign to her and the assumptions of primordial belonging did not apply. In China Molly is an outsider – she does not possess any perceived inherent connection to China, nor can she overlay her American lived experience to understand the people and culture she encounters. However, the roles and expectations she associates with kin allow her to selectively extend the boundaries of belonging across national borders and cultural differences. By imagining nanny as a distant relative Molly moulds a stranger into kin (Hertz, 2009).

As evidenced by the Elmses' experience, adoption tours facilitate travels through time. However, the bonds of the past have no hold on the kinships of the present. While these two families (and two nations) might 'share a sister,' as Molly stated, families envision a clear break between their daughter's institutional life and her new life with a loving family (Duncan, 1993; Yngvesson, 2005).' Nanny was like your first mother and Mom is like your second,' Molly explained in the van heading back to the hotel. Karen corrected her, 'Nanny is more like her second. I'm her third mother.' Thus, families envision a linear and bracketed version of time in order to root the adoptee firmly within her American family.

Adoptive families, like the Elmses, travel to come to terms with abandonment and institutional beginnings. They also return to China to memorialize connection. As one brochure explained, agencies create opportunities for families to 're-capture the sweet memories during their first initial meeting with their adorable little ones.' In these locales, for parents, even the most 'banal objects and spaces may be perceived as powerfully loaded with meaning' since these are the sites where the imagined bonds of kinship finally became tangible (Marschall, 2012: 330). As one mother detailed: 'Madeline became our daughter in a conference room at the Gloria Plaza Hotel in Nanchang on the night of 10 November 2005. I'll never forget those anxious last minutes spent waiting in our hotel room for the all-important call.'[6]

By returning, parents memorialize the transfer of their child, and breathe new life into origins stories for those members of the family too young to remember. As 'gatekeepers' of family memory, mothers return with their adopted daughters to extend relational ties back towards an imagined China (Hurdley, 2007; Kaell, 2012; Miller, 1998). Through travel, they welcome those without direct memories to envision themselves in the past. For example, as adoptive mother Allyson recounts her return to the 'red couch' at the White Swan hotel, she overlays the present onto her memories of the past like semi-transparent layers of film, and invites her daughter to travel with her through time:

> In the hotel, we took pictures of their indoor waterfall and of 'The Red Couch,' with all of the girls seated upon it. To see them all sitting in the same couch ten years later looked so funny because they are much bigger now than when they were babies.[7]

Allyson's daughter Jessica, however, recognizes the 'red couch' not from memory, but as a key feature in a cherished family photograph. 'I liked visiting the red sofa at the White Swan because my mom and dad had showed me a picture of 6 babies sitting on this sofa 10 years ago. I can't believe it has been 10 years since I sat on that sofa.'[8] Encounters with symbolic elements offer Jessica the opportunity to take ownership of her personal biography. Homeland tours thus offer families new platforms for retelling origin stories where adoptees can now be active agents in their own narration.

Yet, as Winter has explained, 'when performing the past, we never dip our toes in the same stream twice. Rituals and commemorations change their meaning even while appearing to retain an older grammar of remembrance' (2010: 17). Adoptees add their own traces to these journeys. As experiences on the homeland tour become legends and tall tales, told and retold over the items travellers return with, the interpretive frames used to recall the journey demonstrate how families define their boundaries and articulate their identities. Shopping offers families the opportunity to socialize children regarding middle-class touristic values and tastes, and the souvenirs they return with become constant reminders of the adoptee's rightful place within her American family. Unlike travellers to Ghana and Israel who souvenir a form of imagined and extended kinship, adoption homeland tourists collect 'chipped off pieces of the Other' (Love & Kohn, 2011: 53) to affirm the kinship bonds of the nuclear unit. Raised on 'culture bites' (Anagnost, 2000) – the easily accessible, decontextualized, and dehistoricized symbolic aspects of Chinese culture – adoptees souvenir kitsch-ship.

'Shopping is perhaps the most ubiquitous of all tourist activities and an extremely important leisure pursuit' (Collins-Kreiner & Zins, 2011: 17). Research shows that when there are more opportunities to shop and more venues for shopping, visitors find the place more appealing (Moscardo, 2004; Timothy, 2005). Yet, in China, adoptive families were not that interested in stopping at the many itinerary-included 'factory' stores. These stops were presented as exclusive 'behind the scenes' opportunities to buy direct from the manufacturer. Billed as attractions unto themselves, these factory stores failed to meet the needs and interests of adoption homeland tourists. Whereas large tour groups of Western retirees, alumni organizations, or upper-middle-class 'pseudo-adventurers' come ready to spend and see their expensive souvenirs as status markers (Bruner, 2005), the families I travelled with did not see themselves as typical leisure tourists and did not like being treated as such. We were on a homeland tour, our very presence was grounded upon the assumption that there was a relational connection between the adopted daughter and her homeland – yet, the structure of our journey appeared to cater to any general tourist. The large parking lots, well air-conditioned showrooms, and English-speaking salesclerks were meant to serve large Western tour groups. While we had signed up for a guided journey through China, the parents wanted a mediated yet intimate encounter with roots and connectedness that one does not get at an itinerary-included 'factory store.'

'When we adopted Farah, we bought really nice, expensive souvenirs for our families, so this time we were just looking for funny or cute little inexpensive things for our friends and family,' Karen explained. Adoptive families were not first-time visitors intent on commemorating their journey by means of conspicuous consumption. Since parents had already been to China they had no strong desire to collect souvenirs to remind them of a 'once-in-a-lifetime' journey (Collins & Zins, 2011). On the contrary, parents felt they were already familiar with China owing to their original adoption journeys, and enjoyed watching their children delight in the stereotypical and commercially available cheap souvenirs that entice first-time visitors (Smith & Olson, 2001). Instead of the big-ticket items for sale at 'factory' stores, the girls were more interested in the mass-produced stuffed pandas and Olympic memorabilia – items to be found in any street-corner souvenir shop.

As one photograph of Anna posing in front of a display case full of stuffed pandas suggests, she *enjoyed* the overly materialistic world of touristic space. And because the children do, so do their parents. This photo of Anna is one of her mother's favorites because 'Anna has always been a panda nut. She has a huge collection of stuffed pandas and her most beloved stuffed creature that she sleeps with is a panda. To see her in front of *so* many stuffed pandas – and in China, the birthplace of the panda – really makes me smile.' The stuffed pandas, jade charms, and Chinese calligraphy on display complement their own symbolic models of culture keeping, thus confirming the bonds of the family. Converting experience into a souvenir, this photograph presents a frozen moment of family togetherness, documenting 'the project of "our family"' (Lofgren, 1999).

Much of tourism is a search for the photogenic, a scavenger hunt during which tourists try to accumulate iconic images of the Other that will later be used to animate identity and narrate personal and family memories and stories. Photographs and souvenirs serve as 'mnemonic device[s] for storytelling' (Bruner, 2005: 24), cultural referents that reflect the preconceived notions and ideals tourists bring with them. For example, while Karen and her family balked at the factory tours, they later recalled with delight how they had 'spent a few days on a hunt for the funniest butchered English tee shirts for friends who would appreciate the humor.' Like the pilgrimage tourist returning with religious souvenirs that reaffirm their religious identity, the homeland tourist maintains and reinforces their American social bonds and identities through their souvenir purchases (Kaell, 2012).

Ordinary items can have sentimental value and become a souvenir as a result of the manner in which it was acquired (Gordon, 1986). Key to the experience was bargaining over the prices of t-shirts, back scratchers, and table-top 'butt-less frogs.' As Karen explained, 'Bargaining for souvenirs was the most important thing for us – we had fun getting good deals.' Children discover no strict blueprint exists in China to structure an economic exchange. The homeland tour was a way for Karen to nurture a certain identity in her children. As she continued, 'I've had a lot of experience with that (Mexico, Greece, Morocco), but it was a first for the kids.' Interactions in the border zone are thus exercises in socialization. When parents like Karen introduce their children to the kinds of interactions permissible in foreign locales, they foster a certain touristic consciousness thus furnishing children with opportunities to *become* tourists and see themselves as Americans abroad. 'There is cachet connected with international travel,' states Nelson Graburn (1979: 2–3), and adopted children access that symbolic value through acquiring kitschy souvenirs. Instead of using the souvenir to connect, the souvenir thus reveals the adoptee's distance and her identity as a travelling American.

Conclusion

'A tour is a story in the making,' Edward Bruner (2005) reminds us. The experience of being away might be brief, but the memory of the journey lives on in the mementos we return with and the stories we share. In our retelling, 'like snapshots in a family album,' (MacCannell, 1976: 15) we connect the disparate pieces of our journey together and craft one overarching narrative. For the homeland tourist, this is a tale of 'getting back to the self.'

The places homeland tourists travel to resonate since these are places of primordial, ancestral and natal origin; these are travels to *roots*. Thus, like the personal heritage tourist, the homeland tourist travels in order to find evidence of a shared culture and a shared past. However, in the present, rootedness implies a sense of familiarity, a comfortable intimacy and a natural closeness – a feeling of connectedness based upon a shared essential 'common grammar.' While this sort of fundamental connection is thought to occur 'by virtue of some unaccountable absolute import attributed to the very tie itself' (Geertz, 1973: 259), the attachments to home are created by familiar routines and regular daily interactions (Fried, 2000). These attachments therefore involve a banal familiarity with backstage spaces that homeland tourists do not possess. To bridge this distance, homeland tourists transform encountered others into distant kin – while away, perceived kin are seen everywhere.

Heritage is thought to be a natural, almost genetic or primordial phenomenon, but as I show, in the end, it is something that needs to be engaged with to be achieved. Across all three cases, tourists use kinship to extend the boundaries of belonging and engage with heritage. For travellers to Israel and Ghana, kinship is based upon a shared fundamental primordial bond, that manifests differently based on different histories and personal experiences. For adoptive families, kinship is based on a shared set of practices and obligations. This legitimizes the created bonds of adoption and allows these bonds to exist alongside natal allegiances. While kinship is extended for different reasons, it affectively resonates because it offers space for the mundane and the sacred to blend. It involves the assumptions of connectedness that come from a natural affinity plus the sense of intimate closeness that is based on a shared everyday banality. Thus, kinship is a powerful framework for bridging the distance between Self and Other.

While homeland tourists are interested in encountering an Other that also represents the Self, as we see, this encounter can sometimes be troubling. Homeland tourists travel with baggage. They spend most of their time in touristic spaces, are approached and seen as outsiders – tourists – and, might not even desire connecting in the first place. However, when they recall their journeys, they do not highlight the discomfort that comes with liminality. The neatly constructed story, told through the souvenir, is one of success. Souvenirs, across all cases, are 'objects of transition, of in betweenness, which mediate the past and the present and the domestic and the public' (Morgan & Pritchard, 2005: 46). Valued for their ability to transport the homeland tourist back through time, souvenirs serve as totems for multisensory memories. Held within the souvenir are stories of encounter and ultimate transformation based on the resolution of Self and Other.

Travel is challenging, as Karen explained: 'I feared that I made a terrible mistake bringing my children halfway around the world on my own.' However, she continued, 'everything worked out by that first morning and I felt a huge sense of accomplishment when we made it back to the U.S.' Although theirs was definitely a structured tour – and structured tours are chosen precisely because they manage variability – Karen's comment suggests that even that kind of travel can transform novice tourists into accomplished travellers. Together, as a unit, they bargain, explore, get lost, overpay, and must come together to understand the varied interactions they have. When family members look upon the souvenirs they return with, they remember a great adventure. 'Which, like all adventures,' as one adopted father explained, 'would bring us closer together.'

Notes

(1) I use pseudonyms for respondents and small organizations and disguised or omitted identifying details. Quotations from respondents are transcribed from recorded interviews unless otherwise noted. When citing open source material, I have not changed any of the names, since they are publicly available.

(2) Maurice and Marilyn Cohen Center for Modern Jewish Studies Website. See http://www.brandeis.edu/cmjs/researchareas/taglit-birthright.html (accessed 15 June 2012).

(3) Maurice and Marilyn Cohen Center for Modern Jewish Studies Website. See http://www.brandeis.edu/cmjs/pdfs/Herzilya.0221081.pdf (accessed 7 March 2011).

(4) 'Birthright gives students new perspectives on Judaism, Israel,' Kevin Criscione. Thursday February 2, 2012. *The Tufts Daily*. See http://www.tuftsdaily.com/birthright-gives-students-new-perspective-on-judaism-israel-1.2694092#.UNI6WLakBzR (accessed 19 December 2012).

(5) 'Birthright recruits participants despite international conflict,' Sophie Barrios. September 21, 2014. *The Miami Hurricane*. Student Newspaper. See http://www.the

miamihurricane.com/2014/09/21/birthright-recruits-participants-despite-interna
tional-conflict/ (accessed 10 April 2015).
(6) 'The Chinese Adoption Effect,' Diane Clehane. August 2008. *Vanity Fair.* See http://
www.vanityfair.com/culture/features/2008/08/adoption200808 (accessed 6
November 2015).
(7) Gladney Heritage Tours. Stories. Allyson & Jessica Macci. Seehttp://gladneyasia.org/
pages/stories/macci.html (accessed 27 August 2013).
(8) Gladney Heritage Tours. Stories. Allyson & Jessica Macci. See http://gladneyasia.org/
pages/stories/macci.html (accessed 27 August 2013).

References

Alba, R. and Nee, E. (2003) *Remaking the American Mainstream: Assimilation and Contemporary Immigration.* Cambridge MA: Harvard University Press.
Anagnost, A. (2000) Scenes of misrecognition: Maternal citizenship in the age of transnational adoption. *Positions – East Asia Cultures Critique* 8 (2), 389–421.
Anderson, L.F. and Littrell M.A. (1996) Group profiles of women as tourists and purchasers of souvenirs. *Family and Consumer Sciences Research Journal* 25 (1), 28–56.
Bhabha, H.K. (1994) *The Location of Culture.* London: Routledge.
Birtwistle, M. (2005) Genealogy tourism: The Scottish market opportunities. In M. Novelli (ed.) *Niche Tourism* (pp. 59–72). Oxford: Butterworth-Heinemann.
Brubaker, R. (2004) *Ethnicity without Groups.* Cambridge, MA: Harvard University Press.
Brulotte, R. (2012) *Between Art and Artifact.* Austin, TX: University of Texas Press.
Bruner, E. (1996) Tourism in Ghana: The representation of slavery and the return of the black diaspora. *American Anthropologist* 98 (2), 290–304.
Bruner, E. (2005) *Culture on Tour: Ethnographies of Travel.* Chicago: University of Chicago Press.
Carter, S. (2004) Mobilizing *Hrvatsko*: Tourism and politics in the croatian diaspora. In T. Coles and D. Timothy (eds) *Tourism, Diaspora and Space* (pp. 188–201). London: Routledge.
Cohen, E. (1984) The sociology of tourism: Approaches, issues, and findings. *Annual Review of Sociology* 10, 373–392.
Cohen, E. (2000) Souvenir. In J. Jafari (ed.) *Encyclopedia of Tourism* (pp. 547–548). London: Routledge.
Collins-Kreiner, N. and Zins, Y. (2011) Tourists and souvenirs: Changes through time, space and meaning. *Journal of Heritage Tourism* 6 (1), 17–27.
Darieva, T. (2011) Rethinking homecoming: Diasporic cosmopolitanism in post-Soviet Armenia. *Ethnic and Racial Studies* 34 (3), 490–508.
Dunbar, E. (1968) *Black Expatriates.* New York: Dutton.
Duncan, W. (1993) Regulating intercountry adoption – an international perspective. In A. Bainham and D.S. Pearl (eds) *Frontiers of Family Law* (pp. 46–61). London: Wiley and Sons.
Durkheim, E. (2001 [1912]) *The Elementary Forms of Religious Life.* New York: Oxford University Press.
Dwyer, O. (2000) Interpreting the civil rights movement: Place, memory, and conflict. *Professional Geographer* (52), 660–671.
Ebron, P. (1999) Tourists as pilgrims: Commercial fashioning of transatlantic politics. *American Ethnologist* 26 (4), 910–932.
Edensor, T. (1997) National identity and the politics of memory: Remembering Bruce and Wallace in symbolic space. *Environment and Planning: Society and Space* 2 (15), 175–194.
Fairhurst, A., Costello, C. and Holmes A.F. (2007) An examination of shopping behavior of visitors to Tennessee according to tourist typologies. *Journal of Vacation Marketing* 13 (4), 311–320.

Fried, M. (2000) Continuities and discontinuities of place. *Journal of Environmental Psychology* 20, 193–205.

Garrido, M. (2010) Home is another country: Ethnic identification in Philippine homeland tours. *Qualitative Sociology* 31 (1), 177–99.

Geertz, C. (1973) *The Interpretation of Cultures: Selected Essays*. New York: Basic Books.

Glazer, N. and Moynihan D.P. (1970) *Beyond the Melting Pot: The Negroes, Puerto Ricans, Jews, Italians, and Irish of New York City*. Cambridge MA: MIT Press.

Gordon, B. (1986) The souvenir: Messenger of the extraordinary. *Journal of Popular Culture* 20 (3), 135–146.

Gordon, E.T. and Anderson M. (1999) The African diaspora: Towards an ethnography of diasporic identification. *Journal of American Folklore* 112 (445), 282–297.

Graburn, N. (1979) *Ethnic and Tourist Arts: Cultural Expressions from the Fourth World*. Berkeley, CA: University of California Press.

Graburn, N. (2004) Authentic Inuit art: Creation and exclusion in the Canadian North. *Journal of Material Culture* 9 (2), 141–159.

Graburn, N. (2004) The Kyoto Tax Strike: Buddhism, Shinto, and Tourism in Japan. In E. Badone and S.R. Roseman (eds) *Intersecting Journeys: The Anthropology of Pilgrimage and Tourism* (pp. 125–39). Urbana: University of Illinois Press.

Haldrup, M. and Larsen, J. (2006) Material cultures of tourism. *Leisure Studies* 25 (3), 275–289.

Harris, E.L. (1992) *Native Stranger: A Black American's Journey into the Heart of Africa*. New York: Vintage Books.

Hartman, S. (2008) *Lose Your Mother: A Journey Along the Atlantic Slave Route*. New York NY: Farrar, Straus and Giroux.

Hertz, R. (2009) Turning strangers into kin: Half siblings and anonymous donors. In M.K. Nelson and A.I. Gary (eds) *Who's Watching?: Daily Practices of Surveillance among Contemporary Families* (pp. 156–174). Nashville: Vanderbilt University Press.

Hitchcock, M. (2000) Introduction. In M. Hitchcock and K. Teague (eds) *Souvenirs: The Material Culture of Tourism* (pp. 1–17). Aldershot: Ashgate.

Hochschild, A.R. (2000) Global care chains and emotional surplus value. In W. Hutton and A. Giddens (eds) *On The Edge: Living with Global Capitalism* (pp. 130–136). London: Jonathan Cape.

Holsey, B. (2008) *Routes of Remembrance: Refashioning the Slave Trade in Ghana*. Chicago: University of Chicago Press.

Hurdley, R. (2007) Objecting relations: The problem of the gift. *The Sociological Review* 55 (1), 124–143.

Jacobson, H. (2008) *Culture Keeping: White Mothers, International Adoption, and the Negotiation of Family Difference*. Nashville: Vanderbilt University Press.

Jenkins, D. (1975) *Black Zion: The Return of Afro-Americans and West Indians to Africa*. London: Wildwood House.

Kaell, H. (2012) Of gifts and grandchildren: American Holy Land souvenirs. *Journal of Material Culture* 17 (2), 133–151.

Kean, R. C., Niemeyer S. and Miller N.J. (1996) Competitive strategies in the craft product retailing industry. *Journal of Small Business Management* 34 (1), 13–23.

Kelner, S. (2010) *Tours that Bind: Diaspora, Pilgrimage, and Israeli Birthright Tourism*. New York: New York University Press.

Kuhn, A. (2002) *Family Secrets: Acts of Memory and Imagination*. London: Verso.

Littrell, M.A. (1990) Symbolic significance of textile crafts for tourists. *Annals of Tourism Research* 17, 228–245.

Littrell, M.A., Anderson L.F. and Brown P.J. (1993) What makes a craft souvenir authentic? *Annals of Tourism Research* 20, 197–215.

Littrell, M.A., Baizerman, S. *et al.* (1994) Souvenir and tourism styles. *Journal of Travel Research* 33 (1), 3–11.

Lofgren, O. (1999) *On Holiday: A History of Vacationing*. Berkeley, CA: University of California Press.

Louie, A. (2004) *Chineseness Across Borders: Renegotiating Chinese Identities in China and in the U.S.* Durham NC: Duke University Press.

Love, L. and Kohn H. (2001) This, that, and the other: Fraught possibilities of the souvenir. *Text and Performance Quarterly* 21 (1), 47–63.

MacCannell, D. (1976) *The Tourist: A New Theory of the Leisure Class*. University of California Press.

MacCannell, D. (2011) *The Ethics of Sightseeing*. University of California Press.

Marschall, S. (2012) 'Personal Memory Tourism' and a wider exploration of the tourism-memory nexus. *Journal of Tourism and Cultural Change* 10 (4), 321–335.

McKercher, B. and du Cros, H. (2002) *Cultural Tourism: The Partnership between Tourism and Cultural Heritage Management*. New York: Haworth.

Mead, G.H. (2010 [1929]) The Self, the I, and the Me. In C. Lemert (ed.) *Social Theory: The Multicultural Readings* (pp. 224–229). Philadelphia: Westview Press.

Miller, D. (1998) *A Theory of Shopping*. Cambridge: Cambridge University Press.

Morgan, N. and Pritchard A. (2005) On souvenirs and metonymy: Narratives of memory, metaphor, and materiality. *Tourist Studies* 5 (1), 29–53.

Moscardo, G. (2004) Shopping as a destination attraction: An empirical examination of the role of shopping in tourists' destination choice and experience. *Journal of Vacation Marketing* 10 (4), 294–307.

Newland, K. and Taylor, C. (2010) Heritage tourism and nostalgia trade: A diaspora niche in the development landscape. *Migration Policy Institute*. September 2010. See http://www.migrationpolicy.org/pubs/diasporas-tradetourism.pdf (accessed 31 July 2012).

Parrenas, R. (2001) *Servants of Globalization: Women, Migration, and Domestic Work*. Stanford, CA: Stanford University Press.

Pierre, J. (2004) Black immigrants in the United States and the 'cultural narratives' of ethnicity. *Identities: Global Studies in Culture and Power* 11 (2), 141–70.

Popelka, C.A., Fanslow A. and Littrell M.A. (1992) Profiles of success: Mexican textile handcraft entrepreneurs and their businesses. *Home Economics Research Journal* 20 (4), 235–253.

Powers, J. (2011) Reimagining the imagined community: Homeland tourism and the role of place. *American Behavioral Scientist* 55 (10), 1362–78.

Rawidowicz, S. (1987) *Israel: The Ever-Dying People and Other Essays*. Fairleigh Dickinson University Press.

Register, C. (1991) *'Are Those Kids Yours'? American Families with Children Adopted From Other Countries*. New York: Free Press.

Richardson, D. (1989) Slave exports from west and west-central Africa, 1700–1810: New estimates of volume and distribution. *Journal of African History* 30 (1), 1–22.

Said, E.W. (2000) Invention, memory, and place. *Critical Inquiry* 26 (2), 175–192.

San Juan, E. (1992) *Racial Formations/Critical Transformations: Articulations of Power in Ethnic and Racial Studies in the United States*. Amherst, NY: Prometheus Books.

Shepherd, R. (2002) Commodification, culture and tourism. *Tourist Studies* 2 (2), 183–201.

Smith, R.K. and Olson L.S. (2001) Tourist shopping activities and development of travel sophistication. *Visions in Leisure and Business* 20 (1), 23–33.

Smith, S.L.J. and Reid, L.J.N. (1994) Souvenirs of tourism scholarship. *Annals of Tourism Research* 21 (4), 855–857.

Stewart, S. (1993) *On Longing: Narratives of the Miniature, the Gigantic, the Souvenir, the Collection*. Durham: Duke University Press.

Strauss, A. and Corbin, J. (1998) *Basics of Qualitative Research: Techniques and Procedures for Developing Grounded Theory* (2nd edn). Thousand Oaks, CA: Sage.

Swanson, K. and Timothy, D. (2012) Souvenirs: Icons of meaning, commercialization and commoditization. *Tourism Management* 33 (3), 489–499.

Till, K.E. (2001) Reimagining national identity: 'Chapters of Life' at the German Historical Museum in Berlin. In P.C. Adams, S. Hoelscher and K.E. Till (eds) *Textures of Place: Exploring Humanist Geographies* (pp. 273–299). Minneapolis: University of Minnesota Press.

Timothy, D.J. (1997) Tourism and the personal heritage experience. *Annals of Tourism Research* 24 (3), 751–754.

Timothy, D.J. (2005) *Shopping Tourism, Retailing and Leisure*. Clevedon: Channel View Publications.

Turner, V. (1966) Liminality and communitas. In V. Turner (ed.) *The Ritual Process: Structure and Anti-Structure* (pp. 94–130). Chicago: Aldine Publishing.

Urry, J. ([1990] 2002) *The Tourist Gaze*. London: Sage.

Wimmer, A. (2013) *Ethnic Boundary Making: Institutions, Power, Networks*. New York: Oxford University Press.

Winter, J. (1999) Forms of kinship and remembrance in the aftermath of the Great War. In J. Winter and E. Sivan (eds) *War and Remembrance in the Twentieth Century*. Cambridge University Press: Cambridge.

Winter, J. (2010) Introduction: The performance of the past: Memory, history, identity. In K. Tilmans, F. Van Vree and J. Winter (eds) *Performing the Past: Memory, History, and Identity in Modern Europe* (pp. 11–34). Chicago: University of Chicago Press.

Wohlgelernter, E. (2000) The arrival of an idea. *The Jerusalem Post*, January 7, p. 05b.

Yngvesson, B. (2005) Going 'home' adoption, loss of bearings, and the mythology of roots. In T.A. Volkman (ed.) *Cultures of Transnational Adoption* (pp. 25–48). Durham, NC: Duke University Press.

Zachary, P. (2001) Tangled roots: For African Americans in Ghana, the grass isn't always greener – seeking the 'Motherland', they find echoes of history and a chilly welcome. *Wall Street Journal*, March 14, Section 1A, 1–2.

8 Returning, Imagining and Recreating Home from the Diaspora: Tourism Narratives of the Eritrean Diaspora in Italy

Anna Arnone

Italy is currently at the frontlines of the European migration juncture and its watery borders are constantly stained with the blood of migrants trying to reach Europe by boat. The present 'migration crisis' has been widely analysed in the way European and Italian structural apparatuses are failing to safeguard the lives of millions of people both in their crossing of the Mediterranean and in the detention centres that host them once they cross Europe's borders (Mezzadra & Neilson, 2012; Mountz, 2011; Pinelli, 2015). Such securitization strategies are also becoming a great source of anxiety and insecurity for the local population (Orsini, 2016) demonstrating that we are confronted with a systemic dysfunction (O'Kane & Arnone, 2016) which urgently needs to be dealt with both academically and politically. Migration in Italy is not a novelty, but the European peninsula has been dealing with transient, diasporic communities for decades with diverse socio-political approaches (as seen in Grillo & Pratt, 2002) and outcomes (i.e. Carter, 1997; Cole, 1997). Categories of people and citizenship have been building up a particular morality of welfare where voluntarism has become a systemic strategy (Muhlenbach, 2012) also to supply outreach to recent migrant arrivals in Milan and elsewhere. The Eritrean community in Milan provides an insight into such long-term diasporic relationships with Italy, not only in terms of the Eritrean transnational politics of identity, but also because the Ertitrean presence shows colonial and postcolonial ties and negotiations with Italian political discourses and apparatuses (Arnone, 2014, 2017).

The Eritrean community in Milan is small and difficult to estimate in numbers since many individuals are not inhabiting the city with a regular permit and many do not dwell in Milan for a long period; others are on the move to different countries. Many migrants may be using city spaces and meeting the rest of the Eritrean community in Milan, but reside in the hinter-land and would thus not be registered among the city's residents. ISTAT (2015) counted 1579 Eritreans in 2003, rising up to 2819 in 2011, and back to 1610 by 2015. The community of Eritreans in Milan is important first of all because it was one of the first migrant communities in the city, and most of all because the Eritrean transnational politics in Milan was particularly lively and visible. Eritreans in Milan were actively participating in the struggle of the Eritrean Peoples' Liberation Front (EPLF) and their political loyalty was transferred to the ruling party, the Eritrean People's Front for Democracy and Justice (EPFDJ). In Milan this faithfulness has been particularly strong and opposition particu-larly silent compared to other Eritrean communities in Europe (Al-Ali et al., 2001; Koser, 2003). The supportive political stance that the Eritrean commu-nity held towards the Eritrean Government seems to be changing intensity, even in Milan (Martigoni, 2014). However, by describing the narratives of those who return we are able to understand the meanings Eritrea holds for these subjects and the political statements that return produces.

The political situation in Eritrea has become widely criticized by the international community. Researchers, intellectuals, journalists and human rights activists working on Eritrea are concerned about the political situation to the point that the negotiations with, and reproductions of, such power by the local population and its diaspora are often not contemplated enough in recent studies. The aim of my work on the Eritrean community has been to find people's responses amidst this troubled political environment by looking at the 'politics of little things', i.e. the actions of those who are not outspoken against the political status quo but who continue to engage with their coun-try, notably by returning 'home' during the summer. I have illustrated else-where how narratives of summer holidays in Eritrea exhibit the diaspora's touristic gaze and its objectification of Eritrea as a space where to find leisure and heritage (Arnone, 2011b). I described migrants' return as a sort of dia-sporic tourism and questioned its impact. Return can be understood as a neo-colonial reproduction of power relations by the Italian Eritrean Diaspora (Arnone, 2017). The importance of Italian status symbols which reflect power and work relations experienced by Eritreans in Milan resonates when they seek to reverse it during their holidays in Eritrea. When describing their holiday they are adamant to transform their belonging to the lower social class they inhabit in Italy to an identification with an 'Italianized' version of the upper middle class while in Eritrea.

This chapter aims at highlighting the political position of the returning diaspora by looking at the way in which people remember their home coun-try, their touristic practices and their narratives of tourism. It also sets to show how these narratives and memories are passed on to the second genera-tion through family tours of Eritrea. This research is the outcome of a 12-year-long engagement with a variety of Eritrean people in Milan. I carried out ethnographic fieldwork between 2003 and 2004 for my DPhil and have regularly returned to the field ever since to continue inquiring about the issues mentioned above. As Eritreans from Milan often moved on to other locations, some interviews were collected in Leiden and London in 2015. All the names of the informants have been changed to ensure anonymity, unless I describe their participation in a public speech or act.

The main methodology used for this specific chapter is narrative collection and analysis, in the form of descriptions of people's return to Eritrea both before departing from Milan and after the journey. Coleman and Crang (2002: 9) define narratives as a fundamental part of tourism studies:

> ... Tourism as a practice is not just gazing and viewing [...]. We see tourists fashioning stories about their travels – not in academic idiom, but through the collection, editing and sorting of photographs, travel diaries and memorabilia.

Not only have these narratives been noticed in the form of discursive developments of collective practices but also by observing the objects, pictures and practices linked to the diaspora's summer return. The narrative about returning is formed by the process of remembering their journeys home, which gives meaning to their lives.

> Rather than the circulation of people amid fixed places we need to notice the mobilisation of places through objects [...]. In other words we look at the dissemination of place. [...] it is not that place is eroded through tourism, but rather that the roles it performs in subjectification can no longer be equated with stability. (Coleman & Crang, 2002: 11)

This chapter therefore analyses narratives of returning home in order to understand what role Eritrea, as a space in the mind, has among the diaspora. Memories of collective struggles from exile are powerful in the making of Eritrean history and play a key role in the actual construction of Eritrea as a touristic place that the diaspora then describes. Remembering and returning home have a very peculiar relation to both the touristic practice of 'othering' oneself and at the same time 'belonging' to Eritrea by placing emphasis on certain aspects of history and heritage. Experiences of Eritrean return have not been clearly analysed by differentiating the migrants' subjectivities in previous research. This chapter instead presents a distinction of the narratives by the members of the first generation and the descriptions of the second-generation youth and highlights the impact that the adults' memories have on the youth.

Eritrean Transnational Participation

The Eritrean-Italian diaspora underwent a great deal of pressure over the years to continue its intimate relationship with the dominant class which took the lead of the newly born Eritrean state in 1993. The diaspora has been part of nation building (Arnone, 2014) and played into Eritrean politics while creating the nation. Here I quote part of an interview with Teodros, a man in his early 60s who explains what their transnational participation was like:

> The history I am about to tell you starts in the first years of the '70s, from the exiles, who were in Europe, starting from Germany, let's call them the intellectuals, who departed from the '68 movement around the world. That is when we can say the liberation movement really started with a clear intention, with the [Eritrean] university students' support from abroad. The exiles organised their political activities in *c'enfer* (cell) *Milan, c'enfer Turin, c'enfer Germany,* etc. All these cells were sections of a movement which regularly met locally and then annually in Bologna with all the European sections. From abroad we organised to give the freedom fighters, who were struggling in Eritrea, all the support they needed, economically, politically and by broadcasting the struggle in the public discourse. (Interview conducted during the 2004 festival in Milan)

Their power in the early rise of the Eritrean state has even prompted Ruth Iyob (2000) to call Eritrea a 'diasporic state'. Between the 1970s and 1993 the number of Eritreans abroad amounted to one fourth of the total national population: 1 million Eritreans abroad against only 3 million in Eritrea (Koser, 2003). Most of them left the country during the struggle for independence from Ethiopia, when the war became too violent to live safely in the country. The exiles who migrated in this period 'fought' the liberation war from abroad; they created networks and political organisations, developed political, social and cultural frameworks, linked their fight to other world struggles and were widely recognized for their political presence. Most Eritreans living outside the country made an effort to support the liberation movements by raising money to invest in Eritrea and worked on strategies for nation building (Arnone, 2008, 2014; Conrad, 2005; Hepner, 2009a; Matsuoka & Sorenson, 2005; Sorenson, 1990, 1991; Tecle, 2012). Conrad's (2005) informants told her how this affected their relationship with their children for whom they had less time since all their attention was focused on their nationalist struggle. Even my own informants remembered how their lives were dedicated to the cause which often meant that many did not even manage to build a family.

In Italy, the Eritrean network grew enormously, incorporating political ideologies and practices mostly linked to the EPLF movement. The latter network based in Italy was again connected with others scattered in Europe and the rest of the world. Italy became internationally important especially after organising the Eritrean Festival in Bologna where people of Eritrean origin from all over Europe and the world came to celebrate a common dream of self-determination and liberation from the Ethiopian empire and from the super powers previously playing a part in the Cold War and intruding into the Horn of Africa's geo-political affairs (Arnone, 2014). Milan was a stronghold of such movements with restaurants and bars owned by members of the EPLF, whose incomes directly fed into the movement. A vibrant community had been active since the 1970s and then it was officially registered as an association in the town hall in 1985, by Padre Marino, a Capuchin friar who supported the EPLF cause. People told me that it was he who signed the letting contract of the community hall space and registered the community's association statute. Before 1985 Eritreans in Milan had obtained permission to share the space of the Centro Sociale Leoncavallo, in its former venue in Via Leoncavallo. The Leoncavallo formed one of the most socially and politically active collectives of squatters in Milan until the mid-90s. It hosted the Eritrean EPLF militants and gave them the use of a room on the top floor, where the Eritrean exiles passed on their knowledge of Eritrean culture, politics and their native Tigrinya language to the youth (Andall, 2002). Such youth organisations were active in other Eritrean communities around the world. Eritrean youth organisations were called Red Flowers, *Keih Imbaba'* in Tigrinya, the official Eritrean language. The adults in Milan described how adamant they were to teach Tigrinya to their youth and to introduce them to their home country's history and culture.

When I was carrying out my fieldwork in Milan in 2003–2004, I heard frequent comments about the lack of spaces to share community life in Milan, be actively involved, discuss community matters, grieve for the death of loved-ones, have Tigrinya language classes for the children and Italian for the adults and many other activities that migrants used to run in the former community hall. In 1999 the community hall was closed due to the end of the lease and conflictual relations between the leading community members and the consulate. Eritreans were left with no community because no other suitable place had been found but also because nobody wanted to be the guarantor of the collective space which was acquiring a more and more politically loaded meaning of confrontation with the Eritrean political party in power. In 2005 the consulate moved to a bigger location with a community hall, which they hired thanks to the economic contributions of the local Milanese-Eritreans throughout the years. The choice of a hall run by the consulate and located inside the consular space was met with apprehension and disaffection by the people who had wished for a plural space where to share community life. Alganesh, in a conversation in 2014, argued that 'the community hall before was for all, this one is not'. By using the words 'for all' she was indeed hinting at the initial national project of the EPLF that aimed at forging national culture out of diversity (Woldemikael, 1993), which she did not find in the new location. In 2014 I asked Eritreans in Milan what they thought about the new community space: most did not even identify the consulate's space as 'the community', the only 'community' they acknowledged was the former one located in 'Via Friuli', run by various members of the community including members from the religious sphere, the women's activist groups, the EPLF supporters, and the youth organisation.

The organized activities aimed at the youth had thus been put on halt for many years and the second generation was integrated in the community by attending rituals of life cycles in religious contexts or celebrating national successes such the Liberation anniversaries. There is, however, an association of young Eritreans still active around the world, the National Union of Eritrean Youth (NUEY), which in Milan is run by the consulate. The NUEY is the association which organizes the *Zura Hagerka*, 'know your country' tour, for the youth to experience the places in Eritrea that are found significant to the history of the country.

Eritrean 'Bio' and 'Necro' Politics among the Diaspora

In 1991 Eritrea was liberated and in 1993 it was officially separated from Ethiopia. After more than 20 years, Eritrea is still under the same unelected leadership, the EPFDJ, formed by the activists of the EPLF. Soon another war began against Ethiopia (1998), lasting two years, causing an enormous number of casualties on both fronts and leading the country to an even worse economic situation than before. After 2000, when the Badme war ended, a strong change in the EPFDJ governing strategies occurred: a militarized reinforcement of the state took over civil society and people's daily lives became impregnated with state surveillance and increasing obligations towards the government. Since then Eritrea has enrolled all young men and women from the age of 17 into a social system that incorporates all citizens in an indeterminate national service, *hagärawi agälglot* in Tigrinya, to carry out various duties for the state (Bozzini, 2011). These duties essentially amount to forced labour and there are wide spread fears that such use of labour is being employed even by foreign companies (Anderson, 2015). The thousands of Eritreans currently arriving in Europe *en masse* and seeking asylum in various countries are crying out against this use of forced labour and the annihilation of human rights in Eritrea. The infrastructure of the country is maintained by an army of unwaged Eritreans. The outcome of such a militarized system has been analysed in various ways (Bozzini, 2011; Gaim Kibreab, 2009; Hepner, 2009a, 2009b; Hepner & O'Kane, 2009; Müller, 2012) and Eritrea has recently been labelled as one of the most repressive countries in the world (Evans, 2012 and UN statement on 16 March 2015) with very low or inexistent freedom of expression.

The Eritrean state's networked system of social control is not only enacted in Eritrea but even employed to constantly supervise the diaspora. The most discussed and noticeable practice of power by the state is the enforcement of a taxation system (Al-Ali et al., 2001; Koser, 2003), which enables the Eritrean state to trace migrants around the world in every move-ment they make from one country to another. A capillary system of surveil-lance (Bozzini, 2011) is in place to collect such diaspora-tax revenue. This taxation system acts as a *sine qua non* if migrants want to keep their relation-ship with the home country alive and even protect their family members at home (Tecle & Goldring, 2013). The latter prosecution is more visible in the most recent migration since the families in Eritrea of those fleeing from mili-tary service are often asked to pay a sum to the Eritrean state for their rela-tive's disappearance (Müller, 2012). Many studies are showing the effects of the Eritrean state's social control of the diaspora via the various forms of forced transnationalism (Al-Ali *et al.*, 2001; Campbell, 2009; Hepner, 2009a, 2009b; Koser, 2003). This complex relationship that the Eritrean state is enacting has been described by O'Kane and Hepner (2009) as 'biopolitics', drawing on Foucault (2009), whereas Bernal (2014) emphasizes practices of 'necropolitics' (see also Mbembe, 2003). The Eritrean state is forcefully implementing strategies and mechanisms through which not only the lives of people in Eritrea and the diaspora are controlled and managed, but even their deaths. By adapting to this structural apparatus the diaspora keeps their relation with their home-country alive and secures their families from being accused of harbouring possible oppositional positions and ideas (see Müller, 2012). The Eritrean state's monopoly of collective spaces in Milan and its overall use of force had great impact on the diasporic political participation which many people feel is going in 'a one-way direction'. My interlocutors in Milan were seldom openly critical of Eritrean political affairs in Eritrea during my early research in 2003–2004. Recent interactions (last year) pro-duced more outspoken responses. Just after the Badme war ended (late in the year 2000), people were still puzzled about the situation in Eritrea and fear-ful of saying anything. With the passing of time people realized that the situ-ation might not change; some are hence prepared to comment in private conversations about the current political stagnation. For example, in 2014, Lettebrahan, a lady in her late 50s, told me with a disillusioned voice:

Ah, these ones (meaning the government and their supporters) are crazy! I don't want to get involved because I'm scared of what could happen to me and my family if I say anything. I keep away from everything and everybody. I just work and see my family. Sometimes I go back to my country but I keep to myself.

Eritreans in the diaspora have demonstrated levels of disenchantment with the politics of the EPFDJ (about issues of political opposition among the diaspora see Al-Ali *et al.*, 2001; Hepner, 2009a) since it monopolized political power, excluding the participation of other political parties and any form of election. Bernal's (2014) latest book on the participation of Eritreans in online discussions shows that there is a strong polarization of different types of political discourses, creating great tensions which are nevertheless still linked by an inclination towards nationalism and dedication to Eritrea as a country. Eritrea is still perceived as the mother of all narratives. Bernal (2014), whose husband is Eritrean, states that she thought she had married an individual but realized that she had married a nation. Eritrea remains an essential part of one's identity and history whichever political position one holds. The politics of identity involved in such a diasporic group is central when trying to analyse how people understand, narrate and remember their return journeys to Eritrea during their holiday. It is however very important to note that, firstly, those who are actively participating in opposition groups do not return to Eritrea, and secondly, that not all people who visit their family in Eritrea reproduce the kind of narratives we are about to investigate.

Return for Holidays in Eritrea

Diasporic tourism is often referred to as a sort of heritage tourism carried out by members of diasporas. Mostly cited are the Jewish diaspora (Feldman, 2010; Kelner, 2010), the trans-Atlantic African diaspora (Bruner, 1996; Ebron, 1999), and the Scottish diaspora (Basu, 2004). Recent research has concentrated on Chinese descent returnees (Louie, 2004) and, interestingly, also adoptees of Korean birth from all over the world (Kim, 2010). In diasporic tourism, memory is triggered by the experience of 'returning' to an ancestral land, or home and visiting places that embody a collective identity with a heritage they start to 'remember' and recognize as theirs. Among returning Eritreans, it is extremely crucial to differentiate between those who return to the country of birth, where they grew up (first generation) and those who visit their parents' home country (second generation). Like many other diasporic tourists, members of the second generation of Eritrean diaspora presumably undertake such journeys to discover aspects of themselves, their ancestry, ethnic culture, and their parents' place of birth but for the first generation the meaning of these return journeys is more arduous to define. Time and space have transformed the migrants' status and their relationship with their home country. Moreover, the place itself changes (Coleman & Crang, 2002); Eritrea is no longer only home but also the country to be visited from abroad. Returning to Eritrea is, on the one hand, connected to a search for an individual and collective past in a heritage-tourism guise and, on the other hand, it is experienced through leisure tourism. In tourism, there is often something that links the 'outsider' with the place to visit and the tourist's travel with some degree of knowledge of the place (Selwyn & Scott, 2011: xvi). In their introduction to 'Thinking through Tourism', Selwyn and Scott (2011: xvi) argue that tourism seems to be explaining much of the complex world that we inhabit, in the sense that it is a lens through which to understand political, spatial, cultural and economic complexities. Diasporic tourism carried out by the returning migrants and their offspring offer a rich example of the meanings that such intricate practice unveils.

The Eritrean diaspora's experience of Eritrea as a place where they could be tourists in the country of personal or parental origin is interestingly marked by the way they return with tokens of holiday-making. Visits to places such as Asmara and Massawa were narrated with descriptions of the weather, leisure facilities and other characteristics that created nice and clear portraits of holiday locations for the members of both the first and second generation. Adults and youths of Eritrean origin in Milan spoke about the beautiful sights in Asmara, the petite, clean and safe capital, where they could find a variety of amusements, bars and restaurants. The weather and especially temperature in Asmara was always exalted as perfect for good health and pleasant living, contrasted with the heat in Massawa, which served to exoticize the seaside city. Emphasis was put on how impossible it was to go to the beach as much as they wanted to, since the temperature reaches 45/50 degrees Celsius. People thus spoke about recovering in air-conditioned hotel lounges, leisurely waiting for the heat to cool down. Their accounts of seaside attractions in Massawa and Dahlak islands reproduce tropes of sandy holidays on the Red Sea with camel rides, exotic fruits and air-conditioned hotels. Being accommodated in hotels in Massawa was described as a way of 'staying away from head lice and fleas'.

When speaking to both generations, Eritrea was not only described as the place to relax and pass time in cafes and hotels. For the adults of the first generation, in particular, it is also where a specific sort of history can be revisited and emphasized. Alongside other descriptions of his holiday, Adonay, a man in his 50s, had photographs of Nakfa, a town in the North West part of Eritrea, located in the Sahel mountains. Nakfa is by far the most meaningful and symbolic place for remembering the EPLF liberation movement. It is an important part of Eritrean liberation history narratives because it was the first town to be 'liberated' from the Ethiopian regime and it thus became the hub of the struggle. For this very reason, Nakfa is also the name chosen for the Eritrean currency introduced in 1997. Adonay described:

> Nakfa is where the EPLF started their successful struggle, since the town's liberation in 1977, Nakfa remained in the hands of the EPLF. After Nakfa's complete destruction by the Ethiopian forces, the EPLF started to build underground. There was a school, the press, a radio station and even a hospital. Local people used to help too, by bringing food and primary goods.

The town is also surrounded by trenches where the fighters fought, which still stand as a reminder of the struggle and its success.

This participant visited Nakfa on his month-long holiday in Eritrea. Reaching this town is not easy and it might take a ten-hour drive from

Asmara. He told me he had gone with a general, the general's son and the driver of the four-by-four vehicle. At the trenches, Tesfay had taken pictures of the general's son. On showing me the photos, he emphasized that the young man had been born there in those very trenches where he was depicted smiling for the camera. For Adonay returning to Milan with such pictures allowed him to show people what the liberation managed to do. All this was experienced more intensely because he visited the site with a freedom fighter whose son had been born in that very place. Thus the value of Nakfa was not only relegated to its embodiment of a precise history, particularly meaning-ful to the birth of the nation and its independence. The experience of visiting Nakfa was animated by the presence of a young man born in the EPLF's underground hospital. The grasp of a life history narrating Nakfa as the place for celebrating both life and death, those trenches echoed the successes of the liberation through time. Showing the picture of a young man born in those trenches Adonay put particular emphasis on how the liberation can be seen as having a living result, the boy pictured as the attainment and continuation of the liberation movement. Not many had managed to visit Nakfa in their summer Eritrean tours but it is a place which everybody nominates when describing the important sites where Eritrean history can be revisited.

Many also spoke about the National Martyrs' Park, a natural reserve instituted in 2000 in a location called *Ts'elot* on a hill on the outskirts of Asmara. 'It is situated on such a beautiful spot, the panorama is stupendous, if you go to Eritrea you should visit it', Haddas told me. The National Martyrs' Park is particularly symbolic for the diaspora because there was an important flow of donations and other sorts of fund raising which took place in 1998 among Eritreans living abroad for its establishment (Bernal 2014: 85). The liberation struggle lasted 30 years; not only did it claim the lives of an estimated 65,000 freedom fighters and tens of thousands of civilians, but it also had a grip on the exiles' lives, by riveting their time, passion and eco-nomic investment. The National Martyr's Park focuses on the glorification of the Eritrean 'martyrs', which includes those who died during the last struggle. Taddesse, a man in his 60s, told me that in Eritrea he visited such places where 'history can be celebrated and remembered with respect for those who struggled for our freedom'. The liberation struggle has become an important trope for diasporic tourism and people's narratives show their quest for sites such as museums and memorials to remember their collective history and honour the dead. Going to Eritrea is part of remembering their participation and personal experiences; these are sites where their Eritrean identity can be asserted and their participation as a diaspora remembered. By remembering and talking about their visit, members of the diaspora restore the intensity of their own commitment and reinvigorate the meaning that such struggle has had for the Milanese community of Eritreans.

The practice of bringing pictures and stories of their journey back from Eritrea served to remind others of this past, and ensured the continuation of such memory among the young Eritreans who have not experienced it. Amin, a man in his late 60s described the importance of transferring that memory:

> We need to pass down our history to the youth who have not experienced what their parents had done, the history of the Eritrean liberation and the struggle of their parents, their commitment to support the fight from exile. [...] The message to these young people is to think about their parents as the makers of such history, to think of them as young people who years ago set off to fight for their belief, for their ideals as Eritreans abroad fighting for the Eritrean liberation cause. (Milan, interview 2010)

Among Eritrean interviewees in Milan, ethnic traditions were not overly emphasized; rather they preferred to portray Eritrea as moving towards development. Tesfay for example brought back a pair of Western-style white trainers 'made in Eritrea' for his teenage son. He said that Eritrea was growing, 'developing'. Tesfay was a nationalist working as an 'odd-job man' for the Eritrean Council. His wife complained about his underpaid position: 'he is practically doing voluntary work for this government'. The act of bringing his son a pair of shoes made in Eritrea can be interpreted as part of the process of reproducing a specific political narrative about Eritrea, one that asserts that the nation needs no aid, no NGOs, no foreign interference. 'Eritrea is a unique country in Africa because it is self-reliant but nevertheless developing'. For those supporting the political status quo in Eritrea returning from the holidays was a way to reinforce the rhetoric that explains the extradition of many foreign NGOs, and even embassies, from Eritrea and the refusal to undergo any UN investigation in the country. The state thus speaks about self-reliance arguing that Eritrea manages without any outside donations and intrusions. Such narrative reproduced by those who return from Eritrea enacts a specific discourse about Eritrea. The gift for his son was part of the first generation's commitment, described by Amin, to pass on to the second generation not only the memory of the past but also a specific political understanding of the present.

Collective memory, Feldman (2010: 10) argues, brings the members of the group or community together while legitimating and fixing its bounded institutions. With such theoretical statement he is describing Jewish memory and continues by noting that memory allows the group to recognize itself through time and ensures the group's continuity by transmitting collective memory from one generation to another and by giving specific relevance to a variety of symbols. The narratives and signifiers of Eritrean first-generation migrants show some similarities with Feldman's description of Jewish collective memory. The way adults are remembering Eritrea and producing a collective memory seems to have an intrinsic scope which fits exactly in the production of a narrative that ensures continuity and legitimacy to the Eritrean people and their political leadership. Moreover, collective memory is there to be perpetuated and transmitted to the next generation. How is such collective memory reproduced? And how are Eritrean adults trying to lead the youth to recognize such symbols and meanings? The next section describes the first hand experiences of the second generation who is taught about the collective memory of Eritrean history.

Eritrea as Adopted Territory

Many Eritrean migrants living in Milan have managed to build or buy a physical place to call home in Eritrea, some investing in such a home for their summer holiday returns, others in preparing for a possible permanent return. Their home in Eritrea also sought to give security to family members living in Eritrea who can benefit from the use of the property all year round. Having a home in Asmara or elsewhere embraces members of the extended family and reinforces strong emotional ties. For the Eritreans in Milan who regularly return to Eritrea during their holidays, being able to share a space called home with their family signals one of the successes of their migratory project (Arnone, 2017). It also means being able to transfer their emotional attachment to Eritrea onto their children by allowing them to visit Eritrea as much as possible.

The Eritrean state recognizes the importance of the diaspora's return and greets them at their arrival with welcoming banners. It also organizes a variety of welcoming events to give a cheerful face to the city of Asmara (Conrad, 2006; Tecle, 2012). The government's 'know your country' tours targeted at the second generation, were mentioned earlier. Moreover, in 2003 the Eritrean government bought a few airplanes and launched the Eritrean Airline which many migrants supported and used to fly to Asmara that summer. The company was set up to allow a fixed-rate 500–euro-budget return flight for the Eritrean diaspora in Europe to increase diasporic return during the holidays. The financial officer of the Eritrean consulate stated that the prices would have stayed low even for the following year, to enable people to go back home more easily using a national company. The Eritrean Airline still flies but it is no longer allowed to land in Europe after its aircrafts were found to be unsafe (European Commission, 2012). In 2003 and 2004 people cherished the novelty of these flights for many reasons. Many commentators emphasized the idea that their country is now independent even in regards to air mobility which had previously been dominated by foreign airlines like Alitalia and Yemenite Airlines. As mentioned in the previous section, such argument is also one of the strongholds of the Eritrean government itself, which portrays Eritrea as unique and different form other African nations, said to be dependent on foreign aid and assistance. This is again connected to the belief that the government is fighting first of all against 'being invaded', including in an economic sense. Moreover, there was a perception among interviewees that by the government controlling all economic activities in the country, it was fighting corruption. In 2003 several young second-generation informants argued that the government had offered cheap flights because that year the names of the casualties of the 1998–2000 war were released (Arnone, 2014; Bernal, 2014). The members of the first generation saw the low price as a kind of appeasement by the government and a good-will gesture towards fostering family re-conjunction in Eritrea and giving people the opportunity to mourn together. One second-generation informant, on the contrary, thought that the government had dropped the price because people didn't want to go to Eritrea any longer and had even returned their tickets after the publication of the list of martyrs. 'When we go, we want to have fun, enjoy ourselves, we don't want to see the country mourning: it's too depressing' Mikal said. Such comment reflects a different emotional attachment felt by the two generations where the second generation does not seem to be engaging not only with the consequence of war on the family but also on the nation. This example is emblematic for showing the relationship of the different generations towards the 'mother land', the war and the Eritrean collective memories connected to nation building. Narratives around going to Eritrea turned out to be fundamental to understanding dynamics between generations, but also between the diaspora and Eritreans at home.

Because of the various conflicts and tensions Eritrea underwent, second-generation youth were not able to savour a transnational relationship with their parents' home country. Some managed to travel to Eritrea during the first half of the 90s but more or less, visits had to be put on halt during the last years of that decade and for the first few years of the following one. At the same time in the same period, there had not been any social space where to engage in extensive Eritrean cultural activities in Milan. The young second-generation adolescents from Milan who visited Eritrea during the aftermath of the Badme war had not been able to follow the full community life prior to the closure of the Via Friuli hall and many had not been engaging in Tigrinya classes or cultural activities with the Red Flowers which used to reconnect the youth to their parents' background. As Conrad argues (2006) with regards to the Eritrean second generation in Germany, Eritrean heritage is no longer part of their day-to-day lives in Milan as it used to be, especially before the 1991 liberation. Nowadays second-generation Eritreans in Milan can experience the individual, religious and national celebrations but they no longer follow institutionally organized Tigrinya classes and there are few opportunities for immersion in their parents' history through Eritrean socio-political and cultural youth activities.

The Eritrean government's *Zura Hagerka* and the parents' insistence on family visits to the home-country ensure the youth find some kind of connection with Eritrea. Visiting Eritrea was sought to encompass the previous Eritrean cultural activities organized in the diaspora. Eritrea thus became an 'adopted territory' – a term used by Kim (2010) to refer to Korean adoptees' politics of identity when returning to Korea – for most of the second-generation youth who sometimes visited the country for the first time as adolescents. They thus started new relationships, or continued fragmented ones, with relatives and friends, as they had had little possibility to visit when they were younger. The 'adoption' of Eritrea was not easy as their encounter with the local population produced ambivalent outcomes as we will notice further along in this section.

Diasporic youth who visited Eritrea were encouraged by parents and the government to empathize with the local history, and engage with the collective memory that is so important to their parents and their parents' generation of Eritreans inside and outside the country. They were thus invited to visit Eritrea where they did not only enjoy the country's landscapes, the food and the folklore but also embarked on tours to the most significant places to arouse an understanding of the country's history. Second-generation interlocutors remembered their visit to the Italian Cemetery and the Italian Railway station in Keren, the Eritrean second biggest city. The adults had told me that this city was in fact the favourite city by the Italian colonials because of its weather conditions which are milder and allow the agriculture to flourish. Keren, like Massawa, was described as being more Muslim and having a different type of architecture and culture compared to the more Abyssinian, Christian, capital of Asmara. Massawa, Green Island and other Dalhak Islands, were mentioned for their access to the Red Sea 'the most beautiful sea in the world' and snorkelling. Massawa was also cited for having been one of the most important locations from which the EPLF managed to counteract the Ethiopian occupation, a place where the liberation movement can be commemorated. There are in fact buildings which stand as a remainder of the hiding places of the EPLF. Fzum, a second-generation 14-year-old boy, recalled family stories of his grandfather who had donated his property in Massawa to the EPLF. As mentioned above, Nakfa is the most emblematic location where to commemorate the liberation movement's success, yet none of my second-generation interlocutors had visited this site, because it is far from both Asmara and Massawa, the two most targeted cities. However, those who go on the *Zura Hagerka* are brought to visit Nakfa and other nationally emblematic areas like Sawa, where most of the military training camps of Eritrea are based. An interesting further perspective is that the second generation are also encouraged to engage with the collective memory through singing. Conrad (2006) and Rena (2011) describe how learning EPLF Eritrean songs initiates the youth to this politicized national culture and allows them to embody its symbols and meanings. Such tours show how places in Eritrea embody the heritage of their parents' country and how tours allow the youth to learn about it through observing, speaking and singing.

The youth had thus acquired some knowledge of the history of Eritrea from this touristic experience and they would 'recall' Eritrean national history when in Milan. They also learned to engage with Eritrea, enjoy its spaces, find its riches, its history and pursue leisurely activities. Both second-generation youth and adults portrayed Eritrea as sufficiently traditional to be identified as the right place to experience an exotic adventure holiday on the Red Sea. In fact, most members of the Italian Eritrean diaspora privileged staying at hotels instead of sleeping at relatives' houses when they do not stay at their own property. The youth especially described local life with an emphasis on dirt, nits, and all sorts of unhygienic practices like being on the coach with animals; adults too supported this vision saying they are no longer used to local practices of daily life.

> Elisa: Although my father drove me twice to Massawa last summer, I once also went by coach.

> Natzennat: What? You went on the 30–nakfa [corresponding to 1 pound 31 pennies] coach? That's disgusting: you shared the space with chickens and sheep! Were there lots of squashed people standing all the way to Massawa? We [a group of 15 second-generation diaspora from all over Europe] hired two minibuses for the three days that we spent in Massawa and we were the only people to make use of this transport. (Fieldnotes, 2004)

The youth had a conflictual idea of Eritrea which they described once they returned to Milan. Mostly noticed were the contradictory statements which signalled their desire for Eritrea to be recognized as modern and at the same time arguing the opposite about its inhabitants and infrastructure. In a group interview four teen-age Milanese-Eritreans were adamant to talk about their summer experiences in Eritrea and the conversation was full of dichotomies. Eritrean people's eating practices were described as 'disgusting' since they eat from the same plate and share the same food. The second generation too share 'ngera, the spongy pancake layered in a communal plate and topped with spicy stews such as Shuro', Zighini, Alecha' and several other traditional condiments. Nevertheless, their comments were mostly about whom to share such dishes with, stating that they were used to sharing with their mother and people they recognized as intimate. These comments revealed how distant the second-generation perceived their relatives in Eritrea with whom they felt uncomfortable to share food from the same plate. Even more estranging for them was to go on a bus journey with local people.

The diaspora's encounter with the Eritreans who had not migrated created other tensions (see also Arnone, 2011b). The returning migrants in Eritrea are called beles, prickly pears: sweet but prickly fruits which mature every year in July and August, during the Eritrean winter season (also in Conrad, 2006; Tecle, 2012). As local Eritreans perceived the members of the diaspora as supporting the present government (Conrad, 2006; Tecle, 2012) and being intimate allies, receiving a warm welcome may have been easy among close kin, and members of the state, but when confronted with other local people, the encounter was not as easy. For example, Natzennat had to 'run away from children throwing stones at the returning youths', and Conrad (2006) described an episode she had witnessed where serious attacks were made against the young people embarking on the tours organized by the government. Mebrat, like many other first-generation Eritreans, explained her offspring's experience in this way:

> I noticed that my son and daughter are having problems with Eritrea. For example my daughter did not want to come with me this year. She said 'mum, why should I come to Eritrea? They treat me as a foreigner and kids throw stones at me. I feel a stranger there too!' so we have to confront ourselves with issues we did not expect: expectations... (Interview in Milan, 2010)

Teodros in his 20s said that he did not want to return 'I was shocked by the poverty and the situation in Eritrea, I did not feel I belonged there, it made me feel very uncomfortable'. Fzum on the other hand admitted that he only went 'because my parents want[ed] me to; I get bored in Asmara, there is nothing to do'. Some second-generation teenagers suffered from the conflictual relationship with people in Eritrea and many chose not to return there because they are treated as foreigners even in the place that their parents have so often emphasized as their home. For some of the youth it is a dreadful moment in which milestones that were solidly built by the adults fade away, leaving their life in Milan as the only tangible reality to trust.

Others were extremely enthusiastic and felt their holiday in Eritrea was their first experience without the complete supervision of their parents and an exciting opportunity to meet other diaspora second-generation youth with whom to share their experience of Eritrea. However, all these young people were empowered by meeting other members of the Eritrean diaspora with whom to share their family experience of migration and compete over their Tigrinja language skills and their knowledge of cultural practices. Of course, the second generation describe their interactions with their relatives in Eritrea (Arnone, 2011a; Conrad, 2006; Tecle, 2012) but their comments show that going to Eritrea did not end with a complete unconditional participation in local life. The outcome of such visits was a sort of detachment from the local population and a recognition of the quality of their holiday. The youth ended up mingling with the rest of the Eritrean diaspora and emphasized their shared identity and experiences with people coming from abroad with the same 'bonding' intention. Returning to Eritrea hence became a way to enhance their feeling as part of the diaspora (Conrad, 2006; Tecle, 2012). In their descriptions of their summer trips to Eritrea 'we', the youth from the diaspora is always compared with 'they', the local people living in Eritrea.

Even the second generation often remember diasporic holiday experiences when they are back in Milan and the act of recalling such experiences produces strong emotions. The intensity of the second-generation's narratives can be included in Kelner's concept of nostalgia:

> For those who would use the homeland tourism as a medium of diasporic socialization, this nostalgia is one of the crucial products of the group experience. Unlike the group itself, nostalgia can outlast the tour. [...] nostalgia can motivate the former tourists to try to recapture what they once had. The experience of being on a homeland tour with that particular group of people at that particular time in their lives can never fully be recaptured, though. [...] Tour sponsors hope that the emotions generated by the group experience will attach to the symbols embedded. (2010: 168)

Surely the families and the Eritrean government who organize such tours around Eritrea are hoping that the emotional attachment, and subsequent nostalgia produced by the holiday will motivate the youth even more to share in the collective memory the organizers wanted them to acquire.

Conclusions: Diasporic Tourism and Sacrificial Nationalism

Eritreans in Milan felt like being homeless before Eritrea's liberation both because of their hardship in Italy and the impossibility to return. Eritrea was felt as the place to liberate and the home to regain from illicit occupation. In a presentation to students of Italian as a second language in 2004, Ainom Maricos, a left wing political activist in Milan, described: 'we left a country called Ethiopia and wanted to return to a country called Eritrea.' Unfortunately, changing the name and leadership was not enough to bring people back to their former lives. 'Nobody can understand home better than one who has not got one.' This was the conclusive remarks by a formerly homeless person during an anthropology lesson in London about the meaning of home. 'Only a man who has no mother knows what a mother means' a Crimean Tartar nationalist in Ukraine told Ignatieff (1994: 10). My student's explanation matched this nationalist longing. Memories of hardship emphasize present overcoming of hardship. A small, cemented and bare corner adjacent the car park of a block of flats, where my student could sit outdoors and drink with his friends became 'my garden where I can grow flowers'. This conversation reminded me of the emotionally charged narratives produced by the members of the Eritrean community living in Milan around Eritrea and its liberation. In Benedict Anderson's (1983) concept of nation, those belonging to the imagined community are bonded by very close emotional ties. Even more so this emotional relationship with the homeland can be noticed among the members of the Eritrean diaspora who became able to make a return to Eritrea during their holidays. For many members of the diaspora who return, Eritrea is still perceived as the home country that they themselves helped to liberate.

Eritrean exiles in the world portray themselves as active participants in the organisation of associations of every sort, expressing opinions and promoting debates, creating a wide variety of events to support the liberation struggle. After 1993 the diaspora's participation in politics and nation building was slowly absorbed by the apparatuses set up by the Eritrean government. The latter now organizes many of the social events, such as the festivals and the liberation day, previously run by the diaspora, leaving little space for the diaspora's engagement and negotiation in the official discourse. An example of this monopoly is the state's reach of Eritrean social spaces in Milan, in Eritrea and in the world. The diaspora's vehemence with regard to the liberation struggle and former EPLF slogan *Awet N' Hafash!* (Victory to the Masses!) is no longer emphasized by the Eritrean government. In official events organized by the state, embassies and consulates, the word *hafash* (masses/people) remains the last feeble echo of the former loud cry. The diaspora thus started to actively participate in the imagination of Eritrea as a place where tourism could become a means for remembering, giving importance to their collectivity and emphasising their belonging to the liberation movement in which they had once been active subjects. Diasporic tourism thus idealized some aspects of Eritrean society making them a 'trope' from which to describe their migration and the country (Arnone, 2011b).

The returning diaspora is actively participating in what Bernal (2014) describes as 'sacrificial citizenship', which in this chapter is signified by their economic devotion and their compliance with the practices of 'forced transnationalism.' The diaspora's fervour for the National Martyrs' Park is an apt example to show how the returning diaspora has embodied sacrificial nationalism. The National Martyr's Park is a memorial of the casualties of the wars. It emphasizes that those who died while enrolled in the military have sacrificed themselves for the nation, as Anderson put it. As I have stated elsewhere (Arnone, 2014), the use of the denomination of 'martyrs' to define all war casualties ignores the significant element of force used by the present government in the recent national service. Those who died in the more recent war were forcibly recruited by the state; they did not choose to sacrifice themselves for the national cause. The exaltation of martyrdom, among the diaspora as well as the Eritrean state, thus reverberates stronger meanings than what even Anderson suggested. Eritreans who commit themselves to the Eritrean cause are all martyrs. Most of the returning Eritrean diaspora insist on describing their lives as devoted to their country: martyrdom is a reflective concept; martyrs are not only those who die at war but also those who dedicate their lives to Eritrea. Bernal digs into the role of the martyr in Eritrean nationalism today in a profound way:

> The martyr [...] not only is a key figure in the Eritrean national imaginary, but represents the essence of the social contract between Eritreans and the state in which the citizen's role is to serve the nation and sacrifice themselves for the survival and well-being of the nation. I call this 'sacrificial nationalism'. (Bernal, 2014: 33)

Whichever way we might analyse their attachment, the returning diaspora prefers to describe their return as holiday-making; this is their way of describing how they still participate in the newly born nation, culturally, economically, socially and politically. The returning diaspora approves and economically supports the creation of monumental structures such as the Eritrean Martyrs' Park. The diaspora supports the creation of physical spaces where to reiterate the symbols constituting collective memory. The erection of a space where to commemorate those who live and die for the state such as the Eritrean Martyrs' Park emphasizes the necropolitics played by the Eritrean state. Monuments are structures of power displayed to exalt symbols which narrate and glorify one aspect of society. Lewis Mumford (1961) described how monuments are erected when there is the need to disguise some form of social crisis: the Eritrean Martyrs' Park is there to remind people that sacrifice is glorified and disguise what happens to those who do not sacrifice themselves for the state. This is the message the diaspora wants to hear and broadcast to exalt their historical importance in Eritrea. The returning diaspora's compliance and support in such project is thus very significant.

The returning diaspora is engaged in this type of sacrificial nationalism. Their former desire 'to return to a place called Eritrea' is granted because the place they wanted to return to is now called Eritrea. They exalt such commitment by returning to Eritrea, and they now struggle to transfer their own passion to their offspring. They introduce the youth to Eritrea through tours which describe the history of the nation, focused on politically motivated narratives which the youth assimilate in a discursive way. The narratives of the youth's holidays in Eritrea do not exalt the emotional attachment to engrained family relations and traditional day to day life of Eritrea. By focusing on the national narratives of war and sacrifice, the youth finds it difficult to engage and sustain a more intimate relationship with the country's inhabitants. The role of the diaspora in continuing their sacrificial citizenship seems to be interfering not only with the way the country portrays itself but also the future relation between the diaspora and the local population. On the contrary the second generation is engaging in what Kelner (2010) defines as 'tours that bind' the Eritrean diaspora together rather than binding Eritreans as a whole.

References

Al-Ali, N., Black, R. and Koser, K. (2001) Limits to 'transnationalism': Bosnian and Eritrean refugees in Europe as emerging transnational communities. *Ethnic and Racial Studies* 24 (4), 578–600.

Anderson, B. (1983) *Imagined Communities: Reflection on the Origin and the Spread of Nationalism.* London: Verso

Anderson, M. (2015) Canadian mining company accused of exploiting Eritrea's forced labour. *The Guardian*, 19 August 2015.

Andall, J.M. (2002) Second Generation Attitude? African-Italians in Milan. *Journal of Ethnic and Migration Studies* 28 (3), 38–407.

Arnone, A. (2008) Journeys to exile: The constitution of Eritrean identity through narratives and experiences. *Journal of Ethnic and Migration Studies* 34 (2), 325–340.

Arnone, A. (2014) The Eritrean festival in the time-warp. *Journal of Social Evolution and History* 12 (2), 73–96.

Arnone, A. (2011a) Talking about identity: Milanese-Eritreans describe themselves. *Journal of Modern Italian Studies* 16, (4), 516–527.

Arnone, A. (2011b) Tourism and the Eritrean Diaspora. *Journal of Contemporary African Studies* 29 (4), 441–454.

Arnone, A. (2017) Tourism and the Eritrean Diaspora from Italy. In N. Frost and T. Selwyn (eds) *Returning Home.* Oxford: Berghahn.

Basu, P. (2004) Route metaphors of roots-tourism in the Scottish Diaspora. In Coleman, S and Eade, J. (eds) *Reframing Pilgrimage: Cultures in Motion.* London: Routledge.

Bernal, V. (2014) *Nation as Network. Diaspora, Cyberspace and Citizenship.* Chicago, IL: University of Chicago Press.

Bozzini, D.M. (2011) Low-tech surveillance and the despotic State in Eritrea. *Surveillance & Society* 9 (1/2), 93–113.

Bruner, E. (1996) Tourism in Ghana. The representation of slavery and the return of the black diaspora. *American Anthropologist* 98 (20), 290–304.

Campbell, J. (2009) Caught between the ideology and realities of development: Transiting from the Horn of Africa to Europe. *LSE Migration Studies Unit Working Papers*, No. 2009/01.

Carter, D.M. (1997) *States of Grace. Senegalese in Italy and the New European Immigration.* Minneapolis, Minesota University Press

Cole, J. (1997) *The New Racism in Europe: A Sicilian Ethography.* Cambridge, Cambridge University Press

Coleman S. and Crang, M. (2002) Grounded tourists, travelling theory. In S. Coleman and M. Crang (eds) *Tourism between Place and Performance* (pp. 1–20). Oxford: Berghahn.

Conrad, B. (2006) When a culture of war meets a culture of exile: 2nd generation diaspora Eritreans and their relations to Eritrea. *Revue Européenne des Migrations Internationales* 22, (1), 59–85.

Conrad, B. (2005) 'We are the prisoners of our dreams': Exit, voice and loyalty in the Eritrean diaspora in Germany. *Eritrean Studies Review* 4 (2), 211–261.

Ebron, P. (1999) Tourists as pilgrims: Commercial fashioning of transatlantic politics. *American Ethnologist* 26(4), 910–932.

European Commission (2012) See http://ec.europa.eu/transport/modes/air/safety/air-ban/doc/list_en.pdf (last visited: April 2015).

Evans, R. (2012) U.N. rights chief accuses Eritrea of torture, killings. *Reuters*, Geneva, June 18.

Feldman, J. (2010) *Above the Death Pits, Beneath the Flag. Youth Voyages to Poland and the Performance of Israeli National Identity.* Oxford: Berghahn.

Foucault, M. (2009) *Security, Territory and Population. 1977–1978 Lectures at the college de France.* USA: Picard.

Grillo, R. and Pratt, J. (eds) (2002) *The Politics of Recognizing Difference. Multiculturalism Italian-style*. Aldershot: Ashgate

Hepner, T.R. (2009a) *Soldiers, Martyrs, Traitors and Exiles: Political Conflict in Eritrea and the Diaspora*. Philadelphia: University of Pennsylvania Press.

Hepner, T.R. (2009b) Seeking asylum in a transnational social field: New refugees and struggles for autonomy and human rights. In D. O'Kane and T.R. Hepner (eds) *Biopolitics, Militarism, and Development: Eritrea in the 21st Century*. New York: Berghahn.

Hepner, T.R. and O'Kane, D. (eds) (2009) *Biopolitics, Militarism, and Development: Eritrea in the 21st Century*. New York: Berghahn.

Ignatieff, M. (1994) *Blood and Belonging: Journeys into the New Nationalism*. London: BBC Books.

Iyob, R. (2000) The Ethiopian-Eritrean conflict: Diasporic vs. hegemonic states in the Horn of Africa, 1997–2000. *The Journal of Modern African Studies*, 38, 659–682.

ISTAT Online See http://dati.istat.it/Index.aspx?DataSetCode=DCIS_POPSTRCIT1& Lang=en (accessed 11 October 2015).

Kelner, S. (2010) *Tours That Bind. Diaspora, Pilgrimage, and Israeli Birthright Tourism*. New York: NYU Press.

Kibreab, G. (2009) *Eritrea: A Dream Deferred (Eastern Africa Series) Woodbridge*. Suffolk: James Currey.

Kim, E.J. (2010) *Adopted Territory: Transnational Korean Adoptees and the Politics of Belonging*. Durham, NC: Duke University Press.

Koser, K. (2003) *New African Diasporas*. London: Routledge.

Louie, A. (2004) *Chineseness across Borders: Renegotiating Chinese Identities in China and the United States*. Durham, NC: Duke University Press.

Martigoni, M. (2014) Fuori dai confini dello spazio della narrazione. Esperimenti di (in) visibilita'. In V. Deplano, L. Mari and G. Proglio (eds) *Subalternita' Italiane. Percorsi di ricerca tra letteratura e storia* (pp. 139–160). Ariccia: Aracne.

Matsuoka, A. and Sorenson, J. (2005) Ghosts and shadows: Memory and resilience among the Eritrean Diaspora. In V. Agnew (ed.) *Diaspora, Memory and Identity: A Search for Home*. Toronto: University of Toronto Press.

Mbembe, A. (2003) Necropolitics. *Public Culture* 15 (1), 11–40

Mezzadra, S. and Neilson, B. (2012) Between inclusion and exclusion: On the topology of global space and borders. *Theory, Culture & Society* 29 (4–5), 58–75.

Mountz, A. (2011) The enforcement archipelago: Detention, haunting, and asylum on islands. *Political Geography* 30 (3), 118–28.

Muhlenbach, A. (2012) *The Moral Neoliberal. Welfare and Citizenship in Italy*. Chicago: Chicago University Press.

Müller, T. (2012) From rebel governance to state consolidation – Dynamics of loyalty and the securitisation of the state in Eritrea. *Geoforum* 43 (4), 793–803.

Mumford, L. (1961) *The City in History: Its Origins, Its Transformations, and Its Prospects*. San Diego: Harcourt Inc.

O'Kane, D. and Arnone, A. (2016) Behind the humanitarian crisis in the Mediterranean: Political incoherence, systemic dysfunction, and a border that kills. *Anthropology Today* 32 (5), 26–27.

O'Kane, D. and Hepner, T.R. (2009) *Biopolitics, Militarism and Development. Eritre in the Twenty-First Century*. NY and Oxford: Berghahn Books.

Orsini, G. (2016) Securitization as a source of insecurity: A ground-level look at the functioning of Europe's external border in Lampedusa. *Studies in Ethnicity and Nationalism* 16 (1), 135–147

Pinelli, B. (2015) After the landing: Moral control and surveillance in Italy's asylum seeker camps. *Anthropology Today* 31 (2), 12–14.

Rena, R. (2011) Role of musical songs in the independence struggle of Eritrean people. *International Journal of Human Resources Development and Management Review* 1 (1–2), 123–138.

Selwyn, T. and Scott, S. (eds) (2011) *Thinking Through Tourism*. Oxford: Berghahn.

Sorenson, J. (1991) Eritrean nationalism and politics of exile. *Journal of Modern African Studies* 29 (2), 301–317.

Sorenson, J. (1990) Opposition, exile and identity: The Eritrean case. *Journal of Refugee Studies* 3 (4), 298–319.

Tecle, S. (2012) The paradoxes of state-led transnationalism: Capturing continuity, change and rupture in the Eritrean transnational social field. *FES Outstanding Graduate Student Paper Series* 18 (3), Faculty of Environmental Studies, York University.

Tecle, S. and Goldring, L. (2013) From 'remittance' to 'tax': The shifting meanings and strategies of capture of the Eritrean transnational party-state. *African and Black Diaspora: An International Journal* 6 (2), 189–207.

Woldemikael, T. (1993) Political mobilisation and nationalism: The case of the Eritrean People's Liberation Front. *Africa Today* 38 (2), 31–42.

9 Travelling to the Homeland over a Double Diaspora: Memory, Landscape and Sense of Belonging. Insights from Transylvanian Saxons

Andrea Corsale and Monica Iorio

Introduction

In the current age of globalisation and increased mobility, even if the traditional notions of home, identity and citizenship linked to defined territories appear to be changing, places, either real or imaginary, continue to have crucial importance in everybody's life. The idea of home, and homeland, is still an essential element for individual and group identity (Archibald, 2002). The notions of collective memory and identity have been critically discussed by Rothberg (2009), Graves and Rechniewski (2010) and Erll (2011), who introduced the concepts of 'multidirectional memory', 'transcultural remembrance' and 'travelling memory' to stress the dynamic and ever-changing relations between history and social practices. Nevertheless, collective memories remain a powerful source of personal identities and subsequent actions.

Even in the presence of full integration in a new place of residence, the memory and feeling of nostalgia for homeland, people and places and the desire to seek or strengthen cultural and social identities are strong factors compelling trips back home (Coles & Timothy, 2004; Hirsch & Spitzer, 2002), and these attachments can reappear even after several generations (Nguyen & King, 2002). People often maintain cultural and psychological attachments to their places of origin and these ties with the homelands help them cope with new lives, displacement or discrimination (Baldassar, 2001; Stephenson, 2002).

One of the most common ways to keep bonds with the homeland is travelling with the aim of preserving or strengthening personal memories and emotional links and to re-discover places. Connections to homelands are major motivators of tourism flows for migrants and their descendants who wish to re-discover their roots, to re-experience the former homeland and thereby to re-locate their identity.

Motivations for diasporic travel (and, specifically, to visit a homeland) are varied and complex. They include visiting relatives and friends, searching for roots, experiencing the land of the ancestors, maintaining cultural identities, attending festivals or celebrations and engaging in different forms of tourism. Usually, the travel motivation varies according to the generation. For many first-generation migrants, travelling to the homeland is a way to address a sense of nostalgia (Baldassar, 2001) and to seek comfort in an environment in which they left a part of themselves (Lowenthal, 1985; Pickering & Keightley, 2006). However, their experiences may be varied and prior expectations are not always met. Standards of living, social norms and political structures of the homeland may have changed since the migrants left and living conditions in the receiving society may be vastly different from those in the homeland. Thus, a true homecoming may not be possible and the idealised picture of the homeland often collides with the reality of a place that has substantially changed (Brah, 1996; Levy, 2004; Markowitz, 2004; Read, 1996). The fear of facing these changes and the difficulty of accepting them are reasons why many former migrants decide not to travel back to their homelands (Baldassar, 2001). Disjunctive experiences in the homeland may also cause home to be detached from homeland, with a sense of belonging re-routed to the receiving society, or even up-rooted completely, producing a feeling of 'homelessness' (Rapport & Dawson, 1998). Alternatively, the homeland may remain a mere cultural and spiritual entity, a land of descent and identification, yet not a place of everyday belonging and social participation (Kelly, 2000; Voigt-Graf, 2008).

For migrants' children and subsequent generations, the experience may be rather different. They do not have their own individual memories about the homeland in past times. They may know family stories or cultural traditions related to the homeland, but they generally have weaker links with specific local places. However, many roots tourists seem to achieve the sense of identity affirmation and belonging that they initially desired (Basu, 2007; Bruner, 1996). Travelling to the ancestral homeland, in these cases, is motivated by a desire to seek or revive personal and familial roots by researching genealogies, family histories and significant historical events. Even when little is known about individual ancestors or the exact villages or houses where they lived, there can still be a strong desire to experience and spiritually reconnect with these landscapes of personal heritage (Basu, 2007; Bruner, 1996).

This chapter explores the issues related to identity, memory and tourism through the case of Transylvanian Saxons, an ethnic German population who, over a long period of time, experienced a double diaspora, first away from Germany and later away from Transylvania, Romania. This peculiarity led to the appearance of different homelands: at the first round of the diaspora, the homeland was represented by the distant and mainly imagined Germany, at the second round, it was represented by Saxon Transylvania in Romania.

The authors focus on the way Saxons perceived their homeland over the two diasporas and analyse the visits to the homeland made by the first generation of Saxons resettled in Germany, who can be defined as 'homesick tourists' (Marschall, 2015). This study highlights the influence of the rediscovered landscape on their sense of belonging to home(land) and the direct and indirect implications for roots tourism development and heritage management.

Prior to entering the field, a range of secondary sources was consulted. A review of literature on diasporic-roots tourism was undertaken to provide a broad academic context for the research. Data were collected through on-site observations and investigations carried out in several former Saxon villages and towns of Transylvania between 2012 and 2014. The investigation included 24 semi-structured and unstructured interviews with emigrated Saxons living in Germany and travelling to Transylvania. Interviewees were approached at the entrance of the Saxon fortified churches, as these are the most important tourist attractions and identity landmarks in each village and town. They were asked to talk about their migration histories, their bonds to Transylvania and Romania, their motivations and experiences of travelling to this land, their feelings about which places they consider to be home, their desire to keep links with Transylvania and their opinions about the development of roots tourism in this region. The interviews were partly done in English, when they were fluent in the language, and partly in German, with the presence of a local interpreter.

According to the research findings, the consequences of Saxons' return to Transylvania as homesick tourists, together with the management of their cultural and architectural heritage left in the region, open new perspectives and raise new questions about the relations between memory and tourism.

The History of a Double Diaspora

Transylvanian Saxons are an ethnic German population who settled in several parts of Transylvania, in present-day Romania, mainly between the 12th and 13th centuries. Their migration was part of a wider German eastward demographic expansion (*Ostsiedlung,* also commonly known as *Drang nach Osten*) which lasted for several centuries and created a scattered 'colonization diaspora' stretching from the Danube to the Baltic Sea and into Russia.

The German colonisation of Transylvania was started and promoted by the Hungarian King Géza II (1141–1162), who encouraged colonists to settle along the south-eastern borders of the Kingdom of Hungary, sparsely inhabited at the time by a mixed Hungarian, Romanian and Szekler population (a subgroup of the Hungarian people), in order to defend it from the repeated attacks by Turkic nomadic peoples, such as Pechenegs and Cumanians. Besides military purposes, these German settlers were also invited to move to the area due to their renowned expertise in mining, crafting, trade and agriculture (Gündisch, 1998).

The colonists mostly came from the Western regions of the Holy Roman Empire; the origin of the collective term 'Saxons' is still disputed, as Saxony was only marginally concerned by this migration (Gündisch, 1998; Wagner et al., 1982).

The first waves of migrants settled in and around the fortified city of Hermannstadt (Sibiu in Romanian), subsequently expanding their presence towards Bistritz (Bistrița) in the north and Kronstadt (Brașov) in the East. Further waves of settlers founded a number of villages, towns and cities and were temporarily joined by Teutonic Knights who built a series of castles and fortresses to further strengthen the border.

King Andrew II (1177–1235) awarded the colonists with many privileges, rights and obligations through the *Diploma Andreanum* of 1224. This document substantially conferred upon the German population living in the region both administrative and religious autonomy, along with obligations towards the kings of Hungary.

The core of the territory which was colonised by Germans reached an area of about 30,000 square kilometres. Within each village, social interaction was strictly regulated through neighbourhood associations, while guilds dominated urban life (Riley & Dinescu, 2007; Rouček, 1971).

After the devastating Mongol invasion of 1241–1242, about 300 fortified churches (*Kirchenburgen*) were built in villages and towns in order to protect population and faith. These Romanesque and Gothic churches were equipped with towers and massive walls. About 150 of these structures still exist and define the landscape in many parts of central, southern and south-eastern Transylvania up to the present day.

During the Middle Ages, the rapid development of the Saxon urban centres, led by flourishing crafting and trading activities, generated the German name of *Siebenbürgen* for the whole of Transylvania, referring to seven fortified towns generally identified with Bistritz (Bistrița), Hermannstadt (Sibiu), Klausenburg (Cluj-Napoca), Kronstadt (Brașov), Mediasch (Mediaș), Mühlbach (Sebeș) and Schässburg (Sighișoara).

The privileged status of the Saxon population was confirmed in 1438 by the *Unio Trium Nationum* pact, which divided political and social power among Hungarians, Saxons and Szeklers, thus excluding the Romanian population. The Saxon assembly, which was part of the Transylvanian Diet, was established in 1486 and was called *Universitas Saxorum*.

The printer and scholar Johannes Honterus, from Kronstadt, introduced Lutheran Reformation to Transylvania in the first half of the 16th century. The rapid, enthusiastic and generalised conversion of Transylvanian Saxons to Lutheranism, with distinct churches, holy books and services, in a region where Roman Catholicism, Calvinism and Orthodoxy were dominant, would prove crucial for the consolidation of their unique identity and for the strengthening of their bonds with Germany. As Saxon schools were also run by the church, generations grew up with the self-consciousness to be German-speaking and Lutheran, and very rarely did they marry outside the Saxon community. Thus, their religion, language, legal status, experience spheres and judgmental values, created a special sense for togetherness. The Saxons managed to preserve their specific features, but also their isolation. In some way they remained aliens to their environment (Keul, 2009; Nagy-Szilveszter, 2011; Ştefănescu, 2013; Teşculă, 2012).

Although the relations with the Catholic Hapsburg monarchy were half-hearted, owing to religious disputes, the alliance between Saxons and Hungarians also deteriorated during the 19th century, because of increasingly heavy Magyarisation policies and progressive erosion of the old privileges. This led Saxons to dismiss Hungary and side with Romania after the dissolution of the Austro-Hungarian Empire (Gündisch, 1998).

In 1918 Transylvania was annexed by Romania according to the Treaty of Trianon and Transylvanian Saxons, together with other ethnic German populations living in other regions of Greater Romania (Banat, Bessarabia, Bukovina, Crişana, Dobrudja and Maramureş), became part of a larger but more heterogeneous German minority in Romania, numbering 745,000 people in 1930, 4.1% of the total Romanian population, according to the Romanian Census results.

Opposition against Romanian nationalist attitudes, assimilation policies and land reforms, led Transylvanian Saxons to become more and more attracted by National Socialism throughout the 1930s and during World War II, when, as a direct consequence of Nazi ideology, hostility toward Jewish and Roma/Gypsy communities deeply penetrated into the German population (Paikert, 1967).

When Romania signed a peace treaty with the Soviet Union in 1944, the German army began evacuating the Saxons from Transylvania, as happened in other German-speaking areas of Central and Eastern Europe during the same period. This operation involved, in particular, the Saxons living in the Bistriţa region, an area briefly re-annexed by Hungary following the Vienna Award of 1940. Although Romania decided not to expel Germans, as did neighbouring countries at the end of the war, around 100,000 Germans fled the country before the arrival of the Soviet Red Army, suddenly creating a large Transylvanian Saxon diaspora mainly located in Germany. More than 70,000 Saxons were arrested by Soviet and Romanian communist authorities and deported to labour camps in Dobrudja and Ukraine for alleged cooperation with Nazi Germany; many of them never returned.

After the early post-war turmoil, the German minority in Romania lived through calmer times, but its politically conservative and free-market-orientated *elite* was largely marginalised by the communist government (Müller, 2009; Steigerwald, 1985).

After World War II, the constant weakening of Saxons' economic and social status and the very critical situation of Romania under Nicolae Ceauşescu, led Saxons to emigrate *en masse*. Indeed, the size of the Transylvanian Saxon population in Romania significantly decreased during the second half of the 20th century, with the last emigration wave occurring in the last two decades of the century, before and after the fall of Ceauşescu's regime, mainly relocating to the Federal Republic of Germany (FRG) and, secondly, to Austria, the US, Canada and other countries (Cadzow *et al.*, 1983; Illyés, 1982; Verdery, 1983, 1985).

West Germany was the favourite emigration target, as it presented welcoming policies, high standards of living, political freedom and high probability of integration (Gräf & Grigoraş, 2003). In 1978 the German Chancellor Helmut Schmidt signed an agreement with Nicolae Ceauşescu establishing an emigration system where about 10,000–12,000 ethnic Germans were allowed to emigrate from Romania every year, against a payment of approximately 5000 German Marks per person by the FRG. Both sides agreed on keeping that additional provision secret, but it was well-known to the people involved (Gräf & Grigoraş, 2003; Koranyi & Wittlinger, 2011).

Poverty, human rights' violations and rampant nationalism undermined the once ethnically diverse Transylvanian society, and the effects of those dynamics, even after the reintroduction of democracy and the free market economy in the early 1990s, further weakened the historical ethnic minorities of the region, including the Saxon community.

According to the Romanian population censuses, the size of the German minority in Romania, including Banat Swabians and smaller communities left in the counties of Satu Mare, Maramureş, Suceava and Bihor, and in the capital city Bucharest, decreased from 745,421 (1930) to 384,708 (1956), 359,109 (1977), 119,462 (1992), 59,764 (2002) and just 36,042 in 2011. Within this broader community, the Transylvanian Saxon population decreased from 237,416 people in 1930 to 18,208 in 2002 and 11,643 in 2011, reflecting the magnitude of emigration and the extent of assimilation. As many of them are now elderly people, the next census, due for 2021, is expected to record significantly smaller numbers.

The size of the Transylvanian Saxon diaspora is difficult to estimate, due to mixed marriages and dwindling association membership. Based on demographic calculations, it is about 400,000 people, mostly concentrated in Germany, particularly in the *Länder* of Bavaria (Bayern), Baden-Württemberg, Rhineland-Palatinate (Rheinland-Pfalz) and Hesse (Hessen) (Michalon, 2003). The Transylvanian Saxon language, which belongs to the West-Central German group of High German dialects, is currently still spoken by about 200,000 people around the world, with only 10,000 of them living in Transylvania, and is considered 'severely endangered' by the United Nations (Gündisch, 1998; Moseley, 2010; Schuller, 1999). It is mostly spoken by older generations, but it is not transmitted to the younger ones, and there are no significant or effective efforts to keep it alive. Bilingual Romanian-German schools in Romania only teach the standard German language.

Yet, in spite of these negative indicators, the re-establishment of a German political party (*Demokratisches Forum der Deutschen in Rumänien*, or Democratic Forum of Germans in Romania) in 1989 has been followed by a series of surprising successes at administrative elections in several towns, and, even more significantly, by the election of Klaus Johannis, former mayor of Sibiu, as President of Romania in 2015, showing that, in spite of its reduced size, the Transylvanian Saxon community in Romania still holds a visible cultural, economic and political role in the country (Cordell & Wolff, 2003).

These complex historical events forged a solid national identity which, in spite of its progressive dwindling and its physical dispersion, is still clearly perceived as closely-knit by the diaspora members and by other nationalities, such as Romanians, Hungarians and other German groups.

The Memory of a Distant German Home(land)

Saxons always had a 'dual ethnic identity' (Custred, 1991). On the one hand, and mostly on the basis of their autonomous status within Transylvania, at least until the abolition of the *Universitas Saxorum* in 1876, they developed a specific self-consciousness. Settlers and their descendants perceived themselves, and were perceived by the other ethnic groups, as *Saxones* in Latin language (Transylvanian Saxons). This identity was mainly rooted in the local German dialect (*Sächsisch*) and folk costumes, and in local institutions, most of all the Lutheran church in Transylvania (Gündisch, 1998). On the other hand, the constant relationship with the German cultural space moulded a German identification, after which Saxons were named in the 17th century *germanissimi germanorum*, the most German of all Germans, according to the German poet Martin Opitz (Cornis-Pope & Neubauer, 2006; Evans, 2006). This remark would be later used and reused in order to convey a feeling of hierarchical superiority compared to other Transylvanian ethnicities, e.g. Romanians, Roma and Jews (Davis, 2010; Gündisch, 1998). Symbolic structures (the Black Church in Kronstadt/ Braşov) and symbolic boundaries (the Carpathians mountains) were used as reference points to stress their identity as Westerners (Cercel, 2012).

The feeling of belonging to the distant German homeland, continuously expressed by the Saxon population from any social class, had a vigour that varied according to the political events that affected Saxons. It was particularly vivid whenever Saxons' autonomy and privileges were under peril and whenever it was necessary to distinguish themselves from the other ethnicities – in particular the Hungarian and Romanian ones. At the same time, the strength of these bonds used to vary according to the way Germany, over time, acted towards the German communities abroad.

From 1867 onwards, during the increasingly heavy Magyarisation pressure (Philippi, 1994), disinterest from the central authority in Vienna, and impressive military and political successes of Bismarck's Germany, led a significant part of the Saxon élite to be strongly influenced by Germany both in cultural and political issues. Bismarck's Germany was perceived as a protective element for Saxons. Articles in the press of the time emphasised this desiderata (Teşculă, 2012).

Following World War I and the Romanian annexation of Transylvania, the economic, political and social influence of the Saxon community further decreased. Thus, during the interwar period, as a reaction for being considered as a relic from the past, Saxons, in particular the educated middle class, reinforced their collective sense of belonging to a broader German nation (Judson, 2005). This was also the result of the increased interest towards 'Germans Abroad', in Germany itself, after World War I (Davis, 2009). The raising German nationalism conceived German communities outside Germany, the unique Motherland (*Heimat*), as members of a broader German ethnic community (*Volksgemeinschaft*) (Judson, 2005). Germans abroad received material, cultural and technical aid from various private organisations in metropolitan Germany, which provided a lifeline for the organisations upon which the Saxon intelligentsia depended for their livelihood, like Lutheran churches and German language schools, whose social role had been weakened by the centralised Romanian State (Philippi, 1994). A great number of young Saxons from middle-class families were sent to study to Germany. Saxon intellectuals and scholars started writing about Saxon folk costumes for a metropolitan audience and visited Germany on speaking tours to illustrate how Saxon folk culture embodied 'Germanness' (Teşculă, 2012). This was a proof of the significant Saxon contribution to the *Volksgemeinschaft* and, at the same time, of the distinctiveness of Saxons with respect to their non-German neighbours (Davis, 2009, 2010). Germanness was embodied in landscape, architecture, family traditions and domestic spaces, which included the speaking of standard German alongside with *Sächsisch*, playing German music and singing German songs (Davis, 2010). Moreover, education courses for young Saxon men and women included extensive components on German literature, music and history. The years of National-Socialist influence brought renewed ties with Germany, now known as the 'Reich', as Saxon political and cultural organisations frequently adopted Nazi-oriented models.

After World War II, the collective memory of the German homeland remained anchored in local history, institutions, dialect and folk customs and continued to be very popular throughout the time of the Cold War. Indeed, the myth of Germanness received an impetus and was nourished by the welcoming policy adopted by the FRG. Over the 1950s, the West German constitution recognised the right of Germans who had lived within the borders of the German Reich prior to 1938 to 'return' to the homeland, and this provision was later expanded to include all *Volksdeutsche* (Gallagher & Tucker, 2000). For ethnic Germans who could claim Germanness by descent, this meant not only that they could gain formal legal citizenship of the FRG but also financial support, as well as access to programmes that would aid their integration. In the context of this policy, Saxons' feeling of belonging to the German homeland reinforced and ultimately persuaded most of them to 'return' to the Motherland (Koranyi & Wittlinger, 2011). Furthermore, the link with the Motherland appeared to be reciprocated when, in 1977, Helmut Schmidt reached the aforementioned agreement with Nicolae Ceauşescu regarding the 'purchase' of exit visa, rendering the impression that the German homeland was welcoming them, while the Romanian home was willing to get rid of them (Koranyi & Wittlinger, 2011). Finally, in a climate of adverse economic and political circumstances in Romania, the calling of the imagined German homeland, affluent and free, materialised itself with Saxons leaving Romania *en masse* after the fall of the communist regime.

The Memory of a Close Transylvanian Home(land)

As mentioned earlier, Transylvanian Saxons experienced a double diaspora, even though over a very long period of time. This unique history let them build a complex memory of home(land). For centuries, within the Saxon community in Transylvania, the German lands had been perceived, at least in an imaginary way, as a sort of distant home, a *Kulturnation*, and a place of belonging. This, together with the welcoming policies promoted by the FRG over the 1980s, led Transylvanian Saxons to think that (re)assimilation in Germany would be an easy and inevitable achievement. However, many Saxons encountered a homeland that did not match the image conjured up during the Cold War (Koranyi & Wittlinger, 2011). The wealthy and free German world that had attracted them was gradually re-evaluated and seen with scepticism. Moreover, they started confronting contrasting and contradictory memories. Having left what many perceived to be an anti-German environment in which anti-fascism determined public discourses on the past, the majority of Saxons arrived in West Germany during the boom of 'Holocaust memory'. In Germany itself, the decline and disappearance of the German communities abroad, in Central and Eastern Europe, was widely seen as an inevitable consequence of World War II. These elements were widely interpreted by Saxons as a challenge to their own strong notion of victimhood and their depoliticised memory of involvement during the war. Moreover, the absence of an institutional forum in which to discuss their experiences during communism in Romania made many of them feel marginalised in Germany

(Koranyi & Wittlinger, 2011). Furthermore, Transylvanian Saxons were in a difficult position when they decided to leave their closely-knit Transylvanian world. Even though they received recognition by the German State due to the law defined as *jus sanguinis*, the situation was not so straightforward with the everyday 'native' German. Because they came from Romania they were called Romanians, although they expected to be recognised as Germans. This unexpected situation pushed them to promote their specific culture, make themselves noticed by the 'native' Germans and strengthen the memory of the land they left, *Siebenbürgen*, which had ultimately become their new homeland. Its memory has been cultivated in a variety of ways – from taking part in online forums devoted to matters of interest for the Saxon diaspora, to participating (actively or as observers) in cultural activities in Germany, to being members of local Saxon organisations, like the so-called *Landsmannschaften* (Paul, 2013). Transylvanian Saxon memory is also collectively celebrated and authenticated through the Transylvanian Museum of Gundelsheim, opened by Transylvanian Saxon associations in 1968, which received the status of national museum in 1991. The museum shows an ever-growing exhibition of material and immaterial aspects of Saxon culture, collected through donations and acquisitions (http://www.siebenbuergisches-museum.de).

Many Transylvanian Saxons living in Germany engage in cultural activities that aim to preserve their memory of the homeland and their present community, as is demonstrated by the importance of the 'Association of Transylvanian Saxons' (*Verband der Siebenbürger Sachsen*) (Iorio & Corsale, 2013). This association dates back to the 1950s and is part of a wider Federation of Transylvanian Saxons, which has branches in Germany, Austria, the US and Canada. It aims at representing the diaspora and keeping Saxon identity and heritage alive. It also offers social assistance and is in direct contact with several Transylvanian-based associations and organisations, such as the German Democratic Forum. The capillary diffusion of the Saxon newspaper *Siebenbürgen Zeitung*, which publishes news and information concerning the Saxon community, is further evidence of German Saxons' interests in Transylvanian matters. They also attend events related to Saxon culture, such as folk dancing performances, and the *Heimattag* meetings, a kind of 'homeland celebration day', the most important of which has been held annually since 1951, over Pentecost, in the town of Dinkelsbühl, Bavaria. *Heimattag* is an important occasion for Transylvania Saxons, entailing art and book exhibitions, seminars, fairs, social events and dancing (Iorio & Corsale, 2013; Paul, 2013). Approximately 20,000 people, mainly from Germany, Austria, Romania and North America attend it every year (http://www.siebenburgen.de/). A similar annual event is held in Transylvania, usually in the village of Birthälm/Biertan. Folk customs, food recipes, family tales also contribute keeping the Transylvanian Saxon memories alive.

There are Transylvanian Saxon emigrants to Germany who are deeply involved in projects and actions for the preservation of Saxon heritage, like the members of the music group *Bürger7* that mainly sing in the Saxon dialect, in both Germany and Romania, with the aim of preserving the language and transmitting themes related to the Saxons' diaspora (Iorio & Corsale, 2013). Several documentaries have been produced in order to narrate Saxons history (Auner, 2006). History and art books on Transylvanian Saxon heritage are frequently published both in Germany and in Romania, in many cases by Saxons themselves (e.g. Gündisch, 1998).

The emergence of prominent Romanian-German figures, such as Herta Müller (Nobel Prize in Literature in 2009) and Klaus Johannis, the current President of Romania, has re-enforced the memory and the social closeness to the homeland, as did the successful choice of Sibiu as European Capital of Culture in 2007.

Travelling to the Homeland

Maintaining social connections with *Siebenbürgen* through organisations and associations, including the Internet, is not the only way through which Transylvanian Saxons in Germany keep their memory of home alive. Indeed, the desire to strengthen it and, most of all, to relive it, pushes them to travel to Transylvania as homesick or roots tourists (respectively first and following generation members). They include Saxons who left Romania in the 1940s, the 1980s and 1990s; elderly people who directly experienced migration during their life; younger generations who have never seen Transylvania through their own eyes; generations who are highly assimilated into the German society; and groups of people who still clearly perceive themselves as different. People of such diverse backgrounds produce different expectations and perceptions, but the uniqueness of the Transylvanian Saxon history binds them and clearly manifests itself through their travels.

Aspects of such travels have been highlighted by the authors in an earlier publication (Iorio & Corsale, 2013). For the present chapter, part of the material collected at that occasion, in particular the interviews, was revisited to reflect specifically on Saxons' homesick tourism to *Siebenbürgen*.

The results show that they engage in such a travel to see and sense places and sites meaningful to them, and to share the memory of the homeland with their travel companions - partners, children or friends, as well as telling their relatives and friends in Germany after the journey. Indeed, the interviews show that the 'memory gaze' (Marschall, 2012) lead first-generation émigrés recognise in the landscape the signs of what is familiar to them, of what recalls their past and let them live those emotions again. Saxon homesick tourists engage in a variety of commemorative activities during their travelling, in order to rediscover the landscape of their childhood or even of their adult life. They visit houses, churches, schools, workplaces or graves related to their families, although many of those places are now abandoned or in bad conditions after years of neglect. Seeing, smelling and touching these places offers a sensory engagement that lets them re-experience the past through the materiality of being again in the familiar places. This can be a very emotional experience, as shown by the words of some of the interviewed:

> I visited the streets where I grew up in Mediasch and walked by the school, then over the bridge to the marketplace and the church in the centre, and also to the cemetery [...] I stayed in front of the housing block where I spent my childhood and I could almost hear our laughter again. I could even still tell which family lived at what floor. I really felt inundated by memories and emotions'. (Uwe, Mediaş, 2014)

> I travelled to Transylvania with my two children, they wanted to see the places where their dad was born. I am glad that they already know the importance of their roots'. (Peter, Prejmer, 2012)

The visit also recalled painful memories:

> The horrible time when Ceauşescu was fighting against the people came to my mind again ... and then I remembered the experience of my journey to the 'free West' when I was eighteen. (Uwe, Mediaş, 2014)

Whether recalling joyful or sad memories, visiting sites and places of one's past in the native land elicits deep feelings of belonging, since those places are personal 'sites of memory' (Nora, 1989). Symbolic monuments embedding historical narratives in the landscape, enable visitors to tangibly engage with collective and familial beliefs about history and ancestry through sensory experiences. This desire to trace the physical remnants of personal and family pasts constitutes, as Basu (2007) observed, a 'spatialization of memory', where such sites function as sources of identity and places from which the identity of the self is perceived to derive. However, as emerged through the interviews, the experience of the homeland landscape may also produce feelings of disillusionment or disappointment, especially when this landscape is perceived as different from the one stored in memory. Saxons visiting the homeland often experience this sort of feeling.

The typical traditional rural landscape of Saxon Transylvania was characterised by linear villages of colourful houses and farms dominated by gothic fortified churches and surrounded by agricultural lands and forests. Urban settlements often kept their Gothic, Renaissance and Baroque architecture and medieval fortifications well into the 20th century (Akeroyd, 2006).

At the end of the 20th century, particularly after the last big waves of Saxon emigration from Transylvania, this typical rural and urban landscape profoundly changed. The urban landscape, in particular, was deeply modified during the 1980s by the construction of big standardised blocks of flats of poor quality, often after the demolition of historical districts and buildings.

After the mass emigration of the Saxons, the population of their villages and towns has almost entirely been replaced by incoming groups of different ethnicity, religion, language and identity, principally Romanians and Roma. The new inhabitants do not feel emotionally attached to Saxon heritage, which does not represent them, and, consequently and understandably, they started to mark their identity, values and ways of living through changes to their acquired homesteads, including alterations to Gothic, Renaissance, Baroque and Art Nouveau house façades. At the same time, most of the Lutheran fortified churches and their annexed cemeteries, particularly in the rural settlements, are neglected and the construction of Greek-Orthodox churches, often built in neo-Byzantine style, has modified the traditional ambiance. Dialects, legends, customs, songs, dances, recipes, dresses, skills and crafts have largely been replaced by different ones. The old traditions basically survive only within the diaspora. Thus, the landscape remembered by the Saxons of the diaspora does not correspond to what they encounter during their travel there. Some Saxon homesick tourists feel disappointed at seeing such a deeply changed landscape, as narrated by Gerda, Heidi and Katherine: 'I was disappointed. The houses of the people I knew and who had emigrated all looked very different. It was loud, dusty and chaotic. It was not a good feeling. I almost cried' (Gerda, Dacia, 2012). 'Many things have changed and look much worse in the village of Petiş and in the surroundings where I went to school and I grew up. I did not expect it to be that run down' (Heidi, Petiş, 2014). 'The economy is so poor, valuable arable land is abandoned, many houses have collapsed, cultural life has declined a lot' (Katharine, Moşna, 2012).

At the same time, the perception of cultural and architectural rupture is an occasion for some interviewed to wonder who has to be blamed, eventually accusing Saxons themselves. Dirk reports:

> Look at the conditions of the Saxon villages: they are ruined, collapsed, abandoned [...] but it is our fault, we left. We should do something to save our homeland, but up to now I cannot see any signs of shared action. (Dirk, Agnita, 2012)

Others perceive negative changes occurring in Transylvania mostly related to 'westernisation' of the country, especially in urban areas, as stated by an interviewed:

> After communism ended, everything changed. Even people have changed. Previously, there was more 'togetherness' than today. Capitalism has made men more selfish. I do not want to give the wrong impression: I am

glad that communism has had its day, but people have developed to their detriment. This is my personal opinion (Hans, Sighişoara, 2014).

These visitors react to the changing landscape by developing a sense of nostalgia for the 'old good days', when life in Saxon Transylvania was simple, close to nature and surrounded by solidarity. The change in the appearance and ethnic composition of the former Saxon towns and villages creates risks of disinheritance among the diaspora, as the signs of 'Germanness' that were so strongly impressed over the centuries have been vanishing fast over the past few decades.

Homeland, Home, Belonging

Although Saxon homesick tourists tend to feel a strong sense of connection with the places they visit, the landscape has deeply changed since their departure and often collides with the remembered one. The comparison with the positive sides of living in Germany ends up producing, in some cases, a sort of detachment and separation between homeland and home, as observed by White (2002). For most of those who were born there, *Siebenbürgen* is the *Heimat* (homeland), the place where they spent their childhood and a place connected with happy memories. This is well expressed by Sonya: 'Siebenbürgen is my Heimat. It will always remain my land, because I spent my childhood and youth there' (Sonya, Cristian, 2012). However, 'home' (*Zuhause*) is in Germany, the place where they live at present, where they have most of their relatives and friends, as reported by Erika: 'My home is my present place of residence: Germany' (Erika, Viscri, 2012).

Consequently, a difference arose between *homeland* and *home*, where homeland is mostly immaterial and made up of emotional attachments, memories, identification, culture and spirit, while home is materiality and real-life experience. Thus, *Siebenbürgen* is discursively constructed in ways that make it familiar and special, a cultural homeland rather than a real home or place of residence. The latter was generally identified with the place of present life and work, of everyday belonging and social participation. However, homeland and home are not antithetical, as stated by Jürgen and Rainer: 'I feel at home in Germany, I work and live there, but I feel my homeland is Siebenbürgen. They do not exclude each other' (Jürgen, Sibiu, 2014).

Feelings of 'home' and 'homeland' are not mutually exclusive and are anchored to fixed, physical territories even though they are expressed in dynamic, multiple and flexible ways, being adapted to different life circumstances and migration contexts. This perceived growing gap between the memory, or image, and the reality generates further delicate and controversial issues when heritage conservation and tourism development overlap conflicting identities.

Transylvanian Saxon Heritage as a Tourist Attraction

The long presence of Saxon inhabitants is still evident in the landscape, which retains a valuable architectural heritage that includes impressive Lutheran fortified churches, mainly built in Romanesque and Gothic style, and traditional rural settlements consisting of colourful farmhouses located along the streets of the villages (Akeroyd, 2006).

Starting from the 1990s, this heritage has been the object of various initiatives in order to turn into sources of attraction for an international tourism market. Leading actors of this process have been the United Nations Educational, Scientific and Cultural Organization (UNESCO), together with a British non-profit foundation called Mihai Eminescu Trust (MET).

The starting point of this process was the inscription of the fortified church of Biertan in the World Heritage List in 1993, followed by the fortified churches and villages of Biertan, Câlnic, Dârjiu, Prejmer, Saschiz, Viilor and Viscri in 1999. The motivation for the inscription was that 'these Transylvanian villages with their fortified churches provide a vivid picture of the cultural landscape of southern Transylvania. The seven villages inscribed, founded by the Transylvanian Saxons, are characterised by a specific land-use system, settlement pattern and organisation of the family farmstead that have been preserved since the late Middle Ages. They are dominated by their fortified churches, which illustrate building styles from the 13th to the 16th century' (UNESCO, 1999). This definition implies a strong pressure for the conservation of the traditional landscape and the rural social structures, in spite of the changes in the ethnic composition of the settlements.

A 1994 encounter between the writer and ICOMOS (International Council on Monuments and Sites) consultant, Jessica Douglas-Home, already active in the preservation of Romanian cultural heritage during the difficult years of the Ceauşescu regime, and a Saxon activist woman from the village of Viscri in central Transylvania, led to the foundation of the Mihai Eminescu Trust, in 1999. The Trust, bearing the name of one of the most famous Romanian poets, works for the preservation of traditional architecture and landscape in Transylvania, almost exclusively focusing on the former Saxon villages.

Douglas-Home, thanks to her network of acquaintances, was able to involve Charles, Prince of Wales as Royal Patron of the Trust; his purchase of a house in Viscri helped promote the actions at the national and international levels. The Trust describes its activities as follows: 'The Trust concentrates in the Saxon villages of Transylvania, a special case because of the age and richness of their culture and the emergency caused by mass emigration of the Saxon inhabitants to Germany in 1990. These villages – farmers' houses and barns built around fortified churches, substantially unchanged since the Middle Ages – lie in spectacular beautiful surroundings. The hills and valleys are rich in wild flowers' (http://www.mihaieminescutrust.org/).

Great emphasis has been put on tangible heritage, through the restoration of the Lutheran fortified churches in several Transylvanian Saxon villages, opening them to visitors, providing information on their history, and restoring the façades of traditional houses belonging to the Saxon architectural style. The MET also addressed the promotion of mixed forms of cultural and rural tourism. In each of the 12 villages where the Trust operates, a 'model guesthouse' was opened to encourage similar initiatives in areas where rural tourism had never been previously practiced (Corsale & Iorio, 2014).

As already observed, Transylvanian Saxon architecture and traditions received great emphasis, as the image presented to the outside world is basically that of Lutheran Saxon villages (Hughes, 2008; Klimaszewsky & Nyce, 2009; Klimaszewsky et al., 2010), even though the population is almost exclusively Romanian and Roma and follows the Orthodox religion. Tourists take pictures of Saxon houses bearing freshly restored and re-painted German names and writings; the visit to the Lutheran fortified churches is the highlight of the stay and the guesthouses supported by the MET, even those managed by Romanian and Roma families, display a distinct Saxon architectural style. Since the Saxon churches and houses are recognised and indicated by guidebooks, websites and tour operators as the highlights of many of these towns and villages (e.g. Viscri, Biertan, Prejmer), the Romanian and Roma families involved in tourism tend to arrange their guesthouses according to Saxon traditions.

Even though tourism is developing fast in the area, highlighting the success of the various initiatives undertaken over the last years, exploiting the charm of former Saxon medieval towns and villages in Transylvania is particularly challenging for many reasons (Corsale & Iorio, 2014). First of all, the population change implies that the Saxon appearance of the places does not reflect the identity of the current inhabitants. Secondly, financial efforts deployed on the preservation or restoration of Saxon architecture are not necessarily seen as a priority in a region deeply affected by widespread poverty. Finally, the Saxon diaspora might no longer recognise this restored heritage, now in the hands of Romanian and Roma people, as their own. Indeed, this approach to Saxon heritage tourism is largely disconnected from the Saxon diaspora and their homesick tourism. The relations between the MET and Saxon organisations, both in Romania and abroad, are difficult, as the former basically accepted the population change and tries to turn Romanians and Roma into custodians of the Saxon heritage in order to provide them with a useful tool for tourism development, while a large part of the latter still has a problem with accepting the end of their presence in Transylvania.

One of the most controversial issues concerns the fate of the fortified churches, as the MET openly supports their reuse as museums, community buildings or even Orthodox churches, in order to create a sense of belonging among the Romanian and Roma communities, while Saxons still insist on preserving their original Lutheran religious function, even where only a handful of elderly people still frequent them.

These delicate issues show the importance of memory in tourism and, more generally, in local development processes. They also raise questions about the potentially contrasting visions and expectations that homesick tourists, more general tourists and local people, may have. This aspect needs to be further investigated both in Romania and elsewhere.

Conclusions

Even though collective memories do not necessarily coincide with individual histories, Transylvanian Saxons clearly share a feeling of belonging to a double diaspora, resulting in complex memories of homeland. At the first round of this diaspora, the homeland was represented by Germany, at the second one by *Siebenbürgen*.

The ultimate fluctuation toward the German homeland occurred when, in a climate of adverse economic and political circumstances in Romania during and immediately after Ceauşescu's regime, Saxons left Transylvania *en masse* and relocated to Germany. At this point, a new homeland started to emerge – Transylvania. Thus, for the Saxons, homeland has never been the actual home, the place where they lived, but the external one, be it Germany or *Siebenbürgen*, in Romania.

Once in Germany, Saxons started to keep the memory of Transylvania in a variety of ways; they also felt the desire to relive that memory by travelling to Transylvania as homesick tourists and visiting sites of personal memory. However, the re-encountered landscape and relived memories played an ambivalent role in (re)defining their relationship to 'home' and 'homeland'. On the one hand, travelling confirmed a sense of belonging to the homeland, on the other hand, it reaffirmed the identification with their current home, Germany, hence affirming unique hybrid identities. It follows that different historical, social and personal events shape the attachment to these places, making diaspora members feel bound, or unbound, to the homeland. The experience of Transylvanian Saxons shows that homesick tourism is a chance to redefine the meaning of 'home', as a symbolic place of roots and past life, and at the same time as a material place of present life in the new country. Transylvanian Saxons seem to constitute a fluid diaspora.

Since the Romanian German diaspora currently exceeds 1 million people globally, and around 400,000 of them are Transylvanian Saxons, the potential of homesick or roots tourism is evident. However, up to now, no specific policies have been adopted to promote this type of tourism. Marketing programmes and actions by the Romanian Government and by county and municipal authorities could strengthen roots tourism. In particular, there is an opportunity to reach a broader audience of second and subsequent generations, and to encourage and aid reluctant first-generation emigrants to visit their homeland. Partnerships with Germany could strengthen marketing policies and the creation or opening of archives, registers and cadastral maps could provide further important tools.

Economic and cultural policies could be introduced in order to turn diasporas into resources for local development. However, for such policies to be well grounded, further investigation of residents' attitudes towards hosting homesick and roots tourists would be very useful, as well as an exploration of their willingness to preserve the heritage of diasporic groups, particularly in areas characterised by deep social, economic, political, cultural and demographic changes. In the case of Transylvanian Saxon heritage, its total disappearance would undermine the link between memory and tourism and destroy one of the main chances for roots tourism development in many rural settlements. However, there are already signs of protection of Saxons' heritage and part of it is already used as a tourist attraction for a wider tourism market, which highlights the connection between the niche area of personal memory tourism and more general and mainstream forms of tourism. This connection should be more developed for the benefit of both tourists, and for local population, although we acknowledge this may be a challenge.

References

Akeroyd, J. (2006) *The Historic Countryside of the Saxon Villages of Southern Transylvania.* Bucharest, Romania: Art Group International.

Archibald, R.R. (2002) A personal history of memory. In J.J. Climo and M.G. Catell (eds) *Social Memory and History: Anthropological Perspectives* (pp. 65–80). Walnut Creek, CA: Altamira Press.

Auner, D. (2006) *Leaving Transylvania.* Germany, Ireland, Romania: Dieter Auner Production.

Baldassar, L. (2001) *Visits Home: Migration Experiences between Italy and Australia.* Melbourne, Australia: Melbourne University Press.

Basu, P. (2007) *Highland Homecomings: Genealogy and Heritage Tourism in the Scottish Diaspora.* Abingdon: Routledge.

Brah, A. (1996) *Cartographies of Diaspora: Contesting Identities.* London: Routledge.

Bruner, E.M. (1996) Tourism in Ghana: Representation of slavery and the return of the Black Diaspora. *American Anthropologist* 98 (2), 290–304.

Cadzow, J.F., Ludanyi, A. and Elteto, L.J. (1983) *Transylvania. The Roots of Ethnic Conflict.* Kent, OH: Kent University Press.

Cercel, C. (2012) Transylvanian Saxon symbolic geographies. *Civilisation* 60 (2), 82–101.

Coles, T.E. and Timothy, D.J. (eds) (2004) *Tourism, Diasporas and Space.* London: Routledge.

Cordell, K. and Wolff, S. (2003) Ethnic Germans as a language minority in Central and Eastern Europe: Legislative and policy frameworks in Poland, Hungary and Romania. In G. Hogan-Brun and S. Wolff (eds) *Minority Languages in Europe* (pp. 99–119). London: Palgrave-Macmillan.

Cornis-Pope, M. and Neubauer, J. (eds) (2006) *The Literary Cultures of East-Central Europe series: History of the Literary Cultures of East-Central Europe: Junctures and disjunctures in the 19th and 20th Centuries. History of Literatures in European Languages.* Amsterdam, Netherlands: John Benjamins Publishing Company.

Corsale, A. and Iorio, M. (2014) Transylvanian Saxon culture as heritage: Insights from Viscri, Romania. *Geoforum* 52 (2), 22–31.

Custred, G. (1991) Dual ethnic identity of the Transylvania Saxons. *East European Quaterly* 25 (4), 483–491.

Davis, S.E. (2009) Maintaining a 'German' home in Southeast Europe: Transylvanian Saxon nationalism and the metropolitan model of the family, 1918–1933. *The History of the Family* 14 (4), 386–401.

Davis, S.E. (2010) Our faithfully kept, age-old inheritance: Transylvanian Saxon folk customs, particularism and German nationalism between the Wars. In E. Smith (ed.) *Europe's Expansions and Contractions* (pp. 199–220). Adelaide, Australia: Australian Humanities Press.

Erll, A. (2011) Travelling memory. *Parallax* 17 (4), 4–18.

Evans, R.J.W. (2006) *Transylvania Saxons in Austria, Hungary and the Habsburgs, Essay on Central Europe, c. 1683–1867* (pp. 209–227). Oxford: Oxford University Press.

Gallagher, J.J. and Tucker, P.N.J. (2000) Aussiedler migration and its impact on Braşov's ethnic German population and built environment. *GeoJournal* 50 (2/3), 305–309.

Gräf, R. and Grigoraş, M. (2003) The emigration of the ethnic Germans of Romania under communist rule. In C. Lévai and V. Vese (eds) *Tolerance and Intolerance in Historical Perspective* (pp. 53–71). Pisa, Italy: Edizioni Plus.

Graves, M. and Rechniewski, E. (2010) From collective memory to transcultural remembrance. *Journal of Multidisciplinary International Studies* 7 (1), 1–15.

Gündisch, K. (1998) *Siebenbürgen und die Siebenbürger Sachsen.* Bonn, Germany: Langen-Müller.

Hirsch, M. and Spitzer, L. (2002) We would not have come without you: Generations of nostalgia. *American Imago* 59 (3), 253–276.

Hughes, A. (2008) Will there be conflict? Identity and values tensions in Transylvania's Saxon villages. Europolis. *Journal of Political Science and Theory* 4, 309–328.

Illyés, E. (1982) *National Minorities in Romania.* New York: Columbia University Press.

Iorio, M. and Corsale, A. (2013) Diaspora and tourism: Transylvanian Saxons visiting the homeland. *Tourism Geographies* 15 (2), 198–232.

Judson, P.M. (2005) When is a Diaspora not a Diaspora? Rethinking nation-centered narratives about Germans in Habsburg East Central Europe. In K. O'Donnell, R. Bridenthal and N. Reagin (eds) *The Heimat Abroad: The Boundaries of Germanness* (pp. 219–247). Ann Arbor, MI: University of Michigan Press.

Kelly, M.E. (2000) Ethnic pilgrimages: People of Lithuanian descent in Lithuania, *Sociological Spectrum* 20, 65–91.

Keul, I. (2009) *Early Modern Religious Communities in East-Central Europe: Ethnic Diversity, Denominational Plurality, and Corporative Politics in the Principality of Studies in Medieval and Reformation Traditions.* Leiden, Netherlands: Brill Academic Publishers.

Klimaszewsky, C., Bader, G.E., Nyce, J. and Beasley, B.E. (2010) Who wins? Who loses? Representation and 'restoration' of the past in a rural Romanian community. *New Library World* 59 (2), 92–106.

Klimaszewsky, C. and Nyce, J. (2009) Does universal access mean equitable access? What an information infrastructure study of a rural Romanian community can tell us. *New Library World* 110 (5–6), 219–236.

Koranyi, J. and Wittlinger, R. (2011) From diaspora to diaspora: The case of Transylvanian Saxons in Romania and Germany. *Nationalism and Ethnic Politics* (17), 96–115.

Levy, A. (2004) Homecoming to the Diaspora: Nation and state in visits of Israelis to Morocco. In F. Markowitz and A.H. Stefansson (eds) *Homecomings: Unsettling Paths of Return* (pp. 92–108). Lanham, MD: Lexington Books.

Lowenthal, D. (1985) *The Past is a Foreign Country.* Cambridge: Cambridge University Press.

Markowitz, F. (2004) The home(s) of homecomings. In F. Markowitz and A.H. Stefansson (eds) *Homecomings: Unsettling Paths of Return* (pp. 21–33). Lanham, MD: Lexington Books.

Marschall, S. (2012) Personal memory tourism and a wider exploration of the tourism-memory nexus. *Journal of Tourism and Cultural Change* 10 (4), 321–335.

Marschall, S. (2015) 'Homesick tourism': Memory, identity and (be)longing. *Current Issues in Tourism* 18 (9), 876–892.

Michalon, B. (2003) Migration de Saxons de Roumanie en Allemagne. Mythe, interdépendance et altérité dans le 'retour'. Thesis Géographie, Université de Poitiers, France.

Moseley, C. (ed.) (2010) *Atlas of the World's Languages in Danger.* Paris: UNESCO Publishing.

Müller, H. (2009) *The Hunger Angel.* London: Granta Books.

Nagy-Szilveszter, O. (2011) Notions of belonging in 20th-century Romanian-German literature. In M. Brie, S. Şipoş and I. Horga (eds) *Ethno-Confessional Realities in the Romanian Area: Historical Perspectives (XVIII–XX centuries)* (pp. 227–242). Oradea, Romania: Eurolimes.

Nguyen, T.H. and King, B. (2002) Migrant communities and tourism consumption: The case of Vietnamese in Australia. In C.M. Hall and A. Williams (eds) *Tourism and Migration: New Relationships between Production and Consumption* (pp. 221–240). Dordrecht, Netherlands: Kluwer Academic Publishers.

Nora, P. (1989) Between memory and history: Les lieux de mémoire. *Representation* 26, 7–25.

Paikert, G.C. (1967) *The Danube Swabians. German Populations in Hungary, Romania, and Yugoslavia and Hitler's Impact on Their Patterns.* The Hague, Netherlands: Nijhoff.

Paul, L. (2013) Transylvanian Saxons' migration from Romania to Germany: The formation of a 'return' diaspora? PhD thesis, Loughborough University. Leicestershire. See https://dspace.lboro.ac.uk/2134/11541 (accessed 24 March 2015).

Philippi, P. (1994) Nation und Nationalgefühl der Siebenbürger Sachsen 1791–1991. In H. Rothe (ed.) *Die Siebenbürger Sachsen 1791–1991* (pp. 69–80). Cologne, Germany: Böhlau Verlag.

Pickering, M. and Keightley, E. (2006) The modalities of nostalgia. *Current Sociology* 54 (6), 919–941.

Rapport, N. and Dawson, A. (1998) Home and movement: A polemic. In N. Rapport and A. Dawson (eds) *Migrants of Identity: Perceptions of Home in a World of Movement* (pp. 19–38). Oxford: Berg.

Read, P. (1996) *Return to Nothing: The Meaning of Lost Places.* Cambridge: Cambridge University Press.

Riley, B. and Dinescu, D. (2007) *Transylvania.* London: Frances Lincoln.

Rothberg, M. (2009) *Multidirectional Memory: Remembering the Holocaust in the Age of Decolonization.* Stanford, CA: Stanford University Press.

Rouček, J.S. (1971) *Contemporary Romania and her Problems: A Study in Modern Nationalism.* Manchester, NH: Ayer Publishing.

Schuller, W. (1999) *Die Mundart der Siebenbürger Sachsen.* See http://www.siebenbuerger-sachsen-bw.de/buch/sachsen/12.htm/ (accessed 8 January 2010).

Ştefănescu, B. (2013) Confessionalisation and community sociability (Transylvania, 18th century–first half of the 19th century). In M. Brie, S. Şipoş and I. Horga (eds) *Ethno-Confessional Realities in the Romanian Area: Historical Perspectives (XVIII–XX Centuries)* (pp. 15–25). Oradea, Romania: Eurolimes.

Steigerwald, J. (1985) *Tracing Romania's Heterogeneous German Minority from its Origins to the Diaspora.* Winona, MN: Translation and interpretation service.

Stephenson, M.L. (2002) Travelling to the ancestral homelands: The aspirations and experiences of a UK Caribbean community. *Current Issues in Tourism* 5 (5), 378–425.

Teşculă, N. (2012) The media, the idea of German affiliation and the Transylvanian Saxons in the 1860s. *Studia Universitatis 'Babeş-Bolyai', Historia* 57 (2), 29–38.

UNESCO (1999) Villages with fortified churches in Transylvania. See http://whc.unesco.org/en/list/596/ (accessed 14 November 2011).

Verdery, K. (1983) *Transylvanian Villagers: Three Centuries of Political, Economic, and Ethnic Change, 1700–1980.* Berkeley, CA: University of California Press.

Verdery, K. (1985) The unmaking of an ethnic collectivity: Transylvania's Germans. *American Ethnologist* 12 (1), 62–83.

Voigt-Graf, C. (2008) Transnationalism and the Indo-Fijian diaspora: The relationship of Indo-Fijians to India and its people. *Journal of Intercultural Studies* 29 (1), 81–109.

Wagner, E., Schneider, E.R., Gross, M. and Intscher, M. (1982) *Transylvanian Saxons: Historical Highlights.* Cleveland, OH: Alliance of Transylvanian Saxons.

White, J.J. (2002) A Romanian German in Germany. The challenge of ethnic and ideological identity in Herta Müller's literary work. In D. Rock and S. Wolff (eds) *Coming Home to Germany? The Integration of Ethnic Germans from Central and Eastern Europe in the Federal Republic* (pp. 171–187). New York: Berghahn.

10 Domesticating Dark Tourism: Familial Roots Trips to the Holocaust Past

Carol A. Kidron

Introduction

The concept of dark tourism has been defined as a fascination with death (Lennon & Foley, 1999) or a desire to become acquainted with deathworlds that have been sequestered from everyday late modern life (Stone & Sharpley, 2008; Walter, 2009). Seaton (1996), however, has described death tourism more broadly as the experience of the sublime, numinous, and/or the mystical experience of the extraordinary (Seaton, 1996). Scholarly accounts of dark tourism have sustained one of the foundational dichotomies in tourism research, namely the differentiation between tourism and everyday life (MacCannell, 1999). Recent scholarship has questioned the above gap between everyday lived experience and both pale tourism (Haldrup & Larsen, 2003; Larsen, 2008; Obrador, 2011) and dark tourism (Walter, 2009). Critical scholars call for studies of the way individual and familial everyday relations inform tourist motivations and shape tourist experiences (Larsen, 2008; Obrador, 2011). Although the scholarship has examined familial relations in leisure tourism (Haldrup & Larsen, 2003; Noy, 2007; Obrador, 2011) and pale heritage tourism (Gouthro & Palmer, 2010), there has been almost no attempt to explore mundane 'homely feelings' (Obrador, 2011) and familial we-relationships (Wang, 1999) in dark tourism.

A growing number of survivors of mass violence are accompanying their children and/or grandchildren on voyages to sites of personal suffering and survival. In the process they are often also undertaking what has been termed homesick/homeland tourism visiting pre-war homes and neighbourhoods (Marschall, 2015b: 333) and even returning to their war-time hiding-place (Kidron, 2013). Although potentially triggering harrowing memories of displacement, loss and often traumatic suffering, these sites ultimately intertwine dark touristic experience with the more positive experience of

200

familial nostalgia. Families seek out the we-relations of those who thrived and survived together in challenging conditions of domesticity in conditions of duress (Kidron, 2013). Despite the empowerment of survival, this duress entailed the perpetually threatened loss of life and often the actual violent loss of loved ones. Descendant tourism to these sites therefore involves dissonant experiences of familial death and loss on the one hand and empowering homely feelings on the other. In this way, these visits constitute a phenomenological bridge between the motivations and experiences of dark tourism and homeland tourism.

In the absence of survivors who have passed away, descendants are discovering their own embodied memories of ancestral pasts (Marschall, 2015b). Descendants are also seeking alternative tourist configurations that might act as surrogate mediators in their journeys to ancestral sites. Surrogate formations include trips with siblings, with ethnic heritage organizations, or school roots trips (Kidron, 2015). These alternatives allow descendants to pool the memories of other descendants so that they may more easily disclose previously tacit transmitted and embodied familial memory. Together, descendants recall and re-enact past familial ties to their challenging heritage and/or (re)-construct future familial ties to erased sites of ancestral domesticity (Kidron, 2013; Marschall, 2015b). The phenomenon of family and/or surrogate family dissonant homeland tourism will be shown to create a nexus between 'extraordinary' secular pilgrimage (Cohen, 1992) and 'ordinary' familial 'sociality on the move' (Larsen, 2008).

This study examines the motivations and lived experiences of Israeli adult children and grandchildren of Holocaust survivors (hitherto descendants) who set out on dissonant homeland tourism to pre-Holocaust heritage sites, pre-Holocaust homes and sites of hiding, accompanied by their survivor parent or by surrogate yet no less 'familial' tourist formations. In both cases the chapter will explore the way family relations emerge in particular ways when emplaced in dissonant heritage sites.

Heritage Tourism and the Post-Tourist in Search of a Home

Heritage tourism entails the search for cultural, familial and/or collective legacy. Whether situated in historical knowledge, material objects, architecture or landscapes (Basu, 2004; McCain & Ray, 2003; McIntosh & Prentice, 1999), heritage tourism seeks out the past as resource for the present (Graham & Howard, 2008). Personal, familial or national heritage is socially constructed, re-presented and performed within the confines of the heritage museum or the more authentic archive, or imagined within distant landscapes where the tourist conjures 'ghosts of place' (Bell, 1997). It entails the 'discovery of connectedness and continuities beyond the self' (Basu, 2004: 38).

Recent heritage scholarship has shifted towards a person-centred approach (Caton & Santos, 2007), perhaps situated in postmodern conceptions of the atomized self in search of a home. As victim of modernity's global mobility, displacement and familial fragmentation (Giddens, 1991), the 'post-tourist' seeks belonging to restore ruptured roots and give form and content to identities. Even when seeking national or ethnic identity (McIntosh & Prentice, 1999) or the *communitas* of collective mass touristic religious or secular pilgrimage (Cohen, 1972), studies gauge individual motives and consumption (Poria *et al.*, 2006). Thus, although the recently outlined diversity of subjective motives deconstructs tourist typologies, a new monolithic tourist 'type' – the solitary post-tourist – has emerged, eliding an examination of family tourism (Obrador, 2011).

The subfield of legacy or genealogy tourism too has emerged as primarily person-centred, where generational consciousness and newfound kin provide the solitary tourist with a sense of re-containment within a personalized family history (Santos & Yan, 2009: 63). When 'hunting for ancestors' (Basu, 2004: 370), it is not merely the genealogical information that is sought but rather the personal connection to ancestors (McCain & Ray, 2003: 713). Although the affinity between legacy tourists and their ancestral roots constructs relatedness, the lone-self remains the focus of memory-identity work. One might ask whether recovered roots impact relations with living family members and whether these roots are not central to the process of intergenerational transmission of familial and/or ethnic identity. What role do family heritage/legacy tours play?

There have been a number of recent studies on family reunions (Ramirez *et al.*, 2007) and 'return visits' of migrant families to their homelands (e.g. Duval, 2004). While these studies explore the way family visits maintain or construct transnational networks of kin relations, they do not focus on the way family relations emerge in particular ways when emplaced in heritage sites. Gouthro and Palmer's (2010) study of family heritage trips to industrial mining sites does explore family tourist engagement with the heritage site as secular pilgrimage. However, person-centred meaning making and identity work of post-modern pilgrimage takes precedence over an analysis of familial emotional sociality. Moreover, the above studies do not examine dark family tourism.

Dark Tourism, Atrocity Heritage and Dissonant Heritage

In contrast to the broader umbrella category of dark tourism, referring to general visitor interest in sites of death and suffering (Lennon & Foley, 1999), atrocity heritage tourism (Ashworth & Hartmann, 2005) anchors the visiting descendants within ancestral landscapes, re-connecting the self to victimized forebears. Tours to slave plantations, prisons, or concentration camps trace personal roots to dissonant heritage sites (Tunbridge & Ashworth, 1996) where ancestors were murdered, incarcerated or from which they were brutally displaced (Bruner, 1996). While earlier approaches to dark and/or atrocity tourism (often used interchangeably) depicted a thanatouristic fascination with death (Lennon & Foley, 1999; Seaton, 1996), recent studies have 'normalized' dark tourism, highlighting complex motives. Stone and Sharpley (2008) and Walter (2009) propose that as death is intertwined in everyday mundane reality, atrocity tourism need not be mystified as an extraordinary experience sought out by necrophilic tourists. According to these authors, atrocity tourism should rather be conceptualized as an opportunity to confront death. Biran *et al.* (2011) assert that motives for visiting death-related sites are diverse, including a desire to experience a wide range of emotional modalities such as pathos or catharsis. Numerous scholars show that empathic identification with ancestors who survived or were murdered at sites of atrocity intensifies emotional responses and overall interest in the site as part of one's project of the self (Jamal & Lelo, 2010; Poria *et al.*, 2006). Feldman (2008) depicts the simulation of empathic family relations between survivor witnesses and non-related Israeli students at Polish sites of atrocity, in this way enabling memory transmission.

However, despite the interest in diverse emotional responses to dark tourism, in ruptured ancestral ties or in simulated familial ties, the scholarship cited above sustains what Feldman refers to as the Turnerian binary of extraordinary dark/atrocity tourist experience and mundane everyday life (Feldman, 2008; Turner, 1973). The Holocaust pilgrim, whether re-imagining the presence of absent pre-Holocaust Jewish life in Poland, or paying homage to the dead in the crematoria at Auschwitz, is portrayed as undertaking a sacred commemorative quest (Feldman, 2008). Scholarship on dark pilgrimages has ignored the more mundane motivations and 'homely' experiences of the family dark tourist. With the exception of Stein's (2009) exploration of the identity work of American Holocaust descendants, there has been no scholarship on family tours to Holocaust sites.

Moreover, the above binary of dark and extraordinary tourist experience and mundane everyday life has overshadowed the liminal phenomenon of homesick/homeland tourism to pre-war homes and to erased ruined landscapes of subsequently displaced ancestors (Kadman, 2010; Marschall, 2015b). Even less work has been done on trips to sites of war time hiding. Considering the ultimate fate of those forcibly displaced and their traumatic loss and suffering, visits to these sites might be classified as dark/atrocity heritage tourism. Yet for those who lived and survived together in these sites, the sites simultaneously emplace and often preserve critical traces of mundane lived experiences, we-relations and homely feelings. These sites may therefore enable descendants to re-discover empowering ancestral and familial ties. Although distinct in important ways from Macdonald's concept of perpetrators' dissonant or difficult heritage (2010: 1–4), one might conceptualize the above visits as dissonant or difficult homeland/heritage tourism.

Whether descendants return to the above sites on their own, with survivor parents/grandparents or surrogate mediators, homeland tourism entails complex forms of familial memory work and emotion work (Kidron, 2013). Yet once again, scholarship on person-centred and binary pale/dark tourism appears to have elided the examination of these 'grey' zones of dissonant heritage tourism.

The Invisibility of Family Tourism and the Binary of Home and Away

Both Obrador (2011) and Larsen (2008) account for the paucity of research on family tourism, claiming that the paradigm of the solitary tourist, detached from everyday domesticity and familial sociality, discursively constitutes the invisibility of family tourism. The authenticity of the extraordinary experience of the idealized lone tourist is thought to depend precisely upon 'breaking the bonds of everyday existence' (MacCannell, 1999: 159). The radical separation from everyday life and bonds configures the family as an obstacle to creative identity work. Exceptions such as the rare accounts of the family holiday, the mass family tourist experience, or pale family heritage more narrowly examine either consumer motivations and/or fleeting and superficial familial sociality.

The idealization of the solitary tourist experience has also elided an analysis of the dialectic between 'home' and 'away'. We know little of the way the familial lived experience is re-emplaced at tourist sites thereby re-shaping the contours of the otherwise 'extraordinary' practice. Neither do we know how family relations are re-constituted within the very different context of the tour.

According to Larsen et al. (2007: 245) reading of family holidays, the 'home is made while away.' Both Haldrup and Larsen's (2003) study of family photography and Noy's (2007) auto-ethnographic recollections of family holidays at the beach depict the way tourist practices enable the performance of familial sociality and emotion work. Family trips are 'resources for shared experience' (Noy, 2007: 154) transforming that experience into familial memory. Obrador's (2011) study of beachside holidays highlights family corporeal co-presence, intimacy and belonging. Building on Wang's (1999) conceptualization of existential authenticity, Obrador (2011) asserts that by permitting the mobilization of 'homely feelings', family holidays enact 'authentic we-relationships' and family holidays sustain and even stabilize family relations that may otherwise be precarious (Carr, 2011: 26; Minca & Oakes, 2006; Haldrup & Larsen, 2003). The trajectory from the home to the tourist site enables 'domestic' thick sociality. Yet can the above insights pertaining to familial pale tourism be applied to family dark tourism and to the grey zone of pre-war homes, neighbourhoods and hiding places?

In the absence of survivors, descendants are discovering diverse ways in which alternative tourist configurations might act as surrogate links to the above ancestral sites. These surrogate formations include trips with siblings, with ethnic heritage organizations, or school roots trips. These alternatives allow descendants to pool together and explore transmitted and embodied familial memory related to ruptured pasts. Descendants either re-enact past familial relations and/or reconstruct future familial ties to erased sites of ancestral pre-war or war-time 'domesticity' (Kidron, 2013; Marschall, 2015a). This study therefore asks what are the descendants' self-perceived motivations to undertake roots trips at pre-Holocaust personal heritage sites and at liminal sites of 'difficult domesticity'? What is sought and ultimately experienced? How do the family or surrogate familial configurations shape the tourist experience?

Methodology

The present study on familial roots tourism builds on a broader research project that explored the private and public memory work of Holocaust descendants in Israel, with relevant data being extracted from the extensive body of interview material collected between 2000 and 2005 (Kidron, 2009). The broader project included 55 in-depth ethnographic interviews conducted with children of survivors and 25 interviews with grandchildren of survivors. Second-generation respondents ranged in age from 35 to 55, and third generation ranged in ages 16–28, with equal gender representation. The great majority was born in Israel to survivor parents/grandparents who emigrated from Europe in the late 1940s and early 1950s after surviving Nazi extermination camps, forced labour camps, ghetto incarceration, or extended periods of hiding. The majority achieved middle- to upper-middle-class status and had some form of higher education. The Snowball Method was used to recruit participants. Semi-structured ethnographic interviews took place in respondents' homes or in cafés and lasted two to four hours. The interview was propelled by a topic guide listing open-ended questions eliciting responses relevant to the study (Denzin, 1970).

During the first half of the interview, demographic questions were posed, followed by an open-ended question: 'Was the Holocaust present in your home and, if so, in what ways?' This question elicited two to three hours of accounts (in each interview) about the silent or partially verbalized presence of the Holocaust in the childhood past. In the second half of the interview, questions were asked such as: 'Do you participate in collective forms of Holocaust commemoration? Have you asked your parents about their Holocaust experience?' Particularly relevant to the present study, questions were posed regarding roots tourism. For example: 'Did you go on a roots trip? Were you accompanied by family members? Why did you choose to go? Can you tell me about the trip? What were the highlights of the trip?' Interviews were taped and transcribed. Dominant and recurring themes that were shared across participants were identified and thematic files were created for analysis, containing interview segments or vignettes from the various participants.

Out of the wider sample of 75 descendants, 40 had undertaken one or more roots trips to their survivor parent's homeland and/or sites of atrocity/heritage (most commonly Auschwitz-Birkenau, Treblinka, Majdanek). Nineteen of the 40 descendants made the trip with one or both of their survivor parents. Interviews took place no more than five years after the trip. Descendant accounts have been selected as illustrative of the wider sample. All names in the following section have been changed to preserve confidentiality.

Being there with the Survivor: From Heritage Tourism to Emotive Familial Experience

Yoav's survivor father requested that his son accompany him on his return to the sites of his childhood in Belgium so he might transmit his history to his children. Yoav (approximately 50 years old) sought out the more distant Jewish heritage. As a cultural heritage tourist his trip was a sacred salvage mission (Bruner, 1996) unearthing the cultural life-worlds ruptured by the Holocaust. Father and son visited the survivor's childhood haunts in the Jewish neighbourhood of Brussels. Despite intentions to 'skip' sites of atrocity, it was impossible to tour the old country without, as Yoav says, 'stumbling across' traces of the Holocaust past. Yoav describes their unintended visit to The Jewish Museum of Deportation and Resistance' in Mechelen (see http://www.gedenkstaetten-uebersicht.de/en/europe/cl/belgien/inst/juedisches-deportations-und-w/) as an unexpected highlight of the trip:

> My father walked into the museum and it was as if he was hit by lightning. He says to me, looking at the photos on the wall, 'that's my father, that's my mother, that's my sister and mother.' There were 12 enlarged pictures of his family on the museum walls that he had never seen, he didn't know they existed, and no one could tell us how they got to the museum ... He hadn't seen his family since they were taken away.

The shaken father and son discovered more photos in the Museum archives and a letter containing an eye witness account of Yoav's grandfather's presence in the concentration camp one year after Nazi records recorded his death. Although the photos could be considered familial pre-war heritage, they evoked the Holocaust past and the presence of the Holocaust dead. What stands out in Yoav's memories of the trip is not however the information accessed regarding his grandfather's fate but rather his father's emotional shock in the museum and his subsequent 'breakdown':

> Although he was overwhelmed in the museum ... that night in the hotel (long pause) he ... fell to pieces. In ... 53 years ... I've never seen him cry ... he broke down ... He just totally fell apart. I was really afraid ... that the man would not survive ... he broke down and cried uncontrollably ... I was overwhelmed ... because I had never seen him cry, he has always been very introverted ... I got to see a side of my father I had never seen ... what was always brimming under the surface. The trip was a real turning point, I really connected with my father; it was phenomenal.

The second highlight of the trip was Yoav's attempted entry into his father's hiding place. As his father was a young child during the Holocaust, his most vivid childhood memories of 'home' were of his recollections of years spent with his family in the hiding place. A return to the site thus marked a very ambivalent form of 'homecoming' for the survivor and the descendant. Epitomizing the complexity of 'difficult heritage' (Logan & Reeves, 2008; Macdonald, 2010), the site encapsulated otherwise incompatible memories of belonging and nostalgia tainted by suffering and loss.

Y: We went to the house where he hid. But we couldn't get in the building because it was locked. But we went around the back and looked in the window – I saw the attic. He [his father] then told me that this uncle was there, and that aunt was over here ... as if it was just yesterday that he was there. It really hurt me that we couldn't go in. He described how they used to pass the time. You would not think that in these situations people lived family lives ... but they did.

C: Why did you want to go in, you did look inside?

Y: I don't know, I wanted to go inside with him to get a feeling of ... to see what it was like ...

C: If you looked in the window, what feeling would you get from going inside?

Y: I wanted to stand there with him, walk around the room, see if he could tell me what it was really like – to be hidden, to wait for others to bring you food, to wait to be caught ... I left really frustrated. I'm still frustrated ... I still want to get in.

Shared presence in the hiding-place would allow Yoav to get an empathic 'feeling' of 'what it was really like to be hidden', while also accessing parental memories of the more mundane moments of domesticity. The power of the site to disclose the sensual and emotional experience of the everyday life of survival recalls Bell's (1997) description of 'ghosts of place'. According to Bell, when visiting sites from our past, our emotional communion with surviving traces can evoke and materialize the virtual presence of absent figures and distant experiences. Yet how could Yoav identify with his father's 'ghosts of place'?

The answer lies perhaps in Yoav's claim above that his father's breakdown permitted him to see a part of his father that had been 'brimming under the surface.' Implying that he had long since been empathically aware of his father's tacit feeling world, I asked Yoav to explain what was 'brimming under the surface':

> When I was a child I would watch my father become, you know, all quiet ... sad. I knew he was remembering his dead, thinking about the period in hiding. I would try to ask questions, sit with him, but my mother protected him, she would say 'leave him alone'. Seeing him cry like that, it was like opening up all those moments. With all the history books I've read and photos I found, it was that night shared with my father that made it all real to me. It brought us even closer together.

In contrast to 'the history books', the tourist site evokes the above display of emotions necessary to 'open[ing] up all those moments' of repressed Holocaust presence in everyday familial life. Father and son's 'corporeal co-presence' (Obrador, 2011: 410) at sites of atrocity thus allowed the descendant to share in previously tacit emotional legacies by enacting intimate familial relationships.

Erez (approximately 40 years old) set out on solitary trips to Germany to explore his German-Jewish heritage. According to Erez, these trips were journeys of self-discovery: 'I wanted to understand if and how the past had made me who I was'. As post-tourist, Erez sought, in his words 'to bring to light parts of myself I've never understood that don't seem to fit Israeli culture'. However, once again ambivalence regarding Jewish European heritage is resonant in the descendant's account. Erez explains:

> What was I supposed to feel when I heard German music, looked at their art? It might be my heritage, but it was the German who turned my grandfather in. But ... it was also a German that saved my father's life. So is this who I am or who I want to be?

Erez's pre-war heritage is interlaced with parental tales of atrocity and survival. Although he intended to explore only pre-war German-Jewish life he ultimately sought more personal familial *milieux de mémoire* so that he might 'fill in the gaps' of parental silences. Re-tracing his father's journey as a child survivor, Erez met relatives in Germany who told him about his father's childhood and he accessed historical documentation of his father's incarceration in the labour camp. Yet historical knowledge was far from satisfying:

E: I realized there are gaps that can't be bridged, at least not alone. I couldn't construct a picture ... of what really happened there.

C: What do you mean by what 'really happened'?

E: I don't know how he really lived ... what it felt like, who took care of him, how did he feel about them ... how he survived. There's something mysterious about survival, something happened there, something happened there to these people that allowed them to survive. I realized only if I go there with him, to these places, might I understand what it was like. I didn't want historical details. I had found those on my own. I wanted to go with him there – to his childhood home, to his hiding place, and the camp where he prevailed. I thought, if I saw those places with him – spent time with him there, I might be able to share something with him, something that I had always felt but couldn't put my finger on.

The descendant realized that solitary trips and knowledge accessed couldn't unravel 'the mystery' of his father's lived experience. Repeated accounts of Erez's wish to know 'what happened' were often followed by references to his desire to 'share' in the feeling world of survival. When Erez explains what it would mean to 'share' the experience, he returns to his childhood memories:

We had a great childhood. None of the trauma they speak about. But there were moments when the Holocaust was more present. Like when I caught my father bathing my grandfather – and saw the scars on his [the grandfather's] back ... I stared in shock [at the grandfather's back] and my father yelled at me to get out of the bathroom ... It was always there, but he [my father] would never share with us, we never really understood what he felt, how it was for him to hide, to be hungry, scared. I thought if we go there ... in the places where it happened, he [my father] might say more, or, well, at least he would remember and react and we could ... feel a bit what he felt. Without this, we just really don't know what happened, and well, actually who this man really is.

Despite the tacit presence of the Holocaust in the everyday life of Erez's childhood, the survivor-parent resisted descendant identification. Erez therefore seeks shared parent–child 'corporeal co-presence' (Obrador, 2011: 410) in authentic topos, so that he might witness a more explicit enactment of the feeling world of survival. Resultant descendant empathic identification would allow him to better 'know' who his father 'really is'.

Erez and his brother ultimately travelled to Germany with their father. They walked the streets of Berlin, visiting the survivor's childhood hometown. They also went to the Sachsenhausen concentration camp. Despite my questions, Erez did not provide any details regarding the sites, how long they spent there, or even the historical knowledge he acquired from his father. Rather he repeatedly refers to his emotional experience of shared presence at sites previously attended alone. He recounts attempted identification with his father's experience as follows:

> We stood there with him, it was very tense, we watched him – searched his face – we saw gestures of great sadness ... we hoped he might tell us what it was like then, there. What it felt like to hide, to be afraid, to be imprisoned, trapped. But he didn't. He just shut down on us again.

The climax of failed sharing occurred at the survivor's basement hiding place, now part of a restaurant. Erez's brother got into a brawl with the restaurant owner who told them they could not enter the basement. Only after their father begged them to leave did the brothers reluctantly agree to give up what Erez insisted should have been 'the highlight of the trip'. When I asked why this place was important enough to fight over, Erez responds: 'If we had been inside with him, in the actual place, he might have told us there what it felt like to hang on and to survive. If nothing else, we would have been there with him and seen it on his face. We could have shared that experience, shared that part of his life.' Asking Erez what his father might have told him about 'hanging on' he added: 'All those months of hiding were not like in the movies – just the moment when the Nazis break in or when the liberators free the victim – what about all the rest of the time ... hours and hours of living there that no one knows about?'

Be it through verbal testimony or embodied facial gestures, Erez aimed to vicariously experience what had eluded him at home and on his solitary trips – the lived experience of survival. Co-presence in the 'actual' site and emotive re-experiencing of the feeling world of survival could have permitted an 'existentially authentic' moment of 'we-relations' (Wang, 1999) where the descendant might have 'shared that part of his [father's] life' that was forever elusive. Even 'being there together' and the desperate attempts at bonding could not compel the wounded survivor to share his emotive legacy. Four of the forty descendant accounts examined for this research similarly culminated in failed bonding.

Family Roots Trips without the Survivor

Miriam, a third-generation descendant recounts her experience during numerous roots trips with her family in Rhodes, Greece. After four centuries in Rhodes, a pogrom drove Miriam's great-grandparents to flee to Egypt where her grandfather was born and from which he subsequently immigrated to Israel. Miriam describes her first of many trips to Rhodes with her grandfather (who had previously never stepped foot in Greece), her mother and her siblings to revitalize their roots on the island:

Miriam: Although my grandfather was born in Egypt he considered himself Greek. They spoke Greek at home, ate Greek dishes, and listened to Greek music. Growing up we'd all make fun of him and we'd say whatever we don't understand – okay it must be a Greek thing. And then we go to Rhodes – and we leave him at some café while we go to the beach and when we come back he's sitting with all the old men, eating his favourite fish fry, arguing in fluent Greek and well...they're all like my grandfather so he's finally at home.

Carol: What else did you do during the trip?

Miriam: We went looking for his family home in a small village near Rhodes. We met locals who showed us where a few Jews lived. But we couldn't be sure which house it was. He walked the alleys, became serious. We didn't ask questions but you can't go to these places without thinking about why people left. They never chose to leave. With all the nostalgia for Greek culture there's always this sense that they kicked you out. But I felt I sort of understood how my grandfather had this bitter sweet thing about Greece. It was there every time we asked him questions. A sparkle in his eye and then ... something else – sadness and a warning about ... you know the fate of the Jews.

Carol: Was there another place in Rhodes that made you think of those moments?

Miriam: Yes. In the synagogue. They have plaques there with the names of all the families that were killed in the Holocaust. Even though their immediate family was in Egypt, their family name is there on the wall. It's very moving. You meet all the Israeli tourists there, many of them Greek Israelis. When you can't find your home, this house of worship [Beit Tfila – house of prayer] ... it's the closest thing to it.

Recalling Erez and Yoav's tales above, Miriam too recounts the unexpected identification and understanding of previously tacit familial lived experiences. The re-emplacement of their grandfather in his ancestral home allows for new found comprehension of his previously inexplicable Otherness as well as the more complex recollections of moments of expellee nostalgia. Reading her account as a narrative whole, one can trace a full range of tourist experiences in Miriam's account – ranging from pre-war heritage tourism in the café, to dark atrocity tourism in the synagogue with the more liminal experience of heritage/dissonant homecoming in the village. Recalling Marschall's (2015b) description of expellee homecoming at sites of erasure, Miriam depicts the way in which one might be both nostalgically homesick while no less cognizant of the contexts of forced displacement. After four family visits to Rhodes, Miriam has created contemporary newly shared lived memories of the familial homeland, bridging the period of absence between present familial life in Israel and their pre-Holocaust lives in Greece that ruptured familial continuity.

Heritage Organizations and High School Trips as Surrogate Families

As the survivor generation dwindles, second- and third-generation descendants turn to heritage organizations as mnemonic surrogates, supplementing their own 're-memory' (Marschall, 2015a; Tolia-Kelly, 2004) and thereby facilitating access to familial heritage on the brink of absence and erasure. *Landsmannschaften* (voluntary ethnic organizations) have become an additional site of Israeli Holocaust heritage work and pre-war Jewish heritage work in Israel. *Landsmannschaften* are also important meeting places where some survivors feel 'safe' to break their silence with like others while preserving their mother tongues and ruptured folk traditions. Descendants have recently become active in these voluntary organizations, seeking traces of their pre-war and Holocaust heritage.

Pazit describes her activities at the Greek *Landsmannschaft* as 'filling in the blanks' left behind after her father had passed away. Lectures by survivors, Greek food fests and music performances enable immersion in one's familial heritage – both the dark and pale heritage. It is at these events that descendants pool the remnants of their family histories in preparation of their trips. According to Pazit, 'meeting the last survivors or other descendants in the organization helped us rediscover our connection to our past. It was like having a large extended family to support your own.' During her roots trip in Thesaloniki, Pazit experienced a sense of 'déjà-vu' as a product of both her own embodied memories and her new 'surrogate' family:

> I walked the streets feeling as if I had already been there before. I had to go, I had to make the place concrete after years of just imagining it. I heard bed time stories from my parents as a child about this shop and that alley. It becomes this mythic place, like sleeping beauty. So I just had to make it concrete. But when you go there you realize that no matter how fairytale-like it was, it did become a part of you ... and you feel at home in those streets because they already took you there. It's eerie and wonderful at the same time. But I have to admit that without the

organization, I couldn't have done it. You just can't put the pieces of that puzzle together on your own. Maybe it's a matter of the courage they give you, maybe it's hearing other people's stories that help you remember yours. My only regret is that I couldn't see my father's home. The people wouldn't let us in. Some friends warned me though that the locals might not want to let the Jews back in ... In a way I can understand them. But I stood outside for a while. It's not the same thing ... but I was close. I know they lived there 60 years ago, but maybe it's better that I didn't go inside – this way I can still imagine ... what it would have been like ... to be there with my father.

Descendant recollections of parental tales come alive as Pazit walks the streets of Thessaloniki. She reflexively explains that her innate sense of familiarity and belonging in memoryscapes not her own, are products of 'mythic tales' of the homeland told at bedtime. The lived experience of parental tales of Thessaloniki became 'a part of her', an example of descendant 're-memory' (Marschall, 2015b). In contrast to the joint survivor and descendant trips above, one might assume that the absence of the survivor parent would make it impossible for Pazit to utilize the trip to re-experience the emotional traces of pre-war communal life tacitly present in her childhood. However, with the help of organizational activities, Pazit's visit jump-started her lived memory of the presence of Thessaloniki. In fact, Pazit claims her experience of déjà -vu results from having been 'taken there'. Thus bedtime stories about Thessaloniki are depicted as virtually 'being there together' with her parents. In this way her roots trips are narratively framed as 'concretizing' virtually 'shared' familial visits to her ancestral homeland. Although when failing to gain access to her ancestral home, Pazit was confronted with moments of dissonance between the 'wonderful' experience of nostalgic homecoming and Holocaust dark tourism, she is far more accepting of the inevitable local responses to returned 'expellees' than Erez in the interview above. Despite the obvious obstacles of time and place, for Pazit being 'close' to her parental home was not only sufficient but preferable as it permitted the illusion of shared co-presence.

Although Israeli high school trips to Poland have primarily entailed visits to sites of Holocaust atrocity for the past 30 years (Feldman, 2004), educators have recently encouraged third-generation Holocaust descendants to seek information regarding their heritage from their survivor grandparents and/or second-generation parents – information that would permit customized visits to the remnants of pre-Holocaust family heritage (Balberg-Rotenshtreich, 2004). Seventeen-year-old Maya, recalls her experience of searching for her grandfather's pre-war home during her high school trip to Poland. Prior to the trip, Maya's family and teachers had joined forces to plan the search mission designed as one of the key events on the itinerary. Her parents went through old family documents while her mother and aunts struggled to recall fragmented and forgotten parental tales of pre-war life. In Maya's case the 'treasure hunt' was all the more moving as her grandfather had recently passed away, transforming the trip into a familial salvage mission. Maya recounts how, with directions in hand, she, a Polish guide and her teacher went in search of the apartment. After finding the site, Maya excitedly encircled the building and to her great surprise she met tenants who knew of a Jewish family that had lived there. They then introduced Maya and her entourage to their elderly father who remembered Maya's grandfather. As Maya recalls: 'this was unbelievable, I was not only there and saw his home ... but I actually met people who knew him, from then! It sounds strange, I know, but talking to them made me feel, well, as if time had not passed. As if it was still my grandfather's house.'

The height of her achievement was not only to be at the authentic site of material pre-Holocaust familial presence, but to actually meet someone 'from then' who had personally survived the passage of time and could authenticate Maya's discovery. Maya immediately called her parents and adopted the new role of third-generation mediator and recounted the tale to her group. The descendant's experience soon became a mythic hero's journey into the heart of Jewish re-presence in Poland to be told and retold throughout the school.

A month later, on Holocaust Remembrance Day, Maya's school staged a post-trip discussion. In addition to the student body, 'veterans' of the trip, teachers, school management and parents attended the event. During the event, Maya stated excitedly:

This trip was so meaningful to me, I found my grandfather's home. This is not just important for me – but for my entire family. I see myself as a messenger. I allow all of us to reconnect with the family past. My family and I are now planning a family trip to Poland to retrace the lives of our ancestors. Soon we'll all be there together. I wish my grandfather would be alive to go with us ... but with the help of the school we found our way there and he is with us in spirit.

The above institutionally organized roots trip engenders new forms of present and future familial memory work and sociality. In the case of Maya, the school encourages her family to recall tacit moments in her family's everyday life regarding survivor pre-war heritage. These are the tacit moments potentially overshadowed by sacrilized Holocaust memory disseminated and perpetuated by state sanctioned national commemorative ceremonies at national monumental sites of memory. Capitalizing on the school's existing resources and connections with local municipal officials and tour guides, it facilitated access to a former survivor home and conversation with fearful/resistant locals to enact survivor and descendant virtual co-presence in the past. Finally, it sustains the family's presence in the past as third-generation students like Maya become mediators ushering their entire family into the ancestral past so that they may together weave their heritage into their future.

Discussion

This study examined the motivations and lived experiences of Israeli descendants of Holocaust survivors who set out on family roots trips to pre-war heritage sites and sites of dissonant homeland tourism accompanied by their survivor parents and/or other descendants in search of the familial past. Post-trip semi-structured interviews disclosed the gradual marginalization of historical memory work in favour of emotive familial sociality. In the case of trips accompanied by survivors/refugees, co-presence in sites of atrocity enabled the performance of survivor-descendant we-relations tacitly present in the home, evoking descendant identification. In this way, roots trips facilitate familial bonding and the enactment of the family. Surrogate formations with descendant siblings, with ethnic heritage organizations and school roots trips allow descendants to pool mnemonic resources to ultimately disclose previously tacit transmitted and embodied familial memory and once again sociality on the move, even in the absence of the survivor. Together, descendants recall and re-enact past familial ties to their difficult heritage and/or (re)-construct future family ties to erased sites of ancestral domesticity.

Findings call for the further deconstruction of binaries such as ordinary/extraordinary, mundane/sacred, and home/away. Findings also problematize the mystification of dark tourism and suggest a nuanced reading of secular family pilgrimage.

Despite the proven limits of tourist typologies (Biran et al., 2011; Uriely, 2005), all descendants can be classified as heritage tourists (Basu, 2004; Cohen, 1979) and legacy tourists (McCain & Ray, 2003). Descendants report studying ethnic history before the trip, visiting parental childhood homes, neighbourhoods or hiding places and salvaging genealogical documents. By traversing the landscapes embedded in survivor tales, they restore the continuity of the family's past, ruptured by forced displacement (Basu, 2004; Bruner, 1996). Although some descendants were also motivated to consume Holocaust atrocity heritage (Ashworth & Hartmann, 2005), others sought out only pre-war heritage. Consistent with Stein's depiction of the way descendants seek out previously silenced survivor pasts (2009), they hoped that the re-emplacement of their parents in landscapes of their youth would 'fill in the gaps' in their familial history.

However, as the narratives of their trips unfold, the descendants move beyond their initial motive to access historical knowledge in favour of emotively intense experience (Obrador, 2011). They do not seek the experience of self-transformation or a person-centred pilgrimage to new found identity and meaning (Guthro & Palmer, 2008). Instead, by staging corporeal co-presence/proximity to familial sites of domesticity, either with the parent/grandparent or their organizational surrogates, descendants hoped to evoke the performance of the feeling world of rupture, displacement and survival (Larsen *et al.*, 2007; Obrador, 2011).

The above evocation of the emotives of survival point to the way dissonant homeland tourism is phenomenologically entangled with thanatourism or dark tourism. Descendants are aware that key emotive experiences in family life such as safety, belonging and generativity, gave way to danger, isolation and the rupture of displacement, ancestral death and parental near-death survival. They hope to experience if and how remnants of family and communal domesticity and sociality – so central to everyday lifeworlds – survive within and even overcome deathworlds. As will be discussed below, recalling their childhoods in post-Holocaust survivor family life, they are also familiar with the way traces of pre-Holocaust and Holocaust domesticity, tainted by death, silently resonated in the survivor lifeworld. As Picard and Di Giovine (2014) assert, tourism is seductive as it permits for the experience of alterity or 'the other within us'. The above nexus between homeland touristic and dark touristic motivations allows descendants to emotively embody the ancestral otherness of ruptured lifeworlds, death and near death 'within them' while continuing to trace the more empowering dialectic between death and survival.

Yet descendants also seek to discover less distressing emotions such as the nostalgia of homeland tourism despite the dissonance of recollections of domesticity under the duress of loss, hiding and subsequent expulsion. In both cases, they seek emotions that might permit for identification, bonding and thick familial sociality with either family members accompanying them on the trip, family members who have remained at home, or even those who have passed away. Findings therefore raise important questions pertaining to the long-term impact of atrocity heritage tourism on familial relations, including on those who did not participate in the journey.

Deviating from scholarly accounts of the 'extra-ordinary' experience of dark tourism and atrocity heritage (Ashworth & Hartmann, 2005; Seaton, 1996), descendants depict their familiarity with and ability to re-access the Holocaust and pre-Holocaust feeling world, claiming it was tacitly embedded within their 'ordinary' domestic social milieu. In keeping with Kidron's (2009) study of non-verbal parent–child interaction in the survivor home, emotive traces of the past were never fully 'silenced' nor absent in the survivor home. Emotional displays at sites of atrocity/heritage are thus conceptualized as materializations and magnifications of the ephemeral and fragmentary presence of the Holocaust and pre-Holocaust past in the everyday lives of survivor families.

The disclosures of emotional undercurrents are depicted as 'amazing' experiences that were (or should have been) the highlights of the trip. The roots trip potentially enables familial intimacy, identification and bonding. Descendant identification with the survivor's display of emotions permits family tourists to experience an 'existentially authentic we-relationship' (Obrador, 2011; Wang, 1999). Descendants seek 'relational knowledge' or the 'knowing' of a significant other's feeling world made possible in moments of empathic interaction (Gergen, 2009).

The above descendant 'relational knowing' at sites of familial heritage appears to problematize Landsberg's (2004) conceptualization of 'Prosthetic Memory'. Landsberg claims that in contrast to the sense of ownership and authenticity one experiences when revisiting one's own memoryscapes, the vicarious experience of the Other's heritage is limited to a 'prosthetic memory' where exposure to mass public forms of representation is necessary to mediate between the otherwise unbridgeable divides of self and other. The descendants depicted above, however, most certainly experience their ancestral heritage as authentic, over which they do feel a sense of ownership. Traces of familial memory (and re-memory) are based on familial interaction which is in no way experienced as an unbridgeable divide between self and other. Finally, the resultant sense of descendant-parent empathy does not preserve the kind of distance Landsberg (2004: 9) claims 'recognizes the alterity' of the Other – in this case their parent or grandparent.

'We-relations' of familial empathy and bonding are associated with domestic 'homely feelings' (Obrador, 2011). However, it is displacement from home that permits the family to constitute 'public niches of domesticity and intimacy' (Sheller & Urry, 2004) bolstering the home while away. The family trip therefore permits for 'home-making' (Larsen et al., 2007) as it enables the exploration of the dissonant roots of present relation and the magnification of previously tacit family dynamics. When emotional memory work succeeds, home making at heritage sites and sites of atrocity also promotes bonding, sustaining the wellbeing of the family unit. Descendant accounts therefore call for the continued deconstruction of the binary of 'home and away' (Uriely, 2011).

The above continuity between domestic everyday life and the family tourist experience raises questions pertaining to pilgrimage in pale and dark tourism. In keeping with the secular pilgrim-tourist type (Cohen, 1992; Collins-Kreiner, 2010), descendants interviewed set out to 'the past as a foreign country' (Lowenthal, 1985) to access the sacred genocidal past or no less sacred erased pre-Holocaust past that profoundly made them who they are. Consistent with Cohen (1979) and Feldman (2008), they undertake personal and familial secular pilgrimage to the ethnic and Israeli national past – or in Turnerian terms they seek their spiritual/ideological 'center out there' and ultimately experience familial *communitas* (Turner, 1973). Yet descendant respondents 'domesticate' the pilgrimage, voyaging to the familial 'emotional centre' rather than to what Feldman (2008) depicts as the national or ethnic collective Holocaust 'centre'. Descendants explore the family's constitutive events, sites, and cultural contexts that shaped the contours of familial emotions, re-examining the relational dynamics in domestic life emergent from this foundational scenario. The family pilgrimage or the surrogate organizational-family pilgrimage aimed to re-enact or restore familial memory thus differs from the solitary journey of non-descendants or the mass pilgrimage (Poria *et al.*, 2006) where the center is staged and re-enacted first and foremost as a collective/national historical event (Feldman, 2008).

Further deviating from the pilgrim type, the descendant does not depict a linear trajectory moving from the ordinary/mundane world of everyday life to the extraordinarily/sacred centre at Holocaust or pre-Holocaust sites (MacCannell, 1999). Instead, descendants continuously shift between childhood memories of heritage-related family relations and the magnified moments of parental emotions at the sites. Unlike Feldman's (2008) tour bus on school voyages to Poland that functions as a demarcated mundane safe haven from the 'death-world' beyond bus perimeters, the border between familial mundane life-worlds at home and death-worlds or dissonant memoryscapes on descendant family tours is porous. Even when moving toward emotional peak experiences, descendants seek to de-mystify collective representations of the difficult past, by staging and magnifying more mundane responses to suffering previously familiar to them from everyday life within the family.

The array of mundane familial motives, heritage tourist practices and emotions depicted above calls upon scholars and brokers in the field to continue to create a dialog between pale and dark heritage tourism (Jamal & Lelo, 2010; Uriely, 2005). The family's domestication of sites of atrocity and dissonant homeland tourism and normalization of the sublime experience of difficult heritage indicates that recent insights regarding the diversity of motives and array of emotions in familial pale tourism and familial leisure practices may be productively applied to dark family tourism without fearing banalization of the sanctity of mass suffering. Demystifying dark tourism, the emotive experience of one's dissonant heritage may be at once spiritually and ideologically meaningful while remaining embedded within ordinary lived experience.

In keeping with Marschall's (2015a, 2015b) insights regarding homeland tourism of expellees, findings pertaining to the re-domestication of sites of dissonant heritage call for further analysis of the very complex emotions of those who come 'home' to sites from which they were forcibly expelled or from which they fled for their lives. Although extensive work has been done on the legacies of refugee psychological distress, future research might examine the often conflicted yet no less empowering experience of return visits of refugees and their descendants. Complex embodied and emotive responses that re-domesticate homes and neighbourhoods (that might otherwise remain either mundane sites where new dwellers erase the past or public sites of collective dissonant memory) create a unique nexus between the proposed demystification of dark heritage tourism and the paradigm of home and away.

Once demystified, further examination of emotion-work undertaken at sites of atrocity/heritage/dissonant heritage may contribute to our understanding of how empathy, identification, bonding and we-relations function in pale family tourism. Aiming to supplement research on the post-modern questions of authenticity and emotions (McIntosh & Prentice, 1999) or hegemonic enlistment of the emotional experience (Feldman, 2008), an ethnographic reading of emotion work in all forms of heritage tourism may decipher how the existential experience of emotion 'works' or fails to 'work' in different sites.

References

Ashworth, G. and Hartmann, R. (2005) Introduction: Managing atrocity and tourism. In G. Ashworth and R. Hartmann (eds) *Horror and Human Tragedy Revisited: The Management of Sites of Atrocities for Tourism* (pp. 1–14). New York: Cognizant Communication Corporation.

Balberg-Rotenshtreich, A. (2004) Educational and humanistic journey or popular adolescent vacation?: Fifteen years to youth trips to Poland. *New Directions* 10, 158–167. (Hebrew).

Basu, P. (2004) My own island home: The Orkney homecoming. *Journal of Material Culture* 9 (1), 27–42.

Bell, M.M. (1997) The ghosts of place. *Theory and Society* 26 (6), 813–836.

Biran, A., Poria, Y. and Oren, G. (2011) Sought experiences at (dark) heritage sites. *Annals of Tourism Research* 38 (3), 820–841.

Bruner, E.M. (1996) Tourism in Ghana: The representation of the slave trade and the return of the black diaspora. *American Anthropologist* 98 (2), 290–304.

Carr, N. (2011) *Children's and Families' Holiday Experience*. London: Taylor & Francis.

Caton, K. and Santos, C.A. (2007) Heritage tourism on route 66: Deconstructing nostalgia. *Journal of Travel Research* 45 (4), 371–386.

Cohen, E. (1972) Toward a sociology of international tourism. *Social Research* 39 (1), 164–182.

Cohen, E. (1979) A phenomenology of tourist experiences. *Sociology* 13 (2), 179–201.

Cohen, E. (1992) Pilgrimage centers: Concentric and eccentric. *Annals of Tourism Research* 19 (1), 33–50.

Cohen, E.H. (2011) Educational dark tourism at an in populo site: The Holocaust museum in Jerusalem. *Annals of Tourism Research* 38 (1), 193–209.

Collins-Kreiner, N. (2010) Researching pilgrimage: Continuity and transformations. *Annals of Tourism Research* 37 (2), 440–456.

Denzin, N.K. (1970) The sociological interview. In N.K. Denzin (ed.) *The Research Act in Sociology: A Theoretical Introduction to Sociological Methods* (pp. 122–143). London: Butterworths.

Duval, T. (2004) Conceptualizing return visits. In T. Coles and D. Timothy (eds) *Tourism, Diasporas and Spaces* (pp. 50–61). London: Routledge.

Feldman, J. (2008) *Above the Deathpits and Beneath the Flag: Youth Voyages to Poland and The Performance of Israeli National Identity*. New York: Berghahn.

Gergen, K.J. (2009) *Relational Being: Beyond Self and Community*. Oxford University Press.

Giddens, A. (1991) *Modernity and Self-Identity*. Cambridge: Polity.

Gouthro, M. and Palmer, C. (2010) Pilgrimage in heritage tourism: Finding meaning and identity in the industrial past. In M. Conlin and L. Jolliffe (eds) *Mining Heritage and Tourism: A Global Synthesis* (pp. 33–43). London: Routledge.

Graham, B. and Howard, P. (2008) Introduction: Heritage and identity. In B. Graham and P. Howard (eds) *The Ashgate Research Companion to Heritage and Identity* (pp. 1–18). Hampshire: Ashgate.

Haldrup, M. and Larsen, J. (2003) The family gaze. *Tourist Studies* 3 (1), 23–46.

Jamal, T. and Lelo, L. (2010) Exploring the conceptual and analytical framing of dark tourism: From darkness to intentionality. In R. Sharpley and P. Stone (eds) *The Tourist Experience: Contemporary Perspectives* (pp. 29–42). New York: Routledge.

Kadman, N. (2010) Roots tourism – whose roots?: The marginalization of Palestinian heritage sites in official Israeli Tourism sites. *Teoros Revue de Recherch de Tourisme* 29 (1), 1–13.

Kidron, C.A. (2009) Toward an ethnography of silence: The lived presence of the past in the everyday lives of Holocaust trauma descendants in Israel. *Current Anthropology* 50 (1), 5–27.

Kidron, C.A. (2013) Being there together: Dark family tourism and the emotive experience of co-presence in the Holocaust past. *Annals of Tourism Research* 41, 175–194.

Kidron, C.A. (2015) Survivor-family memory work at sites of Holocaust remembrance: Institutional enlistment or family agency? *History and Memory* 27 (2), 45–73.

Kirshenblatt-Gimblett, B. (1998) *Destination Culture: Tourism Museums and Heritage.* Berkeley: University of California Press.

Landsberg, A. (2004) *Prosthetic Memory: The Transformation of American Remembrance in the Age of Mass Culture.* New York: Columbia University Press.

Larsen, J. (2008) De-exoticizing tourist travel: Everyday life and sociality on the move. *Leisure Studies* 27 (1), 21–34.

Larsen, J., Urry, J. and Axhausen, K.W. (2007) Networks and tourism mobile social life. *Annals of Tourism Research* 34 (1), 244–262.

Lennon, J.J. and Foley, M. (1999) Interpretation of the unimaginable: The U.S. Holocaust Memorial Museum, Washington, D.C., and dark tourism. *Journal of Travel Research* 38 (1), 46–50.

Logan, W. and Reeves, K. (2008) Introduction: Remembering places of pain and shame. In W. Logan and K. Reeves (eds) *Places of Pain and Shame: Dealing with 'Difficult Heritage'* (pp. 1–14). London: Routledge.

Lowenthal, D. (1985) *The Past is a Foreign Country.* Cambridge: Cambridge University Press.

MacCannell, D. (1999) *The Tourist: A New Theory of the Leisure Class.* Berkeley, CA: University of California Press.

MacDonald, S. (2010) *Difficult Heritage: Negotiating the Nazi Past in Nuremburg and Beyond.* London: Routledge.

Marschall, S. (2015a) 'Homesick tourism': Memory, identity and (be)longing. *Current Issues in Tourism* 18 (9), 876–892.

Marschall, S. (2015b) Touring memories of the erased city: Memory, tourism and notions of 'home'. *Tourism Geographies: An International Journal of Tourism Space, Place and Environment* 17 (3), 332–349.

McCain, G. and Ray, N.M. (2003) Legacy tourism: The search for personal meaning in heritage travel. *Tourism Management* 24 (6), 713–717.

McIntosh, A.J. and Prentice, R. (1999) Affirming authenticity: Consuming cultural heritage. *Annals of Tourism Research* 26 (3), 589–612.

Minca, C. and Oakes, T. (2006) *Travels in Paradox: Remapping Tourism.* Oxford: Rowman & Littlefield.

Noy, C. (2004) This trip really changed me: Backpackers' narratives of self-change. *Annals of Tourism Research* 31 (1), 78–102.

Noy, C. (2007) The poetics of tourist experience: An autoethnography of a family trip to Eilat. *Journal of Tourism and Cultural Change* 5 (3), 141–157.

Obrador, P. (2011) The place of the family in tourism research: Domesticity and thick sociality by the pool. *Annals of Tourism Research* 39 (1), 401–420.

Picard, D. and Di Giovine, M.A. (2014) Introduction: Through other worlds. In D. Picard and M.A. Di Giovine (eds) *Tourism and The Power of Otherness: Seductions and Difference* (pp. 1–30). Bristol: Channel View Publications.

Poria, Y., Reichel, A. and Biran, A. (2006) Heritage site management: Motivations and expectations. *Annals of Tourism Research* 33 (1), 1172–1188.

Prentice, R. and Anderson, V. (2007) Interpreting heritage essentialism: Familiarity and felt history. *Tourism Management* 28 (3), 661–676.

Ramirez, M., Skrbiš, Z. and Emmison, M. (2007) Transnational family reunions as lived experience: Narrating a Salvadoran auto-ethnography. *Global Studies in Culture and Power* 14 (4), 411–431.

Santos, C.A. and Yan, G. (2009) Genealogical tourism: A phenomenological examination. *Journal of Travel Research* 49 (1), 56–67.

Seaton, A. (1996) Guided by the dark: From thanatopsis to thanatourism. *International Journal of Heritage Studies* 2 (4), 234–244.

Sheller, M. and Urry, J. (2004) *Tourism Mobilities: Places to Play, Places in Play.* London: Routledge.

Stein, A. (2009) Trauma and origins: Post-Holocaust genealogists and the work of memory. *Qualitative Sociology* 32 (3), 293–309.

Stone, P. and Sharpley, R. (2008) Consuming dark tourism: A thanatological perspective. *Annals of Tourism Research* 35 (2), 574–595.

Stone, P. (2009) Dark tourism: Morality and new moral spaces. In R. Sharpley and P. Stone (eds) *The Darker Side of Travel: The Theory of Dark Tourism* (pp. 56–74). Bristol: Channel View Publications.

Tolia-Kelly, D. (2004) Locating processes of identification: Studying the precipitates of re-memory through artifacts in the British Asian home. *Transactions of the Institute of British Geographers* 29, 314–329.

Tunbridge, J. and Ashworth, G. (1996) *Dissonant Heritage: Managing the Past as a Resource in Conflict.* Chichester: John Wiley.

Turner, V. (1973) The center out here: Pilgrim's goal. *History of Religions* 12 (3), 191–230.

Uriely, N. (2005) The tourist experience: Conceptual developments. *Annals of Tourism Research* 32 (1), 199–216.

Uriely, N. (2011) Home and away in VFR tourism. *Annals of Tourism Research* 37 (3), 854–857.

Walter, T. (2009) Dark tourism: Mediating between the dead and the living. In R. Sharpley and P. Stone (eds) *The Darker Side of Travel: The Theory and Practice of Dark Tourism* (pp. 39–55). Bristol: Channel View Publications.

Wang, N. (1999) Rethinking authenticity in tourism experience. *Annals of Tourism Research* 26 (2), 349–370.

11 The Articulation of Collective Slave Memories and 'Home' among Expatriate Diasporan Africans in Ghana

Aaron Yankholmes

Initially, when I came down, folks would ask, when are you returning home?
Then I would say, here is home, and they would exclaim, akwaaba *(welcome).*

#17/CC/AA/F

Introduction

Since the launch of the United Nations Educational Scientific and Cultural Organization (UNESCO) Slave Route Project, several researchers have taken an interest in understanding the manifold and pernicious repercussions of the Transatlantic Slave Trade on both continental Africans and those in the diaspora. Considerable attention has been devoted to diasporan Africans' self-conception and cultural identity. DuBois' (1915) seminal collection of essays, *The Souls of Black Folks*, drew attention to the African-American cultural experiences in the US. He put forward the concept of 'double consciousness' to describe facets of the African-American's split personality. Since then a number of theoretical and empirical studies have examined the diversity in African-American identity (Cross, 1991; Gates, 1989; Worrell *et al.*, 2001). As Eyerman (2004) notes, the African-American label was not a natural category to assume, but is rather borne out of the collective memory of slavery.

In the same manner, some of the literature suggests that in a number of Caribbean and Latin American countries, including Brazil, Cuba, Dominican Republic and Colombia, diasporan Africans hold negative attitudes towards their black identity and African heritage (Lovejoy, 2008; Yelvington, 2001). Thus, for people of African descent, the question of cultural identity is fraught with a constant process of (re)negotiation and continual reframing, not only within the contestations over citizenship, socio-economic and civil rights but also their diasporic imagination and (mis)conceptions of Africa as their ancestral home (Angelou, 1986; Appadurai, 1991; Isaacs, 1963; Sundiata, 2003).

Several studies have persuasively demonstrated that continental Africans hold negative stereotyped beliefs about diasporan Africans, in particular, African-Americans (Magubane, 1987; Mwakikagile, 2005; Wamba, 1999). While many of these stereotypes are inaccurate, the search for identity, collective or individual, has a profound effect on the shared interpretations of the past as it touches so centrally on ancestry. Little is known about how identity influences the articulation of slave memories among people of African descent and there have been particularly few sustained efforts at examining the collective slave memories of diasporan Africans who are committed to their black identity and emigrated to their presumed homelands in Africa (Shaw, 2002). While notable exceptions exist for prior research attention, exploring the ideological and political reasons for emigrating to Africa (Gaines, 1999; Lake, 1990, 1995; Lindsay, 1994; Otero, 2010) and the subsequent relations with resident populations there (Okoye, 1971; Wright, 1988), the majority of current research has focused on diasporan African roots tourism experiences (Austin, 2002; Ebron, 2000; Reed, 2006; Schramm, 2004; Timothy & Teye, 2004). This study focuses on the articulation of slave memories and how it influences the search for collective identity and heritage among expatriates who have established relatively long-term residence in Ghana. It is argued that notions of 'home' play a significant role in their identity construction given the context of collective memory.

Although this book focuses on temporary touristic visits of diasporic people to their real or imagined ancestral homes, the current chapter involves those who more or less permanently 'returned' to the land of their slave ancestors. Some have undergone DNA testing and can positively trace their ancestry to Ghana; others are perhaps drawn to the country as a predominantly symbolic homeland. This chapter illustrates that, even for those who can trace their genetic lineage, the socio-cultural context of the ancestral communities makes the connection to 'home' tenuous (Nelson, 2008; Rotimi, 2013). The chapter aims to show how expatriate diasporan Africans in Ghana articulate collective memories of 'home' in a nuanced manner compared to those of diasporan African root tourists. While roots tourists travel to Ghana to remember the experiences of their enslaved ancestors and indulge in reflective lamentations while visiting slavery-related sites, they do not necessarily refer to 'home' in positive terms emphasizing collective identity (Mensah, 2015). In many ways, the nature of tourism produces varied escapist behaviours that often disregard or are unconscious of identity dissonance (Giddens, 1991).

Collective Memory and Collective Identity

A central premise underlying the current study is that collective memory provides a sense of people's identity. In the case of expatriate diasporan Africans, it contends that narrations about 'home' are shaped by the collective memories and articulations of ancestors' experiences during the Transatlantic Slave Trade (Gilroy, 1997). Expatriate diasporan Africans 'recall' memories about slavery and encode their collective experiences of the past, despite not having been directly involved. There is at least one intriguing outcome of the increased scholarly interest in memory: whether memory is an individual or group affair (Kansteiner, 2002; Olick, 1999; Winter, 2010). Funkenstein (1989: 6) argues that

> consciousness and memory can only be realized by an individual who acts, is aware, and remembers. Just as a nation cannot eat or dance, neither can it speak or remember. Remembering is a mental act, and therefore it is absolutely and completely personal.

A considerable stir and, to some extent, irritation was aroused among social scientists and humanists when Maurice Halbwachs (1925 republished in 1992) published his treatise, *The Social Framework of Memory* in 1925, in which he argued against memory as an exclusively individual affair, but rather as the building blocks of collective memory. He contended that individual memories cannot exist on their own but are tied to the collective framework of social reference points that allows them to be recalled in time and space. He notes '[I]t is in society that people normally acquire their memories. It is also in society that they recall, recognize, and localize their memories' (Halbwachs, 1992: 38). Even when individuals have the ability to recall past experiences, he argues, they can be pressured to reconstruct the past in ways that conform to societal norms and values in the present.

> Society from time to time obligates people not just to reproduce in thought previous events of their lives, but also to touch them up, to shorten them, or to complete them so that, however convinced we are that our memories are exact, we give them a prestige that reality did not possess. (Halbwachs, 1992: 51)

This view is important as it constitutes the crux of his argument in regard to the manifold ways different individuals and interest groups within society hold multiple and to some extent contradictory versions of the past. The result is that collective memory is inherently unstable and unreliable.

Not only did Halbwachs make the case for understanding the relationship between memory and society, but he also reinforced his arguments using a connection with identity. Halbwachs argued that social identity essentially defines the content of collective memories. In this way, identity is bound by space or time. Through a sense of identity and shared experiences, people seek new relationships throughout time and space. But some scholars caution us about the entanglement of memory and identity (Gillis, 1994; Megill, 1998), while others see memory as indistinguishable from identity (Assmann & Czaplicka, 1995).

Notwithstanding the epistemological and ontological critiques of the concept of collective memory, it remains relevant and applicable in facilitating our understanding of how expatriate diasporan Africans remember past experiences of their enslaved progenitors during the Transtlantic Slave Trade. Of course, arguing that collective memories are shared representations of the past evokes Berliner's (2005: 208) question, 'Can we really remember something we did not experience? Can someone [who did not actually experience] remember the slave trade?' He asked this in reference to Shaw's (2002) use of 'remembering' in the context of investigating slave memories in Sierra Leone. The answer lies in Halbwachs' (1990) differentiation between collective memory and history. Halbwachs asserts that history aims to be objective, and distanced; it tends to record change and sequence of events over a given time period while collective memory is living, continuous and organic. As an organic phenomenon, collective memory is credible to a number of writers, including Nora (1989: 8) who makes the following distinction between history and collective memory:

> Memory is life, borne by living societies founded in its name. It remains in permanent evolution, open to the dialectic of remembering and forgetting, unconscious of its successive deformations, vulnerable to manipulations and appropriation, susceptible to being long dormant and periodically revived. History, on the other hand, is the reconstruction, always problematic and incomplete, of what is no longer. Memory is a perpetually actual phenomenon, a bond tying us to the eternal present; history is a representation of the past.

Given that there are no survivors of those who experienced the Transtlantic Slave Trade, present-day diasporan Africans are engrossed in recollections of the cruelty and barbarity that their enslaved ancestors suffered. It is this reminiscing and identifying with the past that feeds into their idea of 'returning home', despite the fact that they did not actually experience the Transtlantic Slave Trade or had never been previously domiciled there. In the above case, recounting the past is a means to re-establish collective identity with members of their ancestral communities.

Approaching the question of how expatriate diasporan Africans could remember what they have never directly experienced from this angle immediately brings to mind the social frameworks within which people reconstruct their memories and the limitations of this process. Halbwachs posited that memory reconstruction is constrained by forgetting, especially when remembering traumatic events evokes intense emotions in descendants of the victims. This is particularly true in the context of collective slave memories articulated by members of the African diaspora. As suggested at the beginning of this chapter, the Transtlantic Slave Trade was barely present in humanity's collective memory before the launch of UNESCO's Slave Route Project. While the Slave Route Project has helped rekindle collective slave memories through scientific research, education and cultural heritage tourism, some continental and diasporan Africans are predisposed to forgetting the past, not just because of its strong emotional undercurrents, but also as a means of 'creating space' for new memories. Connerton (2008: 63) notes that such a form of forgetting 'becomes part of the process by which shared memories are constructed because a new set of memories are frequently accompanied by a set of tacitly shared silences'. Therefore, guaranteeing the mnemonic maintenance and survival of collective slave memories is daunting because it serves no purpose for some stakeholders in the management of their identity and ongoing purposes.

Expatriate Diasporan African Community in Ghana and the 'Homeland' Question

The relationship between human mobility, particularly migration and tourism, was until recently a scarcely covered topic by tourism researchers (Hall & Williams, 2002). Given the multiple connotations of migration, it is not surprising that the term 'diaspora' entered the tourism lexicon. Nevertheless, there is no universally fixed meaning of 'diaspora', even though its conceptualization until the 1960s was associated with Jewish, Armenian and Greek forced dispersal and displacement. (For an extensive discussion on the history and evolution of the term see Cohen, 2008.) Safran's (1991) conceptualization is used in this study. He argued that the concept of 'diaspora' applies when members share the following distinctive characteristics:

- they, or their ancestors, have been dispersed from a specific original 'centre' to two or more 'peripheral', or foreign, regions;
- they retain a collective memory, vision, or myth about their original homeland – its physical location, history, and achievements;
- they believe that they are not – and perhaps cannot be – fully accepted by their host society and therefore feel partly alienated and insulated from it;
- they regard their ancestral homeland as their true, ideal home and as the place to which they or their descendants would (or should) eventually return – when conditions are appropriate;

- they believe that they should, collectively, be committed to the mainte- nance or restoration of their original homeland and to its safety and pros- perity; and,
- they continue to relate, personally or vicariously, to that homeland in one way or another, and their ethnocommunal consciousness and solidarity are importantly defined by the existence of such a relationship. (Safran, 1991: 83–84)

Four of the six criteria above make reference to a homeland and eventual return to it. This notion of homeland, which is given relevance in a 'home' environ- ment as the focal point for diasporic identity has been viewed by many as inadequate for capturing the heterogeneity, hybridity and transnational nature of contemporary African dispersions (Akyeampong, 2000; Brah, 1996). Cohen (2008) stresses the virtues of retaining a diasporic identity while abroad and the power of collective identity and memory expressed not just with the homeland but also in the countries of exile with people of other ethnicities. Based on this, he proposed a five-fold typology of diasporas (victim, labour, imperial, trade and deterritorialized) based on the commonalities of experi- ences and the structural processes mediating their experiences. Interestingly, he echoes Safran's (1991) point about a real or imagined homeland in delineat- ing diasporic people. As succinctly pointed out by Lovejoy (1997: 3), 'diaspora' 'ceases to have meaning if the idea of an ancestral home is lost'.

This seems to be particularly true in the case of the African diaspora. Indeed, the initiator of the term, Shepperson (1966), likened the Transtlantic Slave Trade dispersal of Africans to the Jewish experience. While some disagree with the comparison of African diaspora to that of the Jews (Racine, 1982), it lends support to Safran's conception of a neglected or lost nostalgic connection that diasporic people have with an original homeland that is driven by collec- tive memory, vision and myth. In this study, no attempt is made to homoge- nize the African diaspora or standardize its corresponding attributes. This study acknowledges the multiplicities of diasporan Africans and Africans gen- erally. The term 'diasporan Africans' is used here, following Lake (1990: 1), as 'people of African descent born outside of Africa [...]'. Viewed in this context, the 'African diaspora' is conceived both as a political term and an analytical framework. As a political term, it emphasizes the unifying experiences of Africans dispersed by the Transtlantic Slave Trade while as an analytical term, it provides the platform for this study to navigate people of African descent across international boundaries (Patterson & Kelley, 2000).

There are several historical accounts from different periods pointing to the myriad of factors that encouraged freed slaves and descendants of slaves from the Caribbean, North America and South America to relocate or 'return' to Africa (Drachler, 1975; Everill, 2012; Harris, 1982; Sundiata, 2003). Several manumitted Afro-Brazilians, Afro-Cubans and other descendants of slaves from the Caribbean decided to settle or 'return' to Togo, Benin, Nigeria and

Ghana owing to restrictions on employment and ownership of property in the Americas (Lindsay, 1994; Otero, 2010). In the case of African-Americans, the evidence suggests that the purpose of the first wave of migration during the 18th and 19th centuries was to escape racism and attempts to deny their social equality with whites. The migrants (in this case, descendants of slaves) were mostly settled in Sierra Leone in the 18th century and Liberia in the 19th century (Dunbar, 1968; Weisbord, 1973). The quest for land, new economic opportunities as well as exercising absolute right of property ownership were additional motivating factors that propelled African-Americans to emigrate (Walker, 2009).

One of the key points of reference in the discourse on the various repatriation or reverse migration schemes was the idea of a return 'home' (Basu, 2005; Marschall, 2015). With few exceptions, however, research persists in portraying the repatriation as 'homecoming' in terms of a nostalgic longing for the past, omitting reference to collective slave memory (Hosley, 2004; Richards, 2008; Schramm, 2004). Markowitz (1995) reminds us that what at the start of a journey was conceived as a homecoming might turn into a new diaspora. In other words, the early repatriates were not only driven by an insatiable quest to establish filial links with the continent and reaffirm their African-ness but also adopt wider loyalties with members of their ancestral community (Harris, 1992; Walters, 1993). According to Edmondson (1979: 412), the 'search for black roots' was formulated along three dimensions: (1) an inspirational rediscovery of the lessons of the past; (2) a pragmatic search for possibilities in the present; and (3) an ideal conception of the potential for the future. But Patterson and Kelley (2000: 19) note that

> ... diasporic identities are socially and historically constituted, reconstituted, and reproduced; and that any sense of a collective identity among black peoples in the New World, Europe, and Africa is contingent and constantly shifting. Neither the fact of blackness nor shared experiences under racism nor the historical process of their dispersal makes for community or even a common identity.

Suffice it to say that the choice of Ghana for the migrants was by no means arbitrary and the reasons are well documented in the literature (Dunbar, 1968; Gaines, 1999; Weisbord, 1973). Despite being a key supply point for captives during the Transtlantic Slave Trade era, the subsequent British colonization of the coastal areas of the Gold Coast (Ghana's colonial name) in 1844, gave impetus to two types of migration at different time periods; one involving manumitted slaves, and the other involving descendants of slaves. The first movement took place in 1836, and it was the direct effect of the Malê Revolt. It involved mainly former slaves who resettled in Accra (the capital since 1877), which at the time was a major commercial hub with a large population of European and Middle Eastern merchants.

The second wave can best be described as reverse migration; it involved Afro-Caribbeans who were brought in following Britain's take-over of the Gold Coast. Substantially similar to the previous wave but different in terms of the time frame, the next wave of reverse migration involving mostly African-Americans occurred after Ghana formally attained political independence in 1957 (Essien, 2014). Despite local agitations for political independence, the Pan-Africanist Movement spearhead by George Padmore, Henry Sylvester Williams, Edward Wilmot Blyden and W.E.B. DuBois played a tremendous role in the independence of Ghana (Lake, 1990). Ghana became a safe haven and draw for both continental and diasporan African nationalists, liberation fighters, as well as intellectuals who were encouraged to transfer their knowledge and expertise to their local compatriots (Gaines, 1999). Owing to the paucity of data, it is difficult to estimate the current population of expatriate diasporan Africans in Ghana even though Johnson (2014) puts the figure at about three thousand. In some instances, diasporan African immigration to their presumed homelands in Africa take escapist motives, possibly resulting from an attachment to the search for roots or for pleasure (Yankholmes & Mckercher, 2015).

There is a rich body of literature in which early émigrés described their experiences in Ghana (Angelou, 1986; Boadi-Siaw, 2009; Lake, 1990; Magubane, 1987). In particular, African-Americans realized to their chagrin that local residents did not accept aspects of their lifestyle and they, in turn, found no connection with the local cultural context. This resulted in 'uncomfortably' cordial relationships between them. The reasons underlying these frosty relationships between the two groups are still being debated (Osei-Tutu, 2007; Zachary, 2001), but one must not generalize the diasporan Africans' relationships with continental Africans. Skinner (1982: 17) identified five dialectic contradictions in the relations between diasporic people and their ancestral homelands:

(1) anger, bitterness and remorse among the exiles, often among the people at home over the weaknesses that permitted the dispersion to occur;

(2) conflict when the dominant hosts attempt to justify the subordinate status of the exiles, and the latter, in turn, refuse to accept the inferior status thrust upon them;

(3) acrimonious debate among the exiles themselves, and between them and their host and ancestral communities, as to whether the exiles should return to their homelands;

(4) if a return does occur, there is frequently a conflict between the returnees and populations resident there. A corollary is the issue of what effect a return will have on those exiles still in the diaspora; and

(5) the various groups of exiles, their hosts and the people in the homelands face the problem of what to do once the issues arising from the dispersion have been resolved.

It is tempting to analyse the current study on expatriate diasporan Africans along the lines of Skinner's (1982) dialectical continuums, but this is difficult due to the nature of the available data. It is worth reiterating that this study relates primarily to the manner in which expatriate diasporan Africans and members of their ancestral community deal with the reasons for the dispersal. Additionally, this study relates to how expatriate diasporan Africans push their imagination of their enslaved ancestors' experiences to members of their ancestral community as legitimate means of forging a collective identity and to reinforce their sense of 'home'.

Method and Research Setting

This chapter is based on data drawn from a previous research project that examined the 'tourismification' of the slave routes by the Slave Route Project (Yankholmes, 2013). As the current study was not aimed at verifying any specific and operational hypothesis derived from theory, an exploratory qualitative orientation involving semi-structured interviews was adopted.

The informants were 20 expatriate diasporan Africans recruited from Cape Coast, Elmina and Accra in June 2012 (Table 11.1). Twelve were African-Americans; six African-Caribbeans and the rest African-South Americans. Most were female, had lived in Ghana for at least 20 years and had college degrees. With the exception of one informant, most emigrated in 1992, following the First Pan African Historical Festival (PANAFEST) held in Ghana. While the sample is not representative of the expatriate diasporan African community in Ghana, it depicts their locational preferences, which in turn follow the general development trajectory of the country (Lake, 1995).

Because Elmina, Cape Coast and Accra were not just active slave trading spots, as evident in their fortifications, but have also become migrant communities for members of the African diaspora, there is value in highlighting the socio-historical contexts of these locations. Originally, built as trading posts, Elmina Castle (São Jorge da Mina constructed by the Portuguese in 1482); Cape Coast Castle (Fort Carolusburg built in 1664 by the Swedes); and Osu Castle (Christiansburg built by the Danes in 1659 to replace the Portuguese (1640) and Swedish (1652) lodges) were later expanded into castles. During the slaving era, the castles did not only house expatriate staff, traders and later captives in their subterranean dungeons, but also became extended fort communities of mostly Afro-Europeans (Feinberg, 1989; Hernæs, 1996; Lever, 1970).

This last point should be of considerable interest in understanding the socio-political and spatial organization of these fort communities during the slaving era, which lasted well into the post-colonial era. For instance, with increasing competition characterized by power struggles over areas of trade, Accra was fashioned into three European zones of influence: Dutch Accra

Table 11.1 Selected characteristics of the sample

Location	Anonymous	Ethnic identity	Age	Sex	Education	Occupation	Years in Ghana	Year moved
ACC	1	AA	55	F	Degree	Teacher	23	1989
ACC	2	AA	52	M	Degree	Administrator	20	1992
ACC	3	AC	65	F	Degree	Retired nursing assistant	33	1979
ACC	4	AA	62	F	Diploma	Retired administrator	31	1981
ACC	5	ASA	72	F	Degree	Retired accountant	40	1972
ACC	6	AC	45	M	Degree	Business owner	20	1992
ACC	7	AA	53	F	Degree	Registered nurse	23	1989
ACC	8	AA	46	F	Diploma	Beautician	20	1992
ACC	9	AA	75	F	Diploma	Retired/ business owner	52	1960
ACC	10	AC	54	M	Degree	Construction engineer	20	1992
ACC	11	ASA	68	F	Degree	Artist /writer	20	1992
CC	12	AC	52	F	Degree	Accountant	20	1992
CC	13	AA	46	M	Degree	Travel agent	20	1992
CC	14	AA	63	M	Degree	Runs private hotel business	19	1993
CC	15	AC	55	F	Diploma	Business owner	20	1992
CC	16	AA	50	M	Diploma	Social worker	20	1992
CC	17	AA	45	F	Degree	Software analyst	20	1992
ELM	18	AA	68	F	Diploma	Runs family hotel business	23	1989
ELM	19	AC	56	F	Diploma	Sales manager	20	1992
ELM	20	AA	63	M	Diploma	Tour operator	25	1987

Note: ACC = Accra, CC = Cape Coast, ELM = Elmina; AA = African-American, AC = African Caribbean, ASA = African South American; M = Male; F = Female.

(Fort Crevecoeur), English Accra (James Fort) and Danish Accra (Christiansburg) (Parker, 1960). There is compelling evidence that as early as the 1830s, Dutch Accra housed many Afro-Brazilians who were granted land by the local chief (Boadi-Siaw, 2009). It is not surprising, therefore, that many latter émigrés lived in Accra (Skinner, 1963). At present, Accra's status as the national capital with a disproportionate share of infrastructure entices both internal and international migrants. In terms of tourism development, Accra towers over and above all other cities. Besides boasting the only international airport, Accra possesses the lion's share of four and five-star accommodation establishments as well as entertainment centres, museums and cultural institutions.

Of particular relevance to diasporan Africans is the W.E.B. DuBois Centre for Pan-African Culture and the George Padmore Research Library on African Affairs. The city also has a bustling nightlife, many fine restaurants and beaches which are very popular with both Ghanaian and foreign revellers. Initial plans to turn the Christiansburg, which used to be the seat of government from 1877 to 2013, into a tourist site have not come to fruition. On the other hand, Cape Coast and Elmina have become popular tourist destinations in Ghana mainly as a result of deliberate government policy to build attractions and supporting infrastructure in those places. Under the aegis of the United States Agency for International Development (USAID) and other donor agencies, the Cape Coast and Elmina Castles were extensively rehabilitated between 1992 and 1997, while Kakum National Park located 30 kilometres away, was created. Following their rehabilitation, the Cape Coast and Elmina Castles now attract large numbers of visitors, both domestic and foreign.

A better appreciation of the dialectics between expatriate diasporan Africans and resident Ghanaians is premised on an understanding of the criteria for membership in former Slave Trade communities. Like most African communities, there are two contrasting bases for membership: kinship or blood ties and affinity, the latter referring to kinship created on the basis of law (McCaskie, 1995; Perbi, 2004). Therefore, the issue of collective identity depends upon how stringent or permissive members of the ancestral community define consanguinity or affinity. But the degree of strictness or laxness also depends on community members' psychological disposition towards recounting the past, as well as the power relations and social structures of the community.

Both purposive and snowballing techniques were employed in the selection of the informants in each town. The author approached some well-known expatriate diasporan Africans who operate tourism-related businesses in the study locations. These initial contacts were asked to suggest acquaintances that were relevant, available and who might be interested in the study. Inclusion in the study, however, was dependent on the subject's willingness to be interviewed. This non-random approach was suitable because referrals occurred through personal network links and it guaranteed the most suitable people in the sample, especially as further background checks were undertaken by the researcher in keeping with the study's definition of expatriate diasporan African (Allen, 1971). However, the inherent weakness of the purposive and snowball sampling techniques is that informants with larger personal networks may be over-sampled while those with relatively small personal networks could be excluded. This bias was countered by saturating the sampling population in the study areas, thereby capturing informants with the full array of network sizes (Heckathorn, 1997).

The participants were interviewed at their homes. All interviews were semi-structured, lasting about one and-a-half to two hours. The interview started with 'grand tour questions' that elicited descriptions of their personal and family life narratives and issues emanating from the transition into a new social and cultural environment. Within this context, the interview then covered collective slave memories, issues of place attachment and identity, particularly local residents' reactions and attitudes towards their return and opinions about a range of slavery-based heritage tourism related issues, including the conservation and preservation of slave sites. The results used in this study are derived from interview questions on collective slave memories, identity and the transition process.

The data is presented in narrative form in order to capture the words of informants as well as organize and give meaning to their perceptions of identity and how the articulation of collective slave memories influences collective identity construction (Kvale, 1996). Informants' quotes are presented with their anonymous number as well as profile characteristics for which Table 11.1 provides a key.

Results and Discussion

The study's results demonstrate the richness and complexity of participants' articulation of collective slave memories and relationships to their ancestral communities. More importantly, recollecting collective slave memories provides the space for expatriate diasporan Africans to demand acknowledgement of the weakness of their ancestral community that permitted slavery and the dispersion to take place, which in turn legitimates the diaspora's natural right to 'return' to the ancestral homeland. It also facilitates a more nuanced understanding of how the past event is used as a means to (re)negotiate collective identity and ultimately the symbolic representations of 'home'.

Collective slave memories

Most participants were well versed in their genealogical history linked to the Slave Trade. Their sources of knowledge were stories handed down within the family. It was also evident that some had internalized slave narratives from popular history books, films and docudramas. This was not surprising, given the generational changes since the official abolition of slavery in 1807 by Britain, and the subsequent collective silence, disquiet and amnesia that ensued. Second-hand knowledge is very applicable to participants' recollection of their progenitors' traumatic experience since few, if any, collective memories of events can realistically endure for more than 400 years. This second-hand account of memory supports Halbwachs' view that societies in each era reconstruct their contemporary frame of reference. It makes sense, therefore, to say that the participants inferred collective slave memories from various indicators, such as reusable texts, images, rituals and monuments (Assmann & Czaplicaka, 1995). This intuition notwithstanding, an important empirical issue concerns whether participants' articulations of collective slave memories correspond to historical truths. While distinguishing false and historically inaccurate slave narratives is relevant given the political contestations that attend collective memories, what is important here is how expatriate diasporan Africans use slave narratives to imagine or explore the past.

#2/ACC/AA/M .... My fifth great grandmother (sic) used to talk about life on the plantations but she didn't talk about our African ancestry. She couldn't remember the original names of our original African ancestors. I was about twenty years when I found out about our servile origins.

#4/ACC/AA/F ... I never really paid much attention to the stories of my parents about slavery when I was a child. But I realized it was important when I was growing up and during my first year at college. I realized how little those stories had changed when I read some history books back in college. My parents told me Africans were captured from the villages in Africa and sold into slavery.

#6/ACC/AC/M ... Like many Jamaicans, I don't have a lot of family photos. Slave trade defines who I am and it is an emotional thing for me because it was based on race. I found most of the clues to my African ancestry by searching online; my ancestors were captured in Ghana and sent to work in Jamaica's sugarcane plantations.

#18/ELM/AA/F ... The Atlantic Slave Trade always brings on not just feelings of fear but more a feeling of bewilderment in not understanding how people could be treated that way ... it's like saying what did we do? What did we do as African people that someone will treat us like that? You get thrown into cells and you have your freedom taken away from you and all the rest of it ... what did we do wrong for that to happen to us?

Significantly, they were also emotional about the culpability of members of their ancestral communities in the trade.

#10/ACC/AC/M ... I read many historical accounts of the slave trade and am flabbergasted by what happened. But I am even more horrified and deeply affected by the idea that Africans sold their own people as slaves.

And:

#13/CC/AA/M ... How do you forgive your brother who sells you into slavery? The Biblical Joseph did just that. He forgave his brothers who sold him into slavery out of envy! That's why the chiefs apologized and government (of Ghana) initiated the Joseph Project some time ago. But you feel this apology was not sincere. Come to think of it, if there wasn't a sinister motive, why haven't the mutual animosities thawed over the years?

And:

#17/CC/AA/F ... This is very emotional for me because it goes back to what I was saying earlier about my sense of attachment to Ghana. I think both Africans in the diaspora and Ghanaians are living in denial. Ghanaians would have to come to terms with the role they played in the slave trade while diaspor[ic] Africans would have to appreciate that returning to Africa is more than acquiring local names or getting married to natives.

These comments highlight the complicated and political nature of collective slave memories. It is necessary, once again, to return to how Halbwachs explained societies reframing the past to fit the present by adopting different defence mechanisms. In this case, articulation of collective slave memories, particularly the culpability of continental Africans, provides the space for expatriate diasporan Africans to demand acknowledgement of the reasons for the dispersion and this, in turn, provides the most potent way of ensuring the maintenance and survival of collective slave memories and (re)negotiating collective identity around the past as evidenced by the Slave Route Project.

Ancestral 'home' as a place for personal heritage reclamation

Participants' recollections of collective slave memories also helped to explain their relationship with members of ancestral communities. For those who experienced the early uneasy relationships with resident Ghanaians, social exchange was a highly valued element inextricably tied to their search for personal heritage. Informants had a strong affinity to members of the ancestral community who simultaneously connected them to and defined their 'home'.

> #5/ACC/ASA/F … I don't need anyone to tell me I am African. The melanin in my body gives me away. That is who I am, an African and so coming back to Ghana felt like coming back home; home is where your people are. Brazil isn't home; that is where my ancestors were sent and brutalized. Ghana is where I trace my roots and the people are generally nice. Here I feel a stronger connection to my ancestors.

> #14/CC/AA/M … Ghanaians are generally nice people and many were receptive when I returned. I have been here since 1993 and so this is definitely my home. You know what I mean; Ghana is where my ancestors were uprooted and shipped away into slavery. So Ghana is home to me. You don't know your roots until you go back to the very place from where your ancestors were uprooted.

> #17/CC/AA/F … Most folks I come across think I'm Ghanaian because I have been here since 1992 and managed to pick up some slang phrases, which I use all the time. Initially, when I came down, folks would ask, when are you returning home? Then I would say, here is home, and they would exclaim, *akwaaba* (welcome).

When asked the meaning of 'home', informants reiterated the link between collective slave memory and 'home'. For most, it provided the opportunity to belong to the spaces of their progenitors and an opportunity to reframe and familiarize with their agony, even if remembering the traumatic event brought them emotional discomfort or pain. This illustrates Safran's (1995) notion of 'home' among diasporic people. Within the context of expatriate diasporan Africans, the description of 'home' demonstrates the past that they seek to recreate within the present and future. Gilroy (1994) also notes the significance of 'home' as a construct of memory in the dynamics of diasporan Africans remembering and commemorating.

> #10/ACC/AC/M … Home is where you have memory; without memories you have no real relationship to any place. My parents are from Jamaica but moved to Louisiana when I was two years old. So I grew up in Louisiana and my parents continue to live there … But I moved here and have kind of found my roots. … This is where my ancestors were captured and sent across the high seas to the Americas and that's why my parents supported my decision to return. In fact, the other day I was talking to my dad on the phone and he said, he wished he had that kind of courage to do what I have done. So Ghana is home away from home, my ancestral home.

The presence of numerous slave-related sites was the first thing that participants identified with their ancestral 'home'. Though many of these sites are popular tourist places, they served both as tangible and visible reminders of the past as well as reference points for the articulation of collective slave memories.

> #16/CC/AA/M ... The dungeons present a vast store of agonizing experiences of our ancestors ... they are definite reminders of man's cruelty towards man.

> #18/ELM/AA/F ... When you go somewhere and the people welcome you with some meaning to it, you feel a deep connection. That feeling came about when I first visited the castle dungeons [...]. All of a sudden, I was in a room full of women crying and screaming and I began to have queer feelings; shivering all over my body. Then I realized that within the screaming and crying was my own voice; ... in the midst of these women, I could feel hands on me, people just soothing me and telling me it was ok; that I have come home ... this is where I belong. And when I walked out of the dungeons, I knew then before I even talked to my husband who did not come on that trip, he came three months later. But I know when I stepped out of the castle dungeons that I would never be the same person again and that Ghana, Africa, was going to be my home for the rest of my life ... I knew that ...

So participants' articulations of slave memories notarized slavery related sites. It rendered their memories intelligible for members of the ancestral community, thus fostering a sense of bond with their ancestral 'home'. However, not everyone in the ancestral communities was receptive to their 'return'.

> #14/CC/AA/M ... I was surprised at the reaction of some Ghanaians. Whenever I tell them I have finally returned home, they found it hard to believe because they assume I had a good life back in America. For most Ghanaians, it appears that anywhere across the Atlantic was better than being in Africa. They are not aware of the feelings that slavery has instilled in me. But I told them that in America we were always made to feel inferior.

> #20/ELM/AA/M ... The reaction was mixed. Among the enlightened [people], I found open reception. People welcomed my return and made me feel at home ... made me feel that I was at the right place, not a strange place, this is my ancestral home. Then, of course, you have those who considered me a 'stranger' or 'oburonyi' [an Akan word used for foreigners, including diasporic Africans] or 'Whiteman' coming from America; coming from the West and I basically attributed it to their ignorance ... you know ... based on the historical dilemma and dynamics of

what produced the African diaspora. So I did not take offence at that. But most often, I considered it an ignorant response rather than any kind of ill-feeling.

The informants' comments about local residents' reactions to their 'return' reflect a widespread perception among the Ghanaian public that diasporan Africans come to Ghana to be 'knighted' as 'development chiefs' (Benson, 2003). But the phenomenon of 'development chiefs' has become a controversial issue for the chieftaincy institution, particularly because it is plagued by succession conflicts, many of which are traced to the presence of people of slave descent in royal households (Perbi, 2004). The irony here, as the interviews demonstrate, is that even though expatriate diasporan Africans have come to stay, 'bondedness' with some members of the ancestral community does not follow. Regarding the '*oburonyi*' charge, it is premised on what many Ghanaians see as an idealized view of foreigners. As Reed (2006) points out, Ghanaians sometimes call one another *oburonyi* if they have fair complexion, Western education, speak English, hold a white-collar job, travel abroad or exhibit features associated with Western cultures. As a result, the dividing line between Blacks and Whites is obscure. Therefore, the meaning of the designation *oburonyi* can only be established on a case-by-case basis.

Collective identity and belonging

The salience of a 'return' was seen as an inescapable link to the past, a demonstration of the bond with the ancestral 'home' and, ultimately adherence to collective identity. Not only did the 'return' reinforce the participants' self-concept but it also deeply entrenched collective identities based on the horror of the past.

> #3/ACC/AC/F ... This community gives [us] our basic identity. The Transatlantic Slave Trade made this community what it is today and, by implication, who we are as people of African descent.

Interestingly, some participants in Cape Coast and Elmina encountered resistance from some traditional rulers and local residents who were worried about the influence they exerted over community development issues.

> #18/ELM/AA/F ... When we first arrived, we went to the chief's palace to greet him as the Ghanaian custom demands. So we started off on a good footing and we worked hard for everything we have now. But somewhere along the lines some folks in the palace and neighbours were peeved because we told folks to complain about the lack of basic facilities in the community. People come to us for financial assistance all the time and some frankly don't know what kind of help is available from the

traditional authorities. So we decided that the way to do it was to educate them about their basic rights. But you know how it is here, when you step on toes of higher-ups. ... I have no regrets ... none (pause). I have challenges, yes; but I have never regretted the decision that we made to leave America to come back to Africa.

And the relatively strict conditions that expatriate diasporan Africans have to meet in order to qualify as community members induced a sense of social exclusion:

#1/ACC/AA/F ... Erm. To feel a sense of belonging in Ghana does not come from years of association or marriage. It comes from being part of a family or clan. People are nice and friendly but you are considered an outsider. Even if you speak the language, because you don't belong to a clan you cannot be a part of the grain of this society, despite your African ancestry.

#10/ACC/AC/M ... Some Ghanaians look down on Rastafarians. They think we smoke weed, keep to ourselves and dress shabbily. But like other African diasporans whose ancestors were taken away, this is where we belong.

This theme relates to other findings discussed in the extant literature. For instance, Feldman (2016) notes that diaspora Jews who immigrate in Israel constantly have to deal with issues of cultural alterity and identity. As in this investigation, the findings of that study also highlight how the return to the 'homeland' and contact with 'others' impact on the traveller's sense of identity. Although informants may have experienced alterity in their identity construction, this was not the predominant finding in the current study, as settlers did not feel that the marked cultural differences with the locals had anything to do with their assumed identity. Informants are passionate about the collective memory of slavery, which is at the core of their identity and connection to the 'motherland'.

A disconnection was felt at some slavery-related sites. Some informants raised issues about a sanitized past being presented at the Elmina and Cape Coast Castles. Others also recognized slavery-related sites in the northern and southern part of Ghana as places to be carefully negotiated. This resonates with the research of scholars who have described how African-Americans have opposed conservation and preservation efforts at the Cape Coast and Elmina Castles (Hosley, 2008). The current evidence suggests that the driving force behind participants' low engagement at well-known slave sites was the sense of a lack of entitlement to spaces of their forefathers. This idea was captured by two informants who note that:

#14/CC/AA/M ... Here [referring to Cape Coast] it's hard to feel the lamentations of the general population by virtue of the dungeon experience. It's almost like they are separate. There [referring to Salaga in the northern part of Ghana] you feel the people along with the site ... They are all one. You feel people are hurt and have a feeling of tragedy and how it affected them. They seem to be part of it. Here you have to look deeper to see it.

#18/ELM/AA/F ... My subsequent visit to Ghana opened up an area that I was not familiar with in terms of the history of African people and our relationship to the castle dungeons ... back then the castle dungeons had not been desecrated; they hadn't been painted and all the rest of that and it pretty much was a foreboding edifice, which is how it should have stayed forever!

Taken together, these sentiments show that participants were keenly aware of the power of representations. This could be detected in their engagement with local residents and at slavery-related sites. This outsiders' representation in spaces of their forbears does far more than create a sense of apprehension and psychological dislocation, though positively identifying with the ancestral 'home'. It complicates their self-concept, thus decreasing the likelihood of collective-oriented behaviours representing that collective identity. Simmel (1950) offers a way to understanding this apparent paradox. He explains how in comparison to other forms of social distance and difference (such as class, gender, and even ethnicity) the distance of the stranger has to do with his or her 'origins'. This implies that there exists an element of rootlessness even in the ancestral 'home', which in this context poses a social dilemma. It is this dimension of strangeness experienced by expatriate diasporan Africans that a number of previous authors have omitted to investigate.

Conclusions

This chapter demonstrates how identity influences the articulation of collective slave memories among expatriate diasporan Africans in Ghana. The findings can be discussed under three themes: contested identities, ambivalent relations and 'homeland' truths. The expatriate diasporan Africans' view of genealogy and ancestral 'home' is defined by collective slave memories. The articulation of such memories provides the frame and means for negotiating collective identities and forges a role for the past in the present. However, they continue to live with the indignities of the past. Not only does their familial connection to members of their ancestral communities seem tenuous but they were moreover seen as 'strangers'. This situation raised questions about their sense of place and representation. In so far as articulation of collective slave memories concretizes the sense of collective identity, expatriate diasporan Africans' conception of 'home' attains a subtle meaning. Hence, the implicit and explicit meaning of collective identity becomes central to the ontological reality of one's slave ancestry.

An analysis of the relations between expatriate diasporan Africans and members of their ancestral communities reveals ambivalence embodied in the articulation of collective slave memories. At the core of this ambivalence is the weakness that permitted the dispersion to occur. Conscious of the social distance from their ancestral communities, expatriate diasporan Africans articulate collective slave memories as a means of negotiating collective identity construction. This reflects the problematic relationship between reflexivity of behaviour and the degree of fixity in social relations with members of their ancestral communities. Importantly, analysis of their sense of 'home' and belonging was based on the interaction between ancestry and social relationship. As such Cape Coast and Elmina provides a clear illustration of the manifestation of strangeness. In this sense, because collective identity revolves around ancestral 'home', it requires the acknowledgement that it is accessible.

Expatriate diasporan Africans realized that settling in Ghana, in and of itself, did not provide adequate support for belonging to the spaces of their progenitors. In particular, the socio-spatial changes that have taken place in the ancestral communities meant that recollection of the past is constantly reselected and reinterpreted by different stakeholders in response to contemporary needs. In the collective slavery memory process, aspects such as a people's ancestry are suppressed and relationships with different segments of the community are altered. More importantly, the increasing popularity of slavery heritage tourism with its attendant socio-economic benefits to the ancestral communities influences, to a large extent, how members of the community maintain familial ties and how they reinforce their imagination and portrayal of ancestral 'home' for members of the African diaspora.

References

Akyeampong, E. (2000) Africans in the diaspora: The diaspora and Africa. *Africa Affairs* 99, 183–215.

Allen, H.B. (1971). Principles of informant selection. *American Speech* 46, 47–51.

Angelou, M. (1986) *All God's Children need Traveling Shoes*. New York: Vintage Books.

Appadurai, A. (1991) Global ethnoscapes: Notes and queries for a transnational anthropology. In R.G. Fox (ed.) *Recapturing Anthropology: Working in the Present* (pp. 191–210). Santa Fe: School of American Research Press.

Assmann, J. and Czaplicka, J. (1995) Collective memory and cultural identity. *New German Critique* 65, 125–133.

Austin, N.K. (2002) Managing heritage attractions: Marketing challenges at sensitive historical sites. *International Journal of Tourism Research* 4 (6), 447–457.

Basu, P. (2005) Roots-tourism as return movement: Semantics and the Scottish diaspora. In M. Harper (ed.) *Emigrant Homecomings: The Return Movements of Emigrants 1600–2000* (pp. 131–150) Manchester: Manchester University Press.

Benson, S. (2003) Connecting with the past, building the future: African Americans and chieftaincy in southern Ghana. *Ghana Studies* 6, 109–133.

Berliner, D. (2005) The abuses of memory: Reflections on the memory boom in anthropology. *Anthropological Quarterly* 78 (1), 197–211.

Boadi-Siaw, S. (2009) The Afro-Brazilian returnees in Ghana. In K.K Prah (ed.) *Back to Africa Vol. 1: Afro-Brazilian Returnees and their Communities* (pp. 149–153). Cape Town, South Africa: CASAS Book Series.

Brah, A. (1996) *Cartographies of Diaspora: Contesting Identities*. London: Routledge.

Cohen, R. (2008) *Global Diasporas: An Introduction* (2nd edn). London: UCL Press.

Connerton, P. (2008) Seven types of forgetting. *Memory Studies* 1 (1), 59–71.

Cross, W.E. and Vandiver, B.J. (2001) Nigrescence theory and measurement: Introducing the cross racial identity scale (CRIS). In J.G. Ponterotto, J.M. Casas, L.A. Suzuki and C.M. Alexander (eds) *Handbook of Multicultural Counseling* (pp. 371–393). Thousand Oaks, CA: Sage.

Cross, W.E. (1991) *Shades of Black: Diversity in African-American identity*. Philadelphia: Temple University Press.

Drachler, J. (ed.) (1975) *Black Homeland, Black Diaspora: Cross-current of the African Relationship*. Port Washington, NY: Kennikat Press.

DuBois, W. (1915) *The Souls of Black Folk*. Chicago: A.C. McClurg.

Dunbar, E. (1968) *Black Expatriates*. New York: Dutton.

Ebron, P. (2000) Tourist as pilgrims: Commercial fashioning of transatlantic politics. *American Ethnologist* 26 (4), 910–932.

Edmondson, L (1979) Black roots and identity: Comparative and international perspectives. *International Journal* 34 (3), 408–429.

Essien, K. (2014) 'Afie ni afie' (home is home): Revisiting reverse trans-Atlantic journeys to Ghana and the paradox of return. *Ìrìnkèrindò* 7, 47–75.

Everill, B. (2012) Destiny seems to point me to that country: Early nineteenth-century African American migration, emigration, and expansion. *Journal of Global History* 7, 53–77.

Eyerman, R. (2004) Cultural trauma: Slavery and the foundations of African American identity. In J.C. Alexander, R. Eyerman, B. Giesen, N.J. Smelser and P. Sztompka (eds) *Cultural Trauma and Collective Memory* (pp. 60–111). London: University of California Press.

Feinberg, H.M. (1989) Africans and Europeans in West Africa: Elminians and Dutchmen on the Gold Coast during the eighteenth century. *Transactions of the American Philosophical Society* 79 (7), 1–186.

Feldman, J. 2016. *A Jewish Guide in the Holy Land: How Christian Pilgrims Made Me Israeli*. Bloomington and Indianapolis: Indiana University Press.

Funkenstein, A. (1989) Collective memory and historical consciousness. *History and Memory* 1 (1), 5–26.

Gaines, K. (1999) African American expatriates in Ghana and the Black radical traditions. *Souls* 1 (4), 64–71.

Gates, H.L. (1989) What's in the name? Some meanings of blackness. *Dissent* 36, 487–495.

Giddens, A. (1991) *Modernity and Self-identity*. Cambridge: Polity.

Gillis, J.R. (1994) Memory and identity: The history of a relationship. In J.R. Gillis (ed.) *Commemorations: The politics of National Identity* (pp. 3–23). Princeton, NJ: Princeton University Press.

Gilroy, P. (1994) Diaspora. *Paragraph* 17 (3), 207–212.

Gilroy, P. (1997) Diaspora and the detours of identity. In S. Hall and K. Woodward (eds) *Identity and Difference* (pp. 276–300). London: Sage.

Halbwachs, M. (1992) *On Collective Memory*. (L.A Coser. Trans.). Chicago: The University of Chicago Press. (Original work published 1925).

Hall, C.M. and Williams, A. (eds) (2002) *Tourism and Migration: New Relationships between Production and Consumption*. Dordrecht, The Netherlands: Kluwer Academic Publishers.

Harris, E.L. (1992) *Native Stranger: A Black American's Journey into the Heart of Africa*. Simon and Schister: New York.

Harris, J.E. (ed.) (1982) *Global Dimensions of the African Diaspora*. Washington: Howard University Press.

Heckathorn, D.D. (1997) Respondent-driven sampling: A new approach to the study of hidden populations. *Social Problems* 44, 174–199.

Hernæs, P. (1996) European fort community on the coast in the era of the slave trade. In J. Everaet and J. Parmentier (eds) *Shipping, Factories and Colonialism* (pp. 167–180). Brussels, Belgium: Koninklijke Academic Voor Overzeese Wetenschappen.

Hosley, B. (2004) Transatlantic dreaming: Slavery, tourism and diasporic encounters. In F. Markowitz and A. Stefansson (eds) *Homecomings: Unsettling Paths of Return*. Oxford: Lexington Books.

Hosley, B. (2008) *Routes of Remembrance: Refashioning the Slave Trade in Ghana*. Chicago: University of Chicago Press.

Isaacs, H. (1963) *The New World of Negro Americans*. New York: John Day.

Johnson, T. (2014) How to apologize for slavery: What the U.S. can lean from West Africa. See http://www.theatlantic.com/international/archive/2014/08/how-to-apologize-for-slavery/375650/ (accessed 9 September 2014).

Kanesteiner, W. (2002) Finding meaning in memory. A methodological critique of memory studies. *Memory and Theory* 41 (2), 179–197.

Kvale, S. (1996) *Interviews: An Introduction to Qualitative Research Interviewing*. Thousand Oaks, CA: Sage.

Lake, O. (1990) A taste of life: Diaspora African repatriation to Ghana. PhD thesis, Cornell University, Ithaca.

Lake, O. (1995) Towards a Pan-African identity: Diaspora African repatriation in Ghana. *Anthropological Quarterly* 68 (1), 21–36.

Lever, J.T. (1970) Mulatto influence on the Gold Coast in the early nineteenth century: Jan Nieser. *African Historical Studies* 3 (2), 253–261.

Lincoln, Y. and Guba, E. (1985) *Naturalistic Inquiry*. Beverly Hills: Sage.

Lindsay, L.A. (1994) To return to the bosom of their fatherland: Brazilian immigrants in nineteenth-century Lagos, *Slavery & Abolition* 15 (1), 22–50.

Lovejoy, P. (1997) The African Diaspora: Revisionist interpretations of ethnicity, culture and religion under slavery. *Studies in the World History of Slavery, Abolition and Emancipation* 2 (1), 1–21. See http://www.yorku.ca/nhp/publications/Lovejoy_Studies%20in%20the%20World%20History%20of%20Slavery.pdf (accessed 20 March 2013).

Lovejoy, P. (2008) Transatlantic transformations: The origins and identities of Africans in the Americas. In L. Sansome, E. Soumonmi and B. Berry (eds) *Africa, Brazil and the construction of Trans-Atlantic identities* (pp. 81–112). Trenton, NJ: Africa World Press.

Magubane, B.M. (1987) *The Ties that Binds: African-American Consciousness of Africa*. Trenton, NJ: African World Press.

Markowitz, F. (1995) Criss-crossing identities: The Russian Jewish Diaspora and the Jewish Diaspora. *Diaspora* 4 (2), 201–10.

Marschall, S. (2015) Touring memories of the erased city: memory, tourism and notions of 'home'. *Tourism Geographies* 17 (3), 332–349.

McCaskie, T.C. (1995) *State and Society in Pre-colonial Asante*. Cambridge: Cambridge University.

Megill, A. (1998) History, memory, identity. *History of the Human Sciences* 11 (3), 37–62.

Mensah, I. (2015) The roots tourism experience of diaspora Africans: A focus on the Cape Coast and Elmina Castles. *Journal of Heritage Tourism* 10 (3), 213–232.

Mwakikagile, G. (2005) *Relations between Africans and African Americans: Misconceptions, Myths and Realities*. Johannesburg, South Africa: Continental Press: Pan-African.

Nelson, A. (2008) Bio science: Genetic genealogy testing and the pursuit of African ancestry. *Social Studies of Science* 38, 759–783.

Nora, P. (1989) Between memory and history: Les Lieux de Mémoire, *Representations*
26, 7–24.

Okoye, F.N. (1971) *The American Image of Africa: Myths and Reality*. Buffalo: Black Academy
Press.

Olick, J.K. (1999) Collective memory: The two cultures. *Sociological Theory* 17 (3), 333–348.

Osei-Tutu, B. (2007) Transformations and disjunctures in the homeland: African
American experiences in Ghana. In J.K. Anquandah, N.J. Opoku-Agyemang and
M.R. Doortmont (eds) *Transatlantic Slave Trade: Landmarks, legacies, expectations* (pp.
326–342). Proceedings of the International Conference on Historic Slave Route.
Accra: Sub-Saharan Publications.

Otero, S. (2010) *Afro-Cuban Diasporas in the Atlantic World*. New York: University of
Rochester Press.

Parker, J. (1960) *Making the Town-Ga state and Society in the Early Colonial Accra*. Portsmouth
HN: Heinemann.

Patterson T.R. and Kelley, R.D.G. (2000) Unfinished migrations: Reflections on the
African Diaspora and the making of the modern world. *African Studies Review* 43 (1),
11–45.

Perbi, A.A. (2004) *A History of Indigenous Slavery in Ghana from the 15th to the 19th Century*.
Accra: Sub-Saharan Publications.

Racine, D.L. (1982) Concepts of diaspora and alienation as privileged themes in negritude
literature. In J.E. Harris (ed.) *Global Dimensions of the African Diaspora* (pp. 94–105).
Washington: Howard University Press.

Reed, A. (2006) Gateway to Africa: The pilgrimage tourism of Diaspora Africans to
Ghana. PhD thesis, Indiana University, Bloomington.

Richards, S. (2008) Landscapes of memory: Representing the African Diaspora's return
'home'. In N. Opoku-Agyemang, P. Lovejoy and D. Trotman (eds) *Africa and
Transatlantic Memories: Literary and Aesthetic Manifestations of Diaspora and History* (pp.
291–301). Trenton, NJ: Africa World Press.

Rotimi, N.C. (2013) Genetic ancestry tracing and the African identity: A double-edge
sword. *Developing World Bioethics* 3 (1), 151–158.

Safran, W. (1991) Diasporas in modern societies: Myths of homeland and return. *Diaspora*
1 (1), 83–99.

Schramm, K. (2004) Coming home to the motherland: Pilgrimage tourism in Ghana. In
J. Eade and S. Coleman (eds) *Reframing Pilgrimage: Cultures in Motion* (pp. 133–49).
London: Routledge.

Shaw, R. (2002) *Memories of the Slave Trade: Ritual and the Historical imagination in Sierra
Leone*. Chicago: University of Chicago Press.

Shepperson, G. (1966) The African abroad, or the African Diaspora. *Africa Forum* 1 (2),
76–93.

Simmel, G. (1950) *The Sociology of Georg Simmel*. (Kurt H. Wolff Trans.). New York: Free
Press.

Skinner, E.P. (1963) Strangers in West African societies. *Africa* 33 (4), 307–320.

Skinner, E.P. (1982) The dialectic between diasporas and homelands. In J.E. Harris (ed.)
Global Dimensions of the African Diaspora (pp. 17–45). Washington: Howard University
Press.

Strauss, A. and Corbin, J. (1998) *Basics of Qualitative Research*. Newbury Park: Sage.

Sundiata, I. (2003) *Brothers and Strangers: Black Zion, Black slavery, 1914–1940*. Durham,
NC: Duke University Press.

Timothy, D.J. and Teye, V.B. (2004) American children of the African Diaspora: Journeys
to the motherland. In T. Coles and D.J. Timothy (eds) *Tourism, Diasporas and Tourism*
(pp. 111–123). London: Routledge.

Walker, J.E.K. (2009) *The History of Black Business in America: Capitalism, Race, Entrepreneurship* (2nd edn, Vol. 1). Chapel Hill, NC: University of North Carolina Press.

Walters, E.W. (1993) *Pan-Africanism in the African Diaspora: An Analysis of Modern Afrocentric Political Movements*. Detroit: Wayne University Press.

Wamba, P. (1999) *Kinship – A Family Journey in Africa and America*. Penguin Group: New York.

Weisbord, R. (1973) *Ebony Kinship: Africa, Africans, and the Afro-American*. Westport, Conn: Greenwood Press.

Winter, J. (2010) The performance of the past: Memory, history, identity. In K. Tilmans, F. van Vree and J. Winter (eds) *Performing the Past: Memory, History, and Identity in Modern Europe* (pp. 11–34). Amsterdam: Amsterdam University Press.

Worrell, F.C., Cross, W.E. Jr. and Vandiver, B.J. (2001) Nigrescence theory: Current status and challenges for the future. *Journal of Multicultural Counseling and Development* 29, 201–213.

Wright, G. (1988) *Afro-Americans in New Jersey: A Short History*. Trenton: New Jersey Historical Commission.

Yankholmes, A. and McKercher, B. (2015) Understanding visitors to slavery heritage sites in Ghana. *Tourism Management* 51, 22–32.

Yankholmes, A.K.B. (2013) Developing Ghana's Slave Route Project for cultural tourism: Planning and marketing implications (Unpublished doctoral dissertation, School of Hotel and Tourism Management, 2013). The Hong Kong Polytechnic University.

Yelvington, K.A. (2001) The anthropology of Afro-Latin and the Caribbean: Diasporic dimension. *Annual Review of Anthropology* 30, 227–270.

Zachary, P. (2001, March 14) Tangled Roots: For African-Americans in Ghana, the grass isn't always greener. *Wall Street Journal*.

12 *Ongi Etorri Etxera (Welcome Home)*: A Gathering of Homecomings: Personal and Ancestral Memory

John Bieter, Patrick R. Ireland and Nina M. Ray

Introduction

It was late spring of 1889. Jose Navarro and Antonio Azcuenaga, both from the Basque Country's province of Bizkaia and in their early 20s, had gained some success after several years of hard labour in the sheep business in northwestern Nevada in the US. They had heard rumours of better opportunities in Oregon and Idaho and decided to move. They invested in a horse to carry provisions, and began the trek north across the desert.

The area was brown and crackly dry, a world away from the green hills rising above the ocean in their country of origin. Despite having been in the American West for some time, Navarro and Azcuenga had not known what to expect on this journey north and suffered the consequences of poor planning; by the end of the second day they had all but exhausted their water supply. Not knowing exactly how many miles of desert lay ahead of them, continuing north seemed foolish. Two days later, however, the two men finally reached the Owyhee River, plunged in and drank as much as their stomachs could hold.

They decided to unload their supplies and clothing from the horse, and Navarro rode away in search of more water. Azcuenaga remained in the desert with the supplies. Navarro found a creek and returned for Azcuenaga, who by this time was nearly dead from thirst. Navarro lifted him onto the horse and, leaving most of their clothing and supplies behind, returned to the creek with Azcuenaga. They continued on until they reached a small town called Jordan Valley, near the border of the Territory of Idaho. Months later, Navarro and Azcuenaga, two of the first Basque immigrants to Idaho, returned to the spot in the desert where they had nearly died. They wanted the clothes they had left behind (Silen, 1917: 182–183).

One Saturday night in June 1990, a bottleneck of humanity had formed at the main entrance of the old Idaho State Penitentiary in Boise, Idaho. It was taking ten minutes or more just to squeeze through, but once inside, the view was remarkable. Lights shone down on thousands packed into 'Lekeitio Plaza,' what years ago had been the main yard of the prison but, because of its resemblance to an Old Country village square, was chosen by the organizing committee to stage Jaialdi 1990, Idaho's International Basque Festival.

Near the entrance on the festival's main stage, the band Ordago was playing rock with English and Basque lyrics, keeping the ocean of heads, arms and legs moving. Smells of olive oil, garlic and pimientos accented the air where prodigious amounts of Basque and American food were prepared: 'solomo' (pork loin), lamb, 'churros' (deep-fried pastry), croquetas, beans, fish, pork chops with red peppers, and 'txorizo,' the pork sausage popular among Idahoans. There was every kind of souvenir: berets, bota bags, sweatshirts, T-shirts, books, hats, windsocks, stickers, posters and flags, many of them bearing the Jaialdi logo: a dancer on one knee, twirling the Basque flag. Spectators who could not identify the Basque provinces on a map angled 'txapellas,' (Basque berets), on their heads, and stumbled through improvised versions of the 'jota,' a Basque fandango.

The organizing committee for Jaialdi '90 had planned this weekend for more than a year. For weeks, advertisements had trumpeted the festival in Western magazines and newspapers. More than 1000 volunteers contributed to every detail, and on Saturday and Sunday of the festival, an estimated 25,000 people emptied 210 kegs of Budweiser and ate an estimated 5000 pounds of txorizo. During the dance on Saturday night, a visitor from the Basque Country stood near the entrance and looked down on the thousands jammed together trying their best to dance despite the limited space. She remarked, 'I don't know where I am, Boise – or the Basque Country.' The festival now takes place every five years and the one in 2015 was the largest ever.

Legacy Tourism: The Search for Ancestors and Home

Yale (2004: 21) observes that 'the fashionable concept of "heritage tourism" really means nothing more than tourism centered on what we have inherited, which can mean anything from historic buildings to art works to beautiful scenery.' In one sense of inheritance, Basques have an unusually high proportion of Rh-negative blood type (Douglass & Bilbao, 1975: 10–11). Additionally, a recent DNA study conducted at Boise State University, found that 'based upon RST and FST measures, no significant differentiation was found between the Idaho and European Basque populations' (Zubizarreta et al., 2011).

Certainly, the emotions, learned and innate, associated with one's family history are an important part of 'what we have inherited.' A sub-segment of heritage tourism is comprised of tourists who desire to move beyond the scope of general ancestry to find specific links to ancestors or ancestry roots. These legacy tourists travel to seek out information or feel connected to their genealogical or family roots. Defining sub-sets of heritage tourism creates marketing opportunities to reach these segments by understanding their motivations. McCain and Ray (2003a) found that many legacy tourists define heritage as their own family history. The definition of legacy tourism used for this study is adopted from their work; 'travel related to genealogical endeavors.'

Not only is there a large population of history-seeking tourists, but these consumers have demographics favourable to marketers.

Devine (2011: xv) discussed the 'key aspects of human experience' in his book on Scottish migration: '... identity, the relationship between host country and home country, nostalgia.' In some cases, the ancestral homeland is well defined (e.g. Norway) and the present-day boundaries are similar to centuries-old boundaries. In other cases, descendants may wonder where the ancestral homeland lies. For example, America's Scotch-Irish (or Scots-Irish) have no 'homeland' called 'Scot Ireland'. Those engaged in looking for Irish ancestors face the reality of two modern day Irelands. In the case of the Basque Diaspora, the homeland is part of other nations (Spain and France). Does this complication and confusion regarding an ancestral homeland affect the modern-day personal identity of descendants and their memory of home?

Legacy tourism may be a way of satisfying one's yearning for the past without the ability or real desire to travel back in time. While many legacy tourists claim that they wish to see the authentic locations and homes involved with their story and to learn the authentic history of their ancestors, the consumers are really looking for 'authentic inauthenticity' (Brown *et al.*, 2000: 171). According to Davies (2010: 264), a 'fundamental desire is precisely that which the nostalgic yearns for – a stable home, free from the losses of time.' Santos and Yan (2010: 64) comment that developers of legacy sites often purposely try to match the expectations of the tourists. Mkono's research on the authenticity of 'African' dining experiences at restaurants in Zimbabwe found that the food is viewed as a cultural signifier, more than simply a meal (2011: 482), as tourists often made reference to the 'Africanness' of the experience.

Sierra and McQuitty (2007) state that nostalgia can derive both from lived or learned memories (simulated nostalgia). In a classic article on the meaning of tourism, Belk (1997: 23) maintains that 'both physical journeys through time and space and metaphoric journeys are of interest.' The physical journey to ancestral homes joins with the metaphoric journey to meet with personal ancestors as the travellers seek out their records and homes. Legacy tourists are consumers who are looking for tourism experiences to 'link them to others, to a community, to a tribe' (Cova, 1997: 311). They have found their lineage to be the 'linking value' that sustains their community or ancestral tribe connection and the importance of being with fellow tourists on similar quests cannot be overestimated.

Basu (2001) describes the role of the search for identity in 'hunting down home.' He contrasts a modern view which links identity with 'fixity' and a postmodern one which suggests that personal identity and home are found in movement. Within the context of these two approaches, individuals form identity through personal narratives, i.e. telling stories of themselves. He emphasizes the need to address both 'the mobile and the static in these narratives of identity' (Basu, 2001: 336). To Basu, home can be 'deterritorialized' (Basu, 2001: 336) and a myth of homeland can be created. Using the Scottish homecoming as a focus, he shows how 'Scottishness' can be expressed through very observable activities performed by diasporic communities, such as clan societies, their gatherings and Highland Games. In some cases, these heritage elements have been reintroduced into the mother country where such activities may have died out. Being 'deterritorialized' has relevance for the Scotch-Irish who are descendants of mainly those not from the highlands of Scotland, but lowlanders who spent a century in Ulster (more or less today's Northern Ireland) and then left for the New World.

While the idea of a 'home' is often a mythical cognition, what is equally important is that this 'home' is based on a material place and can be visited forming a union of the 'imaginary and the material' resulting in 'sites of memory, sources of identity, and shrines of self' (Basu, 2001: 338). In discussing sites of memory, Basu emphasizes the need for each person to become his own historian and individualize or personalize the cultural identity, thus making the sites of memory into sources of identity and a 'myth of the self' (Basu, 2001: 342). Individuals have the ability to 'invent themselves anew' in the narrative of landscape and identity (Basu, 2001: 342). In discussing 'shrines of self', Basu mentions how the search for personal identity demonstrates the many similarities between pilgrimage and tourism and how the self is the object of a quest. 'Narratives of identity of home and homeland clearly interact in complex ways,' concludes Basu (2001: 346). Many of Basu's concepts and terms of reference ('quest,' 'pilgrimage,' etc.) are used in the empirical data gathering of this research as described later.

Searching for ancestors may be beneficial to one's mental health. Psychologists have shown that thinking about our ancestors increases self-esteem, as the 'ancestor effect' boosts performance on intelligence tests (Fischer et al., 2011). Writing and thinking about ancestors led students to do better on verbal and spatial tests. However, Craig (2005) asked, 'What does it mean to be more-or-less affluent American but trace your origins to the bleak west coast of Co. Clare, an area once famous for the intensity of its privations? ... visits to the West of Ireland began to seem less like episodes of time-travelling and more like a homecoming.' Societal benefits of diaspora/legacy tourism may result when those travelling back 'home' 'will be more interested in sustaining and improving the well-being of the local people, culture and environment' (Huang et al., 2012: 295).

Tourism to 'home and familiar places' certainly relates to diaspora or legacy tourism. VHFP (visiting home and familiar places) is an expansion of VFR (visiting friends and relatives) tourism (Pearce, 2012). VHFP is travel to the locations important in one's own life and places inhabited by one's forefathers. 'The value … lies in emphasizing the roles the past can play in shaping people's travel motivation and identity quests' (Pearce, 2012: 1027). Marschall (2014) researched 'personal memory tourism' which is less about tracking down the homestead where great-grandfather was raised, but more about where the tourist him/herself was raised. The focus of this chapter is embracing of one's ancestry, legacy and the homeland. The experience of tracing one's ancestry and home, and sharing that experience with others, can keep memory alive.

Basques in the American West: Memories and Celebrations of Home

From 1890 to 1990, Basques in Idaho evolved from the status of poor, insignificant immigrants literally staggering (due to often having a lack of potable water) across the border to an ethnic community that attracted thousands to its own festival. Over the century the Basques have been in Idaho, the opportunities of three generations have created a subculture that is neither purely Basque nor purely American. It is a Basque-American subculture, unique, yet representing a tiny cross section of the common American experience.

Most Basques came to Idaho in the first decades of the past century, finding job opportunities in sheepherding. Though this flow was slowed to a trickle by immigration laws in the 1920s – and later by an improved Basque economy that made leaving home unnecessary – that trickle remained steady until the 1970s. The sheer number of Basques made them noticeable in sparsely populated Idaho. Although there might have been more Basques in California or Argentina, few areas had such a high concentration.

When Basques arrived in Idaho, they stayed together. Basque immigrants worked, formed business partnerships and intermarried almost exclusively with other Basques. Compared to other ethnic groups, Basques faced limited discrimination. Their independence, work ethic, honesty and frugality matched American values and over time allowed them to earn the respect of their neighbours. Almost all came with the idea of returning home to the Basque Country after having saved some money. Some did. Many chose to stay (Douglass & Bilbao, 1975; Edlefsen, 1948; Keelan, 1990).

Members of the second generation were Basques at home and Americans outside of it. Their parents instilled in them good work ethics and values that, when coupled with an education, provided a solid base for a successful life in America. Many climbed the social ladder to become foremen, bankers, lawyers and businessmen. In the process, they became more American.

Most of the second generation were not ingrained with exposés about life in the Basque Country, the difficult conditions that had motivated their parents to leave homes and families forever. Instead, their focus was on a promising future. The Basque language, spoken almost universally by the first generation, was largely lost to the second, as children learned English in American schools. Some Americanized their names, moved away from Idaho, married non-Basques and entered mainstream American life. Others married Basques and never left their Basque environment – the majority settled somewhere in between. Some of the second generation did preserve Basque traditions, through dances, picnics, and sporting events. These choices kept the formal culture alive and set the stage for the third generation.

The third generation, the 'ethnic' generation, developed during a period of immense change in the US. It was becoming less fashionable to be simply 'American,' living what many considered to be a bland, 'vanilla' culture, and increasingly popular to be 'from somewhere,' to have an identity that set one apart (Gans, 1979: 1; Gleason, 1980: 54; Novak, 1971: 115). A preservation movement by a number of third-generation Basques in Idaho proved a theory proposed by historian Marcus Lee Hansen (1938), implying that the first-generation immigrant wishes to forget, but grandchildren wish to remember their heritage (Hansen, 1938). Whenever any immigrant group reaches the third generation, he explained, 'a spontaneous and almost irresistible impulse arises' which brings together different people from various backgrounds based on one common factor: 'heritage – the heritage of blood' (Hansen, 1938: 45).

While some immigrants and children of immigrants changed their names to Henry and Frank, some of the third generation named their children Maite and Aitor. 'To what degree do I take on the ways of America?' – the choice presented to the first generation – was inverted: 'To what degree do I take on the ways of Basque culture?' Their choices spread across a wide spectrum, from those with virtually no ties to the Basque community, to those who returned to the Basque Country for the rest of their lives and created their home there. In many ways, third-generation Basques had the best of both worlds: They could claim to be different from the larger American society, yet still feel the security of a community, something many Americans were lacking.

All Basques, from the time of Jose Navarro and Antonio Azcuenaga, contributed to the formation of the Basque-American subculture through their choices based upon opportunities available at that time. Future generations were wondering how to keep the memory of home alive. The Basque Government was too.

The Basque parliament passed law 8/1994, with a plan to 'promote and intensify the relations of Euskadi, the Basque society and its institutions with the Basque communities and centers abroad' (Zubiri, 2005: 5) (see Ray & Bieter, 2014 for a discussion of the success of the law on its 20th anniversary). In brief, the Basque government within Spain provides a number of programs that connect the diaspora with the Basque Country. They include grants for the euskal etxeak/Basque Clubs, economic aid for families in a situation of extreme need, and the possibility for qualifying students to attend the University of the Basque Country. The Basque government established an annual program titled Gaztemundu (youth in the World), which brings together Basque youth from throughout the diaspora to return to the Basque Country and spend time studying the culture of their ancestors. Once every four years, the Basque government also hosts a World Congress as a 'forum for social, cultural, and economic relations among the diaspora communities ... and between the diaspora communities and the Basque Government' (Ley 8/1994).

The Studies Abroad Programs: 'A Shot of Cultural Adrenaline'

Before the 1970s, there were few opportunities for young Basque-Americans to travel 'home' to Euskadi, fewer still to study the language and history of their antecedents. Some might have ventured with their parents, visiting the family farm, struggling to snag words from the galloping table conversation of their relatives. Others, like the group who later formed the Oinkari dancers, saved for months and went on their own. These were generally brief sight-seeing trips, however, from which they would bring back wonderful slides and fond memories of the typically Basque luscious cuisine, but with only a sprinkling of new Basque vocabulary and a vague grasp of Basque history.

This would change after the introduction of the 1972 summer study program in the Basque Country, sponsored by Idaho's Basque Studies Program. A small group involved with the Studies Program travelled for six weeks, spending half the time in the French-Basque town of Ustaritz, the other half in the Spanish Gipuzkoan mountain village Arantzazu. For most, it was their first trip to the Basque Country, offering an opportunity to absorb the Basque language, history and culture.

One member of the group, Dr Pat Bieter (1992), a professor at Boise State University and father of the first author of this chapter, convinced the school to establish a program in the Basque Country. 'As I realized how much I learned and grew to appreciate and love the Basque Country on this trip,' he said, 'it dawned on me that we needed to get others from Idaho over here to meet family and learn more about the history and culture' (personal communication with author 10 March 1992).

In the Fall of 1974, 75 students and five faculty members became the first Americans to participate in an extended study program on Basque soil. More recently, Lagos (2015: 237) discussed the need 'to regard the actual value of foreign study, not simply as a chance to visit a "cool" country but part of an overall educational vision'.

The village of Oñati, located in the province of Guipuzkoa, was in many ways an ideal location. A town of about 10,000, Oñati had a high percentage of Basque speakers, who used a dialect similar to that used by Basques in Idaho. For residents of the small town, it was odd to have so many Americans walking through their streets, conspicuously dressed in sweatshirts and blue jeans. Many were surprised that Americans would take such an interest in their traditions. 'It made us curious,' one Oñati resident said years later. 'We had never met anybody that spoke Basque and not Spanish. It was very nice' (Imanol Galdo, interview with J. Bieter, 31 July 1999). According to Pat Bieter's recollection of the experiences of these travellers, the Americans of Basque ancestry were also surprised, finding the region much different from the image conveyed to them. The illusion of their imagination and the reality of the Basque Country were 'pretty far apart,' one program instructor said later, and they passed through a period of 'disillusion' similar in many ways to that of Basque immigrants who returned to Euskadi after decades in the US. One Idahoan who studied on the program said the people he met in Euskadi 'weren't as Basque as I thought they'd be. Part of that was my understanding of what it meant to be Basque' (Ansotegui, 1992).

Some realized their 'Basqueness' in America was a different species of the culture they observed in the Basque Country, perhaps similar to the experience of African-Americans visiting Africa. One student said of his experience, 'When I got to the Basque Country, I realized I was different from what they were. Ironically, for the first time I realized I was an American – of Basque ancestry. Over time I also came to understand that what had developed in America was its own subculture, distinct from what was going on in Euskadi. I have to admit there was some identity crisis as I tried to sort all this out' (Bilbao, 1993).

Gradually many began to unearth new discoveries about the Basque culture, about what had survived and what had changed since the time their grandparents had emigrated. The program 'changed them and what it meant for them to be Basque,' Pat Bieter said. They saw new Basque dances and new Basque celebrations, made new Basque friends, learned to speak Basque. Some even met their future spouses in the Basque Country. 'It changed me completely,' said Steve Mendive, a third-generation Basque who studied in Oñati 1977–78. 'To know who you are and where you come from is important in directing where you're going in the future.' The Boise State program, he said, was the 'catalyst' for his heavy involvement in Basque culture. He returned to the Basque Country seven times in the next 15 years and became president of the North American Basque Association.

'The program filled a profound need,' said Dan Ansotegui, another third-generation Basque who attended the Oñati program. 'There was definitely a need for people to find out about their roots, and the best way to find out about your roots is to go back to the original land.' 'I have become much more active' in Idaho's Basque community, he said. 'A good part of that is because of my trip.' In fact, Mr Ansotegui later became the owner of 'Bar Gernika' (Gernika is Boise's sister city in the Basque Country), which is located at the beginning of the 'Basque Block' in downtown Boise, near the state capitol. Boise and the surrounding area benefits economically from the Basque heritage, just as the Basque Country does with its ties to its diaspora.

The Basque Country programs, as one Idahoan said, 'put a real shot of cultural adrenaline' into the state's Basque community. It gave the participating students the academic opportunities and background in Basque Country culture that earlier Basque-Americans never had. The Basque subculture in Idaho pushed for authenticity and a revival of the Old Country ways in a manner never previously emphasized, affecting even those who would never get the opportunity to make their own treks to the Basque Country.

For centuries, the 'baserriak,' Basque chalet-like farmhouses, formed the heart of the rural Basque identity and in many cases provided the names for individual Basque families. The adage remains, 'you don't name your farm; it names you.' In fact, the surnames that Basques carried to the new world and that helped expand the Basque identity often came from the location of a family farm, such as one finds for the following Basque names:

- Goikoetxea – 'upper house'
- Etxebarria – 'new house'
- Uberuaga – 'by the warm spring'
- Elizondo – 'by the church'

First built in the late Middle Ages and still common today, these baserriak formed to the geographical surroundings but generally consisted of two or three stories, with steep roofs and exposed beams. Often, these farmhouses contained living quarters as well as a stable and other working areas built as one unit. Because there is so little arable land, the property around each baserri is small, usually six to ten hectares, and frequently right up the side of the hill (Douglass, 1976: 48). This is still the 'home' which is in the memory of many Basques; the home they wish to visit, if for no other reason than to find the origin of perhaps the most important part of their identity – their name (Ezquerra, 2010). Basque farmhouses serve as rural guesthouses that offer accommodations to tourists. *Nekazalturismoa* is this popular form of agritourism; it builds upon the Basque historic identity associated with home and offers a way for the rural sector to remain viable in an ever globalizing economy (see for example www.nekatur.net).

In July 2015 Jaialdi occurred again, bringing in Basques from all over the world and garnering international news coverage (e.g. Johnson, 2015). Interestingly, many in Ireland (especially the North), because of their participation in the Association of European Migration Institutions, know several of the Basque dignitaries who attended Jaialdi and were invited to socialize with their Basque colleagues at the world's largest Basque festival.

Before turning to Ireland and its diaspora outreach efforts, it is worth noting that Basques, like the Irish, and the Scots, share the experience of their homeland being disputed in modern day geopolitical terms. As Leite (2005: 297) said, 'the homeland to which diasporic tourists travel is not homologous with the geographic territory of their destination. It is, instead, a place of the past.' Some hope for specific geographic territories of the future. As mentioned earlier, the Basque Country is split between two nation states, Spain and France, Scotland recently held a referendum about whether it should form its own country or remain a part of the UK, and Ireland has been divided into the Republic and the UK North for many decades. Although Ireland, unlike the Basque Country, has internal religious conflicts, these motherlands share many similarities that warrant a comparison of diaspora experiences and return travel.

Gathering the Irish Diaspora

'From a rock in the middle of the ocean, we have populated the globe with approximately 70 million O'Sullivans, Murphys, and Walshes,' declared the webpage for The Gathering 2013, Ireland's largest ever state-organized tourism initiative, 'not to mention the roughly one million Irish-born people who are currently living abroad' (www.thegatheringireland.com). The US accounts for over 40 million of the first figure and 150,000 of the second, compared to 6.5 million people on the island itself. Its long, intense relationship with the very large diaspora in America has undergone important changes over the past several decades, becoming – as with the Basques – more reciprocal and expansive. Tourism has occupied a central position in the web of transatlantic connections, and official campaigns have been awash in references to memories of the homeland. Recent attempts to gather the Irish Diaspora have been fairly successful in terms of attracting large numbers of tourists. The search for personal identity through family history and links with place, seem to prompt most of these journeys.

The Irish and the American Irish

Ireland's engagement with its American Diaspora has been ambivalent. It has resulted in significant economic benefits in terms of trade, investment, and tourist dollars. The fact that several Irish-American organizations had for decades provided financial and propaganda support to militant republican groups in Ireland helped bring about mitigation of conflict in/about the North by pushing for the Reagan and Clinton administrations to play an important mediating role in the peace negotiations. Many members of the diaspora have flourished abroad, and their triumphs have raised Ireland's international profile and reputation. Emigration has also served as a valuable economic and social safety valve, reducing unemployment rates and the burden on overstretched public finances, and thinning the ranks of the actively disgruntled in Ireland.

At the same time, there has been an image of the emigrant as 'no longer truly Irish' (Nash, 2008: 21), even 'as somehow letting down the country' (McDermott, 2013). Americans of Irish descent are ridiculed for over-the-top 'paddywhackery' (Donnelly, 2012) and 'Eiresatz' St. Patrick's Day cutesiness (Dezell, 2002). Kneejerk anti-British sentiment is met with bemusement, and past financial backing and logistical support for the Provisional Irish Republican Army still rankle in some quarters (Oddie, 2011). Just as 'the prospect of departure seems to make people focus for the first time on the home place' and 'home is the place we start from' (Lunney, 2013: 72–73), perhaps legacy tourists will discover for themselves if such perceptions of home are real. Lunney also wrote how today's Irish are a bit tired of hearing of how 'the best and brightest' were those who emigrated, reflecting negatively on those who stayed behind.

Americans' view of Ireland is coloured by outdated images of the homeland brought with their immigrant ancestors. Nostalgic reminiscences – transmitted through family stories, letters, songs, books and poems – are accompanied by tragic ones relating to the reasons for having to emigrate. Memories of the Great Hunger have been passed down through the generations in the US and have been reinforced by those of the latest arrivals, as they have been stronger and kept more alive in Ireland (Annett, 2013). Since the official sesquicentennial commemoration of *an Gorta Mór* (the Great Hunger) between 1995–97, public memorials have multiplied rapidly, many of them using natural materials from Irish soil (Mark-Fitzgerald, 2014). All of the kitschy 'artefacts of commodity culture' embraced by the maligned Plastic Paddies may help 'to soften the blow of memory' (Thompson, 2012: 75). As seen among the Basques, the imagined homeland can diverge significantly from modern reality.

Most of the Irish discussion focuses not only on ethnic communities, at the expense of newer emigrants, but also on Irish Catholics. Of the five million or so Irish who came to the US between the colonial era and the 1930s, about 40% were Protestants (Ireland, 2012) and more Americans of Irish descent are now from a Protestant than Catholic background. From the 1980s, more nuanced opinion polls on ethnic background, General Social Survey results, and the 1990 US Census – the first to allow respondents to declare a 'Scotch-Irish' ancestry – were drawing attention to the diversity of the diaspora. Irish film, theatrical productions, music, and literature were enjoying exceptional popularity and critical acclaim by the 1990s, and the expansion of 'white ethnic' studies inspired articles and books about the Scots-Irish. The launching of genealogical websites, such as Ancestry.com in

1995, made it easier for individual Americans to explore their family's ties to the Emerald Isle.

As family records have become readily accessible online, many Irish Americans have learned that they have Ulster-Scots (or Scots-Irish) roots. Many of them have been joining those of Irish Catholic descent in travelling to Ireland to trace their personal origins, encouraged by the 'attractiveness and accessibility' of doing so in a country providing archival records in English and the celebrated 'warm welcome' so associated with the myth of the trip 'home' (Nash, 2008: 47). Since three-quarters of all Irish-Americans are also able to claim at least one other ancestry, such pluses are useful in convincing genealogy enthusiasts to climb the branch of their family tree that reaches back to Ireland. Digging up family roots is part of a trend among baby boomers who display a keen interest in cultural and historical sites and opt for hands-on, yet comfortable and safe experiential travel (Ireland, 2014).

The Irish tourist industry has been responding to the developments affecting the American Diaspora, with which it has been interacting for 150 years. Not long after the Great Hunger, American visitors began to return to Ireland 'to scoop up bogwood sculptures, leprechaun figurines, and picture postcards, to buy into a version of Ireland totally mediated through shamrocks and shillelaghs' (Thompson, 2012: 81). An Irish Tourist Association was set up in the 1920s, with a development board and promotion and marketing office emerging in 1952, a couple of years after proclamation of the Republic. (In the North, the Ulster Tourist Authority, also dating from the mid-1920s, became the Northern Ireland Tourist Board (NITB) after World War II). In 1953, authorities in Dublin launched *An Tóstal* ('The Pageant'). It was pitched as 'the welcome which a great motherland extends to her children' (Swastikas & Bedlinen, 2013). While ultimately not very successful over its six-year run, *An Tóstal* left a legacy in continuing events (e.g. the Rose of Tralee and Tidy Towns competitions), a penchant for showcasing culture and history, and the central message of 'welcome home' directed to the Diaspora (see Daly, 2013).

The Celtic Tiger, the Crash, and the 2013 Gathering

Irish tourism officials have struggled 'to reconcile diasporic memory with the realities of a contemporary Ireland' (Cronin & O'Connor, 2003: 15). Some suggested it was time to 'take the sham out of shamrock' (Fletcher & Bell, 2002: 15; McCain & Ray, 2003b). By the mid-1990s, Ireland had entered its 'Celtic Tiger' period of high economic growth and low unemployment and inflation. That unprecedented boom combined with the deepening of the Northern Ireland peace process, 'the global branding of Riverdance, the Irish pub, and the marketing of "craic" [a word for 'fun' and 'entertainment' originating in northern England and Scotland and widely heard in modern-day Ireland] and conviviality to the tourist market' to erase stereotyped images of a quaint but unsophisticated, violent, and poverty-stricken island (Delaney, 2011).

That situation had begun to change when Irish expatriates and their descendants evolved from subjects of indifference into valued 'diasporic communities'. Heralding the conversion was President Mary Robinson's inaugural speech in December 1990, when she dedicated herself to representing those living in the Republic and Northern Ireland, as well as the broader diaspora claiming an Irish identity overseas. In 1996, the Irish government pushed for the indexing of genealogical records, established county-level family research centres, and had tourist promotions promise diasporic visitors a genealogical 'homecoming' (Nash, 2008: 27).

President Robinson's embrace of an expansive, inclusive notion of Irishness fed into and dovetailed with wider political movements. In 1998, the Nineteenth Amendment to the Irish Constitution – necessitated by the Good Friday Agreement (GFA) – was approved by 94% of voters. It came into effect the following December and, among other things, modified the wording of Article Two: it now states that 'the Irish nation cherishes its special affinity with people of Irish ancestry living abroad who share its cultural identity and heritage'. An Irish Abroad Unit was installed within the Department of Foreign Affairs in 2004, and an Emigrant Support Program began to provide welfare services for vulnerable nationals abroad and to support community and heritage projects (Cantwell, 2011).

A new economic development portfolio was added during the financial and economic crisis after 2007. As unemployment rose, first non-Irish nationals and then (Northern) Irish nationals began emigrating, with the outflow soon reaching the highest levels since the Great Famine, a share of it to the US (Sheehan, 2012). Amid fears that the waning of the Northern Ireland conflict might weaken sentimental links to Ireland, engaging with the Diaspora to explore ways to spur recovery and growth became the raison-d'être of the inaugural Global Irish Economic Forum in September 2009. Launched shortly thereafter were the Global Irish Network, comprised of over 300 prominent 'Irish and Irish-connected' members from international business and the cultural and sporting worlds, and the Certificates of Irish Heritage project, by which the government in Dublin (until August 2015) granted official recognition to those with at least one Irish ancestor (Gray, 2013: 109).

A report compiled by the Republic's embassy in Washington, DC, in 2009 noted that despite the strength of Ireland's 'brand' in the US, there was 'a persistent sense ... that we should seek to do even more to capitalize on the asset of our positive image' (Embassy of Ireland, 2014: 6). The elitist nature of the state's 'structured mobilisation of the Diaspora' (DFA, 2012: 6), with corporate leaders in the 'catbird seat', was reflected in the commercialism of the initiatives that followed. Officials in the tourism sector deemed St. Patrick's Day a 'unique' and 'significantly underutilised' asset (DFA, 2011: 28) and announced that it was imperative to 'exploit the Irish Diaspora and Scots-Irish (Ulster-Scots) opportunities' (Tourism Ireland, 2012: 10).

Eager to boost the industry's fortunes, the current tourism development authority, Fáilte Ireland, took inspiration from *An Tóstal* and Scotland's Homecoming 2009 and initiated The Gathering 2013, in collaboration with Tourism Ireland (established as one of six areas of island-wide cooperation under the GFA). It was intended 'to motivate members of [the] diaspora, as well as those with an affinity for Ireland, to come to Ireland to celebrate the best of Irish culture, arts, sports, music, and heritage', and the US was a prime marketing focus (Fáilte Ireland, 2013: 7–8). Rebuilding national pride and refurbishing Ireland's global reputation were likewise important, if less openly advertised objectives (BCC, 2012).

The government added a further €13 million to Fáilte's regular events fund for marketing purposes and to encourage additional activities over the course of 2013. Total third-party cash and in-kind supports amounted to around €8 million. Residents were to invite personally 'anyone with a connection to Ireland to come and visit'; more than one in every three did so (Fáilte Ireland, 2013: 38). In Dublin airport, posters assured arriving members of the diaspora that the country was 'Excited to get you home', and over 5000 'shindigs' [party, celebration] were planned by families, communities, and other groups in every part of Ireland – many in counties not typically regarded as tourist destinations – ranging 'from St. Patrick's Day parties, to family reunions, to celebrations of redheads and left-handed people, and a party where everyone named Clare is invited to County Clare' (McDermott, 2013).

The Gathering did garner its share of criticism, as did Scotland's Homecoming in 2009 (see Ray & McCain, 2012a). Actor Gabriel Byrne, Ireland's former Cultural Ambassador to the US and active supporter of the Irish Arts Center in New York City, condemned it as a 'scam' and a 'shakedown'. Ryanair chief Michael O'Leary rechristened it 'The Grabbing'. Other observers accused organizers of cynically peddling 'the imagined purity of a romantic past' (Feeney, 2013) perpetuating a self-serving, insular attitude toward the Diaspora (Shiels, 2013).

In the end, The Gathering largely fulfilled its stated mission. Between 250,000 and 275,000 tourists travelled to Ireland in 2013, generating an estimated €170 million in revenue. Visitor numbers from North America were up by more than a fifth year over year (Fáilte Ireland, 2013). In-house and independent assessments determined that many of the benefits and impacts were non-monetary: renewed civic pride, lifted spirits, rebuilt social capital, enhanced skills and capabilities, revitalized connections with family and the diaspora, and 'the development of a strong sense of place and memory' (Mottiar et al., 2014: i). 'Family and Clan' as a category accounted for the largest share of events (30%), and 39% of organizers maintained that overseas friends and relatives were their major target audience (Fáilte Ireland,

2013: 20). In fact, it was in the area of genealogy that new tourism potential was most clearly identified.

Toward a New Relationship?

Both the transfiguration of The Gathering into the 'People's Project', in the words of its director, Jim Miley (Fáilte Ireland, 2013: foreword), and the reproaches levelled against it have influenced official policy toward the Diaspora. In spring 2014, the Irish government announced a review of the country's 'diaspora engagement' policies, urging emigrants and members of Irish communities abroad to contribute their views. That July, Prime Minister Enda Kenny appointed the first Minister of State for the Diaspora. And in March 2015, the government published the first policy statement on the Irish abroad that 'recognises that Ireland has a unique and important relationship with its diaspora that must be nurtured and developed' (DFA, 2015: 4). Mentioned specifically are 'the many in North America who identify as Scots-Irish' (DFA, 2015: 17).

The new diaspora policy acknowledges the lessons learned from The Gathering with respect to the 'attachment to place' that 'can be passed down through the generations', 'the strength of the community sector as a driver of diaspora-related tourism', and the very personal desire to trace family history that 'is often the incentive for an individual of Irish ancestry to activate their links to Ireland' (DFA, 2015: 32–33). Officials in Northern Ireland, too, have been investing heavily in genealogy-related services, as well as celebrating country and bluegrass music, seen as a prime cultural link with America's Scots-Irish (Ireland, 2014; Ray & McCain, 2012a). Emotional and person-to-person ties have come more to the fore, as the emphasis shifts to 'developing and deepening long-term relationships' (DFA, 2014: 19) with those who can count Ireland as one of their ancestral homelands.

Links between the Basque Country, Ireland and Scotland

While culturally very different, there are important similarities which have joined the 'homelands' of the Basque Country and Ireland. Bilbao in the Basque Country and Belfast in Northern Ireland are being rejuvenated by urban renewal. The phrase 'the Bilbao Effect' (or 'Guggenheim Effect'), referring to the positive effect a world class museum can have on a declining industrial city, may soon be joined by the term 'Titanic Effect,' based on the new museum in Belfast to commemorate the 100th anniversary of the sinking of the Titanic. As the Basque Country 'brand' has suffered some image problems from the terrorist organization ETA, Ireland has similarly suffered from 'The Troubles.' More importantly in the current context is that both

have recently, at a national level, officially recognized the importance of relations with their diasporas, but potential diaspora returnees are less likely to
'go home' if worried about safety. Sometimes officials active in peace-making
in one location travel back and forth to offer advice to the other nation.
Thankfully, in both locations, ceasefires have mostly held, making it safer
for diaspora tourists wishing to visit 'home'.

The Irish Consul General in Atlanta at the 2014 Ulster American Heritage
Symposium uttered phrases similar to Basques venturing to the Diaspora
(Gleeson, 2014), emphasizing how especially young people in Ulster benefit
from knowing that their Ulster culture (in the formation of the American
Scots-Irish) is alive and well in the New World.

Likewise, the Basque Country has links to Scotland, as portrayed in the
film Gazta Zati Bat ('A Piece of Cheese'), a documentary film produced
thanks to the initiative of the popular movement *Nacioen Munda*, and
directed by Jon Maia in 2012. According to the film's web site, '[t]his documentary presents the Basque conflict in a new/innovative way: it gives us
a[n] ... idea of the big facts, it tells us the story ... to defend the universal
right which all stateless nations must have to decide. Its members dream of
a Basque Country without violence. Its objective is for Basques to be able to
choose their own identity in a peaceful scenario' (Gazta Zati Bat, 2014).

The Basques were keen to see the result of Scotland's September 2014
referendum vote on independence from the UK, potentially redefining their
homeland. In the film, Basque athletes visited Scotland, and Scottish athletes
travelled to the Basque County, where each group participated in each other's
sports, such as *pelota*, wood-sawing, lifting the stone, tossing the caber, etc.
Although on the surface, Scots and Basques may not have much in common,
similar political situations, impacting on residents and diasporas' definitions
of 'home,' and some formal links between the Basque Country and Scotland
have developed, including those based on tourism.

In fact, former prime minister Gordon Brown (2014), in his book, *My
Scotland, Our Britain*, argued for a 'no' vote in the September 2014 referendum
mentioning the nationalist/separatist 'breakaway' movements in Spain (e.g.
the Basques and the Catalans), elaborating about the complexity of national
feeling about one's homeland. It is evident that those who specialize in working with their diasporas are very aware of the strategies that other nations
employ when working with their own diasporas.

Surveying the Basque and Irish Diaspora

A two-page survey was modified from previous legacy tourism projects
conducted since 2005 (see McCain & Ray, 2003a; Ray & McCain, 2009,
2012b). Using convenience sampling, a total of 97 participants were selected
among the attendants of specific events where the researchers had personal

contacts and permission to gather data. Those with Basque, Irish, or Scots-Irish heritage or interest in any of the three were surveyed. Data relevant for this chapter were extracted from the interview material of the past two years. Specifically, a commercial tour to Ireland (both the Republic and the North), which one of the authors joined in 2013, provided six respondents. An Ulster Historical Foundation event in a large Midwestern US city in 2013 provided 56 surveys, and a combination Basque heritage/Ulster Historical Foundation event in Boise, Idaho provided 35 surveys. While exact numbers of total attendees at each event were not available, the response rate is around 50% or more (35 of around 40 attendees, in the case of the combined Basque/Irish event). In all, the sample contained 30 men and 66 women with one respondent not indicating gender. The mean age of the respondents is 63 with a range of ages from 32 to 84. They were all US citizens except for two from South Africa (who were on the tour of Ireland). A couple have dual-citizenship.

Respondents were asked to indicate motivations for legacy tourism, including specific response items generated from Basu's (2004, 2007) research referring to 'home,' 'true home' and homecoming. Other examples of motivations included 'pilgrimage,' 'obligation to ancestors,' 'inward journey,' and 'intellectual challenge'. Participants were asked to indicate family history activities such as searching for information in libraries; a specific location, such as an old homestead; or wishing to find living relatives. Collected data were entered into SPSS and descriptive and simple non-parametric statistics were run.

Results

At least ten in the combined Basque/Irish event indicated that they were there because of their Basque heritage, the others mostly came to learn about Irish, Scots-Irish, or Scottish records. One or two came for more general family history information.

Of several Likert-type items (with 1 = very important and 5 = not at all important), 'visiting places where family is from' (i.e. relevant to concept of 'home') is the most important reason for leisure travel (mean of 1.8). Other items in the section were 'meeting people of similar interests' and 'being together as a family' (second most important).

There are various reasons for undertaking genealogical trips. The majority who have taken these trips do so mainly to find their own ancestry. Finding information in archives and libraries is the top reason listed by 55 respondents, followed by finding a specific location in the homeland (53 respondents), and then finding living relatives (31 respondents). A couple mentioned that the genealogy trip was just a 'fun vacation.' Santos and Yan (2010) also found that travel to archives and libraries should not be overlooked as an important source of tourism.

Simple non-parametric statistics were run to determine if there are any significant differences (at $p < 0.05$) between those most interested in Basque ancestry (10 respondents) versus those of Irish and Scots-Irish ancestry interest. No differences were found on the Likert-type items. The Basques chose 'personal identity' as the most important legacy motivation as did the others, with 'connection to place,' 'intellectual challenge' and 'obligation to ancestors' tied for second. The importance of 'obligation to ancestors' is not surprising in a family history event in Boise, Idaho as the area has a large Mormon (religion of Jesus Christ of Latter Day Saints) population and tracing one's ancestry is encouraged by the Church. So, the results for the Basque group are not really different from the Irish/Scots-Irish sample.

Research based on similar survey questions had been collected in previous projects (Ray & McCain, 2009). To ascertain if motivations for family history interest appear to have changed much over the years (at least based on the data from 2005+; $n = 1057$) and the more recent data, chi-square tests were run on each of the 17 motivation variables. In only two cases, are there significant ($p < 0.05$) differences. More recent respondents (i.e. from 2013–2014) are significantly statistically more likely than those respondents from 2005 to check 'inward journey' and 'quest' as their most important motivations. However, 'inward journey' and 'quest' are not the highest rated (i.e. most often checked) motivations in neither the present, nor previous research. Overall, the authors conclude that, based on the survey questions presented to the samples discussed here, there is little change in 'legacy' motivations over the past decade or so.

Discussion and Conclusion

The low ranking of the 'home'-related response items might be surprising if a researcher has ever experienced legacy tours. Tour guides in Scotland often report how visitors from overseas feel they 'have come home' upon arriving on Scottish soil. Everyone who indicated 'homecoming' or 'true home' was interested in Irish or Scots-Irish ancestry, not Basque. However, the Basque culture has the phenomenon that often the family surname is literally derived from the name of the family home in the Basque Country. Therefore, the concept of 'home' is indeed very much imbedded in Basque identity. And, one might argue that all possible motivations listed on the survey have to do with homecoming and ask what is really the difference between an 'inward journey' and a 'quest', or 'visiting places where family is from' vs 'being together as a family'? The possible response dimensions certainly can overlap.

Ray and McCain (2012a and 2012b) also found that the 'home' items fell relatively low in rankings. It is not that respondents do not ever select 'homecoming' and 'true home,' perhaps it is simply that personal identity and connection with a place (whether that place also qualifies as 'home' or not) are more important. And, it appears that these motivations have not changed much over the past 10 years or so. Certainly, the amount of exposure to interest in family history has increased in the US, encouraged through shows such as the PBS Genealogy Roadshow and others.

Sometimes surprising to first time family history academic researchers is the spiritual motivation. As mentioned earlier, some religions place great importance on tracing one's ancestors. For others, as reported by Leite (2005) and *New York Times* writer, Doreen Carvajal (2014), it might be to locate a place of religious significance and/or perhaps religious persecution. Carvajal (2014), while exploring the Jewish quarter in Segovia, Spain, said 'I felt the pangs of yearning for home – añoranza in Spanish.' It is in regard to this religious meaning that the 'pilgrimage' motive becomes evident. Leite (2005: 276) also found that 'remembering' the ancestral experience intellectually is important. 'Intellectual challenge' was the second ranked motivation for family history in this research reported here.

This chapter has discussed how the memory of home (whether real or imagined) can influence travel and can be greatly personally rewarding. It can also provide strong economic benefits for a host country. That country may not completely coincide politically and geographically with a diaspora community's ancestral homeland. And, the search for homeland identity may be 'reversed' in that those from the homeland may travel to the Diaspora location, such as Basque dignitaries and athletes travelling to Boise, Idaho to participate in the festival, Jaialdi. Most legacy travellers are retired and spurred on in their interest in family history for the sake of 'future generations', while in the cases discussed here, young people mostly engage in legacy travel through home country sponsored programs.

'Troubles' in the homeland matter but when nations reduce their homeland dangers (as both Ireland and the Basque Country have), official government outreach to the Diaspora can be successful, with specific events such as 'Homecoming,' 'Gathering,' or internationally renowned festivals, but also on a continual basis with individual legacy tourists.

Those tourists engage in legacy travel with motivations of enhancing personal identity and a connection to place, often the homeland, whatever their definition of homeland is. Top rated motivations are the intellectual and spiritual dimension of discovering one's ancestors and where they lived. Nations who can help legacy tourists discover the homeland reap economic benefits, whereas the travellers themselves can find the experience deeply rewarding. Motivations for interest in family history and legacy travel do not vary much among groups reported here (those in the Basque, Irish, Scots-Irish Diaspora) and motivations for this travel have not changed much in the past decade, suggesting that researchers and providers of legacy travel will continue to observe the 'coming home' for generations to come.

References

Annett, R. (2013) Memory and migration: Imaginary homelands. *The Future State*, blog post, 12 May. See http://www.thefuturestate.org.uk/memory-and-migration-imaginary-homelands/ (accessed 2 March 2015).

Ansotegui, D. (1992) Interview by J. Bieter, 11 March 1992 available Basque Museum and Cultural Center, Boise Idaho.

Basu, P. (2001) Hunting down home: Reflections on homeland and the search for identity in the Scottish diaspora. In B. Bender and M. Winer (eds) *Contested Landscapes: Movement, Exile and Place* (pp. 333–348). Berg: Oxford.

Basu, P. (2004) My own island home: The Orkney homecoming. *Journal of Material Culture* 9 (1), 27–42.

Basu, P. (2007) *Highland Homecomings: Genealogy and Heritage Tourism in the Scottish Diaspora*. New York: Routledge.

Belfast City Council (BCC) (2012) *Report to the Development Committee on The Gathering*, 20 November. See http://minutes.belfastcity.gov.uk/documents/s66579/The%20Gathering.html? CT=2

Belk, R.W. (1997) Been there, done that, bought the souvenirs: Of journeys and boundary crossing. In S. Brown and D. Turley (eds) *Consumer Research: Postcards from The edge* (pp. 22–45). New York: Routledge.

Bilbao, J. (1993, June 15) Recorded interview 15 June 1993. Archived at Basque Museum and Cultural Center, Boise, Idaho.

Bieter, P. (1992) Interview by J. Bieter, 10 March 1992 and 13 July 1993 available at the Basque Museum and Cultural Center Boise, Idaho.

Brown, G. (2014) *My Scotland, Our Britain: A Future Worth Sharing*. London: Simon & Schuster.

Brown, S., Hirschman, E. and Maclaran, P. (2000) Presenting the past: On marketing's re-production orientation. In S. Brown and A. Patterson (eds) *Imagining Marketing: Art, Aesthetics and the Avant-garde* (pp. 141–184). New York: Routledge.

Cantwell, B. (2011) Australian groups receive just four per cent of emigrant funds, *Irish Echo (Sydney)*, 10 February. See http://www.irishecho.com.au/2011/02/10/australian-groups-receive-just-four-per-cent-of-emigrant-funds/7141 (accessed 24 March 2015).

Carvajal, D. (2014) In Spain, a family reunion, centuries later. *The New York Times*, 4 April. See http://www.nytimes.com/2014/04/06/travel/in-spain-a-family-reunion-centuries-later.html?_r=0 (accessed 29 May 2015).

Cova, B. (1997) Community and consumption: Towards a definition of the 'linking value' products or services. *European Journal of Marketing* 31 (3/4), 297–316.

Craig, P. (2005) Booking passage: We Irish & Americans by Thomas Lynch: The poet undertakes a reviving journey home *The Independent*, 19 August. See http://www.independent.co.uk/arts-entertainment/books/reviews/booking-passage-we-irish-amp-americans-by-thomas-lynch-6143585.html (accessed 5 December 2011).

Cronin, M. and O'Connor, B. (2003) Introduction. In M. Cronin and B. O'Connor (eds) *Irish Tourism: Image, Culture, and Identity* (pp. 1–18). Clevedon: Channel View Publications.

Daly, S. (2013) You know we had a 'Gathering' 60 years ago, right?, *thejournal.ie*, 7 April. See http://www.thejournal.ie/an-tostal-1953-the-gathering-854877-Apr2013 (accessed 15 March 2015).

Davies, J. (2010) Sustainable nostalgia. *Memory Studies* 3 (3), 262–268.

Delaney, E. (2011) Traditions of emigration: The Irish habit of going away, *The Irish Times*, 2 November. See http://www.irishtimes.com/blogs/generationemigration/2011/11/02/traditions-of-emigration-the-irish-habit-of-going-away/ (accessed 18 March 2015).

Department of Foreign Affairs and Trade (DFA) (2011) *The Report of the Second Global Irish Economic Forum*. Dublin: Government of Ireland.

Department of Foreign Affairs and Trade (DFA) (2012) *The 2011 Global Irish Economic Forum-One Year On.* Dublin: Government of Ireland.

Department of Foreign Affairs and Trade (DFA) (2014) *Review of Ireland's Engagement with the Diaspora: Consultation Paper.* Dublin: Government of Ireland.

Department of Foreign Affairs and Trade (DFA) (2015) *Global Irish: Ireland's Diaspora Policy.* Dublin: Government of Ireland.

Devine, T. (2011) *To the Ends of the Earth: Scotland's Global Diaspora 1750–2010.* Washington, D.C.: Smithsonian Books.

Dezell, M. (2002) *Irish America: Coming into Clover.* New York: Anchor.

Donnelly, L. (2012) Yet another Irish Times columnist attacks Irish American identity as not Irish. *Irish Central,* 6 March. See http://www.irishcentral.com/news/yet-another-irish-times-columnist-attacks-irish-american-identity-as-not-irish-141554863–23774 9611.html (accessed 10 March 2015).

Douglass, W.A. (1976) Serving girls and sheepherders: Emigration and continuity in a Spanish Basque village. In J.B. Aceves and W.A. Douglass (eds) *The Changing Faces of Rural Spain* (pp. 45–61). New York: Schenkman Publishing.

Douglass, W.A. and Bilbao, J. (1975) *Amerikanuak: Basques in the new world.* Reno, NV: University of Nevada Press.

Edlefsen, J.B. (1948) A sociological study of the Basques of Southwest Idaho. PhD dissertation, State College of Washington, pp. 48–49.

Embassy of Ireland (2014) *Ireland and America: Challenges and Opportunities in a New Context: A Five-Year Review.* Washington, D.C.: Embassy of Ireland.

Ezquerra, A.S. (March 2010) Professor of History UNED de Bergara, Visiting Professor Boise State University, specialist in Baserriak. Interview by J. Bieter.

Fáilte Ireland (2013) *The Gathering Ireland 2013: Final Report.* Dublin: Government of Ireland.

Feeney, S. (2013) *Dreams of Freedom? Conversations on Aesthetics, Ethics & European Democracies* [Audio podcast]. See http://www.thefuturestate.org.uk/tag/irishness/

Fischer, P., Sauer, A., Vogrincic, C. and Weisweiler, S. (2011) The ancestor effect: Thinking about our genetic origin enhances intellectual performance. *European Journal of Social Psychology* 41 (1), 11–16.

Fletcher, R. and Bell, J. (2002) Hijacking country of origin image, *The Marketing Landscape: Signposts for the Future, Proceedings of the Annual Conference* 2–5 July, UK Academy of Marketing: The Chartered Institute of Marketing.

Gans, H. (1979) Symbolic ethnicity: The future of ethnic groups and cultures in America. *Ethnic and Racial Studies* 2 (1), 1–20.

Gazta Zati Bat (2014) *Synopsis.* See http://www.gaztazatibat.eu/seccion/documentary-2/subseccion/synopsis.

Gleason, P. (1980) American identity and Americanization. In S. Thernstrom (ed.) *Harvard Encyclopedia of American Ethnic Groups.* Cambridge: Harvard University Press.

Gleeson, P. (2014) Consul General of Ireland, Atlanta, Presentation at the Twentieth Biennial Ulster-American Heritage Symposium Athens, GA, 26–28 June.

Gray, B. (2013) Towards the neo-institutionalization of Irish state-diaspora relations in the twenty-first century. In M. Collyer (ed.) *Emigration Nations: Policies and Ideologies of Emigrant Engagement* (pp. 100–125). Basingstroke: Palgrave.

Hansen, M.L. (1938) *The Third Generation: Search for Continuity* (pp. 139–144). Augustana Historical Society Publications.

Huang, W., Haller, W.J. and Ramshaw, G. (2012) Diaspora tourism and homeland attachment: An exploratory analysis. *Tourism Analysis* 18 (3), 285–296.

Ireland, P.R. (2012) Irish Protestant migration and politics in the USA, Canada, and Australia. *Irish Studies Review* 20 (3), 263–281.

Ireland, P.R. (2014) Cracker craic: The politics and economics of Scots-Irish cultural pro-motion in the USA. *International Journal of Cultural Policy* 20 (4), 399–421.

Johnson, K. (2015) A taste of Basque paella amid Idaho's potatoes. *The New York Times*, 4 August. See http://www.nytimes.com/2015/08/05/us/an-ancient-tongue-and-paellas-scent-fill-a-boise-celebration-of-basque-roots.html?_r=0 (accessed 12 August 2015).

Keelan, T. (1990) With the miners came the sheep. *Boise Idaho Statesman Centennial Supplement*. Idaho Statesman: 2.

Lagos, T. (2015) Studying abroad, in travel, tourism and identity. In G.R. Ricci (ed.) *Culture & Civilization* (pp. 233–241). New Brunswick, NJ: Transaction Publishers.

Leite, N. (2005) Travels to an ancestral past: On diasporic tourism, embodied memory, and identity. *ANTROPOlógicas* (9), 273–302.

Ley 8/1994, De 27 De Mayo, De Relaciones Con Las Colectividades Y Centros Vascos En El Exterior De La Comunidad Autónoma Del País Vasco(1) [online]. See http://www.parlamento.euskadi.net/pdfdocs/leyes/ley19940008_f_cas.html (accessed 23 March 2014).

Lunney, L. (2013) Home and leaving home in eighteenth century Ulster. *Familia: Ulster Genealogical Review* (29), 72–82.

Mark-Fitzgerald, E. (2014) Famine memory and the gathering of stones. *Atlantic Studies: Global Currents* 11 (3), 419–435.

Marschall, S. (2014) Tourism and remembrance: The journey into the self and its past. *Journal of Tourism and Cultural Change* 12 (4), 335–348.

McCain, G. and Ray, N.M. (2003a) Legacy tourism: The search for personal meaning in heritage travel. *Tourism Management* 24 (6), 713–717.

McCain, G. and Ray, N.M. (2003b) Taking the 'sham' out of shamrock: Legacy tourists seek the 'real thing'. *European Advances in Consumer Research* (6), 54–59.

McDermott, J. (2013) Ireland's diaspora returns. *Financial Times*, 8 March. See http://www.ft.com/cms/s/2/d845313c-8718-11e2-9dd7-00144feabdc0.html (accessed 11 March 2015).

Mkono, M. (2011) Authenticity does matter. *Annals of Tourism Research* 39 (1/January), 480–483.

Mottiar, Z., Bernadette, M.Q. and Ryan, T. (2014) A study of the social and community impacts of the gathering in counties Kerry and Westmeath. Dublin: Dublin Institute of Technology, School of Hospitality Management and Tourism.

Nash, C. (2008) *Of Irish Descent: Origin Stories, Genealogy, and the Politics of Belonging*. Syracuse: Syracuse University Press.

Novak, M. (1971) *The Rise of the Unmeltable Ethnics*. New York: Macmillan.

Oddie, W. (2011) Archbishop Martin says Irish-American sentimentalism is incomprehen-sible. *Catholic Herald*, 19 April. See http://www.catholicherald.co.uk/commentandblogs/2011/04/19/archbishop-martin-says-irish-american-sentimentalism-is-incomprehensi-ble-but-it%E2%80%99s-dangerous-too/ (accessed 2 March 2015).

Pearce, P.L. (2012) The experience of visiting home and familiar places. *Annals of Tourism Research* 39 (2/April), 1024–1047.

Ray, N.M. and Bieter, J. (2014) 'It broadens your view of being Basque': Identity through history, branding, and cultural policy. *International Journal of Cultural Policy* 21 (3), 241–257.

Ray, N.M. and McCain, G. (2009) Guiding tourists to their ancestral home. *International Journal of Culture, Tourism, and Hospitality Research* 3 (4), 296–305.

Ray, N.M. and McCain, G. (2012a) Homecoming, *Hamefarin* and hijacked country-of-origin perceptions: The motivations of Irish and Scottish legacy tourists. *Journal of Irish and Scottish Studies* 5 (2), 117–139.

Ray, N.M. and McCain, G. (2012b) Nostalgia for the distant land of past: Legacy tourism. *International Business & Economics Research Journal* 11 (9), 977–989.

Santos, C.A. and Yan, G. (2010) Genealogical tourism: A phenomenological examination. *Journal of Travel Research* 49 (1), 56–67.

Sheehan, A. (2012) Emigration 'at famine levels' as 200 leave country each day, *Irish Independent*, 31 December. See http://www.independent.ie/irish-news/emigration-at-famine-levels-as-200-leave-country-each-day-28952883.html (accessed 17 July 2013).

Shiels, D. (2013) Diaspora disregarded? How Ireland is failing her emigrants' memory. *Irish in the American Civil War*, blog post, 16 October. See http://irishamericancivilwar.com/2013/10/16/diaspora-disregarded-how-ireland-is-failing-her-emigrants-memory/ (accessed 2 February 2015).

Sierra, J.J. and McQuitty, S. (2007) Attitudes and emotions as determinants of nostalgia purchases: An application of social identity theory. *Journal of Marketing Theory and Practice* 15 (2), 99–112.

Silen, S. (1917) La Historia de los Vascongados en el Oeste de los Estados Unidos. New York: Las Novedades, Inc.

Swastikas and Bedlinen (2013) Arche Attica: Old things I found in the attic, June 4 2013. See https://archeattica.wordpress.com/2013/06/04/swastikas-and-bedlinen/ (accessed 3 October 2015).

Thompson, S. (2012) The kitsch of the dispossessed. In O. Frawley (ed.) *Irish Studies: Memory Ireland, Diaspora, and Memory Practices* (pp. 75–87). Syracuse: Syracuse University Press.

Tourism Ireland (2012) *Competing to Win*. Coleraine & Dublin: Tourism Ireland, Ltd.

Yale, P. (2004) *From Tourist Attractions to Heritage Tourism* (pp. 1–40). Huntingdon: ELM Publications.

Zubizarreta, J., Davis, M.C. and Hampikian, G. (2011) The Y-STR genetic diversity of an Idaho Basque population, with comparison to European Basques and US Caucasians, *State University Scholar Works, Biology Faculty Publications and Presentations, Department of Biology*. See http://scholarworks.boisestate.edu/ cgi/viewcontent.cgi?article=1233& context=bio_facpubs (accessed 20 February 2015).

Zubiri, A.U. (2005) The foreign action of the Basque Government, current events. *Euskal Etxeak* (71) 8–9.

13 Epilogue: Home, Travel, Memory and Anthropology

Nelson Graburn

This collection goes to the heart of the intersection between contemporary anthropology and key concerns of the world in which we live – home, family, memory, mobility and identity. These cases studies, most of which consider communities who left their home(land)s unwillingly and are unable to ever settle there again, are very poignant and yet familiar to all of us because of the universal distribution of such stories in modern media as well as their current political significance. Reading these chapters is rather like reading a book of short stories; they are very moving and unforgettable, even if not always entertaining. Furthermore, it causes me to reflect on my own life – perhaps not uncommon for someone in his fourth quarter-century – and I find that I have experienced nearly every kind of travel, memory, displacement, nostalgia and homeland described in this book,[1] and some which are not! So, much of this chapter is autobiographical, which is an accepted form of anthropological research and exposition (Okely, 1996). This leads me in the end to focus on the neglected topic of the meaning of homeland, travel and memory for anthropologists. Indeed, as 'human' first I will examine many key topics in this book in the light of my own life experiences stressing the emotions that are involved.

Nostalgia and Memory

Nostalgia is perhaps more closely related to home, memory and travel than any other concept. Its European etymology literally means 'home sickness' as described in the 17th century, as a disease caused by *spatial* (and hence cultural and geographical) displacement that could be cured by going home. But it is by no means limited to Europe or to early modernity. For instance, an identical disease named *mahora* was exhibited by soldiers from Nara and Kyoto as they went to conquer the hinterlands to unify Yamato, the ancient Japanese nation. *Mahora* is an archaic word, no longer used in regular conversation, but is was chosen as the title of the journal of the Kinki

Nippon Institute for Research on the Culture of Travel, founded in Tokyo, July 1993. In common English parlance we now associate nostalgia with *temporal* displacement, a wish to return to a former time period, often an idyllic state of home and family, commonly childhood. But such sentiments must have been universal features of human experience, as the old wish to return to a time of youth, or the wish of the bereaved for a time with former partners, relatives or friends, again implying a 'home-like' sociality. And the desire to return to a previous era or an imagined time, before one was born, a common feature of modern nostalgia in cultural, historical and environmental tourism, has been a feature of all 'hot societies' (Levi-Strauss, 1984) which are conscious of significant changes over historical time, including pre-modern Japan.

Nostalgia is a central topic in all the case studies of this volume, and it appears to be of increasing importance to the contemporary social sciences (Ange & Berliner, 2014), because it is of increasing importance to both modern (MacCannell, 1976) and 'post-modern' generations (Lowenthal, 2015). Marschall points out in the Introduction that a key differentiation must be made between those (relatively few cases) who left a place voluntarily without regret (Scottish, English, Germans to North America) and those who were forced to leave and cannot return (Chernobyl Ukrainians, Eastern European Jews, Chinese adoptees and especially the Palestinians). My own experience bridges both forms of departure: I left England hurriedly by ship for Canada in 1958 in order to avoid my call up for military service – as an anthropology student, I thought I would rather study the colonized peoples of the Empire than learn to shoot them. That made me a deserter and I could not return to the UK for fear of being arrested; I was unable to visit my mother when she was dying of cancer in 1960. However, after the draft was cancelled in 1963, I was able to return to both my homeland and my home and stay with my father and see my friends and family.

Nostalgia is generally a positive sentiment for tourists and travellers – Dann (1994) paraphrased it as 'looking forward to going back.' I now live in California and my daughter moved to Portugal and has her family there. After we first visited her 'new home' in 1988, it has become our 'adopted home' (one of them) and we look forward to going back every year. This may be typical of VFR (Visiting Friends and Relatives) type tourists (Janta *et al.*, 2015). But for exiles and permanent 'refugees,' such as the Palestinians, it turns into an unquenchable angst.

A similar kind of distress may be felt when a return is possible, but there is no 'there there.' In 1981 I took my American children to see Hillside School, my prep. school (elementary boarding school) near Godalming, in Surrey, but when we got there we couldn't find it: the entrances to the property were fenced off and trees and bushes blocked all views in. What had happened to the lovely three-storey country house where I had lived the best part of five years, 1946–50!? Luckily I decided to knock on the door of a small house built where the front lawn had been, and was greeted by 'Hello, Graburn!' from a little old lady who turned out to be the headmaster's widow! Equally important, for analytical purposes, is the distinction between the nostalgia felt by those who actually left a home they remember, and that of their descendants who only heard about the place through family memories, word of mouth, stories, media and so on. This was particularly true of the Eritreans in Italy whose children were less aware of the political involvements, and felt much more like tourists; their engagement with their (parents') homeland was as an 'adopted terrain' that didn't really feel theirs. For many of the more distant descendants of emigrants, their identity with their 'homeland' is much closer to what Anderson (1983) called 'imagined communities' known mostly through books, photos, maps, newspapers, TV, the internet and so on.

Thus nostalgia is intimately tied to the central topic of memory, as we have already seen. We should make a clear distinction between the memories of 'homeland' of those who actually left that 'home' and the memories of those whose ancestors left before they were born. But this is a problematic difference, well considered by Bloch (1998). Many theorists now believe there is little distinction between our 'direct' memories and those we 'inherited' from others or media because in fact direct memories may well be constructions based on the memory of the last occasion we recalled the phenomenon, of constructions based on some original, unmediated experience. Much as Bourdieu's *habitus* (1977, 1984) is tacit embodied knowledge based on forgotten learned experience, we are usually unable to detect the actual origin of each occasion of memory.

This allows us an entrée into the problematic relationship between *individual* and *shared* memories, seeing that our memories usually include memories of other people recalling their own (shared) memories which may appear to us as 'our own' having forgotten the occasion(s) of our reception of that 'memory.' Thus we may 'remember' stories of grandparents and other deceased relatives and, very pertinent to this volume, memories of their homes or homes where their (our) ancestors had lived, as well as stories of travel from (or to) previous homes and homelands. I am sure many readers can recall such networks of memories from their own pasts. From my earliest memories, I heard that my family were 'Malays' and often spoke Malay at home, especially when they didn't want outsiders to understand (Graburn, 1999). They spoke longingly of their homes in Malaya where my father spent 27 years, met and married my mother, and all his siblings except one lived and married (all before World War II). I could probably remember more stories of Malaya, saw more photos of homes, golf courses, etc., and was surrounded by many Malay (and Chinese) utensils, textiles, and furnishing to make me think we were a special kind of English people called 'Malays'. [Later, at boarding school, I discovered other boys were 'Africans' and spoke Swahili, or 'Indians' or 'Egyptians', and, unlike me, they actually went 'home' on holidays and lived there.] They talked of exotic foods, fruits, and 'natives' who were great athletes with good eye-sight; I was proud when they said 'he runs, climbs trees, can see for miles, just like a native.' My father's sister had married an Asian student in London in 1894; they went to live in Amoy, Malaya and Singapore, and retired to England. He was sometimes called a 'native' behind his back by my English family. These were powerful shared nostalgic memories which framed the family and which I could not help being totally swept up in – some have said that's prob-ably why I became an anthropologist. I would like to suggest that anthropolo-gists' identity and memories of these overseas 'homeland' communities are very like those of colonials of long ago who had to learn the local language, cook local foods, etc.

Surprisingly, the afterlife of colonials who return to their 'mother coun-tries' has not featured in this collection. I know of many cases where European and other colonizers have returned or have had to evacuate from the colony to what some would call homelands, especially through indepen-dence or war. Many of these people, such as my Portuguese son-in-law and his siblings were born in Mozambique and had never seen Portugal before they 'returned' short before independence. Others, such as my daughter's Portuguese host family, were forced to leave, never felt comfortable in Portugal, and yet resented those (Africans) who took over what had been their 'homes' for generations. Some returned to Africa but reported, like the German, Jewish and Palestinian cases, that things had been ruined. Others would like to return to the lands of their birth and their ancestors but are ambivalent. My family members chose or were forced to leave Malaya which was occupied by Japan in World War II. A number of them went back after-wards and were warmly welcomed by the local population, especially as they were seen as rebuilding the nation destroyed by a crueller 'colonial' occupier. Similarly, many French, Jews and other Europeans had lived in Algeria for centuries as *colons* or *pieds noir* and had to leave after the Algerian war. They and their children – who often do return – may still consider Algeria to be their 'homeland' even though they may regret what had happened there (Rosaldo, 1989).

This is one example of the key concept of *collective* memory whereby a whole family, community or (sub)cultural group can claim to share stories and memories, keeping alive their common past and hence their contempo-rary identity. The concept of 'collective memory' stems from the work of Halbwachs, as shown in his *Les cadres sociaux de la mémoire* (1925). Memory is always embedded in and determined by the structure and history of the particular society. Individual recollections are configured by group identities: 'It is not possible to have memories that exist outside of the framework of the society in which people live, which determines how to retain and recall such memories' (Halbwachs, 1925: 63, author's translation from French). Here we may usefully draw a parallel between memory, sound and language. Humans are quite capable of hearing sounds, but they are incapable of hearing sounds without interpreting them according to a learned system of meaning. Even if they do not understand the sound – a strange noise in the dark or the distant cry of an unknown animal - they attempt to interpret it within a pre-existing framework.

That does not mean that there is no such thing as individual memory – indeed, unless we believe in Jung's 'collective unconscious' or in Kroeber's (1917: 22–51) 'superorganic' we could turn the question around and ask 'Is culture nothing but the sum of shared memories of a community?' Nevertheless, we can agree with Halbwachs and his ilk that all memory is socially contextualized or mediated. More specifically, for instance, the way we remember a tourist experience, a holiday, is governed to a large extent by the rules of our (sub)culture, e.g. how to speak about it, how to take and share photos, what souvenirs to collect, how to save, display and share them. That in turn will be constrained by our identity within the subset – our age, gender, sexual orientation, kinship and family position – as well as our own individual immediate and long-term experiences, such as family upbringing and holidays. Though memory is not quite so 'shared culturally' as language, it is a close parallel in terms of its sociocultural formation and mediation.

Home and Homeland

These two key concepts have re-merged in contemporary anthropology (Anderson *et al.*, 2013), but this volume is one of the first to focus on *homeland*, as a culturally significant former home, in the sense of a geographical, cultural and historical origin. In addition, the word homeland (in many languages) has become of prime political importance in the past century, both as a claimed 'own territory' by minorities, internal colonies, the Fourth World (Graburn, 1976, 1981) within the larger techno-bureaucratic nations of the modern world, and as a place of confinement or exile from the centers or territories of such nations, as in the case of apartheid South Africa, or the reserves or reservations within Canada and the US, respectively.

One theme, particularly common in more rural areas or older times, is the strong relation of home and 'homestead.' Rural people, settlers and colonizers (of other countries or uninhabited areas) place great importance on their own construction, of houses, extensions and additions, gardens, and even walls and fences; for urbanites the same might also apply to interior furnishings and decoration. This *material* connection is a bond of self and embodiment, much in the same way as commensality or growing one's own food. The loss of such homes, through death, poverty, age or exile is especially wrenching. In Berkeley, I myself constructed walls, terraces and borders, planted trees, bushes and asparagus and helped design a greenhouse and separate 'new house' on the grounds. The former took so much labor and time that I failed to finish my promised volume on Inuit art, which shows how much it meant to me, and to my wife and children who participated and used these facilities. Even the things one grows have a strong connection to 'home.' For instance, asparagus is particularly symbolic of a 'real home.' It takes a lot of room, cannot be harvested till three years after planting and continues to provide sustenance for 30 or more years – ours has! Fruit trees are similarly emblematic of a long-term relationship to foodstuff and the land. These features (and the bonds they establish) probably kept us from moving to a larger house as the family grew.

Many of the chapters are about distant homes and homelands, from which ancestors emigrated, voluntarily or by poverty or coercion. These lands of the ancestors, often many generations back, have a mythical quality and are the destinations of 'Roots tourism'. For the exiled generation, a revisit is poignant and engenders detailed comparisons with the remembered past. But for the descendants, the visit is to a mythical place, now called 'Roots' after Alex Haley's book *Roots* (1976) and TV series, purporting to be about his West African ancestors. In fact, *Roots* was direct plagiarism of a fictional historical ethnography by anthropologist Alex Courlander (1967), for which Haley was sued, found guilty and fined $650,000. Similarly, 'roots' may be 'staged authenticity' (MacCannell, 1976) or far removed from a disconnected historical reality. For transnationally adopted children, tourism to their 'homeland' may be little more than exposure to urban cultural areas of the country which they left, a situation in which they have no agency.

But there are other kinds of roots tourism to diasporic homelands which represent continuity, kinship and even ownership. Links of kinship and marriage may be maintained ad infinitum so that the diasporic community has indeed two permanent homes. Berkeley anthropologist Patricia Nabti married into a Lebanese mountain community which we used to call 'Global Village', after Marshall McLuhan's prediction (1962) that in the future all the world would be connected equally closely by an as yet unknown medium. The 6000 inhabitants of the village of Bishmizzine live permanently on five continents, but all retain some ownership and relatives (less than 2000 at any one time) in the village. They visit this 'home' for important occasions, and especially for the high quality schools which are maintained by remittances. And they usually marry another Bishmizzini, either in the village or arranged through the village (Nabti, 1992). Other diasporic relations may be more episodic, but engender strong and satisfying bonds of kinship and exchange. Seteney Shami, a Berkeley doctoral student, was from Jordan and is of Circassian ethnic origin. The Circassians, originally pagan, then Christian, then Muslim, inhabited the North Caucasus and some emigrated to the Ottoman Empire. But in 1864 the Russians invaded and drove out or killed three quarters of the population (Sochi, the site of the 2014 Winter Olympics was built on the graves and sites of massacre of the Circassians, engendering protests from the diaspora all over the world), who then settled in Turkey, the Balkans, Egypt, Jordan, etc. where they prospered especially in governmental, legal and military professions. In the 1980s affluent Jordanian Circassians wanted to reconnect with their families (about 600,000 of the world's 4 million Circassians still live in Russia) and strengthen their ethnic language and culture, so they chartered a plane and flew to their homeland in the Northern Caucasus (Shami, 1998). Though most never met traceable relatives, the locals treated them as long lost families, and extended hospitality, friendship, business partnerships and even land and farms for sale! There were even marriages which strengthened the 'Circassian-ness' of the diaspora families, and provided a more regular diasporic situation, more comparable to some of the British, Irish, Germans, Nepalis and others described in this book. And almost always, the emigrants try to involve their new relatives and take them 'back home' to show them off and to acquaint them with *their* origins. A particularly poignant example is shown in 'Transnational Fiesta' in which Peruvian Quechua (Inca) peoples from poor villages in the Andes settled and prospered in Washington, DC. They took turns sponsoring the annual fiesta and returning with their new families with great pride (Martinez & Gelles, 1992).

One form of 'tourism and home' that one might call mini-diaspora is the possession and retreat to a 'second home' or country cottage. Called *dasha*s in Russian, they are common in many European civilizations, as well as India, Egypt and elsewhere. These second but very real homes are visited seasonally, usually by family but often with invited guests on vacation. They stand in a 'touristic' relationship to the regular 'working' home: they are for leisure and family bonding, often self-constructed, with gardens or mushroom gathering (in Finland), often near lakes for boating and fishing, and definitely closer to nature, an anti-dote to urban alienation as MacCannell (1976) expressed it. Yet, for many families this is 'more real' than the real home, a retreat where children learn their social and gender roles, where the family can relate 'authentically' (Wang, 1999). One might even say that the second home or 'the cottage' in Canadian terms (Harrison, 2013) is the real backstage in the performance that is life.

Anthropologists, Memory and Home

Berkeley anthropologist Elizabeth Colson presciently wrote (1989: 14):

Our most meaningful experiences are probably associated with field research … For those of us who have been engaged in long-term studies, it is field work and the mulling over the field data that provides a good deal of our own personal sense of continuity. We live between two worlds and feel somewhat detached from both, but each gains meaning through its contrast with the other.

Colson, who started field research work at the Rhodes-Livingstone Institute in Rhodesia in 1946, retired from UC Berkeley in 1984 and in 2002 returned to live in what is now Zambia, nearby the Gwembe Tonga and other peoples she had known in the previous 60 years. This is very comparable to what has come to be called 'life style migration' where people may voluntarily *change* their homes, as reported in Europe (Benson & O'Reilly, 2009), Asia (Yamashita, 2012) and the Americas, when they decide to go and live in those desirable places they had previously encountered as tourists or mobile workers, after retirement or even before as a second home.

For many of us anthropologists our first/major field site becomes an important home to which we wish to return. We often found there a new 'family' and community that has remained very meaningful, and which we followed over time, sometimes daily (in my case 57 years so far), e.g. through Facebook. But the sense of a lost 'home' and profound nostalgia does not mean going back to live there. A visit or even communication can bring back strong intimate emotions typical of family, community and the meaning of the passage of time. I visited the small out of the way village of Kimmirut, Baffin Island as a graduate student and government researcher in 1960 and wrote a report (Graburn, 1963) encouraging the revival of villages in a beautiful coastal area then threatened by abandonment; the Government listened to me and provided passage for Inuit to return from more urban communities nearby! After my return visit in 2000, I wrote this letter to my daughter and grandchildren:

Dear E, P & N and all,   Iqaluit, Nunavut 21st October 2000

... Just got back from the village of Kimmirut (now 400 people – only 93 when I first visited in 1960). Had a good time there; stayed with an older couple ... Busy – a few people there remembered me from my staying there all summer in 1960; but some have died and others have moved away – But there were some more profound moments too. I got quite upset about some of the people who had died – some of my former friends had died only a year or two ago. But a little boy – as cute as [my grandson] Noël if that is possible and about the same age then [see attached photo] – never had a chance to grow up; he was drowned at the age of 12 when he fell through the ice on a lake. And I keep thinking of all the other children who are loved and cared for so hard by their parents, who don't have a chance to grow up – because of illness, or accidents, or whatever. And one of my best friend Akudliksirq's oldest granddaughter aged 15 just hanged herself to death – and she had a baby. And the same friend's youngest sister Pitsiulak, who was seven and still breast-feeding in 1960, moved to Montreal when she was grown up, and was killed by a car while crossing the street. But more than that.

I was in Church last Sunday and I spotted an old friend Jusipi Pallu - I hadn't had a chance to talk to him yet. He looked quite old, but he's only 62. Actually he is the oldest friend, because in 1959 he was on the 'CD Howe' hospital ship travelling back to his village of Kimmirut after a year in hospital in Montreal, and I was on board going from McGill in Montreal to the village of Salluit for the first time – so I got to know him then. And we met each other again and became friends when I went to Kimmirut in 1960. I thought – I hadn't seen him for 40 years – when we were last together we were just beginning our adult lives, and in the intervening years we have done practically everything of real importance in our lives – got married, had children, worked long and hard to achieve in our different lives, and now have grandchildren – he has 16. He has some teeth missing and so on, but he still works full time and hunts a lot, but his wife, an unmarried teenager when I knew her before, had already died last year.

So we have gone from the near beginning to the near end of our active adult lives without meeting in between. Just as I was 22 when I met him, and in Kimmirut it was only my second trip north – I was thinking the other day, that if I am lucky, I may now have 20 years more to live, and I may make one more research trip. It's like my life is in reverse, doing backwards what I was doing forwards then, like a grand circle. After all, this time I was giving back to them photos and information I had gathered from them 40 years before. These thoughts stayed with me through the weeks, especially as I talked to people about their lives since I had last seen them, and I proudly showed pictures of my home and family to them. And 40 years is a long time – 1960 to 2000.

P.S. Montreal, 9th November 2000

This afternoon I went to a meeting with Inuit from a number of villages, most of which I hadn't visited recently. One man, Katchuak, whom I had known since he was a young teenager in Salluit in 1959 (but I saw again in 1964, 1967–68 and 1986), came up to me very excited: 'Apirku (My name 'Anthropologist,' in the *Inuktitut* language), you look so OLD now ....PLEASE come and see us again before you die!' We should never wait so long, never more than half a generation to revisit friends and collaborators. It's a long time from May to November.

Many other anthropologists have described their return to places to family and home(land)s where they had long carried out research (e.g. Adams, 2015; Bruner, 2005), but interestingly enough Adams has also pointed out (in press) that when she returned to Toraja, Indonesia (for the funeral of her 'host mother') the anthropologist and her family were treated exactly the same way as emigrant Torajans who had settled in other countries. It has become commonplace for the formerly marginal Fourth World peoples – previously studied only by anthropologists (Graburn, 1976, 1981) – to have joined the same global flows as the other cases in our chapters. Anthropologists have followed these emigrants usually to urban areas of settlement and work and back to their more rural 'tribal' homelands with complex and ambivalent feelings of both homecoming and alienation – Torajans to Canada, the USA and back (Adams, in press), Batak to urban Medan and back (Bruner, 2005), Inuit to Canadian cities and back to the Arctic (Graburn, 2005), Western Samoans to California, Cook Islanders to New Zealand, Native Americans to Los Angeles and so on. But these minority peoples may not have the time or the funds to visit their distant families and homelands. In some instances, they find community in ethnic theme parks, visiting their co-ethnic friends who are 'performing themselves' in mock up villages, ethnic Indonesians to Taman Mini national ethnic park in Jakarta (Bruner, 2005; Errington, 1998) and Chinese minority *minzu* who visit the Yunnan Provincial Nationalities Village in the capital Kunming (Graburn, 2015).

Sometimes a nostalgic return to a family homeland can be combined with one's anthropological identity. My wife's family came from a rural community Kamou-cho in Kagoshima prefecture, in far southern Japan. She grew up in Los Angeles with parents from Kamou who spoke the local vernacular *Kagoshimago* but only allowed their five children to speak regular *Nihongo*. In 1974 my wife (second generation), her mother Yaguchisan (first emigrant generation), my two children and I stayed for two weeks in Kamou with Yaguchisan's oldest sister in the family homestead and visited the many other relatives there and the 400-year-old family graveyards. My wife was struck by how familiar it all was, even the language and declared 'It's just like home; I see where it all comes from.' We stayed there without Yaguchisan many times again, especially for family reunions such as *Oshogatsu* (New Year), with our children and more recently with our daughter who now lives in Portugal and our grandchildren; as long as our friends and relatives still live there, we feel it is a family home.

Having become interested in the anthropology of tourism (Graburn, 2007), I took advantage of these and other occasions, and we also lived elsewhere in Japan, studying Japanese domestic tourism (Graburn, 1983, 1987). I got to know the village well and saw the despair as old people died, young people emigrated and the economy shrank, houses fell down and gardens and fields were abandoned. In desperation the government renamed the road where our relatives lived *The Street of Samurai Houses;* they built a new *onsen* (hot spring resort), a luxury *ryokan* (traditional hotel) and a big tourist office near the Hachiman Shinto shrine and its famous *kusunoki*, a 1200-year-old camphor tree, the biggest tree in Japan! As part of my studies, I would hang around, introduce myself to the (relatively few) bus tourists and ask them where they came from, what they came to see in the village, and could I show them around my 'adopted home'.

These and many other professional occasions involve a nostalgic return to a home or a homeland or a community that is very meaningful to both the emigrants and their descendants and relatives, and indeed it is equally meaningful for those 'left behind' as many of our chapters show. But we might question the title of the book 'Is this *Tourism*'? These trips are obviously travel and they are visits, if they are not permanent.

Most of the returnees and 'roots' tourists in our cases studies claim they are not tourists either, they are pilgrims or some other form of *serious* visitors. Yet Feldman's (2016) research on Christian 'tourists' to Israel emphasizes how flexible the label is. These guided Christian package visitors reject the label tourist and insist they are 'pilgrims.' Yet when they see the overly demonstrative ritual behavior of other visitors, e.g. Russian or Cypriot Orthodox 'pilgrims', to the same churches, they reject that identity and insist they are sensible (but restrained) tourists. This wish to be labelled something other than tourists is still strong amongst Europeans (McCabe, 2005) though it is diminishing in North America where many middle class people are no longer so concerned about their attributed status (Graburn, in press).

Anthropologists returning to loved communities and past field sites would probably also reject the label 'tourists.' Anthropologists too have been likened to tourists, for their exploratory behavior (MacCannell, 1976) and their interpretations of the social world (Van den Abeele, 1980). Yet, as Boissevain (1977) pointed out long ago, anthropologists are dreadfully afraid of being mistaken for tourists in 'their' communities by the local people, to the point that they often avoid mentioning the presence of tourists in their field sites and even long *avoided studying them!*

The study of homes, travels, memory and belonging has never been more important than it is today. Many people in our affluent world move home a number of times or have multiples homes and even spiritual centers. Some of these are frequently on the move for work or leisure (Clifford, 1997) and are always 'coming or going,' yet we still pity both the rootless affluent and the homeless poor and disabled. Home is still important both as a tap-root of origin and as a centered retreat for life. The essence of home is spiritual but the spiritual is known and experienced through both materiality and sociality. The balance between these is historically and culturally contextualized, for example, for those 'on the move' whether voluntarily, as pastoralists or tinkers, or through coercion or excursions, as with Jews, Roma and the many refugees, the social and the portable *are* home. For people with more stable situations, farmers or urbanites, especially those with long historical roots, the materiality of structures, foods and landscape are more important. Happy and lucky indeed are those of us who can enjoy both sociality and rooted material embodiment, and even happier are those, including many anthropologists, who have multiple families and communities which accept them and who feel comfortable with many abodes, cuisines and landscapes.

Note

(1) In my own case, the Graburn family originally came from Eastern Scotland, settled in Beverley Yorkshire in the 16th century, then moved to Barton-on-Humber, Lincolnshire in the 17th century, lost all their money/property in the 1830s and moved to the London area. The large family had spent some of their youth in these northern regions. My father grew up around London, worked in Malaya where he married my mother, also from the London region. They retired before the war and I was adopted into their home in the Surrey countryside. After school and Cambridge, I fled to Canada, went to McGill in Montreal, started research among the Canadian Inuit and then got my PhD at U. Chicago. After more Inuit fieldwork I was hired at and moved to Berkeley. I married Kathy Yaguchi from Los Angeles, moved into our home on our wedding day, and have remained there for 50 years. After more research trips to Inuit communities, we visited Kathy's parents' natal village in Japan in 1974 and have visited relatives there and elsewhere in Japan many times since. Our children went to elementary school there (and in France); one went to university there and since moved to Portugal; the other went to U. Strasbourg. Since 1991 I/we have visited China more than 15 times, but never more than a month – but our younger daughter has moved there for a year! Since McGill I have also visited or taught for many weeks in Canada and in China and for many months or years in England, France, Japan and Brazil. Retirement has not stopped me – yet!

References

Adams, K. (2015) 2015 'Families, Funerals and Facebook: Reimag(in)ing and Curating Toraja Kin in Translocal Times.' *TRaNS: Trans –Regional and –National Studies of Southeast Asia*, 3 (2).
Adams, K. (in press) Migration, self and other: negotiating identities and 'Home' in Indonesian heritage tourism. In N. Leite (ed.) *Taking Tourism Seriously: Edward Bruner and Interpretive Theory in the Anthropology of Tourism*. Lanham, MD: Lexington Books/ Rowman & Littlefield.
Anderson, B. (1983) *Imagined Communities: Reflections on the Origin and Spread of Nationalism*. London: Verso.
Anderson, D.G., Wishart, R.P. and Vaté, V. (eds) (2013) *About the Hearth: Perspectives on the Home, Hearth and Household in the Circumpolar North*. London: Berghahn.
Angé, O. and Berliner, D. (2014) *Anthropology and Nostalgia* London: Berghahn.
Benson, M. and O'Reilly, K. (eds) (2009) *Lifestyle Migration: Expectations, Aspirations and Experiences*. London: Routledge.
Bloch, M. (1998) *How We Think They Think: Anthropological Approaches to Cognition, Memory and Literacy*. Boulder, CO: Westview.
Boissevain, J. (1977) Tourism and development in Malta. *Development and Change* 8 (4), 523–38.
Bourdieu, P. (1977) *Outline of a Theory of Practice*. Cambridge University Press.
Bourdieu, P. (1984) *Distinction: A Social Critique of the Judgment of Taste*. London: Routledge.
Bruner, E. (2005) *Culture on Tour*. University of Chicago Press.
Clifford, J. (1997) *Routes: Travel and Translation in the Later Twentieth Century*. Cambridge: Harvard U P.
Colson, E. (1989) Overview. *Annual Review of Anthropology* 18, 1–16.
Courlander, H. (1967) *The African*. New York: Crowne.
Dann, G. (1994) Tourism and Nostalgia: Looking forward to going back. *Vrijetijd en Samenleving* 1–2, 75–94.

Errington, S. (1998) *The Death of Authentic Primitive Art and other Tales of Progress* Berkeley: University of California Press.

Feldman, J. (2016) *A Jewish Guide to the Holy Land: How Christian Pilgrims Made Me Israel.* Bloomington: Indiana U Press.

Graburn, N. (1963) Lake *Harbour, Baffin Island: The Decline of an Eskimo Community.* Ottawa: Government of Canada NCRC-63–2.

Graburn, N. (ed.) (1976) Ethnic *and Tourist Arts: Cultural Expressions from the Fourth World.* Berkeley: University of California Press.

Graburn, Ne. (1981) 1, 2, 3, 4 . . . Anthropology and the Fourth World. *Culture* 1: 1, 66–70.

Graburn, N. (1983) *To Pray, Pay and Play: The Cultural Structure of Japanese Domestic Tourism.* Aix-en-Provence: Centre des Hautes Etudes Touristiques.

Graburn, N. (1987) Material symbols in Japanese domestic tourism. In D. Ingersoll and G. Bronistky (eds) *Mirror and Metaphor: Material and Social Constructions of Reality* (pp. 15–27). Lanham, MD: University Press of America.

Graburn, N. (1999) Foreword: Southeast Asia on my mind. In J.Forshee, C. Fink and S. Cate (eds) *Converging Interests: Traders, Travelers and Tourists in Southeast Asia* (pp. v–x). Berkeley: Center for Southeast Asian Studies.

Graburn, N. (2005) From aesthetics to prosthetics and back: Materials, performance and consumers in Canadian Inuit sculptural arts; or, Alfred Gell in the Canadian Arctic. In M. Coquet, B. Derlon and M. Jeudy-Ballini (eds) *Les cultures à l'oeuvre- Rencontres en art [Cultures at work – encounters in art]* (pp. 47–62). Paris: Biro Editeur et Editions de la Maison des Sciences de l'Homme.

Graburn, N. (2007) Tourism through the Looking Glass. In D. Nash (ed.) *Tourism Study: Anthropological and Sociological Beginnings* (pp. 93–107). London: Pergamon Press.

Graburn, N. (2015) Ethnic tourism in rural China: Cultural or economic development. In A. Diekmann and M. Smith (eds) *Ethnic and Minority Communities as Tourist Attractions* (pp. 180–186). Bristol: Multilingual Matters.

Graburn, N. (in press) The tourist (chapter 7). In N. Salazar and J. Coats (eds) *Key Figures of Human Mobility.* Special issue of *Social Anthropology/Anthropologie Sociale.*

Haley, A. (1976) *Roots: The Saga of An American Family.* New York: Doubleday.

Halbwachs, M. (1976 [1925]) *Les cadres sociaux de la mémoire.* Paris: Mouton, 1976.

Harrison, J. (2013) *A Timeless Place: The Ontario Cottage.* Vancouver: UBC Press.

Janta, H., Cohen, S.A. and Williams, A.M. (2015) Rethinking visiting friends and relatives mobilities. In *Reconceptualising Visiting Friends and Relatives Mobilities (VFR).* Special issue of *Population, Space and Place* 21 (7), 585–598.

Kroeber, A.L. (1917) *The Nature of Culture.* Chicago: University of Chicago Press.

Levi-Strauss, C. (1984) *The Birth of Historical Societies.* Berkeley: Hitchcock Lectures. Sept. 23rd [after the French ...]

Lowenthal, D. (2015) *The Past is a Foreign Country – Revisited.* Cambridge University Press.

MacCannell, D. (1976) *The Tourist: A New Theory of the Leisure Class.* NY: Schocken.

Martinez, W. and Gelles, P.H. (producers) (1992) *Transnational Fiesta.* [videorecording] Berkeley: University of California Extension, Center for Media and Independent Learning.

McCabe, S. (2005) 'Who is a tourist?' A critical review. *Tourism Studies* 5(1), 85–106.

Nabti, P. (1992) Emigration from a Lebanese village: A case study of Bishmizzine. In A. Hourani and N. Shehadi (eds) *The Lebanese in the World: A Century of Emigration,* Oxford University Press.

Okely, J. (1996) *Own and Other Culture.* London: Routledge.

Rosaldo, R. (1989) Imperialist nostalgia. *Representations* 26, 107–22.

Shami, S. (1998) Circassian encounters: The self as other and the production of the homeland in the North Caucasus. *Development and Change* 29 (4), 617–646.

Van den Abeele, G. (1980) Sightseers: The tourist as theorist. *Diacritics* 10, 3–14.

Wang, N. (1999) Rethinking authenticity and the tourism experience. *Annals of Tourism Research* 26 (2), 349–370.

Yamashita, S. (2012) Here, there, and in-between: Lifestyle migrants from Japan. In D. Haines, K. Yamanaka and S. Yamashita (eds) *Wind over Water: Rethinking Migration in an East Asian Setting* (pp. 161–172). New York: Berghahn.

Index